CAPE COD

MARTHA'S VINEYARD & NANTUCKET

Orientation

A real-estate agent couldn't have dreamed up an easier sell than this lush peninsula some 60 miles long, crenulated with nearly 600 miles of shoreline, nearly half of it beach, glorious beach. No wonder Cape Cod's praises have been sung by sources as disparate as **Henry David Thoreau** and **Patti Page.**

Yet the Pilgrims were less than impressed when, on 11 November 1620, they pulled into what would someday become **Provincetown**, a protected harbor cupped in the hand of the Cape's "flexed arm." They moved on after a month, convinced the place would never amount to much. Appreciative of profitable pursuits, they might be chagrined to learn that the Cape—which appeals to up to 13 million tourists a year—now generates annual revenues in excess of $1.1 billion.

Of course, the early settlers themselves account for at least part of the mystique. The area is steeped in history—not just the brave exploits of the colonists and the largesse of the indigenous peoples who welcomed them, but the escapades of pirates and patriots, whalers, and farsighted entrepreneurs. And even though modern innovations ultimately eclipsed a lot of their grand schemes (whale oil, for instance, was replaced by kerosene), the settlers left in their wake an extraordinary cache of architectural treasures, enhanced by unspoiled landscapes of surpassing beauty.

Just as Cape residents started migrating to Boston and Lowell in search of factory work (the population declined by one-third between 1860 and 1920), city dwellers began arriving at Thoreau's "wild rank spot" for rustic vacations. By the turn of the century, more than 75 hotels had opened on the Cape. The figure now runs to 10 times that, and tourism revenues make up about 60 percent of the area's economy. Even though commercial development has compromised the Cape's visual appeal—particularly along the southernmost shore—there remain great pockets of preservation lands where, as Thoreau wrote, "a man can stand and put all America behind him."

The famous naturalist was referring to the "Back Side," located on the ocean side of the Outer Cape, a 30-mile stretch of wild dunes and thrashing surf that since 1961 has been under the protective stewardship of the **Cape Cod National Seashore.** Unencumbered by human habitation (beyond the occasional picturesque lighthouse or weather-silvered shack), this seemingly endless beach knows no equal in New England. Though the access points fill up fast on fine days, walk a ways and you're on your own. The placid bays have their charms as well: surf gentle enough for a toddler, and miles of shell-strewn floor to explore at low tide.

The peninsula's idiosyncratic communities all distinguish themselves in some way. History buffs and fans of fine architecture might want to start with a detour to **Plymouth** before they arrive at Cape Cod, then ramble along historic **Route 6A** from **Sandwich** (the Cape's oldest town, founded in 1637) to **Orleans**; the houses lining this twisting road range from colonial to Victorian. The western coast of the Cape offers a peaceful redoubt for families; at the southernmost tip, the tiny village of **Woods Hole**, a ferry port for **Martha's Vineyard** and home to a world-renowned scientific community, represents one of the hipper enclaves in these parts, with laid-back restaurants and watering holes. Old money has claimed the coastline along the Sound, from **Falmouth** to **Hyannisport** by way of **Osterville** and **Centerville**, but there's no charge for ogling these seaside estates, and you can live like a grandee, if only for a night, at a mansion-turned-inn.

Route 28 west of **Hyannis**—unabashedly commercial and unapologetically crass—has been mucked up by overdevelopment, but you'll still find some genteel pockets such as **Harwichport. Chatham**, at the Cape's "elbow," is proof positive that Norman Rockwell-style family values live on: this cozy town is chockablock with inviting shops, and the weekly band concerts draw standing-room-only crowds.

Past Orleans is a wind-scrubbed landscape where you're never more than a mile or two from the sea. Pretty **Wellfleet** is doing a good job of upholding the Cape's tradition of inspiring and supporting artists. Provincetown may have slipped a bit in that regard but remains a haven for sensualists of all stripes, with a European sophistication and a New Orleans-style sense of fun. The **Islands—Nantucket**, Martha's Vineyard, and tiny **Cuttyhunk**—are worlds unto themselves, providing all the advantages of modern-day life (Nantucket's restaurants, in particular, regularly set new standards for the culinary vanguard) but few of its stresses. Once you venture past the whaling towns of Nantucket and **Edgartown**, preserved in all their spiffy glory, you'll find yourself wandering amid rolling moors and scrub-oak forests, with only a few fellow escapists for company.

Except for a handful of larger towns (Falmouth, Hyannis, Provincetown) that remain active year-round, the Cape and the Islands endure a touristic tide, receding into quietude every winter and swelling with visitors come summer. But don't underestimate the allure of the depopulated "shoulder seasons." In fall, the foliage casts a fiery glow across the marshlands and inland hills, and the cranberry bogs gleam with ruby fruits. There's no pleasure so great as revelling in an all-but-empty beach on a toasty Indian summer afternoon. It's no wonder, though, that the Cape attains its peak of popularity in summer. From Memorial Day to Labor Day, when the sand sizzles, so does the social life: teens and twentysomethings converge to worship the sun, sea, and themselves, not necessarily in that order. Families with young children return to rediscover the many little miracles of surf and dune.

Truth be told, however, not all that many visitors ever make it to the attractions listed here, except perhaps during a long spate of rain. They're too busy baking on the beach, engineering sand castles, or consuming massive novels, as their ages and tastes dictate. But it's remarkable how the days drift by, in a daze of time-stilling sensory pleasures. Travel writer **Paul Theroux**, who calls the Cape home, summed up its charms succinctly in an essay for *Cape Cod Life:* "Anyone who grows tired of Cape Cod needs his head examined," he opined. "A perfect summer is a dream of childhood, idleness, and ice cream, and heat."

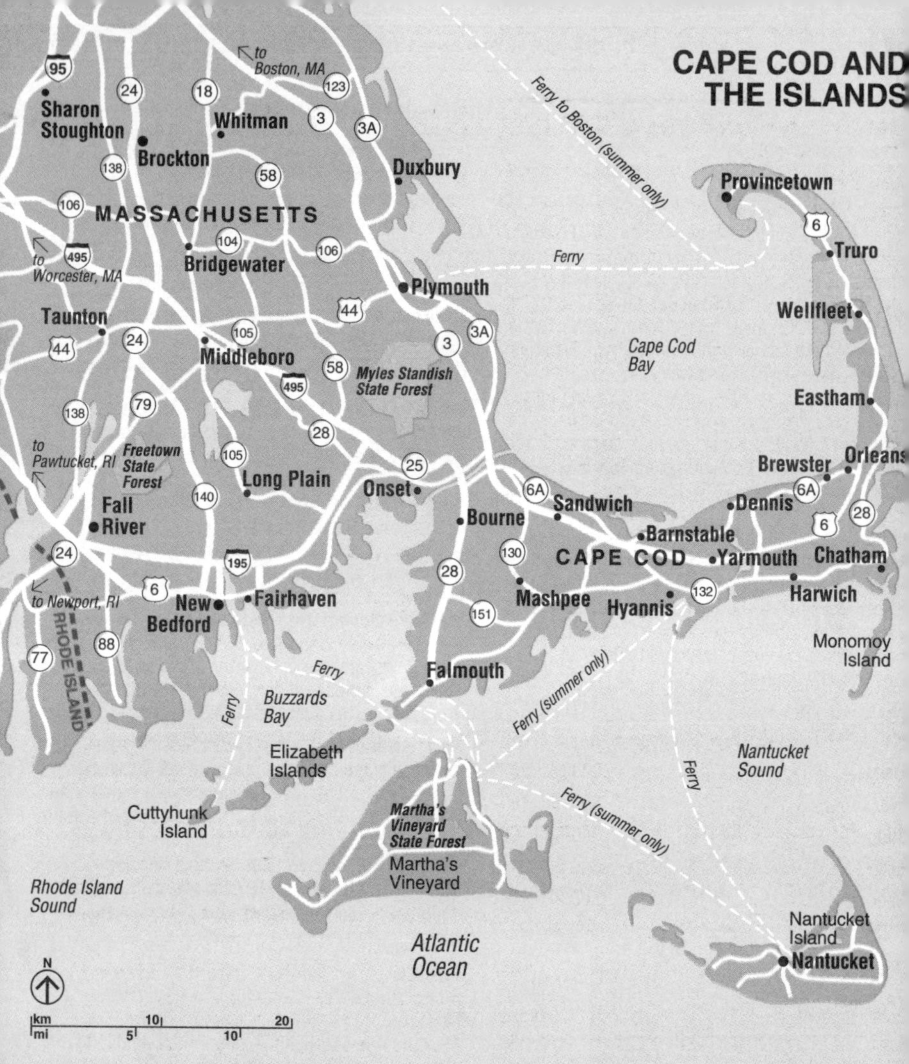

Area code 508 unless otherwise noted.

Getting to Cape Cod and the Islands

Public Airports

Chatham 945.9000
Cuttyhunk Island 997.4095
Hyannis 775.2020
Martha's Vineyard 693.7022
Nantucket 325.5300
New Bedford 992.2264
Provincetown 487.0241

Airlines

Cape Air 771.6944, 800/352.0714
Colgan Air 800/272.5488
Continental Express 800/525.0280
Delta Business Express 800/345.3400
Island Airlines 228.7575, 800/698.1109
Island Shuttle 997.4095
Nantucket Airlines 790.0300, 800/635.8787
Northwest Airlines 800/225.2525
USAir 800/428.4332

Rosa rugosa, those raggedy roses you see everywhere along the beaches, arrived on these shores from the Orient as stowaways on trade ships. They've flourished here on the Cape, providing not only summerlong beauty but also a fall harvest of plump rosehips, which make a tangy tea, rich in Vitamin C, as well as tasty jelly.

Getting around Cape Cod and the Islands

Buses

Bonanza Bus Lines (548.7588, 800/556.3815) links Logan Airport and downtown Boston with Bourne, Woods Hole, Falmouth, and Hyannis; service is also offered to Rhode Island, Connecticut, and New York City. **Plymouth and Brockton Bus Lines** (746.0378, 800/23-LOGAN) travels from Boston and New York to Plymouth, Hyannis, and Provincetown. Falmouth operates an inexpensive shuttle to Woods Hole during weekends in July and August. During these months, Provincetown also runs a low-cost shuttle bus about town. From late spring through early fall, **Martha's Vineyard Transportation Services** (693.1589 for details; 627.7448 for recorded schedule information) operates an inexpensive shuttle-bus service between the towns of Vineyard Haven, Oak Bluffs, and Edgartown, with connections up-island to West Tisbury, Chilmark, and the airport, as well as a town-to-beach trolley in Edgartown. On Nantucket, **Barrett's Tours** (228.0174) runs reasonably priced beach shuttles to Sconset, Surfside, and Jetties.

Car Rentals

The main companies operating locally are:

Alamo	800/327.9633
Avis	800/331.1212
Budget	800/527.7000
Hertz	800/654.3131
National	800/227.7368
Thrifty	800/367.2277

Driving

If you can possibly manage without a car, you'll be doing yourself and the natives a favor, for glutted highways are one of the major headaches of summer on Cape Cod. If you choose to drive, however, be forewarned: The hardest part about getting around the Cape is getting *onto* it. Only two rather narrow bridges—the **Sagamore** and **Bourne**—offer access. Common sense would suggest that you not try to funnel on during the Friday-night crush, or to leave on a Sunday evening. Beyond that, a new service called **SmartTraveler** (617/374.1234) uses remote cameras and airplane spotters to provide up-to-the-minute reports on congestion, as well as on parking availability at the ferry terminals. Few people really need a car on the Islands, and getting one over is prohibitively expensive—that is, *if* you can get a reservation without several months' notice, or score standby by sitting in line for hours. And make sure you've got return passage covered: in peak times, such as summer, reservations are often booked by early winter. All the island-bound ferries have ample pay-per-day parking available (some in satellite areas with a free shuttle bus), so car-free connections are easy. Car rentals can be arranged on-island, if necessary, and off-the-road vehicles are permitted on certain stretches of beach, at specified times; generally, a sticker is required.

The layout of the Cape, once you're on it, is not complicated, though the terminology is. Basically it's divided into the **Upper Cape, Mid-Cape,** and **Lower Cape,** designations that have nothing to do with what's "higher" on the map but rather—as befits a nautical community—which way the higher longitudes lie (the numeration declines as one heads east). Three main roads cover most of the territory. Scenic **Route 6A,** a historic preservation district also known as the Army of the Grand Republic Highway, the Cranberry Highway, and the Old King's Highway (take your pick), is the longest stretch of historic highway in the country; it started out as a native footpath and now wends its way leisurely along the bicep of the Cape's somewhat misshapen "arm." **Route 6,** built for speed, not aesthetics, cuts east-west through the thickest part of the peninsula. **Route 28,** headed south from the bridges, is similarly fast and utilitarian, and its sidekick, **Route 28A,** much prettier; they twine together near Falmouth and then, combined as Route 28, scoop around the outer rim. At Orleans, the three main roads converge, and Route 6 continues up the narrow forearm and into the "fist" of Provincetown (Route 6A reemerges briefly to skim the shore along North Truro and Provincetown). Innumerable secondary roads crisscross among the main drags, and the right zigzag could save you a substantial amount of time—a key consideration if you're racing to catch a ferry.

Note: Beware the dreaded Massachusetts rotary, a device designed to strike fear in all but the most intrepid of drivers. The rule is that those *in* the circle have the right of way and will think nothing of cutting you off. You may have to bide your time before entering their elect number. Another fiendish arrangement is the four- or even five-way stop; here diplomacy—and an instinct for self-preservation—rules.

Ferries

So beautiful are the views from these workaday vessels, tourists often take a day trip just for pleasure, even though the longer rides tend to be rather expensive—astronomically so if you want your car to accompany you. Only the **Steamship Authority** (see below) transports cars, but it and the other ferries welcome bikes, for a small extra fee.

The trip to Martha's Vineyard from the Cape takes less than an hour; to Nantucket, a bit over two. **Bay State** (617/723.7800) makes one six-hour round-trip from Commonwealth Pier in Boston to Provincetown, with a three-hour layover, daily late June through Labor Day, and Saturdays and Sundays only Memorial Day weekend through Columbus Day weekend (the latter time span is usually what is meant by "in season"). Travelers arriving from the south could take **Cape Cod Cruises** (747.2400) from Plymouth to Provincetown, in season, or **Cape Island Express** (997.1688) from New Bedford to Vineyard Haven on Martha's Vineyard. Those bound for the Vineyard from the Cape can leave from Hyannis aboard the **Hy-Line** (775.7185) to Oak Bluffs, in season; from Falmouth aboard the **Island Queen** (548.4800) to Oak Bluffs, in season (it boasts the quickest crossing time, only 35 minutes); from Woods Hole via the **Steamship Authority** (540.2022) to Vineyard Haven, year-round, and to Oak Bluffs (no cars allowed) in season.

Nantucket boats leave from Hyannis: the **Steamship Authority** runs year-round, **Hy-Line** only in season. In addition, Hy-Line travels from Oak Bluffs to Nantucket, in season. **Cuttyhunk Boat Lines** (992.1432) makes one round-trip daily in summer to its tiny namesake, less often during the rest of the year.

Island ferries depart several times daily from Hyannis and Woods Hole, year-round; if you miss one, there's always another, or a good excuse to investigate a new bed-and-breakfast. However, rooms are virtually impossible to find in August and, to a lesser extent, July; be sure to secure one before you show up.

Parking

In addition to the lots maintained by the ferry lines, many private citizens who live nearby convert their driveways and lawns into quick cash cows come summer. They're legitimate and usually charge slightly less than the official lots. You pay up front and estimate your time of return—a good idea in any case, lest you find yourself hemmed in. However, even these spaces tend to fill up by Friday night, so come early in the day, or arrange your trips for a less heavily traveled time. Short-term parking can be tight in many of the Cape's more heavily trafficked towns (such as Sandwich, Falmouth, and Hyannis); in Provincetown it's pretty much impossible.

Beach parking throughout the Cape, as well as on Martha's Vineyard, is a complex matter. Each town has its own sticker system, with information ordinarily available at Town Hall (if not, your innkeeper can steer you in the right direction). You can pay by the day or week or season, but one way or another, you will pay, at all but a handful of beaches (usually not the best). The mammoth beaches within the Cape Cod National Seashore have fairly priced lots, but to take advantage you'll have to show up early (by 10AM at least) or late in the day. Nantucket beaches are all fee-free, mirabile dictu, and depend on (1) scarce cars and (2) careful parkers who neither block the way nor get mired in sand.

Taxis

Taxis will be there to meet all scheduled flights and ferries. Virtually all the towns on the Cape have cab companies; the Islands have many. Check the Yellow Pages of the phone book or ask your innkeeper. Most charge a set fee, rather than by the mile.

Tours

Among the dozen or so companies offering bus tours to the Cape and Islands are **Brush Hill Tours** (617/896.6100), **Maupintour** (913/843.1211, 800/255.4266), and **Tauck Tours** (203/226.6911, 800/468.2825). On Martha's Vineyard, **Adam Wilson** of **AdamCab** (693.3332, 800/281.4462) gives an excellent van tour of the island; actress/historian **Holly Nadler** (693.9321) leads walking tours of Edgartown. On Nantucket, the van to catch is that of 6th-generation native **Gail Johnson** of **Gail's Tours** (257.6557); 12th-generationer **Anita Stackpole Dougan** (228.1861) gives walking tours.

Trains

From late June to early September, **Amtrak's** "Cape Codder" runs from Washington D.C., Philadelphia, and New York City to Hyannis Friday evening, returning Sunday evening; service from Boston and Providence is offered on Saturday and Sunday. For details and reservations, call 800/872.7245.

FYI

Bed-and-Breakfast Inns

Most B&Bs operate like luxurious mini-hotels, where the hosts are combination concierge, cook, cicerone, and (with any luck) newfound friend. They make up in personal attention whatever they may lack in square footage, and the furnishings tend to feed fantasies of idyllic country life. Virtually every B&B on the Cape also packs a lot of history; many are on the **National Register of Historic Places.** The **Massachusetts Office of Travel and Tourism** (617/727.3201, 800/447.6277) offers a free statewide B&B guide. **Destinnations** (800/333.4667), a consortium of several dozen outstanding inns on the Cape and Islands, can arrange an itinerary custom-tailored to special interests or just general enjoyment. The **Provincetown Reservation System** (487.2400, 800/648.0364) will book restaurants as well as lodgings.

Climate

The temperature ranges from an average of 35 degrees in winter to 70 in summer, with spring and fall averaging 50 to 55. The relatively mild climate is a boon for gardeners, who get an extended season: there's rarely more than a few inches of snow in January and February, and an equal amount of rain per month the rest of the year. Vacationers may not appreciate the precipitation so much (you can expect it, typically, 10 days out of every month). However, they do appreciate the fact that when inland Massachusetts broils through the dog days of August, the Cape and Islands generally stay breezy and cool. In fact, old hands pack a cotton sweater and windbreaker even for summer jaunts, since a brisk wind off the ocean can chill you to the bone before you know it.

Drinking

The legal drinking age is 21, and IDs are checked for those whose age appears questionable. Should you be "carded," the only acceptable ID is a Massachusetts driver's license or a state liquor-identification card, issued by the Registry of Motor Vehicles. Drinking in public is illegal; however, at smaller restaurants without a liquor license, you're usually welcome to bring wine or beer (call ahead to confirm). On Martha's Vineyard, all the towns except Edgartown and Oak Bluffs are "dry," so bring your own if need be.

Money

ATMs are ubiquitous throughout the Cape and Islands; among the larger banks are **BayBank**

(800/342.8888), **Bank of Boston** (800/252.6000), **Fleet Bank** (800/841.4000), and **Shawmut Bank** (800/742.9688). It is difficult-to-impossible to change foreign currency on the Cape, however, so do your exchanging at Logan or in Boston. Traveler's checks and credit cards are widely accepted.

Personal Safety

For the most part, the Cape and Islands are still so rural and peaceful that you'll feel comfortable leaving your car unlocked—but it's probably not a good idea: car theft runs rampant in the state, if not in this particular corner of it. Be forewarned that some of the homier B&Bs don't even have room keys. The lifestyle is very casual in any case, so leave your valuables safe at home. In the more populous towns (e.g., Hyannis and Provincetown), you'll want to exercise the customary caution regarding pocket-books and camera bags.

A more pressing concern than pickpockets is another kind of parasite, the Lyme disease-carrying tick, prevalent in tall grass and brush, particularly April through October. As a precaution when hiking, wear light-colored trousers (the better to spot the suckers) tucked into socks, and stick to the center of the trail. Spray your clothes (not skin) with a DEET-based insecticide, and inspect for ticks often. If you find one lodged in your skin, pull it directly upward, taking care not to squeeze the body (which could spread the infection); disinfect with alcohol and take the tick and yourself to a doctor immediately. A red-rimmed rash may signal an undetected bite, so if you see one, even much later, have it checked out. The possible complications entailed by this disease are severe and, in the long term, potentially life-threatening. For further information, contact the **Massachusetts Department of Public Health** (617/727.0049) or the **Lyme Borreliosis Foundation** (203/871.2900). A milder threat is poison ivy, which you can avert by avoiding plants with a cluster of three shiny green leaves, and alleviate somewhat by immediate washing.

Publications

Cape Cod Life, a bimonthly, covers local issues and pleasures. Every June, *Boston* magazine publishes a well-informed, up-to-date guide to the Cape, with a table listing the relative merits and facilities to be found at the public beaches (similar information can be found in the phone book). Other glossies include *Provincetown Arts, Martha's Vineyard Magazine,* and *Nantucket Journal.* The *Cape Cod Times* is the paper of record. Among the many free papers you'll find along the tourist circuit, *A-Plus* is worth picking up for its in-depth coverage of "arts/antiques/ architecture/attitude/ambience" etc.; and *The Little Yellow Cape Cod Guide* for its useful information and even more useful discount coupons.

Smoking

State law requires that any restaurant seating 75 or more must offer a nonsmoking section. Some of the larger hotels offer nonsmoking rooms. An increasing number of B&Bs are switching over to strictly non-smoking, so inquire before you book.

Taxes

In Massachusetts, a 5 percent tax is charged on all purchases except services, food bought in stores (not restaurants), and clothing less than $175. A 9.7 percent hotel tax is also assessed.

Telephones

Calls cost 10 cents from a pay phone; however, calls between counties are usually long distance. Long-distance credit calls can be initiated by dialing "0" before the area code and number. Some hotels charge extra for calls made from the room; usually the fee is posted, but if not, inquire, or hold out for a pay phone.

Tipping

The norm for restaurant meals is 15 percent of the pre-tax total; 20 percent signals exceptional service, or a patron who is aware that tips account for a major portion of a seasonal worker's wages. Personal services also usually entail a tip of 15 to 20 percent, and it's customary to give a dollar or more for help in carrying bags and to leave a few dollars per day for housekeeping services.

Phone Book

Emergencies

Ambulance/Fire/Police......**911**

Coast Guard......457.3210

Legal Aid......800/742.4107

Missing Persons......800/622.5999

Poison Hotline......800/682.9211

Traveler's Aid......617/542.7286

Visitor Information

AIDS Action Hotline......800/235.2331

American Youth Hostels......202/783.6161

Amtrak......800/871.7145

Attorney General's Office......617/727.8400

Cape Cod Baseball League......432.0340

Cape Cod Bird Club......477.3847

Cape Cod Chamber of Commerce......362.3225

Destinnations......800/333.4667

Elder Services of Cape Cod and the Islands......394.4630, 800/244.4630

Golf Pro-Motions of Cape Cod......539.0969

Information Center for Individuals with Disabilities......800/462.5015

Massachusetts Association of Campground Owners......617/927.3180

Massachusetts Commission for the Blind......800/392.6450

Massachusetts Department of Environmental Management......617/727.3180

Massachusetts Office of Travel and Tourism......727.3201, 800/447.6277

TDD/TTY......800/852.3029

Weather Forecast......790.1061

The Cape and Islands by the Book

If you have time for some prefatory reading, the following books should prove worth your while.

Angels without Wings by Jane Vonnegut Yarmolinsky

Cape Cod by William Martin

Cape Cod by Alan Nyiri

Cape Cod by Henry David Thoreau

Cape Cod and the Islands by Eleanor Berman

Cape Cod Architecture by Clair Baisly

Cape Cod: Its People and Their History by Henry Kittredge

Cape Cod Pilot by Josef Berger (alias Jeremiah Digges)

The Cape Itself by Robert Finch

Cape Light: Color Photographs by Joel Meyerowitz

Common Ground: A Naturalist's Cape Cod by Robert Finch

Ghosts of Nantucket by Blue Balliett

The Great Beach by John Hay

The Handbook for Beach Strollers by Donald J. Zinn

Illumination Night by Alice Hoffman

Lighthouses of Cape Cod, Martha's Vineyard, Nantucket: Their History and Lore by Admont G. Clark

Moby-Dick by Herman Melville

Mooncussers of Cape Cod by Henry Kittredge

Nantucket by Robert Gambee

Nantucket, The Other Season by Stan Grossfeld

Nantucket Style by Jon Aron and Leslie Linsley

The Outermost House: A Year of Life on the Great Beach of Cape Cod by Henry Beston

Outlands: Journeys to the Outer Edges of Cape Cod by Robert Finch

Of Plimoth Plantation by Governor William Bradford

Old Provincetown in Early Photographs by Irma Ruckstuhl

On the Vineyard II edited by Peter Simon

A Place Apart edited by Robert Finch

Sand in Their Shoes by Edith and Frank Shay

These Fragile Outposts by Barbara Blau Chamberlain

Walks & Rambles on Cape Cod and the Islands: A Naturalist's Hiking Guide by Ned Friary and Glenda Bendure

The Wampanoags of Mashpee by Russell M. Peter

Cape Cod on the Calendar

April
Daffodil Festival, Nantucket

June
Blessing of the Fleet, Provincetown

July
Barnstable County Fair, Falmouth
Regatta, Edgartown
Wampanoag Powwow, Mashpee

August
Illumination Night, Oak Bluffs
Pops-by-the-Sea, Hyannis
Possible Dream Auction, Edgartown
Road Race, Falmouth
Seafood Fest, New Bedford
Seaport Festival, Hyannis

September
Bourne Scallop Festival, Buzzards Bay
Cranberry Harvest Festival, Harwich

December
Christmas Stroll, Nantucket
First Night Cape Cod (Falmouth, Hyannis, Orleans, Provincetown)

The World Guide to Nude Beaches and Recreation, published by the Naturist Society in Oshkosh, Wisconsin, lists the following for the Cape and Islands: Truro between Ballston and Long Nook beaches; Herring Cove Beach near Provincetown; Sandy Terraces near Hyannis; Gay Head Lighthouse and Lucy Vincent Beach in Chilmark on Martha's Vineyard; and Miacomet, Pebble, Eel Point, and Madequecham beaches on Nantucket. Of course, none of these nude beaches are *official*. In fact, in 1975, the Cape Cod National Seashore was the first (and so far, only) federal beach in the country to prohibit nudity—not out of prudishness, but because oglers were trampling the delicate dunes. Here, rangers routinely issue $50 tickets and occasionally even arrest those using their birthday suits as bathing suits. However, the parks services' repressive measures have only served to foment rebellion: protestors have seized on occasions such as Independence Day to mount organized "nude-ins." Elsewhere, officials tend to turn a blind eye.

Sand castles, observes Brewster architect Malcolm Wells in his charming self-published booklet on the subject, "are environmentally ideal. They create no pollution and they disappear with the next tide."

How to Read this Guide

CAPE COD & THE ISLANDS ACCESS® is arranged so you can see at a glance where you are and what is around you. The numbers next to the entries in the following chapters correspond to the numbers on the maps. The text is color-coded according to the kind of place described:

Restaurants/Clubs: Red **Hotels:** Blue
Shops/ Outdoors: Green **Sights/Culture:** Black

Rating the Restaurants and Hotels

The restaurant star ratings take into account the quality, service, atmosphere, and uniqueness of the restaurant. An expensive restaurant doesn't necessarily ensure an enjoyable evening; however, a small, relatively unknown spot could have good food, professional service, and a lovely atmosphere. Therefore, on a purely subjective basis, stars are used to judge the overall dining value (see the star ratings above at right). Keep in mind that chefs and owners often change, which sometimes drastically affects the quality of a restaurant. The ratings in this guidebook are based on information available at press time.

The price ratings, as categorized above at right, apply to restaurants and hotels. These figures describe general price-range relationships among other restaurants and hotels in the area. The restaurant price ratings are based on the average cost of an entrée for one person, excluding tax and tip. Hotel price ratings reflect the base price of a standard room for two people for one night during the peak season.

Restaurants

★	Good	
★★	Very Good	
★★★	Excellent	
★★★★	An Extraordinary Experience	
$	The Price Is Right	(less than $10)
$$	Reasonable	($10-$15)
$$$	Expensive	($15-$20)
$$$$	Big Bucks	($20 and up)

Hotels

$	The Price Is Right	(less than $100)
$$	Reasonable	($100-$175)
$$$	Expensive	($175-$250)
$$$$	Big Bucks	($250 and up)

Map Key

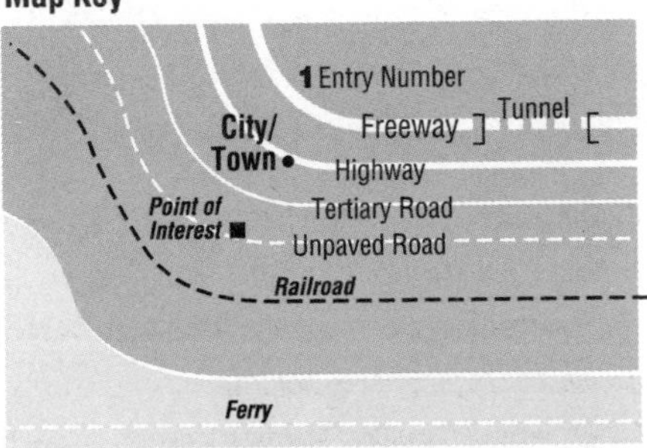

Bests

Alexander Theroux
Novelist and Poet

There is something of the "retreat" about Cape Cod. **Thomas Merton** loved Truro (and found the name haunting). **Henry James** took buggy rides in these parts. (Remember, part of *The Bostonians* is set here.) **Kahlil Gibran** wrote much of *The Prophet* here. **Conrad Aiken** worked here, as did **Edmund Wilson, Nabokov,** and **John O'Hara,** who wrote *Butterfield 8* at the **Oceanside Hotel** in East Sandwich. And did you know **Sylvia Plath's** mother once taught at **Cape Cod Community College?**

Beaches haven't changed since **Thoreau** tramped over them in 1849—wild, splendid, and long. My favorite is **Head of the Meadow Beach** in Truro, where the dunes are high and the crashing surf can tear off one's bathing suit. **Sandy Neck Beach** in West Barnstable is an ecological quiddity: beach, marsh, woods, and desert all at once.

My favorite breakfast place is **The Egg & I** at 517 Main Street in Hyannis. The omelets (try "The Philly," filled with sautéed steak, cheese, and onions) are brilliant. The **Sagamore Inn** in Bourne, with its old decor and tin ceilings, has superb food. And **Jack's Outback** in Yarmouthport has wonderful food (eccentric Jack humorously insults customers and always rings a bell when patrons leave a tip as they pay on the way out). All of these places are, of course, inexpensive, unpretentious, and serve large portions of matchless food. I also like the **Villa Vecchione** for Italian food and **The Pavilion** (with a special luncheon buffet) for perfect Indian cuisine, both of which are located in Hyannis. And the ice cream is handmade at **Four Seas** near Craigville Beach in Centerville.

As for bookstores, there are many, but **Eric Hjulstrom's Bass River Books** in West Dennis and **Tim's Used Books** in Provincetown are the only two of, say, 20 that have ever given me a discount (and I've been buying books for 15 years).

Whale-watching excursions are everywhere, and one always sees the mammals sporting. With someone you love, the ferry ride to **Nantucket** is paradise. Buy a fishing pole and go blue fishing, catch some, bring them home, and fry them (covered in gin, an old Cape Cod tip).

Finally, the woods, which are lovely, dark, and deep. Coves, landings, bogs, inlets—so many hidden, magical places on Cape Cod for those who bother to look. Lurk in them, dream. Cape Cod is a perfect place to drive or walk around and get lost in. The scent of blueberries. Hot pine. Ocean air. **Patti Page's** Cape Cod is still there behind the fudge-shop signs and T-shirt emporia.

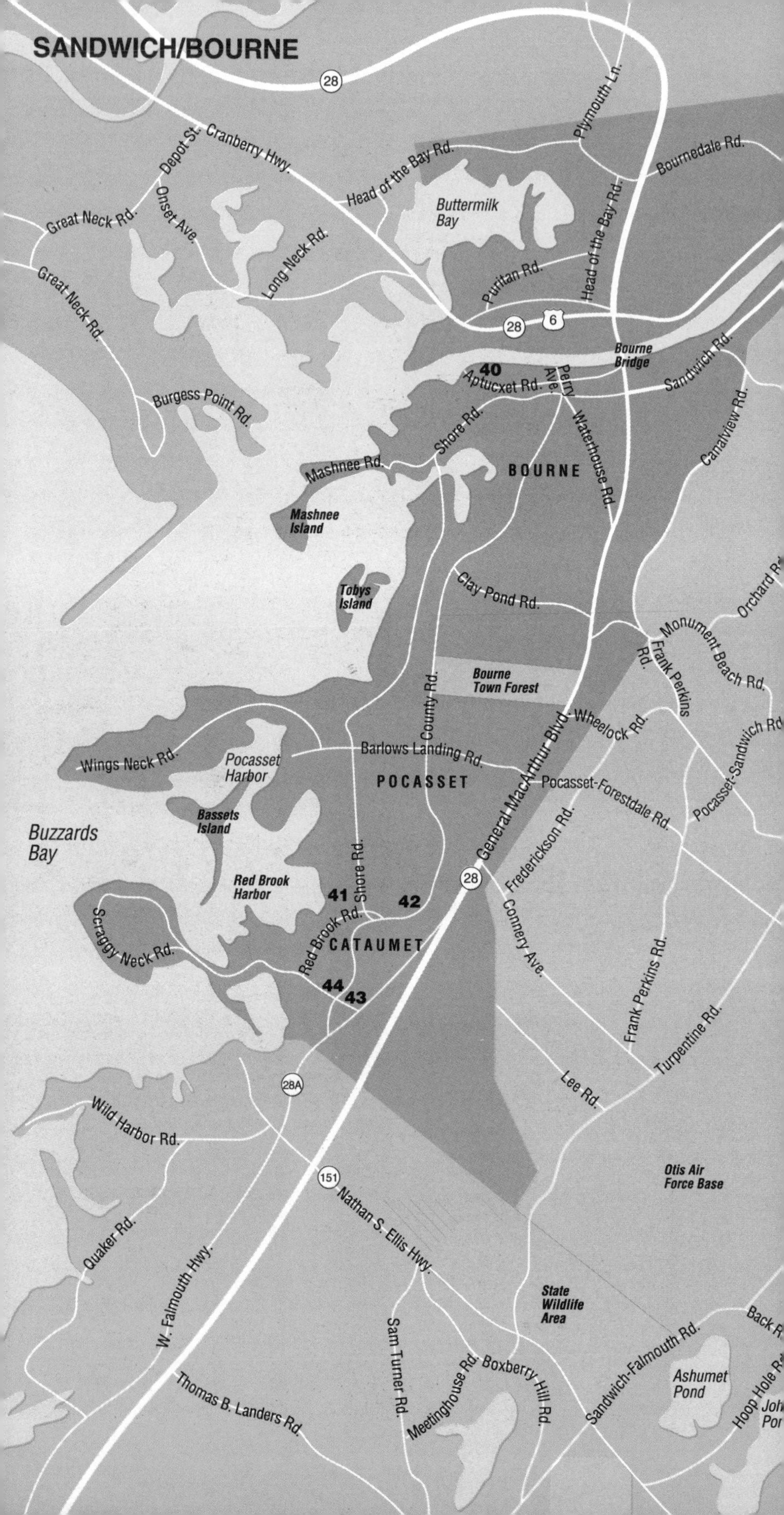
SANDWICH/BOURNE
28
Cranberry Hwy.
Depot St.
Plymouth Ln.
Head of the Bay Rd.
Bournedale Rd.
Onset Ave.
Great Neck Rd.
Long Neck Rd.
Buttermilk Bay
Puritan Rd.
Head of the Bay Rd.
Great Neck Rd.
28
6
Bourne Bridge
40
Aptucxet Rd.
Perry Ave.
Sandwich Rd.
Burgess Point Rd.
Shore Rd.
Canalview Rd.
Waterhouse Rd.
Mashnee Rd.
BOURNE
Mashnee Island
Tobys Island
Clay Pond Rd.
Orchard Rd.
Monument Beach Rd.
Frank Perkins Rd.
Bourne Town Forest
County Rd.
Wheelock Rd.
General MacArthur Blvd.
Barlows Landing Rd.
Wings Neck Rd.
Pocasset Harbor
POCASSET
Pocasset-Forestdale Rd.
Pocasset-Sandwich Rd.
Bassets Island
Buzzards Bay
Fredrickson Rd.
Shore Rd.
Red Brook Harbor
41
42
28
Scraggy Neck Rd.
Red Brook Rd.
CATAUMET
Connery Ave.
Frank Perkins Rd.
44
43
Turpentine Rd.
Lee Rd.
28A
Wild Harbor Rd.
151
Otis Air Force Base
Nathan S. Ellis Hwy.
Quaker Rd.
W. Falmouth Hwy.
State Wildlife Area
Back Rd.
Sam Turner Rd.
Meetinghouse Rd.
Boxberry Hill Rd.
Sandwich-Falmouth Rd.
Ashumet Pond
Hoop Hole Rd.
Thomas B. Landers Rd.

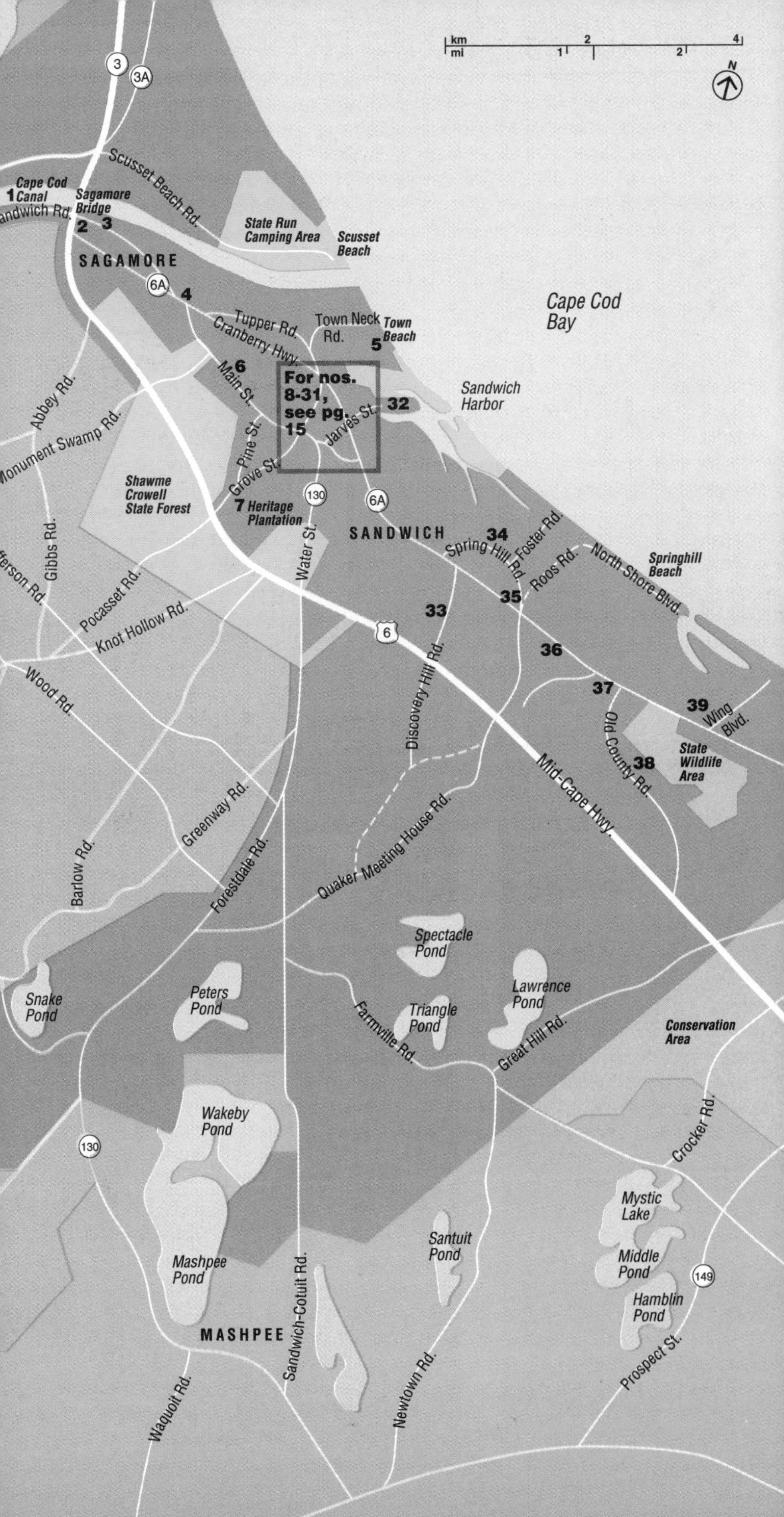

km
mi
2
4
1
2
N
3
3A
Scusset Beach Rd.
Cape Cod Canal
1
Sagamore Bridge
Sandwich Rd.
2 3
State Run Camping Area
Scusset Beach
SAGAMORE
6A
4
Cape Cod Bay
Tupper Rd.
Cranberry Hwy.
Town Neck Rd.
Town Beach
5
6
Main St.
For nos. 8-31, see pg. 15
32
Jarves St.
Sandwich Harbor
Abbey Rd.
Monument Swamp Rd.
Pine St.
Grove St.
Shawme Crowell State Forest
7 Heritage Plantation
130
6A
SANDWICH
34
Spring Hill Rd.
Foster Rd.
Roos Rd.
North Shore Blvd.
Springhill Beach
Gibbs Rd.
Pocasset Rd.
Knot Hollow Rd.
Water St.
35
33
6
36
Wood Rd.
Discovery Hill Rd.
37
39
Wing Blvd.
Old County Rd.
38
State Wildlife Area
Mid-Cape Hwy.
Greenway Rd.
Quaker Meeting House Rd.
Barlow Rd.
Forestdale Rd.
Spectacle Pond
Snake Pond
Peters Pond
Lawrence Pond
Triangle Pond
Farmville Rd.
Great Hill Rd.
Conservation Area
Wakeby Pond
130
Crocker Rd.
Mystic Lake
Santuit Pond
Mashpee Pond
Middle Pond
149
Hamblin Pond
MASHPEE
Sandwich-Cotuit Rd.
Prospect St.
Newtown Rd.
Waquoit Rd.

Sandwich/Bourne

Founded in 1637 by a splinter group of Puritans, **Sandwich** is the oldest town on Cape Cod. According to Plymouth Colony records, "tenn men from Saugust" (now the town of **Lynn** in Massachusetts) were granted "liberty to view a place to sitt down & have sufficient lands for three score famylies." Having found a site rich in local resources—plentiful fish, fresh water, and salt marsh hay as fodder for their livestock—these men did indeed "sitt down," naming their rough-hewn settlement for the town of Sandwich in Kent, England, also renowned for its salt marsh.

The New World Sandwich remained a bucolic retreat, favored for its prolific trout streams (statesman **Daniel Webster** purportedly hooked a few big ones here), until the 1820s, when Boston glass merchant **Deming Jarves** turned it into an industrial center virtually overnight. Jarves recognized in Sandwich an ideal glass-manufacturing site: it had plenty of virgin forest to fuel the furnaces, hay for packing the output, and if the local sand wasn't quite up to snuff, no matter; the raw material could be shipped in, the harbor being handy. By mid-century, the tiny town had two factories that made every type of glassware, from purely decorative knickknacks to strictly functional drinking vessels. These companies eventually put Sandwich on the map as one of the foremost glass capitals of the world.

Sandwich's boom was short-lived, however: in the 1860s and 1870s, competition from coal-powered plants in the Midwest cut into the market, finally diminishing the demand for the more expensive Cape Cod-produced glass, and in 1888, the **Boston & Sandwich Glass Company** shut down for good. In some ways, the resultant depression that left the town moldering until the first wave of automobile-borne tourists arrived in the 1920s was a blessing: Sandwich has retained a town center that is the very picture of a pristine New England village. Prescient planners and generous local benefactors have made sure that colonial-era buildings such as the carefully restored **Hoxie House** and **Dexter Grist Mill** remain intact and open to the public. Captain's houses of the Federal period—typically white clapboards with black trim—lend a formal grace to the tree-shaded streets.

Although Sandwich's bayside beaches don't begin to match the wild beauty of the vast, unspoiled, oceanside stretches of the Outer Cape, they quite suffice for sunbathing, swimming, and perhaps a sunset stroll. The town attracts a more affluent and somewhat older beach-oriented crowd than the towns from **Orleans** up to **Provincetown.** A major draw are the exceptional museums, including the **Heritage Plantation**, a 76-acre complex encompassing noted collections of folk art, and the **Sandwich Glass Museum.** Both provide the visitor with a context for understanding the area's history, as well as a sense of continuity.

West of Sandwich is the county of **Bourne** (which split off in 1864, naming itself for a New Bedford whaling magnate and philanthropist), a place that is primarily rural and decidedly private, making few concessions to draw tourists. Summer homes here, whether grand or simple, have descended through generations, and the inhabitants are content to savor the simpler pleasures of Cape life: intensive gardening, swimming in the protected and relatively warm waters of **Buzzards Bay**, bicycling along winding country roads. If you're looking for diversion here, you may feel frustrated or even unwanted—but focus on the quiet beauty of the place and you'll understand why Bourne residents are happy just to stay put.

1 Cape Cod Canal This remarkable 17.4-mile waterway was under discussion as early as 1697 and espoused by **Myles Standish, George Washington,** and other prominent figures. But it was New York financier **Augustus Perry Belmont** who saw the plan through. Having beat the completion of the Panama Canal by a scant but significant 17 days, Belmont captained the triumphant opening parade of boats on 29 July 1914; among the notables on hand was Assistant Secretary of the Navy **Franklin D. Roosevelt.** And though Belmont backed construction of the canal, it never garnered him much monetary reward (when it was sold to the U.S. government for $11.5 million in 1928, the bondholders—who had put up $16 million—suffered a loss).

Under the jurisdiction of the **U.S. Army Corps of Engineers (USACE)** since 1917, the Cape Cod Canal remains the world's widest sea-level canal—at 480 feet—and transports some 20,000 vessels yearly. Because of strong currents (and busy marine traffic), it's verboten to swimmers, but the banks have been turned into a greensward popular with bicyclists, who enjoy 14 miles of paved paths (seven miles on each side). It's hard to imagine that these bucolic shores were an early 18th-century hotbed of industry. Here, in factories that flanked the canal for a full mile, **Keith Car and Manufacturing** (at one point the largest employer in New England) produced Conestoga wagons, and later railroad cars. Today, the USACE staff offer "bike hikes" from the Buzzards Bay railroad bridge, guided walks around Sagamore Hill (starting at the entrance to Scusset State Park), and other interpretive programs. ♦ 759.5991

2 Christmas Tree Shops As natives know, these giant emporia—with six locations on the Cape, others elsewhere in New England—have nothing at all to do with Christmas, except in the spend-spend-spend sense. Off-price housewares crowd this outsized pseudo-Elizabethan thatched cottage, where you can pick up the odd bargain on things you didn't even know you needed: lawn furniture, gardening supplies, books, toys, even gourmet foodstuffs. How about some fluorescent shoelaces? ♦ Daily 9AM-10PM. 9 Rte 6A (at the Sagamore Bridge), Sagamore. 888.7010. Also at: 655 Rte 132, Hyannis, 778.5521

2 The Bridge ★★$$ You might not think to give this hohum-looking restaurant a second glance, but inside, the **Prete** family has been turning out excellent Italian food (homemade minestrone, tortellini, and more) since 1953. Now, chef and daughter-in-law **Pon** has added her Thai spring rolls and *padt ka prow gai* (chicken with basil, garlic, and peppers), as well as a summer dish, *yum nuer* (sliced sirloin marinated in lemon, peppers, scallions, and spices, served cold with jasmine rice). ♦ Italian/Thai ♦ Lunch and dinner. 21 Rte 6A (at the Sagamore Bridge), Sagamore. 888.8144

3 Pairpont Glass Works Combining 18th-century techniques introduced by **Deming Jarves,** founder of the Boston & Sandwich Glass Company, and by **Thomas J. Pairpont,** a leading glass designer of the 1880s, the Pairpont line has been prized by collectors practically since its inception. Among the less expensive items are commemorative "cup plates" (about $6). Ascending the price scale are hand-blown candlesticks ($130 a pair) and decorative koi fish ($250 and more). It's fascinating to watch this ancient craft applied to tomorrow's collectibles. ♦ Daily 9AM-6PM; glassblowing demonstrations M-F 9:30AM-4:30PM. 851 Rte 6A (at the Sagamore Bridge), Sagamore. 888.2344, 800/899.0953

4 Sagamore Inn ★$$ For your first glimpse of "corny old Cape Cod" (an increasingly scarce commodity), duck into this classic late 19th-century roadhouse with wooden booths and tin ceiling. The food may not be anything to write home about, but it's cheap and plentiful, and you can't go wrong with the steamers—steamed longneck clams to be dunked in their own broth then in melted butter. For connoisseurs of classic diner fare, there's pot roast and Grapenut pudding. ♦ American/Takeout ♦ Lunch and dinner. Closed Tuesday and Dec-Mar. 1131 Rte 6A (between the Sagamore Bridge and Tupper Rd), Sagamore. 888.9707

5 Horizons on Cape Cod Bay $$ Make a beeline for the bay, and this is the first scenic eatery you'll find. The airy interior is generic collegiate, with pennants decorating the rafters, but the deck basks in a broad bay view, spectacular at sunset. Try a fried clam roll, the Cape's ubiquitous low-rent delicacy. ♦ American ♦ Lunch and dinner; Sunday brunch. Closed mid-Oct to mid-Mar. 98 Town Neck Rd (at Freeman Ave), Sandwich. 888.6166

5 Beachside B&B $$ If you can't wait to hit the beach running, here's the first available sleep-over opportunity. This modern three-bedroom B&B offers all one could ask in terms of setting, privacy, and luxury. It's right on a private stretch of **Town Beach,** with a view of the bridge and (on a clear day) Provincetown. The unobtrusive owners live next door, not in-house. There are two sitting rooms: one doubles as an exercise room, with a Stairmaster and Lifecycle, and the other suits more sedentary types who prefer a good book, a comfortable couch, and a crackling fire. Rooms are spacious and thoughtfully equipped, right down to the CD players and Jacuzzis-for-two. ♦ 1-3 Bay Beach Ln (off Freeman Ave), Sandwich. 888.8813

6 **Dillingham House** $ Built by one of the town founders, this circa 1650 house—a three-quarters Cape—reputedly harbored a backroom bar during Prohibition. The former tackroom, with its wood stove, grand piano, and loads of books, games, and puzzles, is a great place to hang out when the weather's uncooperative; when it is, guests have the use of house bicycles. There are five not too fancy, but nice enough rooms, including one with a waterbed (what would the Puritans think?). ♦ 71 Main St (Rte 130), Sandwich. 833.0065

7 **Heritage Plantation of Sandwich** You could—and probably should—devote at least half a day to savoring the Heritage Plantation's various components. The cluster of museums on these 76 acres of landscaped grounds showcase a strange and enchanting amalgam of collections assembled by relatives and friends in honor of **Josiah Kirby Lilly** (of pharmaceutical fame).

For instance, a reconstructed Shaker round barn (copied from the real thing in Hancock, Massachusetts) houses antique automobiles from the era when cars were dazzling chariots of steel; among the holdings is **Gary Cooper's** zooty 1931 Duesenberg. The military museum features an exhibit of Native American artifacts, including a striking Haida blanket made of gray and red wool and decorated with mother-of-pearl buttons. The high point of the art museum isn't the Currier & Ives prints, though they're charming, nor the schoolgirls' samplers, the advertising art, or the children's toys, but rather a working carousel (circa 1912) with 32 hand-carved creatures, including a giraffe and a goat; rides are free. An ostrich, a frog footman, and other peculiar turn-of-the-century mounts ring the room.

An open-sided jitney carts visitors hither and yon, but the grounds, with their labeled flora, invite self-propelled exploration on foot, especially in May and June, when the carefully bred rhododendrons burst forth in infinitely varied shades of delicate pink. ♦ Admission. Daily 10AM-5PM; no tickets sold after 4:15PM. Closed Nov to mid-May. Grove and Pine Sts, Sandwich. 888.3300

Within the Heritage Plantation of Sandwich:

Carousel Cafe ★$$ The perfect picnic spot, and you don't have to lug a basket. This gourmet snack bar, under a striped green awning, offers soups (including chowder and gazpacho), salads, and overstuffed sandwiches. Grab a tasty cranberry cookie for a portable dessert. ♦ Snacks ♦ Lunch and snacks. 888.3300

8  **Old Cemetery Point** It stands to reason that the Cape's oldest town would have some of its oldest graves. This knoll overlooking Shawme Pond has lots of well-kept tombstones (dating from 1683) sporting pithy admonitions and winged death's heads. Most are hand-hewn. You may find it interesting later to match up the various "Here lyes ye body of" with figures whose names are still bandied about town. ♦ Grove St (between Academy Rd and Pine St), Sandwich

9 **H. Richard Strand Antiques** This fine 1800 emporium (shown above) carries only the best furniture, china, and glass, all beautifully arrayed in formal settings. Come early in the season and it looks almost like a normal house, albeit one inhabited by an incurable collector. The quantity of holdings gradually diminishes as the summer progresses, but never the quality. ♦ Daily 9AM-5PM. 2 Grove St (off Main St), Sandwich. 888.3230

10 **Town Hall** Built in 1834 at a cost of $4,138 to accommodate Sandwich's boomtown business, this plain and boxy Greek Revival beauty, with four Doric columns as understated decoration, was made to last, and has: it's still in use as the center of town government. ♦ Rte 130 (as it becomes Main St), Sandwich. 888.0340

11 **The Inn at Sandwich Center** $ One of the "newer" B&Bs in town, this 1750s saltbox aggrandized with an 1850s Federal roofline has five inviting bedrooms decorated in bold bright colors. Owner **Judy Dunn**, who opened it in 1992, serves homemade granola and muffins (you'll wake up to the aroma of them baking). Ask to see the beehive oven's chimney crafted of clamshell plaster. Centrally located, yet peacefully situated on its own hillock, the inn is right across the street from the Sandwich Glass Museum. ♦ 118 Tupper Rd (at Main St), Sandwich. 888.6958, 800/4844.4017 ext 2401

A special exhibit at the Sandwich Glass Museum is dedicated to Hannah Crowell Burgess, a Sandwich native who in 1855, at the age of 22, had to take over the wheel of a clipper ship from her ailing husband off the coast of Peru; "Hannah the Navigator" successfully brought the ship to shore, but meanwhile her husband died, and she returned home a widow. The words "I will never marry again" are inscribed in her wedding ring (now on display).

12 Sandwich Glass Museum Half the history of the town is encased in this extensive collection of glassware, much of it displayed to optimal effect along banks of sunny windows. A good, succinct video introduction explains the rise and fall of the business, from 1828 to 1888. **Deming Jarves'** glass-production system, utilizing local resources and a mostly immigrant workforce, initially worked so well that for the first time in history, even citizens of modest means could afford glassware. His enterprise went swimmingly until coal-powered Midwestern plants undercut and out-produced him. Jarves' ill-timed recourse was to attempt a return to handblown glassmaking, just as his labor force was beginning to bridle after decades of exploitation. His business crashed and burned—but it was only the beginning for collectors who prize the factory's extremely varied output. Even nonaficionados will find much to admire in the products on display, from dolphin-motif candlesticks to pressed "lacy" glass.

The museum (pictured at left) is run and staffed by the nonprofit **Sandwich Historical Society,** and the volunteer docents are happy to fill in with local lore. A gift shop on the premises features related literature and reproductions of Sandwich classics, as well as contemporary work by Cape Cod artisans. ♦ Admission. Daily 9:30AM-4:30PM Apr-Oct; W-Su 9:30AM-4PM Nov-Dec, Feb-Mar. 129 Main St (at Tupper Rd), Sandwich. 888.0251

13 First Church of Christ Built in 1847 by **Charles Bulfinch** associate **Isaac Melvin** of Cambridge, and evidently influenced by the designs of **Sir Christopher Wren** (the spire resembles Wren's masterpiece, St. Mary-le-Bow in London), this elegant church counterposes ornate Corinthian columns (two sets, one miniaturized in the cupola) and a chunky geometric design; the result is at once down-to-earth and celestial. ♦ Service Su 10AM. 136 Main St (at Water St), Sandwich. 888.0434

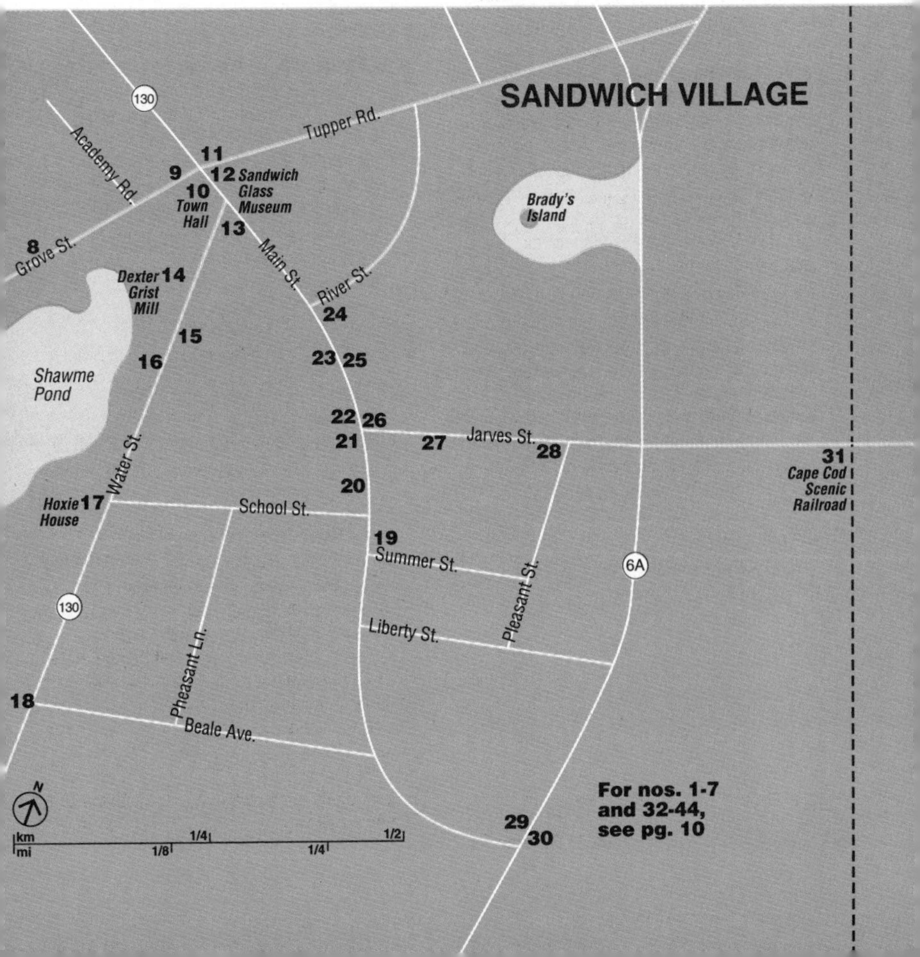

SANDWICH VILLAGE

130
Tupper Rd.
Academy Rd.
11
9
12 Sandwich Glass Museum
10 Town Hall
13
8
Grove St.
Main St.
Dexter 14 Grist Mill
River St.
24
Brady's Island
15
16
23 25
Shawme Pond
22 26
21
27
Jarves St.
28
31 Cape Cod Scenic Railroad
Water St.
20
Hoxie 17 House
School St.
19
Summer St.
6A
Pleasant St.
130
Liberty St.
Pleasant Ln.
18
Beale Ave.
N
km
mi
1/8
1/4
1/4
1/2
29
30

For nos. 1-7 and 32-44, see pg. 10

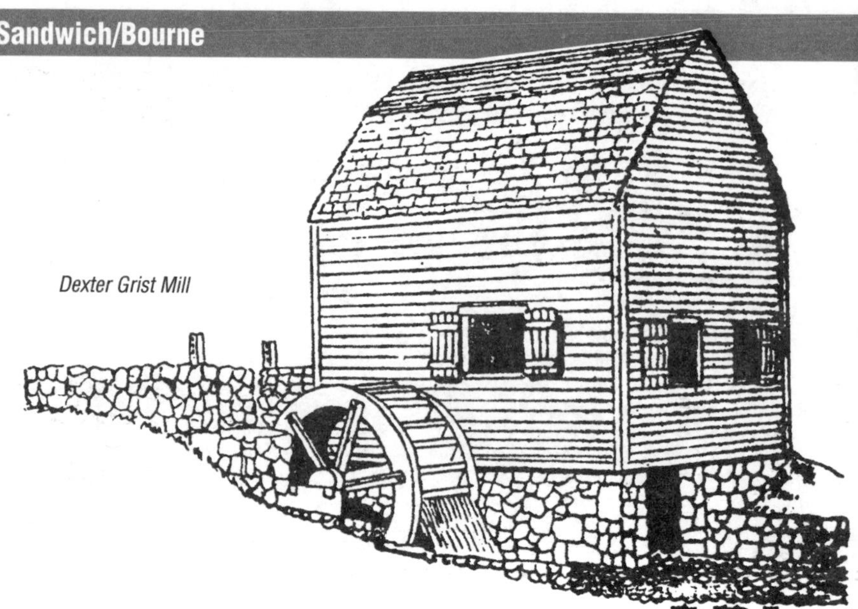
Dexter Grist Mill

14 Dexter Grist Mill During the glass factories' heyday, this circa 1640 mill built by **Thomas Dexter,** was one of several turbine-powered workhorses (a far cry from the quaint site visible today). Its output became obsolete in 1881 (coal-powered Western mills could provide flour more cheaply), and it sat idle until the 1920s, when **Alice Harvey** turned it into a tearoom to attract the new wave of motoring tourists. In the late '50s, the defunct mills surrounding it were demolished, and in 1961, it was reopened as a working mill—and tourist attraction.

Today, using a cypress wood waterwheel and wooden gears (the oldest form of milling machinery in the country), powered by pond overflow, town miller **Leo R. Manning**—a schoolteacher—churns out cornmeal. Offered for sale in cloth bags, it's best when used within 24 hours, and makes terrific polenta, in addition to colonial staples like johnnycakes and Indian pudding; ask for recipes. The mill is also a popular spot with Shawme Pond's feathered friends: a dozen or so swans, geese, and ducks are usually in attendance. ♦ Admission. M-Sa 10AM-4:45PM, Su 1-4:45PM mid-June to mid-Sept; Sa 10AM-4:45PM, Su 1-4:40PM mid-May to mid-June, mid-Sept to mid-Oct. Shawme Pond (next to Town Hall), Sandwich. 888.1173

15 The Dunbar House $ **Mike** and **Mary Bell,** teachers from Somerset, England, rescued this 1741 house from two decades of dereliction in 1990. They've made the most of its prime setting (opposite the Dexter Grist Mill and Shawme Pond), by turning the house into a four-bedroom B&B. Each room is pleasantly, if not dazzlingly, decorated and visitors are treated to home-cooked breakfasts as well as afternoon tea. ♦ 1 Water St (between Main and School Sts), Sandwich. 833.2485

On the grounds of The Dunbar House:

The Dunbar Tea Shop ★★$ This carriage house-turned-tea shop boasts a wonderful blend of antiques, gifts, British comestibles, and books new and old (e.g., a "slightly careworn" collection of Dickens). The tearoom, with its wood stove, couldn't be cozier in winter; come summer, tables are set up in the unstudied splendor of the garden. Lunches feature savories, quiches, and specials such as vol-au-vent; sweets include pies, scones, Scottish shortbread, and wickedly rich "Trafalgar squares." ♦ Daily 10AM-dark. Tea served 11AM-4PM. 833.2485

16 Thornton W. Burgess Museum Local boy and avid conservationist **Thornton W. Burgess** (1874-1965) wrote 15,000 children's stories and 170 books, some of which may seem a bit musty to modern eyes (quoth Peter Rabbit: "With an open mind go on your way/And add to knowledge every day"). But little children love this tiny museum with its original illustrations by **Harrison Cady,** puzzles and games, gift shop, and, best of all, live animal story times (with a real critter on hand) in the summer.

The 1756 cottage, known as the **Eldred House,** was the home of Burgess' eccentric aunt, **Arabella Eldred Burgess,** a teacher who claimed to communicate verbally with both wildlife and plants. A "tussie-mussie" garden shaped like a nosegay and a "touch and smell" garden of aromatic herbs flourish outside. The museum, along with the **Green Briar Nature Center & Jam Kitchen,** is operated by the **T.W. Burgess Society,** a nonprofit organization conceived on the centennial of Burgess' birth by local bookseller **Nancy Titcomb** to commemorate his works and foster his philosophy. ♦ Donation. M-Sa 10AM-4PM, Su 1-4PM mid-Apr to Dec. 4 Water St (between Main and School Sts), Sandwich. 888.4668

17 **Hoxie House** Built circa 1675 by **Reverend John Smith** and named for whaling captain

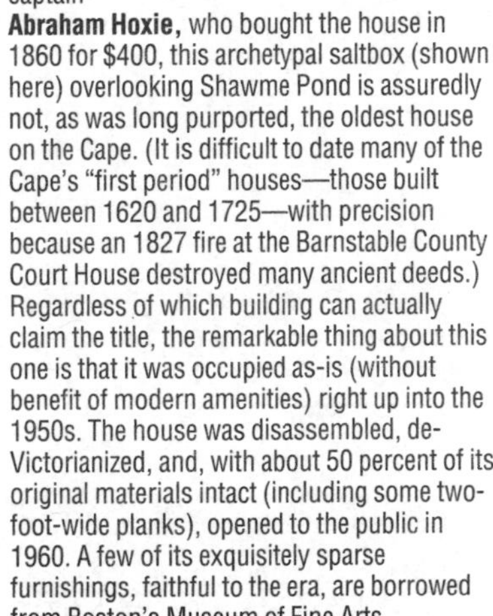

Abraham Hoxie, who bought the house in 1860 for $400, this archetypal saltbox (shown here) overlooking Shawme Pond is assuredly not, as was long purported, the oldest house on the Cape. (It is difficult to date many of the Cape's "first period" houses—those built between 1620 and 1725—with precision because an 1827 fire at the Barnstable County Court House destroyed many ancient deeds.) Regardless of which building can actually claim the title, the remarkable thing about this one is that it was occupied as-is (without benefit of modern amenities) right up into the 1950s. The house was disassembled, de-Victorianized, and, with about 50 percent of its original materials intact (including some two-foot-wide planks), opened to the public in 1960. A few of its exquisitely sparse furnishings, faithful to the era, are borrowed from Boston's Museum of Fine Arts. ♦ Admission. M-Sa 10AM-5PM, Su 1-5PM mid-June to mid-Sept. 18 Water St (at School St). 888.1173

18 **Quail Hollow Farm** So luscious-looking is the produce arrayed at this picturesque, nicely weathered 1840 barn, that it deserves to be painted rather than eaten. The prices (unposted) may give you the impression that you've been charged by the karat, but the payoff is superlative taste as well as looks. Try the locally made canned goods (such as jalapeño pepper jelly or amaretto chocolate topping), and don't miss the tea cakes, usually available in lemon or blueberry; they're moist, dense, and supersweet. ♦ Th-Su 10AM-5PM late May to mid-Oct. Rte 130 (at Beale Ave), Sandwich. 888.0438

19 **Isaiah Jones Homestead** $$ Victorian decor can often be lugubrious, but here it's unabashedly sexy. Several of the five guest bedrooms in this 1849 sea captain's home—its ornate trim painted cream, dusty rose, and slate blue—inspire heated fantasies: *vide* the **Deming Jarves** Room, with its demi-canopy bed draped in burgundy damask (the raised whirlpool tub in the adjoining bath is a thoughtful addition). A gourmet breakfast is served by candlelight (so flattering on those mornings-after), and fireside tea or lemonade on the porch is proffered according to the season. ♦ 165 Main St (at Summer St), Sandwich. 888.9115

20 **Summer House** $ Aptly named and decorated, this circa 1835 Greek Revival house is spacious, airy, and supremely refreshing. Four of the five large corner rooms have fireplaces, and all sport pretty quilts made by owner **Kay Merrell.** The breakfast room is a dazzler, with Chinese-red walls and black-and-white checkerboard floor; expect some rather elaborate eye-openers, such as puff pastries, coffee breads, and fruit cobblers—*plus* a hearty entrée, something along the lines of eggs Benedict. You could probably pass up lunch for the complimentary afternoon tea served on the sun porch: with tea cakes or British biscuits. And the hammocks in the English-style garden are so inviting you may wish that Sandwich didn't have quite so many alluring activities. ♦ 158 Main St (at School St), Sandwich. 888.4991

21 **Home for the Holidays Ltd.** The front parlor of this 1850 home-turned-shop (shown here) observes Christmas year-round; other rooms honor holidays in passing, with seasonally appropriate presents. There's one room set aside for gifting babies and children, and the repertoire tends to the classical, such as Steiff stuffed animals. Among the big-ticket items for adults is a Thomas B. Swain & Co. picnic hamper, fully accoutered, for slightly short of four figures. Whether you're hoping to please a host or hostess, or simply treating yourself, the choices here are truly select. ♦ Th-Sa 10AM-4PM, Su noon-4PM Sept-May; Th-Sa 10AM-4PM, Su noon-6PM June-Aug. 154 Main St (at Jarves St), Sandwich. 888.4388

22 **Captain Ezra Nye House** $ Yet another house to make you wonder why sea captains ever left home. This 1829 Federal manse, hosted by **Elaine** and **Harry Dickson,** has seven appealing bedrooms, including one in pale blue calico with complementary stenciling. Breakfasts are competitive: homemade apple-cinnamon quiche, soufflés. . . . ♦ 152 Main St (at Jarves St), Sandwich. 888.6142, 800/388.2778

Settlers misnamed Buzzards Bay, mistaking the native osprey for the scavengers.

23 The Weather Store An interest in meteorological matters is not a prerequisite for enjoying this store: "weather" is interpreted broadly to incorporate giant lobster whirligigs, scrimshaw, brass lanterns, maps, globes, etc. If you are a weather nut, all the better. Paraphernalia ranges from handsome Maximum instruments (a must for the yacht) to the "weather stick," a $5 "easy to install, no maintenance" device that lets you know when a storm's brewing. Co-owner **Parke Madden** confirms that visitors seeking a gift for the already overequipped rarely leave empty-handed. ♦ M-Sa 10AM-5PM May-Dec. 146 Main St (between Jarves and River Sts), Sandwich. 888.6434

24 Yesteryears Doll Museum Housed in the somewhat shabby **First Parish Meetinghouse** (shown here; an 1833 Gothic Revival structure that replaced the 1638 original) is a fabulous collection of dolls from the past three centuries, lovingly presented in glass cases raised on old church pews. The effect, especially when you happen upon the life-size dolls in the old altar area, is more than a little spooky, as is the parade of forgotten childhood favorites.

Among the holdings is an elegant Queen Anne doll from the 17th century; more recent exemplars include a panoply of Shirley Temples, a bouncy Betty Boop, and "literary dolls" like Eloise. Barbie shares a case with G.I. Joe. But it's the infinite variety of 19th-century German and French bisque dolls who steal the show. New exhibits are organized yearly, and there's a consignment shop/doll hospital in the basement for collectors with a niche to fill or a poppet to put to rights. ♦ Admission. M-Sa 10AM-4PM mid-May through Oct. Main and River Sts, Sandwich. 888.1711

25 The Dan'l Webster Inn $$ It may come as a disappointment to learn that this is not the original colonial parsonage-turned-tavern, destroyed by fire in 1971. That said, this large but sensitively landscaped complex—operated since 1980 by the **Catania** family, owners of the Hearth 'N Kettle chain of restaurants—expertly fulfills the role of town nexus, with 47 luxurious, reproduction-appointed rooms (including eight suites with canopy beds and fireplaces in nearby historical houses). A small outdoor pool with gazebo, access to a local health club, and tru[ly] delectable food (MAP plans are available) round out the amenities. Because of its modernity, it's not as evocative as the many historic little inns in town, but the four-star service more than compensates. ♦ 149 Main St (between River and Jarves Sts), Sandwich 888.3623, 800/444.3566

Within The Dan'l Webster Inn:

The Devil n' Dan Tavern, Conservatory, Webster Room, and Heritage Room ★★★$$$ The inn's four dining areas are all served by the same kitchen, with executive chef **Richard Catania** at the helm. The Tavern seeks to re-create a colonial ambience, and serves a special burger topped with Canadian bacon, barbecue sauce, and various vegetables; it's a local favorite. The Conservatory, skylit and fronting a meticulously tended garden, is a lovely spot for breakfast (try the prime-rib hash), or indeed any meal. It's at dinner that the chef pulls out the stops: in addition to traditional favorites (*fruits de mer* in white wine, rack of lamb in currant sauce), Catania composes a monthly menu to take advantage of seasonal offerings. So dedicated is he to fresh ingredients, the inn has opened its own aquaculture farm, yielding freshwater fish and hydroponic vegetables. The desserts are elaborate and invariably exquisite. ♦ New American ♦ Breakfast, lunch, and dinner. 888.3623

26 The Brown Jug Antiques Art glass (particularly the local product), Staffordshire china, and French and English cameos are the specialties at this homespun little shop, in business since 1935. ♦ M-Sa 10:30AM-5PM, Su noon-5PM May-Oct; by appointment Nov-Dec, Mar-Apr. 155 Main St (at Jarves St), Sandwich. 833.1088

27 The Village Inn at Sandwich $ This 1837 Federal-style B&B (shown above) looks welcoming on the outside, with its broad lawn and wraparound porch; inside, it's even prettier. Co-owners **Winfried** and **Patricia Platz** are responsible for the furniture and decor, respectively. He actually made the chairs and tables, which look like freshly minted Victoriana, while she provisioned the eight bedrooms with bleached floors, feathered comforters, swaths of fabric, and imaginatively angled wooden beds ("I have a thing about straight lines," she confesses). The whole is dramatic and romantic, with a contagious sense of style. ♦ Closed Jan-Mar.

4 Jarves St (between Pleasant and Main Sts), Sandwich. 833.0363

28 Madden & Company Like an upscale general store, this relatively new shop—installed in a late 19th-century church—showcases the must-haves of the late 20th century: esoteric foodstuffs (including an assortment of jams, spreads, and mustards from Canada's Honey Hollow) and tasteful household accessories. A sprinkling of antique ceramic aspic molds are thrown in for good measure. ♦ M-Sa 10AM-5PM May-Dec. 16 Jarves St (at Pleasant St), Sandwich. 888.3663

29 Old King's Row Antiques This small and spanking-clean shop, opened in 1993 by **Lore Garner,** has limited but impeccable stock, from colonial candlestands to 18th-century samplers. ♦ M-Tu, Th-Su 10:30AM-5PM. 158 Rte 6A (at Main St), Sandwich. 833.1395

30 Sandwich Minigolf Trust Sandwich to have a *tasteful* miniature golf course. **Maurice Burke,** who now teaches at a Christian school in Taiwan, started building this 18-hole beauty 40 years ago on what was his family's cranberry bog. He incorporated the architectural vernacular of the region—shingled windmills, covered bridges—as well as nautical wonders into the hazards. There's a whale and a sea horse to maneuver around, plus the world's only floating golf green. ♦ Admission. Daily 10AM-10PM mid-June to mid-Sept; Sa-Su 10AM-10PM mid-May to mid-June, mid-Sept to mid-Oct. 159 Rte 6A (at Main St), Sandwich. 888.1579

30 Maypop Lane Pretty much a flea-market-style hodgepodge, this group store (stocked by seven dealers) is just the kind of place that hints at surprise pickings—perhaps in the area of dolls, quilts, or costume jewelry. ♦ Daily 10AM-4PM. 161 Rte 6A (opposite Main St), Sandwich. 888.1230

31 Cape Cod Scenic Railroad Board a vintage train here for a day trip into **Hyannis** (about 40 minutes away) or a brief jog north to **Sagamore** (10 minutes). For details on dinner cruises and charter trips out of Hyannis, see page 51. ♦ Four departures daily June-late Oct; limited schedule May, late Nov to late Dec. Jarves St (between Rte 6A and Factory St), Sandwich. Main office: 252 Main St, Hyannis, 771.3788

32 The Sandwich Boardwalk When Hurricane Bob blew this 1,350-foot-long, 117-year-old landmark away in 1991, undaunted locals raised $80,000 for a board-by-board replacement. Sponsored "personalized planks," inscribed with messages, were pounded in place under the supervision of the Department of Conservation. Once again, this delicate wooden walkway arches over the marsh and toward the sea, and kids have resumed the summer tradition of jumping into **Mill Creek.** Look for great blue herons stalking their dinner in the shallow tidal pools. ♦ Harbor St (off Factory St), Sandwich

33 Green Briar Nature Center & Jam Kitchen You'll know you've come to the right place when the aroma of slowly simmering jam envelops you like a sweet fog.

Ida Putnam founded her jam kitchen in this late 18th-century house in 1903 and expanded it in 1916 to make room for a new line of "sun-cooked" preserves; her recipes, and those of kindred canners, are sold in the on-site shop and by mail order to this day. Author **Thornton W. Burgess,** who traipsed through the surrounding woods as a young boy, commended her efforts, writing, "It is a wonderful thing to sweeten the world, which is in a jam and needs preserving." Visitors are sure to agree.

Not only can you wander through the cheerful kitchen with its 20 Glenwood burners performing sugary alchemy, there's also a little nature library, a classroom with some skulls and stuffed animals and tiny dioramas of wildlife performing human domestic chores and other neat stuff, and a 57-acre nature preserve named for Burgess' fictive environment, the Old Briar Patch. A take-along trail map identifies local flora, and afterward you can visit the wildflower garden or have a nibble—alongside "Peter Rabbit" in his magisterial hutch—overlooking "Smiling Pool." Visit the shop for some take-home goodies: pear butter, perhaps, or Mae's mincemeat, or maybe just a jug of Squanto's Secret fertilizer and a convincing rubber snake. ♦ Donation. M-Sa 10AM-4PM, Su 1-4PM mid-Apr to Jan; Tu-Sa 10AM-4PM Jan to mid-Apr. 6 Discovery Hill Rd (off Rte 6A), E. Sandwich. 888.6870

Cape waters have snagged thousands of wrecks, starting with the Jamestown-bound *Sparrowhawk,* out of Plymouth, England, which foundered off Nauset Beach in 1626. Chatham historian Joseph A. Nickerson (a 10th-generation descendant of town founder William Nickerson) estimates that over the centuries some 2,000 ships have foundered off the Atlantic Coast between Monomoy Island and Eastham: one of the largest in recent history was the 470-foot Maltese freighter *Eldia,* which ran aground off Nauset Beach in 1984.

34 1641 Wing Fort House Accruing around a basic "peak house" (steep-roofed dwelling) built by **Reverend John Wing** circa 1641, this three-quarters colonial is the oldest house in America owned and lived in continuously by the same family. No Wings are in residence at present, but caretaker **David Wheelock** can provide an in-depth tour, showing how successive generations "recycled" parts of the structure to suit their changing needs. In the Victorian parlor you'll see "gunstock posts" which resemble upright rifles, barrels to the ground; early builders thought that the extra thickness on top might bear more weight, a precaution later proven unnecessary. A "press bed" and half-tester bed, both of which fold up flat to the wall, are the space-saving precursors of a Murphy; their rope underpinnings, which required constant cranking not to sag, may have given rise to the expression "sleep tight." ♦ Nominal admission. M-F 10AM-4PM mid-June to Aug. 69 Spring Hill Rd (off Rte 6A), E. Sandwich. 833.1540

35 Quaker Meeting House On this site, in 1657, the oldest Quaker Meeting House in continuous use in North America was established. The third incarnation of the house, erected in 1810, is as plain inside and out as one would expect: shingled exterior, simple pews arranged around a wood stove. It's a sign of the times—times past, that is—that the building is flanked by carriage barns. Any elegance here awaits the inspired speaker. ♦ Service Su 11AM. Off Spring Hill Rd (off Rte 6A), E. Sandwich. 398.3773

36 Pine Grove Cottages $ When **Patti Page** sang of "quaint little cottages," this is surely what she had in mind. This cluster of 11 shingle-sided cottages, family run for three generations, includes some one-roomers scarcely bigger than a birdhouse. Customers love them, size notwithstanding, assures owner **Kathy Bumstead,** saying, "They're kind of campy." She has freshened them up with lots of white paint, stenciling, and chenille bedspreads. Most visitors head straight for the beaches, but if you want to hang around, there's an aboveground pool as well as badminton and croquet. Children are certain to find peers to play with. ♦ 348 Rte 6A (between Quaker Meeting House and Old County Rds), E. Sandwich 888.8179

Sometimes the early settlers went overboard in their search for meaningful Biblical names: Nathan Bourne of Sandwich, for instance, named his ninth son (born in 1770) Mahershalallashbaz.

Restaurants/Clubs: Red | **Hotels:** Blue
Shops/ Outdoors: Green | **Sights/Culture:** Black

37 The Bee-Hive Tavern ★$ It's a roadhouse, all right, but with dark paneling, booths, banker's lamps, and old paintings and prints; there's even a gaping bass displayed over the bar. Burgers, salads, and sandwiches (including Middle Eastern roll-ups) are the staples, along with plenty of steaks, chops, and traditional fish dishes—such as baked stuffed quahogs, a dish rendering the giant native clam actually palatable by means of microdicing and seasoned stuffing. Prices are reasonable—no worse, really, than at a charmless clam shack. ♦ American/ International ♦ Lunch and dinner; breakfast also on Friday through Sunday from mid-May to mid-Oct. 406 Rte 6A (between Quaker Meeting House and Old County Rds), E. Sandwich. 833.1184

37 Titcomb's Book Shop This well-stocked three-story barn houses new and used books; specialties include regional, maritime, genealogical, and children's titles. There's usually quite a bit of vintage **Thornton W. Burgess** on hand: owner **Nancy Titcomb,** who raised eight children here, spearheaded the revival of interest in his work, and the establishment of the museum and nature center dedicated to his memory. If you need to load up on maps and guidebooks, or just get your bearings, stop in—they'll be glad to help out. ♦ M-Sa 10AM-5PM; Su noon-5PM. 432 Rte 6A (between Quaker Meeting House and Old County Rds), E. Sandwich. 888.2331

38 Nye Homestead This 1685 peak house-turned-saltbox-turned-full Cape colonial (shown above), home to early Sandwich settler **Benjamin Nye,** isn't a must-see, but it's sufficiently interesting if you have a bit of spare time. Marring the whole effect is a modern overhead light fixture, a '40s quilt, and some rather overzealous renovations: the stenciling in the back "borning room," though lovely, looks as if it had been retouched yesterday, as does the mustard-colored painted paneling in the parlor. Among the more interesting artifacts are small wood-and-iron stilts, apparently once used to maneuver through mud, and a housekeeper's tie-on pocket (colonial clothes had none, fabric being scarce). The small room beneath the stairs was installed to help ventilate the fire but has been known to generations of children as "the Bugaboo room." ♦ Admission. M-F noon-4:30PM mid-June to mid-Oct. 85 Old County Rd (off Rte 6A), E. Sandwich. 888.2368

WINGSCORTON FARM INN 1758

39 **Wingscorton Farm Inn** $$ This 1758 Federal farmstead, named for the Quaker/Abolitionist **Wing** family, was once a key stop on the **Underground Railroad;** ask to see the secret room concealed behind a fireplace panel in the library, where fugitive slaves hid until they could be escorted to the beach under cover of darkness. The farm remains a working one; its seven secluded acres harboring horses, a donkey, sheep, pygmy goats, free-range chickens, assorted cats, a pet turkey, and a potbellied pig—in all, "quite a menagerie," says **Dick Loring,** who opened the inn in 1980. The guest list is never very long, with only two upstairs suites, each with a king-size canopy bed (the only nod to modernism); an adjoining single room; plus a two-story carriage house with its own kitchen and a sun deck. All the rooms have working fireplaces and stunningly pared-down period furniture.

Guests invariably partake of the multicourse farmhand breakfast (with nut breads fresh from the oven) at the plank table in the main house. The "keeping room," now a comfortable living room, features what is thought to be the largest colonial hearth in New England: nine feet long, its mantel showcases an array of antique pewter. The inn is as well suited to romantic getaways as it is to family holidays; children delight in this lively domestic zoo. For a memento, take home some fresh eggs or a free-range chicken from the fridge in the barn, where they're sold on an honor system. ♦ 11 Wing Blvd (off Rte 6A), E. Sandwich. 888.0534

"Ice King" Frederick Tudor of Bourne (1763-1864) earned fame and fortune shipping ice to the West Indies and India. His inventor son Frederick, Jr., built the Monument Beach mansion that would become Gray Gables, Grover Cleveland's "summer White House."

40 **Aptucxet Trading Post Museum**
Centuries ago (before the Cape Cod Canal), two rivers almost met at this site; the portage route between them made a natural trading ground, especially with the Wampanoag tribe encamped nearby, and the Dutch accessible to the south.

The Pilgrims built their first trading post here in 1627, using polished fragments of quahog shells (which were known to the Indians as *wampumpeake* or *wampum*) as currency. The year before (in the first official treaty signed in North America), they had assumed the debts of their English backers in exchange for a monopoly on trade with the natives. The original post was destroyed by hurricane, and a second, erected in 1635, lasted only a few decades. However, references in Bradford's account enabled a pair of archaeologists to locate the site and excavate it in 1926; the dig yielded not only arrowheads, tools, and shards, but the original building's foundation.

Today, there's a replica (shown above) of the trading post, ably explicated by curator **Eleanor Hammond.** One room is arranged as it might have been in the days when two paid hands manned the property; the other displays the artifacts found on-site, plus the "Bournedale stone," the threshold to an Indian church built in the late 17th century, which, when turned over, revealed curious inscriptions. No one is sure whether these are Phoenician or Viking—or neither.

This modest complex, operated by the nonprofit **Bourne Historical Society,** contains a couple of other oddities as well, from a small Victorian train station built in 1892 for the personal use of **President Grover Cleveland**—his Monument Beach mansion, "Gray Gables" was the original summer White House—to the windmill that served his fishing buddy, actor **Joseph Jefferson** (renowned for his portrayal of Rip Van Winkle) as an art studio; it's now a gift shop. A shaded picnic area overlooks the canal and the **Vertical Lift Railroad Bridge,** which lowers a 554-foot-long span of track to permit trains to pass. Built in 1935 at a cost of $1.5 million, it's the second-largest bridge of its kind, but no longer very active. The best time to try to catch it in action is evenings between 5PM and 6PM. ♦ Nominal admission. Tu-Sa 10AM-5PM, Su 2-5PM May to mid-Oct. 24 Aptucxet Rd (off Perry Ave), Bourne Village. 759.9487

Sure-Fire Amusements for the Young and the Restless

The Cape's natural attributes of sand and surf fill most kids' fun quotas, but for those occasional instances when inclement conditions (or a case of sunburn) require a retreat from the beach, it pays to have some alternative diversions planned—the better to avoid cabin fever.

Movies, of course, are a godsend; a complement to the usual modern multiplexes, the **Wellfleet Drive-In** (349.2520) broadens the younger ones' cinematic experience beyond the family VCR. They can romp in a playground by the snack stand as dusk descends, then, likely as not, nod off during the feature film. Also, most of the local theaters offer morning and matinee performances specifically for children. Among these are the **Falmouth Playhouse** (563.5922), the **Cape Cod Melody Tent** (775.5630) in Hyannis, **Imagine Theatre for Children** (362.6333) at the Barnstable Comedy Club, the **Cape Playhouse** (385.3911) in Dennis, the **Harwich Junior Theatre** (432.2002) in West Harwich, Orleans' **Academy of Performing Arts** (255.5510), and **Actors Theatre of Nantucket** (228.6325).

A number of nearby museums will capture kids' imaginations—if not their intellects—for a couple hours. For the most part, it's best to forgo the stodgy historical society collections; an exception is the **Barn Museum** (398.6736) in West Dennis, with the fanciful "Driftwood Zoo" collection of artwork. The following also merit a look, depending on age, interest, and attention span. Sandwich's **Heritage Plantation** (888.3300) has an indoor merry-go-round (unlimited free rides with paid admission) as well as a snazzy antique car collection and landscaped grounds for roaming. In Brewster, the **Cape Cod Museum of Natural History** (896.3867) has pioneered a hands-on approach to learning; its nature trails make for enlightening meanders.

Of the various historic mills scattered about the area, Brewster's **Stony Brook Grist Mill** (no phone) is the most enjoyable, thanks to the miller-docents who encourage children to get in on the action. **Plimoth Plantation** (746.1622) in Plymouth is not to be missed: here, costumed interpreters make sure every visitor comes away with a feeling for authentic colonial life.

As for less educational pursuits, the choices are many. Very small children might be wowed by the **Aqua Circus** (775.8883) in West Dennis or the **Bassett Wild Animal Farm** (896.3224) in Brewster. The **Cape Cod Potato Chip Factory** (775.7253), just north of Hyannis, gives a five-minute tour that culminates in a complimentary crunchy snack. Harwich has a couple of sure-fire kid-pleasers in the **Trampoline Center** (432.8717) and **Bud's Go-Karts** (432.4964), while Martha's Vineyard boasts the theme-park-style **Flying Horses Carousel** (693.9481). Peewee Arnold Palmers will want to try their luck at any of the Cape's miniature golf courses.

Chatham's **Play-a-round Park**—a challenging sprawl of play structures designed by **Robert Leathers**—is good for several hours of free play; it's located on Depot Street next to the **Railroad Museum**. The **Charles Moore Arena** (255.2972), a roller skating rink in Orleans, is a great rainy-day resource, and on Friday nights kids ages 9 to 15 can cut loose at their own roller-disco party. Another physical activity to let off steam capitalizes on the Cape's network of bike paths: with cycle rentals (in all shapes and sizes) in no short supply, it's a fun way for the family to see the sights together.

---

41 Chart Room ★$$ Now a comfortably broken-in bar and restaurant, this rehabbed railroad barge used to be a machine shop that produced vessels for use in the Korean War. The Chart Room is one of the few places you can observe ordinarily private-minded Cataumet residents disport themselves—tastefully, of course. It's tucked away amid an active marina, and specialties include swordfish slathered with anchovy butter. ♦ American ♦ Lunch and dinner mid-June to mid-Sept; Th-Su mid-May to mid-June, mid-Sept to mid-Oct. Closed mid-Oct to mid-May. Cataumet Marina, Shipyard Ln (off Shore Rd), Cataumet. 563.5350

Restaurants/Clubs: Red **Hotels:** Blue
Shops/ Outdoors: Green **Sights/Culture:** Black

41 Harbor Casuals For women who find they've come to the Cape overdressed for success, this little shop stocks the kind of clothes that render one an instant native: linen blouses, flower-print pants, madras shorts, cotton sweaters. ♦ Daily 11AM-9PM mid-June to mid-Sept; F 5-9PM, Sa-Su 11AM-9PM mid-May to mid-June, mid-Sept to mid-Oct. Cataumet Marina, Shipyard Ln (off Shore Rd), Cataumet. 563.5129

42 Wood Duck Inn $ Staying in either of the two suites at this 1848 house, which overlooks a working cranberry bog, is like having a place of your own. Each has a small private deck (where innkeeper **Maureen Jason** will gladly bring you breakfast), a full living room with kitchenette and chintz-covered armchairs, a bathroom with stenciled ivy trailing from the skylight, and a cozy bedroom with comforters. Basically, no amenity is overlooked, and if you're interested in the "real" Cape, there's no better place to experience it. Maureen and her husband, **Dick,** who carves decoys (hence the name) can direct you to conservation lands in the area, where you may get to mingle with the nonhuman population. ♦ 1050 County Rd (near Red Brook Rd), Cataumet. 564.6404

43 The Courtyard Restaurant and Pub $$ All-American favorites predominate at this casual family spot, indigenous fare having expanded to include pizzette and chili. Kids get a crack at their favorites, too, such as peanut butter and jelly sandwiches. Among the specialties are such yummy *Joy of Cooking* throwbacks as seafood medley topped with crumbled Ritz crackers. The bar, paneled in barn board with Oriental rugs, can be a comfortable hideout when the weather's discomfitting. ♦ American/International ♦ Lunch and dinner. Cataumet Sq (Rte 28A and County Rd), Cataumet. 563.1818

43 Lee's Antiques This is one of those "everything piled together without rhyme or reason" grab bags that can yield surprise finds. Whether your objective is a weathered wicker couch or antique kitchen utensils, odds are good you'll find it here. ♦ Daily 10AM-5PM mid-June to mid-Sept; Sa-Su 10AM-5PM mid-Sept to mid-June. Cataumet Sq (Rte 28A and County Rd), Cataumet. 563.3261

43 Cataumet Fish Step right up and watch your dinner being gutted, or pluck a live lobster from the tank. This quaint little market only looks old, thanks to the vintage iceboxes and stove used to display designer pasta and Common Crackers, but the fish is as fresh as this morning. Check out the board of nautical knots to see how your Scout training holds up. ♦ M-Sa 10AM-6PM, Su 10AM-5PM mid-May to mid-Oct; Tu-Sa 10AM-6PM mid-Oct to mid-May. Cataumet Sq (Rte 28A and County Rd), Cataumet. 564.5956. Also at: 15 Boxwood Circle, Falmouth. 548.7535; Deer Crossing, Mashpee. 477.4116

44 Emack & Bolio's One of Boston's favorite ice cream emporia has a well-situated outpost here. Try the "Cosmic Cataumet Crunch," a gooey delight shot with caramel. ♦ M-Th noon-8PM, F-Su noon-9PM mid-Apr to mid-Oct. Rte 28A and County Rd, Cataumet. 564.5442. Also at: Main St, Chatham. 945.5506; Oracle Sq, Rte 6A, Orleans. 255.5844

44 Thunder Mine Adventure Golf Follow the yellow diamonds to this 18-hole Astroturf minigolf course with a Gold Rush motif. En route or afterward, you can pick up some penny candy or add to your baseball card collection. ♦ M-Th 10AM-10PM, F-Su 10AM-11PM late May to mid-Oct. Rte 28A and County Rd, Cataumet. 563.7450

Bests

Marie C. Franklin
Journalist, *The Boston Globe*

Chatham Band Concerts—bring your lawn chairs and your nostalgia for Americana. Friday night band concerts are free at **Kate Gould Park** in Chatham in summer.

Chatham Center—a wonderful collection of shops and restaurants. My favorites: the **Mayflower Shop** with its green and white awnings, and **Chatham Squires** restaurant, where locals and tourists alike belly up to the bar for steamers and beer.

Kreme and Kone Restaurant—arguably the best fried clams and onion rings on Cape Cod—located in both Dennis and Chatham.

Flea Market at Wellfleet Drive-in on Route 6 in Wellfleet—bring cash for bargains galore; open seven days a week in the summer.

Antiquing on Route 6A from Sandwich to Provincetown—there's a shop every couple of hundred yards. It's fun even if you don't buy.

Baker's Hardware in South Chatham—the tinkle of the bell above the door gets me every time. The proprietor, **Cyrus Baker,** is in his 80s, and still figures your bill on scratch paper and gives you change from his pocket.

Chatham Fish and Lobster Company, in the Cornfield Marketplace in West Chatham. Name your seafood passion—lobster, clams, swordfish—and you'll find it fresh there. Cooking advice is free.

Off-The-Bay Cafe in downtown Orleans. On nights when we have a baby-sitter, we drink margaritas and play Trivial Pursuit at the bar. The clientele is eclectic, and everyone mixes well.

When the head honchos of the Plymouth Colony checked up on their satellite town of Sandwich in 1655, they found it intolerably lax: many men had taken to wearing their hair below their ears! The Puritans put up stocks and a whipping post, and soon the "teenaged" town was set to rights.

FALMOUTH/MASHPEE

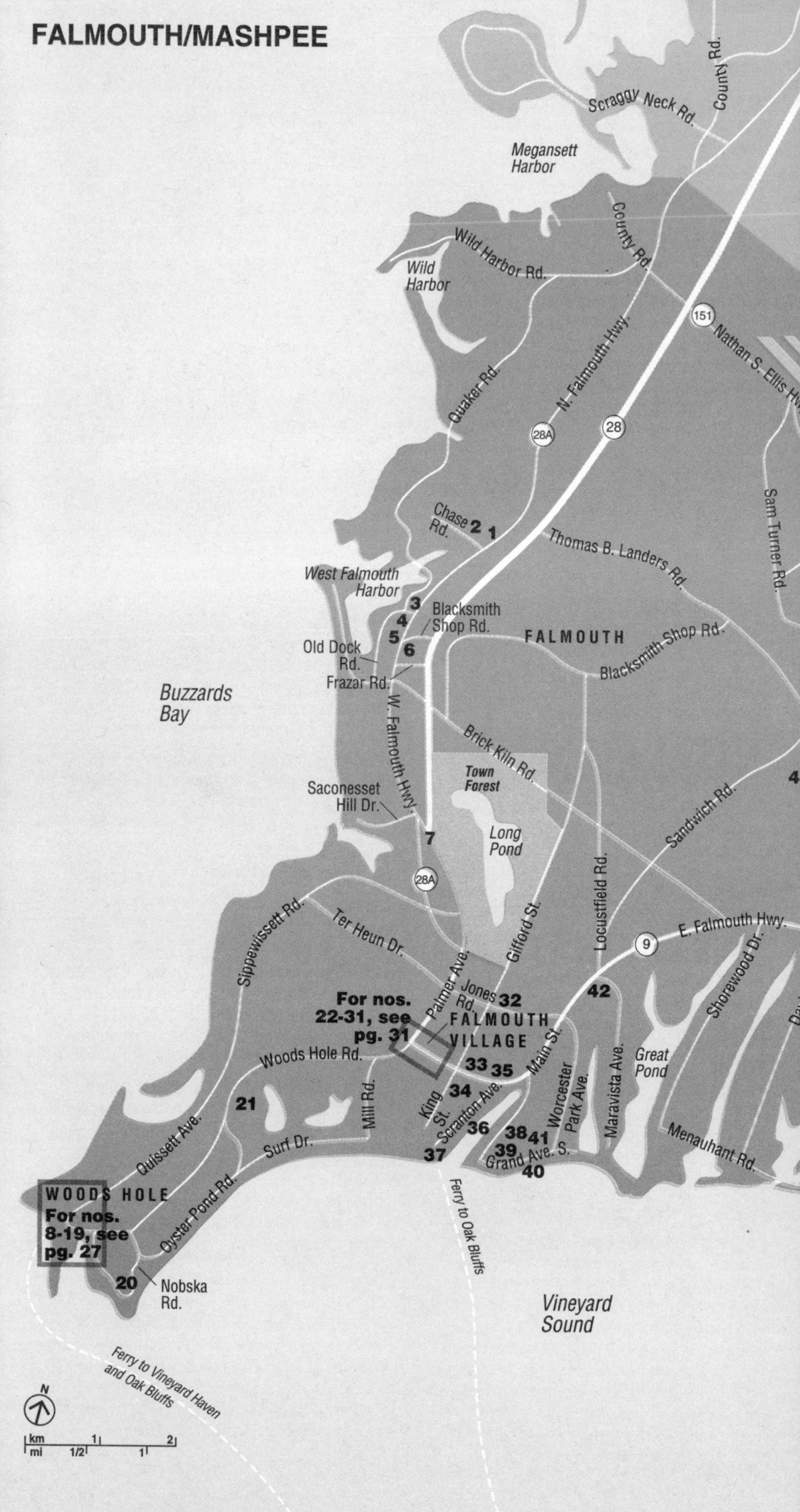

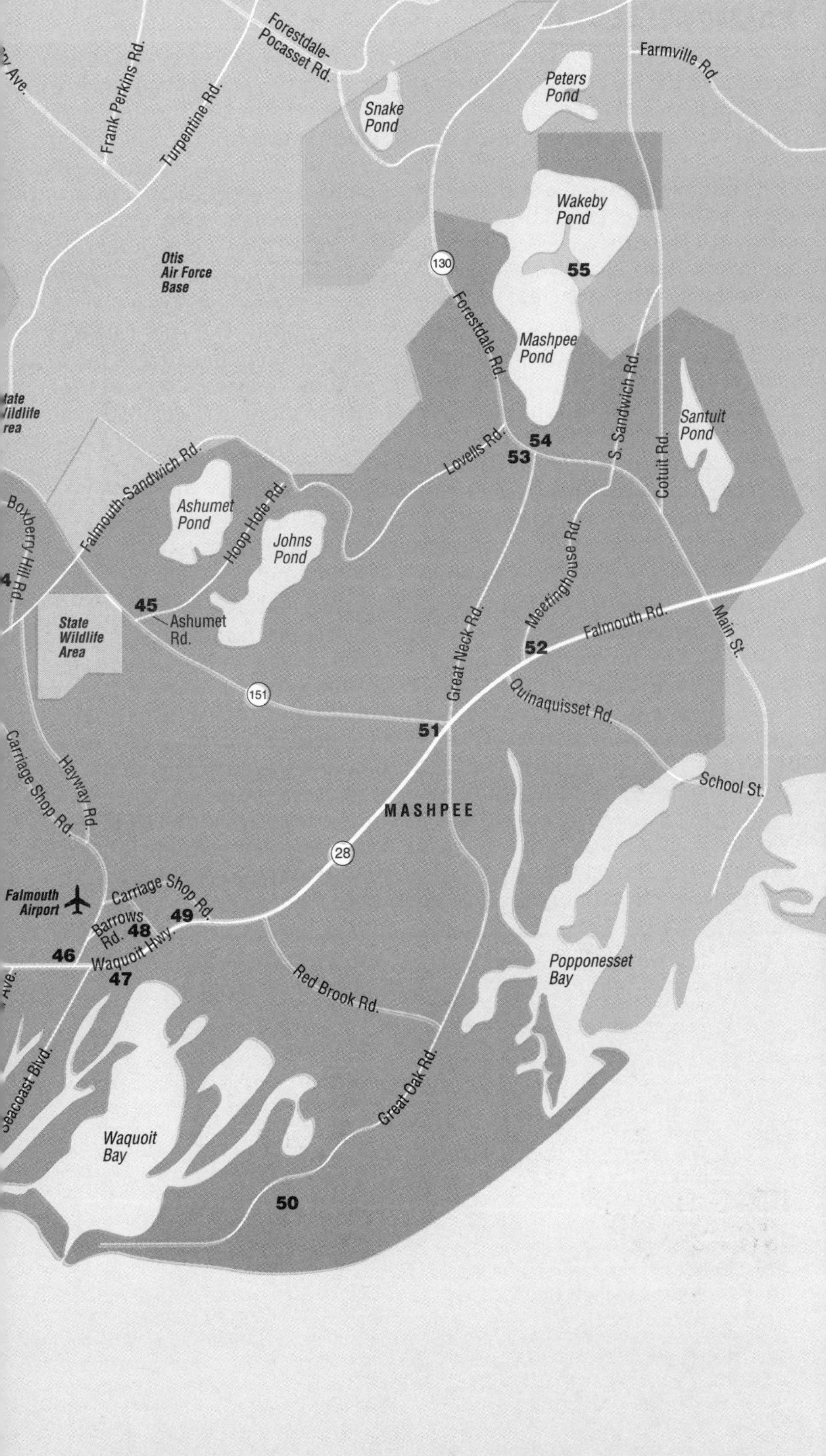

Forestdale-Pocasset Rd.
Farmville Rd.
Frank Perkins Rd.
Turpentine Rd.
Snake Pond
Peters Pond
Wakeby Pond
55
130
Otis Air Force Base
Forestdale Rd.
Mashpee Pond
S. Sandwich Rd.
Cotuit Rd.
Santuit Pond
54
53
Lovells Rd.
Falmouth-Sandwich Rd.
Ashumet Pond
Hoop Hole Rd.
Johns Pond
Boxberry Hill Rd.
45
Ashumet Rd.
State Wildlife Area
Meetinghouse Rd.
Great Neck Rd.
Main St.
52
Falmouth Rd.
Quinaquisset Rd.
151
51
School St.
Carriage Shop Rd.
Hayway Rd.
MASHPEE
28
Falmouth Airport
Carriage Shop Rd.
Barrows Rd.
48
49
46
Waquoit Hwy.
47
Red Brook Rd.
Popponesset Bay
Seacoast Blvd.
Great Oak Rd.
Waquoit Bay
50

Falmouth/Mashpee

Among the most staid and perhaps smug of Cape towns, **Falmouth** takes its allure for granted. For those passing through en route to the Island ferries, it may appear as nothing more than a nuisance, a logjam designed to entrap impatient vacationers. But take the time to savor Falmouth like a native and you'll find it to be a worthwhile destination in and of itself—for its timeless **Town Green**, its narrow but scenic beaches, and its lively mix of shops and exceptional restaurants. The area of **North Falmouth** along Route 28A is especially restful, untouched as yet by tacky tourist traps. **Falmouth Heights**, a cluster of weathered shingle houses on a bluff facing distant Martha's Vineyard, seems to have dozed off at the turn of the century; the nostalgia element here is genuine.

Falmouth, or rather the nine or so villages it comprises, was established in 1660 by about a dozen Congregationalists driven out of **Barnstable** for advocating Quakers' rights. It enjoyed a brief flurry as a whaling port in the early 1800s, after which the population began to plummet, largely because of the lure of new industrial hotbeds near Boston. The town rebounded when tourists discovered it: they began arriving by the trainload in the late 19th century. The railroad reached the tiny port of **Woods Hole** in 1872, a year after the U.S. Commission of Fish and Fisheries had set up a small seasonal collecting station to study marine specimens, a settlement that blossomed into a year-round scientific community of international stature.

Adjacent to Falmouth is **Mashpee**, which served as a summer campground for a number of Native American tribes (its native name meant "land near the great cove") for millennia before the colonists arrived. In 1660, moved by the impassioned speeches of missionary **Richard Bourne**, the Plymouth General Court set aside 10,500 acres in the region of Mashpee, or "Marshpee" as it was then known, as an Indian "plantation"; the arrangement was meant to last perpetually. The very concept of private property was anathema to the native way of life, however, and through gradual transfers out of native hands, the territory has come to be riddled with suburban developments. Only 600 or so Wampanoags still live here, but a great many more, representing other tribes, gather for the annual Fourth of July weekend **Wampanoag Powwow**, an event you won't want to miss if you're in the vicinity.

---

1 Haland Stable Those who can "sit English" will enjoy an escorted trail ride through woods and past cranberry bogs, but rank beginners will need to prepare with a half-hour lesson. Instructor **Hazel Shaw**, who grew up here, opened the stables in 1964, and has transformed many a novice into a devotee. ♦ Fee. M-Sa 9AM-5PM, weather permitting. 878 Rte 28A (between Thomas B. Landers and Chase Rds), W. Falmouth. Appointment required. 540.2552

1 Domingo's Olde Restaurant ★★★$$ In 1979, **Domingo Peña** turned his grandfather's 1841 Greek Revival house into a showcase for his considerable skills as a chef. The decor is understated (stucco walls, glass-topped tables), but the cuisine is decidedly festive, bursting with the bold, sunny flavors of the Mediterranean Rim. Among his signature seafood dishes are escargots Provençale, bouillabaisse, and haddock Portuguese, with celery, green peppers, fresh herbs, and white wine. ♦ International ♦ Dinner. 856 Rte 28A (between Thomas B. Landers and Chase Rds), W. Falmouth. Reservations recommended. 540.0575

1 Whistlestop Ice Cream It's a veritable shack, decorated with old railroad trappings, but the offerings are locally made and especially luscious. Try a cone of the different specials, such as cookie dough or "death by chocolate"—a great way to go. ♦ M-F noon-9PM, Sa-Su noon-10PM mid-May to mid-Oct. 854 Rte 28A (between Thomas B. Landers and Chase Rds), W. Falmouth. 540.7585. Also at: 171 Clay Pond Rd, Monument Beach. 759.4010

2 Sjoholm $ It's nothing fancy, but this 19th-century farmhouse with 15 rooms (including some in a converted carriage house and sail loft) is eminently affordable. The Swedish name, the legacy of former owners, means "safe place surrounded by water," and it fits.

Innkeeper **Barbara Eck** occasionally offers Swedish pancakes and sugary "rosettes." ♦ 17 Chase Rd (off Rte 28A), W. Falmouth. 540.5706

3 **A Propos** This is one of those antiques stores where you can hardly maneuver, it's so packed with goodies. The treasures range from ornate Victorian jewelry to beaded bags, alligator purses, cards of buttons, packs of cards, and on to bigger stuff, like bureaus and beds. Poke around long enough and there's no telling what you'll find. ♦ M-Sa 11AM-5PM, Su noon-5PM late May to mid-Sept; M, Th-Sa 11AM-5PM, Su noon-5PM mid-Sept to Jan; Sa 11AM-5PM, Su noon-5PM Jan-May. 636 Rte 28A (near Old Dock Rd), W. Falmouth. 547.0045

3 **Europea** Vintage kimonos, African straw bags, embroidered T-shirts, offbeat jewelry . . . it's worth seeking out this out-of-the-way outpost for world-beat womenswear (there's great stuff for little kids, too). ♦ M-Sa 10AM-6PM, Su noon-6PM May-Oct; M-Sa 10AM-6PM, Su noon-5PM Nov-Apr. 628 Rte 28A (near Old Dock Rd), W. Falmouth. 540.7814. Also at: 37 Barnstable Rd, Hyannis. 790.0877

4 **Village Barn** This former barn now houses the collections of eight antique dealers (a far neater lot than the livestock). The advantage of having eight perspectives on what's worth preserving is a spectrum of aesthetic slants, one or more of which may coincide with your own. One person is keen on quilts, another on Quimper and glass paperweights—you get the picture. There's also a "junk room" up in the hayloft. It's reassuring, somehow, to know that even pros will pick a dud from time to time, and their rejects may strike you as retro gold. ♦ 606 Rte 28A (near Old Dock Rd), W. Falmouth. 540.3215

5 **Chrisalis Country Home** A combination home furnishings/antiques store, Chrisalis Country Home has some exquisite stock, arranged by owner **Dorothy Donlan** in happy groupings; she has an eclectic eye and unerring taste. ♦ Daily 10:30AM-5PM Mar-Dec. 550 Rte 28A (opposite Blacksmith Shop Rd). 540.5884

6 **Inn at West Falmouth** $$$ Owner/manager **Lewis Milardo** is gifted both as a decorator (he's irrepressibly opulent, lavishing flowers everywhere, inside and out) and as a chef (rustic Italian). This 1900 shingle-style summer house overlooking Buzzards Bay had fallen on hard times when he and partner **Edward Savard** came to the rescue; its multiple lives had spanned private residence, piano camp, home for unwed mothers, and—perhaps the worst insult of all—'50s bachelor pad. Their 1985 renovation brought it back into its own, as the kind of retreat city-dwellers dream of.

Seven of the nine rooms are furnished with unusual European antiques and hand-embroidered linens; the other two have a restful Oriental cast, with grasspaper wall coverings and bold Korean accoutrements, also ancient. Several have fireplaces and/or private balconies, and all adjoin Italian marble bathrooms with whirlpool baths. Breakfast is served buffet style until late morning, so no one need stir who doesn't care to. There's a jewel-like heated pool set in the deck, and below, on the very private and bloom-strewn grounds, a clay tennis court. You don't even need to pack a good book; Milardo lays in stacks of the latest best-sellers. The beach is a 10-minute stroll away. ♦ 66 Frazar Rd (off Rte 28A), W. Falmouth. 540.6503

7 **Peach Tree Circle Farm** ★★$ This sweet little farmstand-cum-lunchroom looks as though it had been *in situ* forever, but it's actually a mid-'80s innovation. Drop by to pick up some cut flowers or produce fresh from the field, and, odds are, you'll want to linger for a light lunch of fresh garden vegetable soup or a salad with its full crunch factor intact. The deli can fix you up with homemade jams and jellies, the bakery with strawberry-almond crunch bars and other treats. ♦ American ♦ Breakfast, lunch, and dinner (to 6PM); breakfast and lunch (to 4PM) only Sept to June. 818 Old Palmer Ave and Saconesset Hill Dr, Falmouth. 548.2354

8 **Woods Hole Gallery** **Edith Bruce** has found a select group of area artists, and has been showing their work since 1963, making fresh discoveries every year. (She restores Old Masters, so knows what to look for in a work of art.) Among her recent finds, for instance, are the compact dunescapes of **Beth Pykosz,** who with resolute smudges of intensely hued pastels manages to convey a fragile, complex world. "All the artists have won awards—they have to," says Bruce. "It's my house, so I can be picky." ♦ M, Th-Sa 10AM-5PM, Su 2-5PM late June to mid-Sept. 14 School St (off Water St), Woods Hole. 548.7594

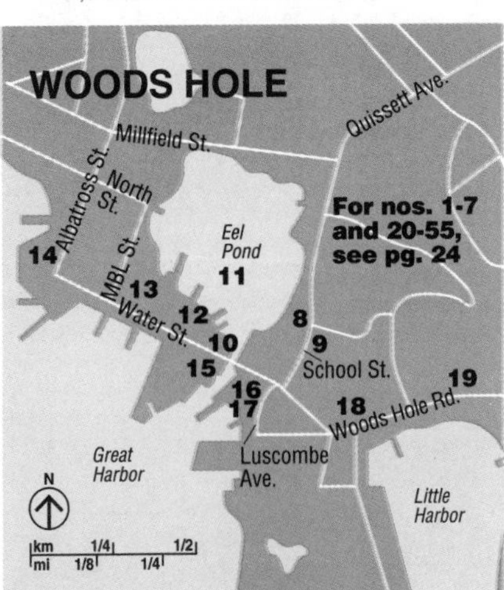

9 Woods Hole Oceanographic Institute Exhibit Center (WHOI) To tell the truth, WHOI (known as "HOO-ey" to habitués) is not all that keen on meeting and greeting visitors: "We have over a thousand scientists conducting research in our labs," says public information officer **Shelley Lauzon.** "We can't disrupt their work." To placate the hordes of tourists who persist in visiting nonetheless, WHOI (the largest independent oceanographic institute in the world, with an $80 million annual budget) maintains a modest exhibition hall that documents the institute's highly successful history.

Initiated by a $2.5 million **Rockefeller Foundation** grant in 1930 and now 80 percent funded by research contracts, WHOI helped the U.S. survive World War II by doing underwater reconnaissance and went on to explore the watery two-thirds of the earth with a phalanx of research vessels, from the 279-foot *Knorr* (which has been cut in half and lengthened like a stretch limo) to the 25-foot *Alvin,* a 1964 submersible built for three that earned headlines in 1966 when it retrieved an unexploded hydrogen bomb in the Mediterranean, and more recently when it probed the *Titanic* in 1986. Capable of descending to depths of 13,000 feet, little *Alvin* (named not for the chipmunk but for WHOI scientist **Alvyn Vine**) has been especially effective in exploring the pitch-dark depths long thought to be inhospitable to life, where, it turns out, the bizarre creatures of the hydrovent communities subsist through chemosynthesis.

The physical exhibits at WHOI's visitor center may not be extensive (check out the pickled "cookie-cutter" shark, and the sea spider almost two feet across), but the short videos that run continuously throughout the day are truly intriguing, the next best thing to a "20,000 Leagues Under the Sea" voyage of your own. ♦ Free. M-Sa 9:30AM-5PM, Su noon-5PM late June to early Sept; M-Sa 10AM-4PM, Su noon-4PM mid-May to late June, early Sept through Oct; F-Sa 10AM-4PM, Su noon-4PM Apr to mid-May, Nov-Dec. 15 School St (off Water St), Woods Hole. 457.2000 ext 2663

10 Black Duck ★$$ A cafeteria by day, restaurant by night, this casual spot has a deck overlooking Eel Pond and a repertory of some 60 soups, chowders, and stews, of which a handful are available at any given time. The rest of the menu is filled out with fairly standard seafood fare. ♦ International ♦ Breakfast, lunch, and dinner; call for off-season (mid-Oct to May) hours. 73 Water St (between Eel Pond and MBL St), Woods Hole. 548.9165

10 Cap'n Kidd ★$$ Seafood—surprise!—dominates the bill of fare at this popular bar/restaurant (primarily bar). A crude mural (circa 1946) depicts the namesake pirate who, legend has it, was brought ashore in **Woods Hole** en route to his hanging in England. The hand-carved mahogany bar with its hefty marble railing is thought to be about 150 years old; as for the institution itself, no one seems to know. "It's pretty old," ventures one bartender. Customers are busy making time, not tracking it, at the barrel tables with keg stools. In winter, the glassed-in deck, with its wood stove, is the pulsating heart of the community. ♦ American ♦ Lunch and dinner. 77 Water St (between Eel Pond and MBL St), Woods Hole. 548.9206

Within Cap'n Kidd:

The Waterfront ★★$$$$ Cap'n Kidd has a civilized side, which comes out only in summer. When the warehouse-size adjoining dining room fills up, diners push right out onto a pier in the pond. Chef **James Murray's** menu is an exercise in unabashed fishploitation: broiled swordfish gets the "Pier House" treatment (braised with mango and papaya, with champagne beurre blanc) and the seafood *en croute* gets its kick from vermouth, brandy, and cream. As for service, the official line is: "The only thing we overlook is the water." ♦ International ♦ Dinner. Closed late Sept to early June. Reservations recommended. 548.8563

11 Susan Jean Captain John Christian's 22-foot shallow-draft Aquasport is usually moored in Eel Pond, but pickups can be arranged virtually anywhere along the shore. A native Cape Codder with 30 years of experience on the water, Christian will lead a maximum of three very serious fish-seekers on a hunt for trophy bass along the **Elizabeth Islands.** (In this company, anything under three feet or so is tossed back to grow a bit.) He knows all the best spots, from **Quick's Hole** to the "hallowed" **Sow and Pigs Reef** at Cuttyhunk, and trips—typically eight hours in length—are timed to take advantage of tides and climatic conditions, even if that means embarking in the middle of the night. "There's a lot of beauty out there," says Christian. "Some days we'll see the moon set as the sun rises—something you can't get with a boat that leaves at six in the morning." ♦ Fee. Eel Pond (off Water St), Woods Hole. Reservations required. 548.6901

The 1796 Paul Revere bell that tops Falmouth's First Congregational Church bears an upbeat inscription, in keeping with the fire-and-brimstone bent of the time: "The living to the church I call, and to the grave I summon all."

12 Shuckers World Famous Raw Bar & Cafe ★★$$ "Never eat lobster in a place where you have to wear a shirt," advises **Glen Waggoner,** whose critical rounds for *New England Monthly* earned him the honorific "The Man Who Ate New England." He'd feel right at home at this tiny restaurant, which has room for maybe a dozen people inside and another 100-plus spilling over onto cafe tables lining the periphery of **Eel Pond.** Start with clam chowder—a modest misnomer packed with fresh crab, shrimp, and whatever marine surplus the chef cares to toss in. Appetizers include "crabcaves" (crab and cheese sauce on toast points), and marinated grilled eel, about which the menu warns: "You order it, you bought it." Entrées run the gamut between cioppino and "traditional lobster boil," consisting of clams, mussels, lobster, and corn on the cob. To wash it down: Nobska Light, brewed right in Falmouth. ♦ International ♦ Lunch and dinner. Closed late Oct to early May. 91A Water St (between Eel Pond and MBL St), Woods Hole. 540.3850

13 Marine Biological Laboratory (MBL) Founded in 1888, the nonprofit MBL (housed in a converted 1836 granite spermaceti candle factory) has a somewhat broader mandate than **WHOI:** the approximately 800 scientists who work here don't focus strictly on marine organisms, but study their relative simple systems as a key to "fundamental biological processes common to all life forms"—human included. (Research on sea urchins, amazingly enough, led to such reproductive breakthroughs as in vitro fertilization, and may someday spawn a birth control pill for men.) The MBL is happy to show visitors around, provided they reserve ahead. The 1½-hour tours consist of a slide presentation; a guided tour, led by a retired scientist, to the holding tanks to view what one staffer alludes to as the "creepy-crawlies" (e.g., eels, squid, sponges, coral, crabs, and dogfish aggressively nosing the surface); and, finally, a visit to a lab for a demo of work in progress. ♦ M-F 1PM mid-June to Sept. MBL and Water Sts, Woods Hole. Reservations required (preferably a week in advance). 548.3705 ext 423

14 National Marine Fisheries Service Aquarium (NMFS) Set up in 1871 as a summer sampling station by the **U.S. Commission of Fish and Fisheries** (the NMFS' predecessor), this is the oldest aquarium in the country and a wonderfully sloppy place in which to experience close encounters of the piscine kind. Little kids revel in the "touch tank" tide pools (adults are wont to dabble as well), and taller tanks painted in bright primary colors harbor further surprises: an "octopus vulgaris," perhaps, looking downright cartoonish. In the wall-mounted tanks, you can observe the graceful glide of loggerhead sea turtles or the scuttling of a natural blue lobster (whose coloration defies 20 million-to-one odds). You might even get to watch a toothy wolffish chow down on a hapless crab. Pause, too, to take in the display on plastics pollution: you'll think twice next time you're tempted to toss a baggie. Every summer, two seals from Mystic, Connecticut, take up residence in a streetside tank; feedings are at 11AM and 3PM. ♦ Free. Daily 10AM-4:30PM late June to mid-Sept; M-F 9AM-4PM mid-Sept to late June. Albatross and Water Sts, Woods Hole. 548.7684

15 Woods Hole Handworks This small but distinguished shop, an artisans' coop, carries the work of some 17 clever creators—most notably, weaver **Gunjan Laborde** (her spectrum-hued chenille shells and shawls drape as beautifully as they glide through the day) and beadworker **Donna Andrews-Maness,** whose jewelry (pins and earrings) hew to motifs of leaves and fishes. Keep coming back: the artists are always evolving, along with the stock. ♦ M-W 10AM-5PM, Th-Sa 10AM-8PM, Su noon-5PM mid-June to mid-Sept; F-Su May to mid-June, mid-Sept to late Dec. 68 Water St (between MBL St and Eel Pond), Woods Hole. 540.5291

16 The Fishmonger Cafe ★★$$ As a footnote on the menu advises, it's a mere "262 leisurely paces" from here to the ferry gangplank, but it's worth waiting for the next boat, if you must, to savor the ebullient natural foods served at "the 'Monger." Operated by chef/owner **Frances Buehler** since 1974, this sunny-yellow harborside cafe, with exposed beams and kitchen, is almost always hopping, yet consummately mellow. The treats trickle by throughout the day. The breakfast special might be lemon-ricotta-soufflé pancakes with raspberry sauce; always on the menu are California omelets (guacamole, salsa, sour cream), and Thai crab-and-pork sausage, packing peanuts, cilantro, and coconut milk. Check the blackboard as the day progresses and you might find the likes of Portuguese kale soup or fresh trout with pesto cream sauce. A folk singer often thrums at night; during the day the accompaniment is the hum of local gossip. ♦ International ♦ Breakfast, lunch, and dinner. Closed M, Th-Su mid-Feb to May; closed Dec to mid-Feb. 56 Water St (between Eel Pond and Luscombe Ave), Woods Hole. 548.9148

17 Landfall ★$$ Run by a local family since 1948, and built almost entirely of salvage, this harborside eatery serves the usual seaside suspects: clams, lobster, swordfish, etc. Surrounding you are relics from shipwrecks and long-gone grand hotels; the massive beams overhead came from a Gloucester pier, the glass panels from horse-drawn trolleys that used to traverse Harvard Square. Successive hurricanes, from Carol to Bob, have tried to reclaim some of this booty, but the Landfall keeps bouncing back. ♦ American ♦ Lunch and dinner. Closed Dec-Apr. Luscombe Ave (off Water St), Woods Hole. 548.1758

18 Bradley House Museum Captain William Bradley bought this house for $339 in 1821 before he was lost at sea; it now houses the **Woods Hole Historical Collection.** What's on view at any given time varies, except for a diorama of the town circa 1895 and a "spritsail" boat made at the turn of the century by local builder **Eddie Swift.** There's a potluck quality to the exhibits. If you'd prefer something more substantial, try one of the free walking tours of town Tuesdays at 4PM during July and August; reservations are required. ♦ Free. Tu-Sa 10AM-4PM mid-June to mid-Sept. 573 Woods Hole Rd (at Water St), Woods Hole. 548.7270

19 Nautilus Motor Inn $$ This establishment doesn't exactly exude ambience: in fact, it has the somewhat drab personality of a stereotypical scientist-nerd (visiting scientists account for a good portion of the clientele). However, the rooms are fine, the views—on the waterside—pretty spectacular, plus there are free tennis courts and a nicely situated sliver of a pool. If you've missed the earth tones of the '60s and early '70s, here's one place you can get your fill. ♦ Closed Nov to late Apr. 533 Woods Hole Rd (between Water St and Nobska Rd), Woods Hole. 548.1525, 800/654.2333

Within the Nautilus Motor Inn:

The Dome ★$$$ **Bucky Fuller** built this dome while at MIT in 1953, and the miracle may be that it's still standing (it's said to be the oldest geodesic structure in the country). The food, frankly, doesn't warrant the tariff: if you just want to get a peek at the retro-futuristic interior, draped in circusy swathes of mauve, mint, ivory, and bronze fabric, duck in for a drink before you commit. The overall effect can be a bit creepy. Unless you're a true fan of '50s kitsch, a brief brush with it may suffice. ♦ American/Continental ♦ Dinner; Sunday brunch. Closed Monday; closed Nov-Mar. 548.0800

20 Nobska Lighthouse This classically proportioned tower is actually an 1876 replacement for the 1828 original; it comprises four impervious cast-iron shells. The light has been automated since 1985, but with or without a keeper on hand, the view of the Elizabeth Islands is nonetheless romantic. ♦ Nobska Rd (off Church Rd, south of Woods Hole Rd), Woods Hole. 547.3219

21 Woods Hole Passage $ Owner-in-residence **Christina Mozo** is an artist, which explains the serene, considered air and distinctive flair of this five-bedroom B&B (illustrated above). The living room in the main building (a converted 19th-century carriage house) is painted sherbet pink; offset by bulky linen couches and a view of the spacious back garden, this bold stroke seems apropos. Four of the bedrooms were carved from a century-old barn; the upstairs rooms, with their cathedral-ceilings, are particularly appealing. Daylong traffic along the main route to Woods Hole might be a deterrent if you weren't going to be out all day anyway, enjoying the area's many attractions. Should you run out of things to see and do, Mozo can suggest some little-known beauty spots, such as nearby **Spohre Garden** and the **Knob.** In any case, she'll send you off with a hearty breakfast—quiche or soufflé, perhaps, or French toast with fresh fruit, maple syrup, and cream. For those with an early ferry to catch, she'll pack a breakfast-to-go. ♦ 186 Woods Hole Rd (between Mill Rd and Oyster Pond Rd), Woods Hole. 548.9575

22 Inn at One Main $$ Known since the '50s as "The Victorian," this 1892 decorative shingled house with Queen Anne accents desperately needed freshening when **Mary Zylinski** and **Karen Hart** (whose mother runs the Village Green Inn, diagonally across the street) took it on in 1993. These two young women have succeeded in infusing it with their own blithe spirits and romanticism. Lace and wicker abound, especially in the turret room, which boasts a brass bed. Breakfasts are far from mundane: expect the likes of cranberry pecan waffles or gingerbread pancakes. ♦ 1 W. Main St (at Locust St), Falmouth. 540.7469

Restaurants/Clubs: Red **Hotels:** Blue
Shops/ Outdoors: Green **Sights/Culture:** Black

23 Market Bookshop Housed in a century-old former butcher shop (shown above), this is one of those bookstores that is an integral part of the community, and a delight for transient browsers. A massive maple table sits by a hearth (roaring in winter), and the books are arranged in logical groupings on high oak shelves. Owner **Bill Banks** is proud to have mentored preschoolers straight through college over the past two decades plus. The store offers an out-of-print search service ($1 per title), and same-day follow-through on contacting publishers with special orders. You'll probably find all you need right here, though, particularly if it's Cape Coddiana you're after. ♦ M-F 9AM-9PM, Sa 9AM-5:30PM, Su noon-5PM late June to mid-Sept; M-Tu, Th-Sa 9AM-5:30PM, W 9AM-9PM, Su noon-5PM mid-Sept to late June. 15 Depot Ave (off N. Main St), Falmouth. 540.0480. Also at: 22 Water St, Woods Hole, 540.0851

Behind the Market Bookshop:

Market Barn Gallery The barn out back, with its whitewashed interior, makes a great place to show New England artists, as well as to conduct readings and signings. ♦ M-F 9AM-9PM, Sa 9AM-5:30PM, Su noon-5PM late June to mid-Sept. 540.0480

24 Highfield Theatre In 1972, the 650-acre **Beebe Woods** estate, where two brothers had built matching mansions in the 1870s, was about to fall prey to developers when local benefactor **Josiah Lilly** stepped in and bought it for the town. The buildings were deeded to the **Cape Cod Conservatory,** and although one mansion was too far gone to be rehabilitated, **Highfield Hall** remains—a glorious, hulking but uninhabitable relic. The real prize, however, was the estate's former horse barn, converted by New York producer **Arthur Beckard** into an Equity theater in 1946. That initial venture fizzled, but in the succeeding two decades a series of college companies put on plays in the barn. In 1969, Oberlin administrator **Robert Haslun** came up with the idea of an intercollegiate company, culled nationwide, and the **College Light Opera Company (CLOC)** was born. Each season, this independent, nonprofit educational institute plucks its 32 players from universities across the country, along with 17 musicians to fill out the full-size orchestra pit (a welcome anomaly in this age of synthesized sound). The young hopefuls—many of whom go on to tackle Broadway—mount an astounding nine musicals in as many weeks, much to the delight of the usually 100 percent capacity audience. During the off-season, the theater is used for Conservatory exhibits and recitals, and for productions by the amateur—as in enthusiastic—**Falmouth Theatre Guild.** ♦ CLOC performances Tu-W, F-Sa 8:30PM; Th 2:30PM, 8:30PM July-Aug. Depot Ave Extension (off N. Main St), Falmouth. 548.0668

25 Food for Thought ★$$ Housed in a small-scale shopping arcade of pleasing shingled facades, this little eatery is nothing to make a special trip for but convenient if you're in the neighborhood and in need of a nosh. "Caj" (as in casual) is the operative word. Breakfast specials run from regional staples like cranberry-granola muffins to such exotic AM fare as burritos; dinners are usually a panoply of ethnic specials. ♦ International ♦ Breakfast; dinner also on Thursday through Saturday. Closed Monday. 37 N. Main St (between W. Main St and Palmer Ave), Falmouth. 548.4498

25 Enseki Antiques The stock here runs from big, bold pieces, such as a carousel horse (a mere $5,650, and that's marked down), to something so humdrum and lovely as a '30s Deco kitchen clock. **Gary Enseki** dealt antiques in England before opening this shop in 1992, and already he's making the same old stuff shown elsewhere in these parts look pretty pallid. ♦ Daily 10:30AM-5PM; call ahead to confirm. 49 N. Main St (between W. Main St and Palmer Ave), Falmouth. 548.7744

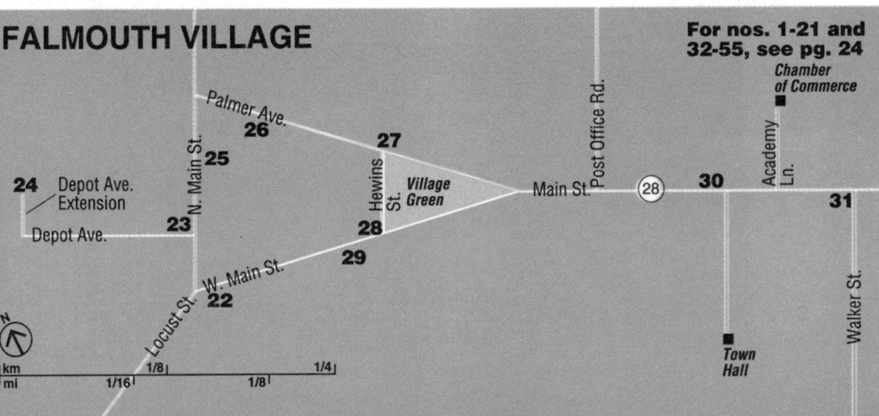

26 The Coffee Obsession The menu at this spare, cathedral-ceilinged cafe, opened in 1992 by **Hugh Brimingham** and **Bill Ventura,** consists of "mostly coffee"—e.g., brew of the day, or perhaps iced cappuccino—plus the odd pastry, biscotti, and a bit of ice cream. The walls are hung with the works of local artists (and the ceiling, inexplicably, with grain sacks), and games, dictionaries, books, and slightly used newspapers are yours for the playing/perusing. Occasionally, of an evening, the space is given over to a poetry reading or open music night. In a solidly bourgeois town, this is what passes for a Generation X hangout, and it gives one hope for the future. ♦ M-Th 7AM-10PM; F-Sa 8AM-11PM; Su 8AM-8PM. 110 Palmer Ave (between N. Main St and the Village Green), Falmouth. 540.2233

26 Aurora Borealis China is the predominant focus of this quirky shop, much of it labeled and exhaustively annotated, so you can educate yourself as you poke around. Prices are reasonable: if you've always yearned for a mid-19th century ironstone chamberpot, you can secure one here for less than $100. Among the other subspecialties are cameos, Japanese prints, and vintage local postcards. ♦ Daily 11AM-4PM May-Oct; Sa 11AM-4PM Nov-Dec; by appointment Jan. 104 Palmer Ave (between N. Main St and the Village Green), Falmouth. 540.3385

27 Falmouth Historical Society Museums Linked by a formal colonial garden researched by landscape archaeologists and maintained by the **Falmouth Garden Club,** the three structures in this complex synopsize the high points of Falmouth's history. Guided tours are given of the **Julia Wood House,** cute as a dollhouse, with its tiny pillared, two-tier porch. It was built in 1790 by **Dr. Francis Wicks,** a smallpox inoculation pioneer who had served as a medical corpsman in the Revolution. His vintage office has been reconstructed, and it's fascinating, if frightening (he doubled as town dentist and veterinarian).

The **Conant House,** originally a half-Cape, was home to **Reverend Samuel Palmer,** minister of the neighboring First Congregational Church (which harbors a 1796 Paul Revere bell) from 1730-75; it's now used to display seagoing memorabilia such as harpoons, sailor's valentines (folk sculptures fashioned from shells), and exquisitely embroidered mourning pictures. One room commemorates **Katharine Lee Bates,** the Wellesley College professor who in 1893 penned the poem/anthem "America the Beautiful." Born at 16 Main Street in 1859, Bates spent her girlhood in Falmouth. (A 1986 statue by Boston University's **Lloyd Lillie** stands in front of the Falmouth Library.)

The **Dudley Hallett Barn** houses the 19th-century sleigh that delivered Dr. Wicks on his rounds, along with assorted farm implements and several grand old flags draped from the hayloft. The Village Green that the complex fronts, which remained a grazing ground for horses into the early 19th century, was initially laid out, in 1749, as a militia training field—just in time for the skirmishes of 1776 and 1812. Historical Society docents lead free, informative walking tours Tuesdays at 4PM, July through August. ♦ Admission. M-F 2-5PM mid-June to mid-Sept. 55-65 Palmer Ave (at the Village Green), Falmouth. 548.4857

28 Village Green Inn $$ This plain 1804 Federal house got gussied up with fancy shingling in the Victorian fervor of 1894 and is all the prettier for it—if a monster to maintain. **Don Long** attends to the woodwork, **Linda Long** to the hospitality. A former schoolteacher, like her husband, Linda is clearly a born innkeeper, with a knack for creating cozy rooms and a baker's gift for breakfast: apple-plum crumble, nutmeg muffins. . . . Each of the five rooms has some unusual feature, such as a bathroom with pressed-tin walls. The roomy bay-windowed suite includes a daybed and a desk, helpful for those who can't seem to leave the workaday world behind. Business will fade soon enough, as you lounge on the porch, surrounded by red geraniums, and sip sherry or lemonade. ♦ Closed Jan to late Feb. 40 W. Main St (at the Village Green), Falmouth. 548.5621

29 Mostly Hall $$ Built by **Captain Albert Nye** to please his New Orleans-born bride in 1849, this plantation-style house—unique on Cape Cod—got its name more than a century ago from a young visitor who marveled, "Why Mama, it's mostly hall!" By rights it should be called Mostly Headroom: soaring ceilings leave plenty of space for queen-size canopy beds in each of six corner rooms. Its official classification is "Greek Revival raised cottage" (it sits on granite pillars, generously set back from the street), but whatever name it goes by, it's a spectacular property, and hosts **Caroline** and **Jim Lloyd,** who bought the B&B in 1986, have brought it into the first rank. It's not just the breakfasts, though they're spectacular, too: the cheese blintz muffins, eggs Benedict soufflé, and peach-poppyseed muffins have already prompted a cookbook. The Lloyds go overboard to ensure that you're happily occupied, listing their various concierge services on a slate should you be too shy to ask. They offer badminton, croquet, six loaner bikes (the **Shining Sea Bikeway** is nearby), and an entire bureau stuffed with brochures and menus, backed by firsthand reports. Pore over the options in the parlor, with its blue-velvet loveseat set, or retire to the widow's walk, transformed—via VCR—into a comfy cockpit for armchair travelers. ♦ Closed Jan to mid-Feb. 27 W. Main St (between N. Main St and the Village Green), Falmouth. 548.3786, 800/682.0565

30 **The Quarterdeck Restaurant** ★★$$ You might not think to poke your head into this Main Street hideaway, which looks like just another dim watering hole from the outside. The interior, however, is surprisingly atmospheric, with modern stained glass and exposed wooden beams, and Culinary Institute grad **Rob Pacheco** does right by the ocean's bounty, pan-blackening scallops with Siberian garlic sauce, for instance, or borrowing from his wife's Azorean background to come up with succulent specials. ♦ International ♦ Lunch and dinner; Sunday brunch. 164 Main St (opposite Town Hall Sq), Falmouth. 548.9900

Laureens

30 **Laureens** Just the place for a pick-me-up, **Laureen Iseman's** snazzy shop/cafe shakes your senses to attention the second you walk in: sure, you could sip a cup of designer coffee (it's delicious), but here you can just as easily inhale it. The deli counter offers breakfast-through-nighttime nibbles, and there's a great array of gifts to take home or bestow—everything from Boyajian caviar (order a day ahead) to books, baskets, spaetzle-makers, croquet sets, and American Spoon Foods by the case, which is how these nonpareil delectables from the wilds of Michigan tend to get consumed. ♦ M-Sa 8AM-6PM, Su 8AM-5PM May-Oct. 170 Main St (opposite Town Hall Sq), Falmouth. 540.9014

31 **Ben & Bill's Chocolate Emporium** Look for the kids invariably clustered outside, draped across wrought-iron benches and raptly indulging in piled-high ice-cream cones. The two dozen fresh-cranked flavors would be lure enough, but candy is also made on the premises, in huge copper pots, and you get to watch, surrounded by glass cases filled with the end results. It's a chocoholic's dream. ♦ Daily 9AM-closing. 209 Main St (at Walker St), Falmouth. 548.7878

The rambling rose was born in the early decades of this century in the Woods Hole gardens of hybridist Michael Walsh.

32 **Coonamessett Inn** $$ If this inn (pictured above), which grew from the nucleus of a 1796 homestead, has a '50s feel, it's intentional. **Edna Harris** opened the Coonamessett Inn beside the river of that name (Algonquian for "place of the large fish") in 1912 and moved it here in 1953. When the property came up for sale in the mid-'60s, an anonymous benefactor—**Josiah Lilly** again, by all accounts—bought it in order to keep it just the way it was. Surrounded by seven acres of gardens and bedecked with blooms (maintained by the full-time "flower lady" on staff), the inn is staid in the best sense and a perennial haven to its patrons: "You can tell time by who comes when," says manager **Mal Hughes.** Only a short distance from the bustling center of town, the inn, with its 16 traditionally decorated suites and eight guest rooms, is at once an oasis and a social center in its own right, one where the passing stranger will be made to feel at home. ♦ Jones Rd and Gifford St, Falmouth. 548.2300

Within the Coonamessett Inn:

Coonamessett Inn Restaurant ★★★$$$ Three dining rooms accommodate up to 300 guests, or conference groups. The largest, the Cahoon Room, features playful primitive paintings by the late Cape artist **Ralph Cahoon** (whose commemorative museum is located 10 miles eastward, in Cotuit) and chandeliers resembling a favored motif, hot-air balloons. Traditional inns such as this often don't augur much excitement in the way of cuisine, but self-taught chef **David Kelley** generates his own. The house-cured gravlax is a silky ribbon, perfectly salted, and nicely set off with crème fraîche and chewy Portuguese bread. Entrées are seasonally influenced; it's worth turning up in May for his lobster sautéed with spring vegetables, tossed with fettuccine and herbed butter. Pâtissier **Karen Dean's** creations are hearty yet subtle and also make maximum use of local bounty. ♦ New American ♦ Lunch and dinner. Jackets requested; reservations recommended. 548.2300

Eli's ★★$$ The tavern, a handsome blend of blond wood, brass, and hunter-green trim, serves more casual fare—some of it fairly studied, though, like the marinated lamb kebabs, with couscous and a feta-strewn salad. Yankee staples like chowder, pot roast, and potpie can always be found on the menu. ♦ American/International ♦ Breakfast, lunch, and dinner. Jacket requested. 548.2300

33 Peking Palace ★★$$ Most towns think their Chinese restaurant is tops, but this one really is a winner. Some inkling of the care put into the preparation and presentation is apparent right from the entryway—bamboo lines the alley to the parking lot, and a small, perfect garden graces the narrow setback. Etched-glass windows and rosewood tables are among the opulent decorative touches, but the proof is in the dishes themselves—all 265 of them, encompassing Mandarin, Szechuan, Cantonese, and Polynesian specialties. The shrimp in various sauces are invariably plump, and a dish like "Blessed Family Happiness in the Nest" (an edible nest, that is) will deliver on its promise. In summer, Peking Palace stays open into the wee hours, in case you get a late-night craving. ♦ Chinese/ Takeout ♦ Lunch and dinner (to 2AM in summer). 452 Main St (between King St and Lantern Ln), Falmouth. 540.8204

34 Betsy's Diner ★★$ Who cares if it represents packaged nostalgia? This 1957 diner, imported from Pennsylvania by entrepreneur **Larry Holmes** in 1992, is an absolute peach, down to the neon cup of coffee "steaming" evocatively in the window. The fixtures are all original, and an added-on dining room features enamel-top tables and vintage advertising art. The jukebox is stocked with period platters (from "Hound Dog" to "Chapel of Love"), and the prices feel like rollbacks, too: burgers cost half of what you'd pay at a fern bar, and the blue-plate turkey dinner sells in the single digits. Breakfast is served anytime—now, that's class—and the pastries, including meringue pies, are made fresh on the premises. No wonder the joint is jumping from dawn past dark. ♦ American/ Takeout ♦ Breakfast, lunch, and dinner. 457 Main St (between King St and Lantern Ln), Falmouth. 540.4446

35 Falmouth Artists Guild Stemming from an informal interest group in the early 1950s, the guild coalesced into a nonprofit corporation in 1969 and set up shop in the Old Town Infirmary. Some 8 to 10 shows are held a year, half of them juried, and the work is, as a rule, superior to what you'll see in many more moneyed galleries. It's a great place to catch rising stars. Prices at a recent exhibit ranged from $20 for a creditable watercolor to $3,000 for a magnificent shoreline quadriptych in pastels by **Jane Lincoln.** Another incentive to buy: at least 60 percent of the purchase price goes to the artist, reversing the typical commission ratio imposed by commercial galleries. ♦ M-Sa 10AM-3PM. 744 Main St (at Scranton Ave). 540.3304

36 The Flying Bridge ★★$$ This longtime local favorite was slightly on the skids when Hurricane Bob came along to clear the deck in '91. **William Roberts** bought it, treated it to a total makeover, and reopened for business in 1993. Now, the 600-seat restaurant is as spiffy as can be, sparkling with harbor light and enthusiastically staffed. The menu is extensive, but the blackboard specials are your best bet, and for the best water views—right about mast height—head upstairs past an amusing sand mural decorated with sea urchins, globs of tar, and half a rotted skiff, along with the usual buoys and traps. There's often in-house entertainment, and on Thursday nights in summer, you can stroll to the nearby **Harbor Band Shell** for a bit of patriotic oompah-pah. ♦ American/Continental ♦ 220 Scranton Ave (between Main St and Clinton Ave). 548.2700

The Regatta

37 The Regatta of Falmouth By-the-Sea ★★★★$$$ **Brantz** and **Wendy Bryan** are widely credited with awakening the Cape from its culinary doldrums. Their airy perch at the mouth of Falmouth Harbor, decorated in ever paler shades of mauve and pink, sets a standard of elegance that only their other restaurant, **The Regatta of Cotuit at The Crocker House,** can hope to match. The plates, for instance, are not just Limoges, but a Limoges design of Wendy's own devising, with two entwined roses. Of course, it's what goes *on* the plates that counts, and chef **Vincent Ditello,** an accomplished saucier, fills them with unalloyed artistry. The Regatta classics include corn-and-lobster chowder, wild mushroom strudel, and lamb *en chemise* stuffed with *chèvre,* spinach, and pine nuts, enrobed in puff pastry, and drizzled with a Cabernet Sauvignon sauce. Among the newer dishes are Thai-style lobster and shrimp, with homegrown Asian greens, ginger, and cilantro. If you're inclined to self-indulge, go for the dessert sampling; otherwise, "chocolate seduction" should suffice. ♦ International ♦ Lunch and dinner. Closed mid-Sept to mid-May. 217 Clinton Ave (off Scranton Ave), Falmouth. Reservations recommended. 548.5400

37 **Patriot Party Boats** This three-vessel fleet has something for everyone. The magnificent *Liberté,* modeled after a 1750s Pinky schooner, sails the Vineyard Sound; the speedy *Minuteman* was custom-designed to serve expert sportfishers; and the homely *Patriot Too,* with its fully enclosed deck, is ideal for families who want to try "bottom fishing" for scup, bass, fluke, and the like. Tackle and instruction are included, and kids under five ride free. The *Patriot Too* also goes out on scenic cruises, and with any luck **Bud Tietje's** father, who started the business, will ride along: he knows every house along the shore, including a twin set created when neither member of a divorcing couple would agree to give up the house. Back at the shack, ask Bud to show you the collection of old photos of their humble headquarters standing up to assorted hurricanes over the past 40 years; Hurricane Carol, in '54, was the real kicker. Tietje's fleet also conducts bird-watching day trips to the Elizabeth Islands with the **Audubon Society,** and fills in as a backup ferry to Martha's Vineyard, transporting the island's hockey team for after-hours winter games and regularly coming to the rescue of other off-schedule passengers. ♦ 227 Clinton Ave (at Scranton Ave), Falmouth. 548.2626, 800/734.0088

At Patriot Party Boats:

The Clam Shack ★★★$ It's nothing fancy, but has repeatedly garnered *Cape Cod Life's* "best clam shack" award. This rustic joint—it would be pretentious to call it unpretentious—consists of one long counter, five drop-down tables suspended by chains, and a million-dollar view. The bellied clams served here are the Cape Codder's homegrown foie gras. ♦ American ♦ Lunch and dinner. Closed mid-Sept to late May. 548.2626

38 **Holiday Cycles** **Bob Mollo** stocks and services all the regular bikes, from three-speeds to ten-speeds, spanning six-speed "cruisers" with extra-wide handles. He's also got tandems and bright-red Italian-made "surries" with fringe on top, capable of transporting a family of six with some fancy footwork (these he rents only by the hour, because, cute as they are, "they do have some weight to them"). The tiny shop, where you can leave your car for free, is located a short jog from the Falmouth Heights beach, and he's happy to steer seasoned cyclists to a 23-mile loop through bucolic Sippewissett that ends on the Shining Sea Bikeway, with the wind (and sun) to their backs. ♦ Daily 9AM-6PM mid-May to mid-Oct. 465 Grand Ave (between Main St and Worcester Park Ave), Falmouth Heights. 540.3549

38 **Shrubs'** ★$ Carbo-depleted cyclists aren't the only ones piling into this classic roadstand. Anyone in need of a good feed would appreciate the "U-Boats" (overstuffed subs) and a tempting sandwich like the "Tina Tuna": tuna grilled with bacon and Thousand Island dressing. **Richard Breton** has been fueling ravenous beachgoers since 1984, while adding to the movie memorabilia collection that adorns the walls. ♦ American/Takeout ♦ Breakfast, lunch, and dinner. Closed for dinner mid-May to late June, mid-Sept to mid-Oct; closed mid-Oct to mid-May. 465 Grand Ave (between Main St and Worcester Park Ave), Falmouth Heights. 540.0080

39 **Peacock's Inn on the Sound** $$ The 1880 shingled cottage enjoys a perfect setting, inside and out. The 10 breezy rooms are decorated in an unfussy country mode; the common room is graced by a substantial stone fireplace and several sea-blue couches arranged so that you can drink up the bluffside sea view, straight out to Martha's Vineyard. For all its beachside style, this is a jeans-and-barefoot kind of place. Owners **Phillish Niemi-Peacock** and **Bud Peacock** don't stand on ceremony, but do stand ready to refer you to the area's best restaurants, including some hidden gems. To tide you over, they serve all-out breakfasts: fresh fruit, custom-blended juices, apple muffins, Belgian waffles with fruit butter, banana-stuffed French toast. . . . The beach is just a short roll—or rather, stroll—down the bluff. ♦ 313 Grand Ave South (between Main St and Worcester Park Ave), Falmouth Heights. 457.9666

"Never was there a lovelier town than our Falmouth by the sea," wrote "America the Beautiful" author Katharine Lee Bates of her birthplace, continuing: "Tender curves of sky look down on her grace of knoll and lee."

The Wampanoags, who maintained summer camps in the area that is now Falmouth, called the region Suckanesset, which translates roughly as "where the black wampum is found."

Restaurants/Clubs: Red **Hotels:** Blue
Shops/ Outdoors: Green **Sights/Culture:** Black

The Straw-Hat Circuit: On Stage around the Cape

America's "little theater" movement got its start in a Provincetown parlor, where in 1915 a cadre of artists and writers, including **John Reed** (who wrote *Ten Days That Shook the World,* about the Russian revolution), put on some homegrown plays for their own pleasure and edification. Playwright **George ("Jig") Cram Cook,** who with his wife, **Susan Glaspell,** was a ringleader of the group, opined stirringly: "One man cannot produce drama. True drama is born only of one feeling animating all the members of a clan, a spirit shared by all and expressed by the few for the all." With this idealistic mandate, the spirited young company began presenting radical one-act plays. The reception was so warm that they had to move to larger quarters: a Lewis Wharf fish house, where an audience of 60 paid 50 cents apiece to see history in the making. In the second season, **Eugene O'Neill,** attracted by rumors of this promising new enterprise, came to Provincetown, but was too shy to present his work to the troupe; Reed had to lead Cook to him. The fish house, its doors cast open to the sea, offered a ready-made set, and O'Neill himself played a part in the premiere of his *Bound East for Cardiff.* Buoyed by the positive response, the cast moved the operation to Greenwich Village; only then did they begin calling themselves the **Provincetown Players.** Their success became legendary (as did O'Neill's stature), but they never returned to their town of origin.

In 1923, a group called the **Wharf Players** tried to take up the banner left by the Provincetown Players and immediately spawned a dissident offshoot, the **Barnstormers.** The Wharf Players survived until 1940, mounting a market-driven bill of old chestnuts and Broadway hits until a blizzard carried their theater out to sea. Meanwhile, the rival Barnstormers, directed by **Frank Shay** and headquartered in his barn playhouse, staged an inaugural season of new O'Neill works. Among the other budding playwrights they encouraged was **Raymond Moore,** who turned producer in 1926. After one season in Provincetown, he decamped to **Dennis,** where he founded the **Cape Playhouse.** Moore had no great affection for the threadbare production values of little theater; indeed, his vision for the Cape Playhouse was big, bold, and professional, and his goal nothing short of outdoing Broadway. His theater, he promised in a 1927 prospectus, aimed "to stand for the best in the field of art and to establish something infinitely more important than a mere commercial theater." To an astonishing degree, it succeeded.

The physical setting was, and still is, magnificent: a 1790 meetinghouse adapted by Theater Guild designer **Cleon Throckmorton** to seat 500. On 4 July 1927, **Basil Rathbone** opened in *The Guardsman,* and the rest is theatrical history. During the Playhouse's stellar early days, there was only one brief but significant bout of competition: starting in 1928, the **University Players** performed for a few summers in **Falmouth,** featuring such stars-in-the-making as **James Cagney, Orson Welles, Mildred Natwick, Margaret Sullivan, Josh Logan, Tallulah Bankhead** and **Jimmy Stewart.** Meanwhile, a steady parade of celebs and celebs-to-be trod the boards of the Playhouse, including **Bette Davis** (who started as an usher), interns **Gregory Peck** and **Anne Baxter,** pre-matinee idols **Robert Montgomery, Henry Fonda,** and **Humphrey Bogart,** and grandes dames **Judith Anderson, Ethel Barrymore, Eva Le Gallienne,** and **Gertrude Lawrence,** who served as the Playhouse's guiding spirit during the rocky post-World War II years. A 41-year-old divorcée, Lawrence had come to the Playhouse in 1939 to try out for the Broadway-bound play *Skylark,* and there became enamored of the manager, Boston Brahmin **Richard Aldrich.** When they married on 4 July 1940, she received an ebullient telegram from her dearest friend, a fellow British child-star: "Dear Mrs A/Hooray Hooray/At last you are deflowered;/On this as every other day/I love you. Noel Coward." Before her sudden death in 1951, while playing Anna opposite **Yul Brynner** in *The King and I* on Broadway, she and Aldrich spread out across the Cape like theatrical Johnny Appleseeds, starting up the **Falmouth Playhouse** in 1949 and raising—literally—the **Cape Cod Melody Tent** in 1950.

Although that golden age has never quite been replicated, all sorts of theater flourishes to this day on the Cape and the nearby islands. A town-by-town sampling:

Barnstable: The **Barnstable Comedy Club** (385.2159) develops original comedies and kids' shows.

Brewster: The Cape Cod Repertory Theatre (896.6140) presents Shakespeare in an outdoor amphitheater.

Chatham: At the Monomoy Theatre, the **Ohio University Players** (945.1589) perform musicals and dramas.

Dennis: The **Cape Playhouse** (385.3911) stages the only Equity productions on the Cape, and favors new Broadway productions; the children's theater imports a changing roster of companies.

Falmouth: At the Highfield Theatre, the **College Light Opera Company** (548.0668) performs musicals, including Gilbert & Sullivan productions; the **Falmouth Playhouse** (563.5922) mounts summer standards, particularly musicals.

Martha's Vineyard: Year-round productions at the **Vineyard Playhouse** (693.6450) are small but polished; local amateurs mount summer productions at the **Tisbury Amphitheater** in Vineyard Haven (693.6450).

Nantucket: The **Actors Theatre of Nantucket** (228.6325) specializes in slightly offbeat comedies, the **Theatre Workshop of Nantucket** (228.4305), and tried-and-true musicals and dramas.

Orleans: The **Academy Playhouse** (255.1963) offers the gamut from musicals to Shakespeare to modern drama.

Wellfleet: The **Wellfleet Harbor Actors' Theater** (349.6835) is probably the most avant-garde company on the Cape, though the quality is often uneven.

40 **The Wharf Restaurant** ★$$$ If you favor seafood with a heavy salting of sea breezes, head straight for this waterfront eatery—as generations have since the turn of the century. Their photos line the entryway, and a moosehead with a seen-it-all smile presides over the usual nautical hodgepodge. The menu is indistinguishable from those at hundreds of similar establishments. But owner **Bill Sweeney** is so committed to fresh fish, he sees to some of the daily catch himself. His motto: "If our fish was any fresher, you'd have to slap it." If something so simple as a fisherman's platter—an assortment, fried or broiled—would hit the spot, this is as good a spot as any in which to partake. ♦ American ♦ Lunch and dinner. Closed Jan-Apr. 281 Grand Ave S. (between Main St and Worcester Park Ave), Falmouth Heights. 548.2772

Within The Wharf Restaurant:

Casino by the Sea Outside, the surf is pounding, and inside, the music's throbbing. So you never heard of the bands—the college crowds couldn't care less. Thursday is "their" night, but so are all the rest. Wednesdays are for country western (lessons included). On Saturday afternoons, there's a volleyball-and-beer combo (Busch draft for less than a buck); on Sunday afternoons, the competitive sport is raft-racing. ♦ Cover. M-F 8PM-1AM; Sa-Su 3PM-1AM May-Sept. 548.2772

41 **Lawrence's** ★$$ Back in the 1890s, when this was **Lyman Lawrence's Sandwich Depot,** the house specialty came on bread baked on the premises and cost a nickel apiece. Expanded in 1930 by architect **Gilbert E. Boone** in a vaguely Tudor style (dark beams, herringbone brick), this local institution doesn't have the most exciting menu—same old seafood, basically, plus Continental staples like duckling and filet mignon—but it's comfortable, and a stone's throw from the beach. ♦ American/Continental ♦ Lunch and dinner. Closed mid-Oct to May. Indiana Ave (off Grand Ave S.), Falmouth. 548.4411

Fascinated by the numerous windmills that dotted the countryside of Cape Cod, Henry David Thoreau described them as looking "loose and locomotive, like huge wounded birds, trailing a wing or a leg."

42 **Amigos Mexican Cantina & Restaurante** ★$$ No, in case you were wondering, **Michael Sweeney** is not Hispanic. But he visits Mexico several times a year, reads a lot of cookbooks, and can flip a mean burrito; he also has an affinity for Cajun cuisine. Then again, maybe it's the 17-ounce margaritas that keep packing the regulars into this unprepossessing minimall. ♦ Mexican/American/Cajun ♦ Lunch and dinner. 31 Main St/Rte 28 (between Worcester Park and Maravista Aves), Falmouth. 548.8510

43 **Tony Andrews Farm and Produce Stand** East Falmouth was once the strawberry capital of the world; this is one of the few farms left where you can still "pick your own"—or buy your own, for that matter, if you're not up for a few grueling hours in the high summer sun. **Tony Andrews** has been coaxing the fruit forth since 1927, and the scent hangs heavy and luscious in the shimmering heat. ♦ Picking: daily 8AM-noon mid-June to mid-July. Farmstand: daily 9AM-6PM mid-June to Sept. 398 Old Meeting House Rd (between Old Barnstable and Carriage Shop Rds), E. Falmouth. 548.5257

44 **Falmouth Playhouse** This 600-seat summer theater (pictured above) started out as the **Coonamessett Ranch,** a country club financed by plumbing heir **John Crane** and designed by renowned New York theater architect **Thomas Lamb.** During World War II, it served as an officers' club and was maintained by German POWs. After the war, it housed a nightclub that hosted several fund-raising events for the British Overseas Relief Fund. That's when British actress **Gertrude Lawrence** came across it and saw a potential theater. Retrofitted by architect **E. Gunnar Peterson,** the Falmouth Playhouse opened in 1949 with **Tallulah Bankhead** in *Private Lives;* to christen the venture, she sipped

champagne from her shoe. Over the past four decades, a "Who's Who of Mid-Century Theater" has paraded through this big old barn of a place, and the head shots lining the walls show them at young, tender ages: **Hume Cronyn, Julie Harris, Tony Perkins,** and countless others trod these boards. Several significant premiers have taken place here, too, from *An Evening with Nichols and May* to **Arthur Miller's** *A View from the Bridge.* Alas, in recent years, the fare has been considerably less adventurous: mostly proven Broadway vehicles starring second- and even third-string TV stars. For the price (top seats go for less than $25), it's still a relative bargain, but it would be great to see some new life breathed into this straw-hat survivor. ♦ Admission. W-Th 2PM, 8:30PM; F 8PM; Sa 5PM, 9PM; Su 7PM. 59 Theater Dr (off Boxberry Hill Rd, next to Cape Cod Country Club), Falmouth. 563.5922

45 Ashumet Holly and Wildlife Sanctuary A 49-acre preserve, whose Wampanoag name means "water near a spring," Ashumet contains more than 1,000 holly trees (some 65 varieties) cultivated by the late **Wilfred Wheeler,** the state's first commissioner of agriculture, who was concerned by the attrition among native hollies caused by excessive holiday harvesting. Following Wheeler's death in 1961, the property was placed in trust under the aegis of the **Audubon Society** by **Josiah Lilly.** Some 133 species of birds have been spotted passing through, and about four dozen swallows have returned to nest in the barn every April since at least 1935. In fall, the most sought-after sight is a blooming franklinia, a member of the tea family, which produces large white flowers. Walkers can follow a self-guided map through wildflowers and heather, and around a glacier-formed kettle pond abloom every summer with Oriental lotus flowers. ♦ Admission. Tu-Su dawn-dusk. 286 Ashumet Rd (off Rte 151), E. Falmouth. 563.6390

46 Oysters Too ★★$$ Just another ranch-style roadside restaurant? Look again, because, although this place is relatively new (owners **Bob** and **Jim Knight** opened it in 1992, springboarding from the decade-long success of their family-style restaurant **Cherrystones,** on Route 151), the decor is quite tasteful—lots of dark wooden booths, illumined by hanging Depression-style glass lamps—and chef **Michael Dias'** dishes are not only delectable but a steal for this price range. His sea scallops, flash-broiled and brushed with lemon-butter, are simplicity itself, but superb; the scampi *Amareuse* are sautéed with tomato *concasse,* almonds, and anisette and served atop angel-hair pasta. Dessert may be nothing fancier than homemade bread pudding, but what could be more delicious? ♦ American/Continental ♦ Dinner. 876 Rte 28 (between Central Ave and Edgewater Dr), E. Falmouth. 548.9191

47 Waquoit Bay National Estuarine Research Reserve Estuaries, where freshwater rivers meet the ocean, are among the most fertile—and fragile—segments of the coastal environment. Traditionally dredged, filled, and otherwise manipulated to suit commercial needs, these delicate ecosystems have come under the protective scrutiny of the **National Estuarine Research Reserve System (NERR),** created by an act of Congress in 1972. One of four such sanctuaries in New England, the Waquoit Bay property (added to the NERR roster in 1988) is a shallow embayment covering 2,250 acres, including a 500-acre state park at South Cape Beach. State funds have been secured to turn the old **Swift Estate** mansion into a headquarters with exhibition space; meanwhile, you can find your own living exhibits by walking its paths. During summer, resident naturalists offer guided walks (covering such topics as birds, plants, and dune ecology) and "Evenings on the Bluff," family-oriented educational programs. ♦ Tu-F 1-4PM July-Aug. 149 Waquoit Hwy/Rte 28 (between Seacoast Blvd and Barrows Rd), E. Falmouth. 547.0495

48 Bed & Breakfast of Waquoit Bay $ **Tom** and **Janet Durkin** are former owners of the Longwood Inn in Marlboro, Vermont, long beloved by the classical musicians of the **Marlboro Music Festival,** as well as their cultured camp followers. The Durkins are jazz fans themselves, and their new venture, a four-bedroom B&B set back on several acres of tree-shaded grounds along the bucolic **Child's River,** is like a mellow improv. The '20s-era common room resembles a cross between a chapel and an Arts-and-Crafts bungalow; it's adorned with bold paintings by their daughter, and a piano for visiting musician/friends. It's not that the decor is so outstanding—though it's quite nice. Janet's "Waverly fabric fetish" has resulted in some very handsome rooms, and the Europeans who've already discovered this hideaway appreciate both the private baths, complete with bidets, and, off one bedroom, a secluded roof deck, seemingly custom-designed for sunbathing *au naturel.* All these extras aside, it's the Durkins themselves who make the place cook: their interests are many and lively, their company invigorating. ♦ 176 Waquoit Hwy (between Seacoast Blvd and Barrows Rd), E. Falmouth. 457.0084

49 Moonakis Cafe ★★$ If it's not past 2PM, come to a screeching halt. Unless you're doing the B&B route, where breakfasting is a competitive sport, you won't come across repasts like these anywhere. The omelets are astounding: lobster-asparagus, bacon-and-Brie, and smoked shrimp, red onion, and chèvre, to name just a few of more unusual special combos. Or perhaps you'd prefer homemade corned-beef hash or chicken-apple sausage? Maybe pumpkin-nut pancakes or Belgian waffles with kiwi? One gets the sense that the owners of this low-key roadside restaurant are operating a test kitchen dedicated to pushing the boring-old-breakfast envelope; in any case, there are plenty of willing—nay, greedy—guinea pigs on hand to help out. Lunch is good, too, if a bit more predictable (sandwiches and burgers), but you can always finish up with a rousing apple brown Betty. ♦ American ♦ Breakfast and lunch; breakfast only on Sunday. 460 Waquoit Hwy (between Barrows and Carriage Shop Rds), E. Falmouth. 457.9630

49 Cape Trader This multidealer shop has the quality vacillations common to group shops but still merits perusal, especially since one of the exhibitors, **Diane Clifford,** is in the habit of buying up whole households. All sorts of interesting stuff tumbles out when it comes time to shake down the inventory. ♦ M, W-Sa 10AM-5PM; Su noon-5PM. 486 Waquoit Hwy (between Barrows and Carriage Shop Rds), E. Falmouth. 457.7850

Recent archaeological evidence suggests that the "People of the First Light" (that is, Native Americans of the Algonquian tribes) may have occupied the "Narrow Land" during the late Pleistocene, soon after the last glaciers receded some 10,000 to 12,000 years ago, leaving behind the "terminal moraine," or ridge of rubble, that now constitutes the Cape and Islands. The tribes subsisted as nomadic hunter-gatherers for about 10,000 years before settling into more permanent winter and summer sites. They had spent a few millennia developing a sustainable agriculture when the English showed up, bearing not only a very different agenda but devastating diseases; from an estimated population of 30,000 early in the 17th century, their numbers dwindled to the hundreds.

50 New Seabury, Cape Cod $$$$ The subject of a long and ultimately futile land rights battle initiated by the Wampanoag tribe, who were granted most of Mashpee in 1660, this enormous resort development—some 1,700 condos spread over 2,000 acres—contains about 170 rentable units, as well as three miles of private beach on Nantucket Sound, two 18-hole golf courses, two swimming pools, 16 all-weather tennis courts, and an indoor recreation complex. The condos are sorted into more than a dozen "villages," of which four are open to transients: **Tidewatch,** a '60s-era hotel complex adjoining the country club; **The Mews,** comprising California-modern villas and houses, along with a Nautilus center; **SeaQuarters,** golfside villas with Jacuzzi solaria; and **Maushop Village,** modeled on Nantucket cottages, with rose-entwined white picket fences, and crushed-clamshell walkways. The latter—named, ironically enough, for the mammoth sea deity whose mission it was to see to the Wampanoags' well-being—is pretty darn cute, if you don't mind some questionable karma. ♦ Great Oak Rd (off Red Brook Rd), New Seabury. 477.9111, 800/999.9033

Within New Seabury, Cape Cod's Maushop Village:

Popponesset Marketplace Within this cluster of white-shingled buildings are about a dozen shops, mostly proffering resortwear and staples. Two spots worth seeking out: The **Smokehouse Cafe** (★$$), which serves a creditable barbecue whose aroma is all but irresistible, and **M. Brann & Co.,** which features a mix of **Maria Brann's** boisterous handiwork (lavishly decorated sunhats, pillows fashioned from vintage chenille) and kitschy retro staples like McCoy vases. ♦ Shops: M-Sa 10AM-5PM, Su noon-5PM late June to early Sept; Sa 10AM-5PM, Su noon-5PM late May to late June, early Sept to mid-Oct. Restaurant: Breakfast, lunch, and dinner. Closed Monday through Friday late May to late June, early Sept to mid-Oct; closed mid-Oct to late May. 477.9111

50 Popponesset Inn ★★★$$$$ Since taking over in 1988, co-owner **Linda Zammer** has lightened up the decor of this venerable 1940s inn-turned-restaurant with a color scheme that's predominantly white (down to the painted Windsors) with washes of pale blue. The whole place—and it's large, accommodating as many as 500 in enclosed decks and tents—seems to embrace the sea, and vice versa. Executive chef **David Schneider** is a veteran of the RockResorts circuit (Carambola, Williamsburg, Woodstock) and does right by local bounty, enrobing seafood *en papillote* and smothering lobster in a brandied cream Newburg. If neither wallet nor cholesterol level warrant an all-out splurge, try the lighter fare in adjoining **Poppy's** ($$$) or just sip a "Poppy Codder" (Absolut, with cranberry juice and a splash of Triple Sec) while imbibing the sea breezes. ♦ Continental ♦ Lunch and dinner. Closed Monday and Tuesday and for lunch Wednesday through Friday Apr to late June, mid-Sept to Nov; closed Nov-Mar. Mall Wy (off Shore Dr), New Seabury. Reservations recommended; jacket preferred. 477.1100

51 **Mashpee Commons** The principals of **Fields Point Limited Partnership** (the same company that developed New Seabury) have gone to great pains to create a 30-acre mall that looks like a traditional New England town (it just happens to be brand-spanking-new). The developers even went so far as to measure and replicate the sidewalks and streets of Woodstock, Vermont, in order to create a pedestrian-friendly "town center" encompassing some 50 shops and eateries. The buildings erected to date (designed by such firms as **Prellwitz/Chilinski, Ellenzweig Associations, Orr & Taylor,** and **A.E. Ferragamo**) are indeed handsome, though the trees have a lot of growing to do. More than a decade into its master plan (formalized in 1979), the complex still has a sterile, reconstituted feel, and is not yet the community-builder it's purported to be. (The next phase, with input from Miami architects **Andres Duany** and **Elizabeth Plater-Zyberk** of Seaside fame, will be an influx of neo-traditional dwellings ranging from half-Capes to "captain's houses" and "courtyard apartments.")

If the development-oriented ethos doesn't disturb you too much, there are several appealing shops worth browsing here. **Signature** (539.0029) features very snazzy crafts, the chic kind as opposed to cutesy. There's a de rigueur **Gap** (477.6668), as well as an **Irresistibles** (477.5853), a women's clothing chain that carries cottons (especially hand-knit sweaters) and the **Segrets** line of vividly printed sportswear. There's also a six-screen movie theater—concealed, of course, behind a tasteful curved arcade—and, on Friday nights in summer, free outdoor concerts ♦ Shops M-Th, Sa 10AM-8PM; F 10AM-9PM; Su noon-5PM. Rte 151 and Falmouth Rd/Rte 28. 477.3887

Within the Mashpee Commons:

Gone Tomatoes ★★$$ Who would expect to find haute North Italian in a mall? This handsome bi-level restaurant, with creamy walls, teal accents, and terracotta floors, does a great ravioli carbonara—unconscionably rich, but no one's likely to complain. Seafood generally turns up in the daily specials, and there are eight types of grilled focaccia pizza always on tap. Service is friendly and prompt—helpful if you're trying to catch a movie next door. ♦ Italian/Takeout ♦ Lunch and dinner; Sunday brunch. 477.8100

52 **Old Indian Meetinghouse** Built in 1684 on Santuit Pond and moved here in 1717, the Old Indian Meetinghouse is one of the oldest church buildings in America, and is still used for worship and meetings. Converted by British missionary **Richard Bourne** (the son of a wealthy shipping merchant), the "Massapee" tribe—spellings varied widely early on—was welcomed into the Congregational fold in 1670. In the mid-1800s, after a succession of indigenous preachers (descendants of the sachem Massasoit), the Mashpee people decided to become Baptists. Volunteer curator **Emma-jo Mills Brennan** can fill you in further; you might also want to buy a copy of **Russell M. Peters'** excellent history, *The Wampanoags of Mashpee.* The interior is inspiringly plain, except for an improbable Victorian chandelier, and much smaller in scale than comparable structures erected by the colonists. Be sure to climb up into the gallery to see the graffiti of masted schooners carved by some restive young churchgoers, probably a century or more ago. ♦ Sa-Su noon-4PM. Service Su 11AM June-Aug. Meetinghouse Rd (at Falmouth Rd/Rte 28), Mashpee. 477.0208

53 **Wampanoag Indian Museum** Housed in a 1793 half-Cape, this collection of tools, baskets, mementos, etc., is not impressive in and of itself; one must read between the lines, or better yet, peruse some of the historical literature offered for that purpose, to gain an entirely new perspective on the glorious saga of colonization. When **Captain John Smith** came reconnoitering in 1614, the Wampanoags of eastern Massachusetts numbered more than 30,000. In 1617, after **Lieutenant Thomas Hunt** had kidnapped six men from the tribe and sold them into slavery, a small band boarded an unoccupied ship in retaliation—and there encountered plague, which swept through the community. People died by the thousands, and the whole fabric of society unraveled. (This is why the Pilgrims were able to take over an abandoned farm site when they arrived a few years later.) Very little of the Wampanoag's beleaguered history is

immediately evident in this modest museum, which uninformed visitors have been known to dismiss as "kind of sad," but there's a vast store of wisdom underlying the meager artifacts, and an in-depth visit is a prerequisite to understanding the anomalies now present in the region. ♦ Donation. Tu-F 9:30AM-2PM. Rte 130 (between Great Neck and Lovells Rds), Mashpee. 477.1536

54 **The Flume** ★★★$$$ This pared-down yet striking restaurant is named for the ladder that fish climb to spawn. Owner **Earl Mills** is both Chief Flying Eagle of the Wampanoag tribe and an extraordinary chef. Here, he serves New England classics, such as clam chowder, codfish cakes, scalloped oysters, baked beans, pot roast, apple-stuffed duckling, and an authentic Indian pudding. Like many Cape restaurateurs, Mills offers a discounted early-bird menu for the benefit of fixed-income retirees and others unable to afford a full-scale night on the town; his is especially generous, encompassing three courses for less than $10. ♦ American/Takeout ♦ Dinner; lunch also on Sunday. Closed Monday and Tuesday mid-Sept to late May. Lake Ave (off Rte 130), Mashpee. 477.1456

55 **Lowell Holly Reservation** This 130-acre woodland preserve was bequeathed in 1943 by former Harvard University president **Abbott Lawrence Lowell** to the Trustees of the Reservation, the oldest private land trust in the country: founded in 1891 by **Charles Eliot**, it now comprises more than17,500 acres of exceptional scenic, historic, and ecological value. In addition to some 500 holly trees, the reservation—an unspoiled peninsula jutting into Cape Cod's largest freshwater ponds, Mashpee and Wakeby lakes—harbors stands of native American beech, untouched for several centuries. Wildflowers-in-residence include beechdrops (a brown parasite that blooms under beeches), silverrod (a slim cousin to the goldenrod), and pink lady's slipper, a native orchid that blooms in spring. ♦ Daily 10AM-sunset late May to Oct; trailhead parking closes at 5PM. Off S. Sandwich Rd (between Farmville and Cotuit Rds), Mashpee. 921.2944

Veteran Cape-observer Robert Finch has a feel for the ennobling potential encoded in Cape Cod's evershifting landscape. "It needs to be known," he wrote in *Common Ground: A Naturalist's Cape Cod* (1981), "not only from soil samples and by planning boards, but in its many moods and expressions, its comings and goings, its various lives and forces that can excite wonder and awe and new ways of seeing."

Restaurants/Clubs: Red **Hotels:** Blue
Shops/ Outdoors: Green **Sights/Culture:** Black

Bests

Douglas Parker

Artist/Art Director, *Bostonia Magazine*

Heritage Plantation in Sandwich. Besides the extensive exhibits of antique autos, firearms, and a great carousel, the collection of rhododendrons hybridized by **Charles Dexter** are mindblowing in May.

Bertha Walker Gallery (208 Bradford Street, Provincetown) is the best gallery in a town where art galleries are profligate. Look for exhibits of **Selina Trieff** and **Robert Henry,** painters unsung but soaring in their milieu.

The **Black Duck Restaurant** in Woods Hole, and the **Black Dog Restaurant** in Vineyard Haven, Martha's Vineyard. These fine community restaurants specialize in local seafood served alfresco in the former and on a screened porch overlooking the harbor in the latter—wait if necessary to be seated on the porch; you'll be glad you did. Try the bluefish—either broiled or smoked.

The Flying Horses, the oldest carousel in America, in Oak Bluffs, has just been restored, emerging as the high point/centerpiece to any visit to "O.B" with children—catching the brass ring (which is not that difficult to do) gives the catcher another ride for free.

Martha's Vineyard has become a quiet destination of distinction for artists escaping urban decay. **On the Vineyard Gallery** (State Road opposite lower Lambert's Cove Road), a remarkable nonprofit exhibit space in a rural setting surrounded by perennial gardens, provides what is probably the best representation of some of the finest resident artists on the island. On Sunday evenings in summer, you'll usually find an opening reception for a new show.

The **Scottish Bakehouse,** farther up the road from the gallery, is a paean to the joy of sweets-eating. In addition to all the expected treats (breads, cakes, and cookies), you'll find fresh shortbread and "hermits" to munch on your circuit of the island.

My favorite place to take visitors is to the beach at **Cedar Tree Neck** on Martha's Vineyard. While difficult to find—take the Indian Hill Road to just before it ends, where you'll see among a group of mailboxes a sign directing you down a circuitous dirt road for about a mile to the reservation—the "walk" through sassafras and misshapen scrub oak with intermittent views of a barrier beach pond has as its destination one of the most beautiful, least disturbed, wild, sandy beaches and cliff walks on the island. A truly transporting and refreshing experience, a walk on this beautiful deserted beach can wash away all your troubles. Take a good friend along and enjoy this unique place.

Wintertide Coffee House, Vineyard Haven, is a long-lived community gathering spot for the finest in folk, fusion, singer/songwriter, and instrumental music. It is the annual site of a retreat for musicians interested in spending some intense creative time with fellow artists in a beautiful setting.

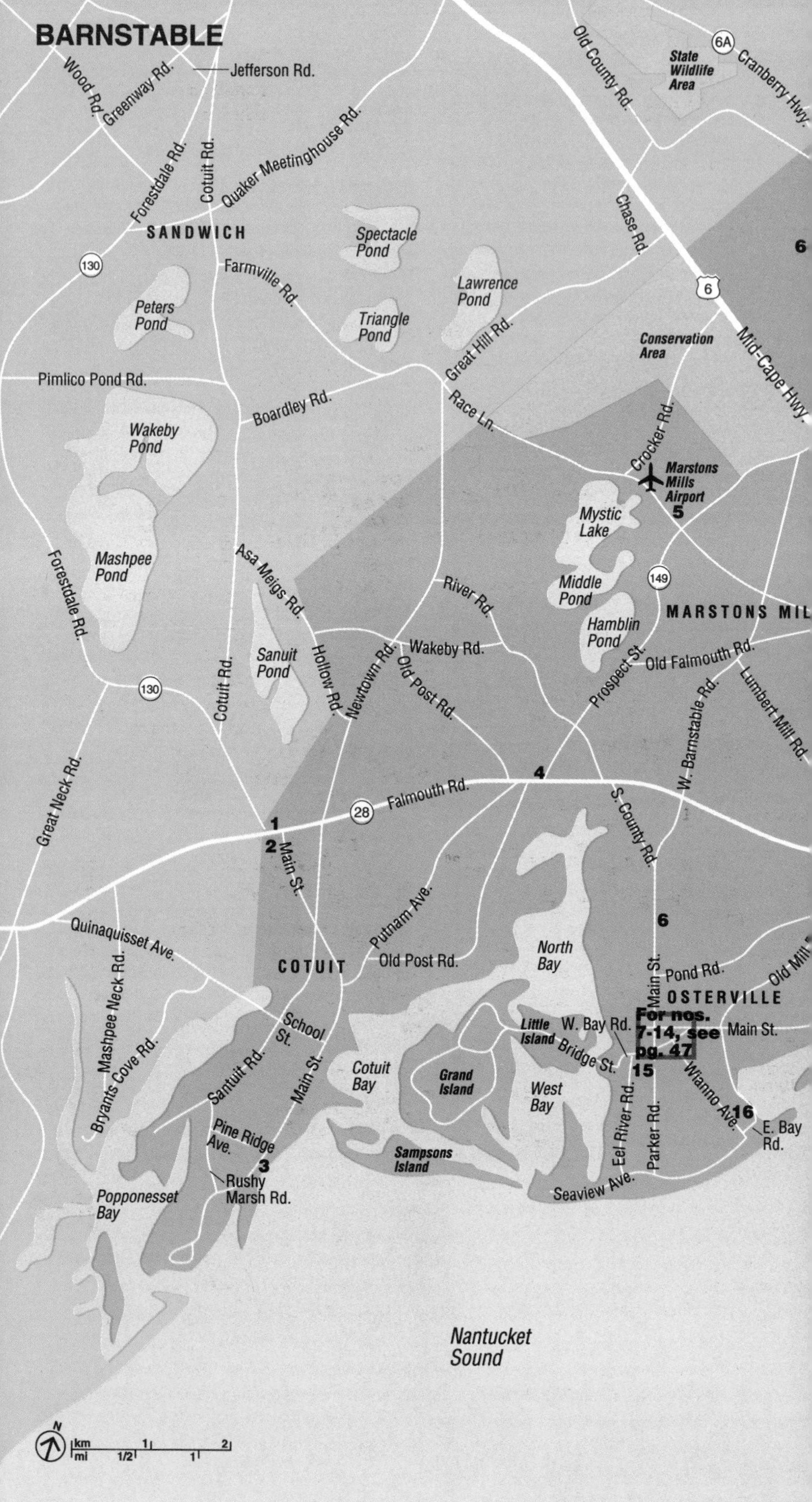

BARNSTABLE
Wood Rd.
Greenway Rd.
Jefferson Rd.
Forestdale Rd.
Cotuit Rd.
Quaker Meetinghouse Rd.
Old County Rd.
6A
State Wildlife Area
Cranberry Hwy.
SANDWICH
130
Farmville Rd.
Spectacle Pond
Lawrence Pond
Triangle Pond
Peters Pond
Chase Rd.
6
Mid-Cape Hwy.
Conservation Area
Great Hill Rd.
Pimlico Pond Rd.
Boardley Rd.
Race Ln.
Wakeby Pond
Crocker Rd.
Marstons Mills Airport
5
Mystic Lake
Middle Pond
Hamblin Pond
149
MARSTONS MIL
Mashpee Pond
Forestdale Rd.
Asa Meigs Rd.
River Rd.
Wakeby Rd.
Sanuit Pond
Hollow Rd.
Newtown Rd.
Old Post Rd.
Prospect St.
Old Falmouth Rd.
Lumbert Mill Rd.
W. Barnstable Rd.
130
Cotuit Rd.
Great Neck Rd.
4
Falmouth Rd.
28
S. County Rd.
1
2
Main St.
Putnam Ave.
Quinaquisset Ave.
Mashpee Neck Rd.
COTUIT
Old Post Rd.
North Bay
Main St.
Pond Rd.
Old Mill
OSTERVILLE
School St.
Bryants Cove Rd.
Santuit Rd.
Main St.
Cotuit Bay
Little Island
W. Bay Rd.
For nos. 7-14, see pg. 47
Main St.
Bridge St.
15
Grand Island
West Bay
Wianno Ave.
16
E. Bay Rd.
Eel River Rd.
Parker Rd.
Pine Ridge Ave.
3
Rushy Marsh Rd.
Sampsons Island
Seaview Ave.
Popponesset Bay
Nantucket Sound
N
km
mi
1/2
1
1
2

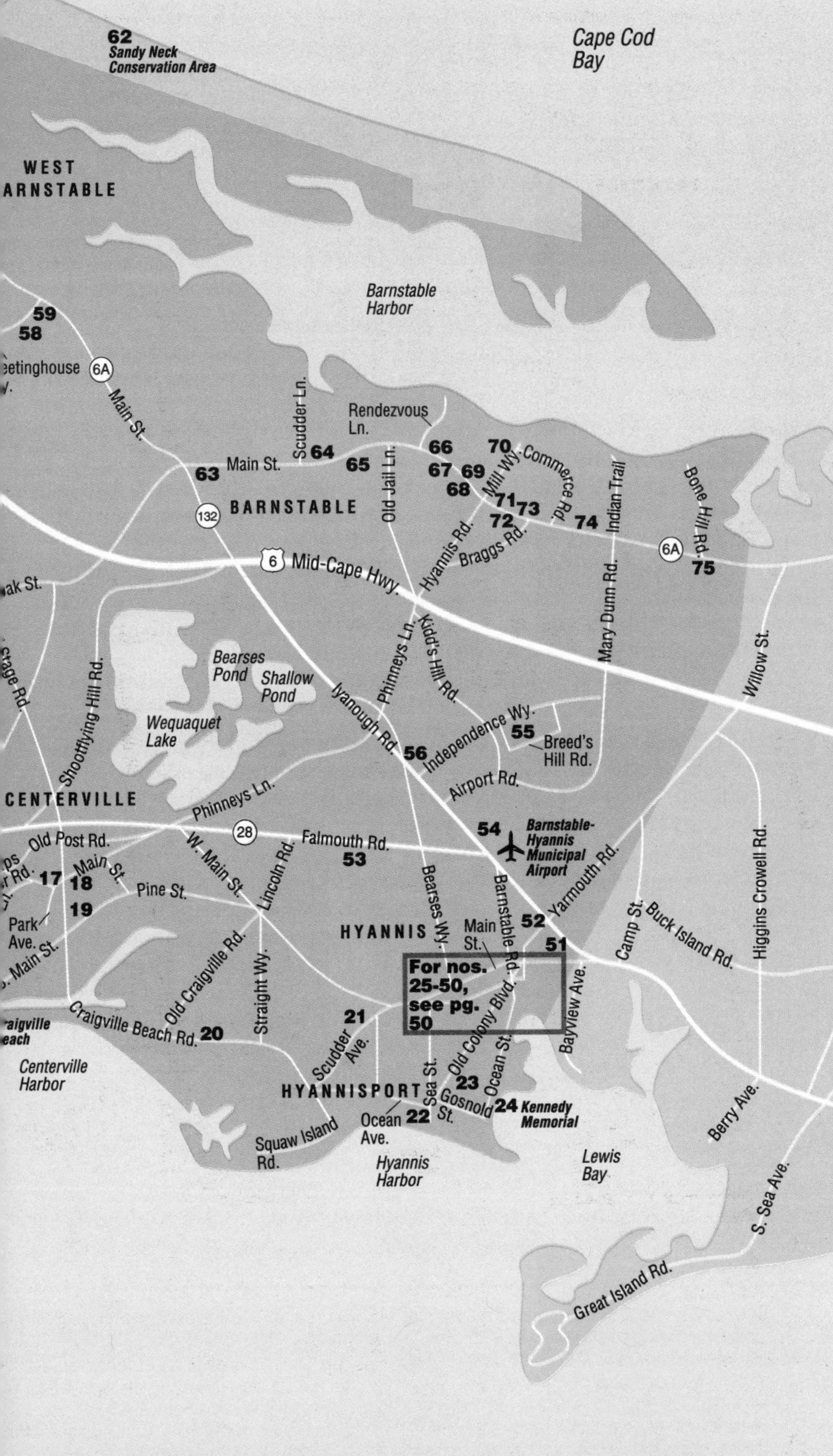

62
Sandy Neck Conservation Area
Cape Cod Bay
WEST
ARNSTABLE
Barnstable Harbor
59
58
Main St.
Scudder Ln.
Rendezvous Ln.
63
64
65
66
67
68
69
70
71
72
73
74
75
Old Jail Ln.
Mill Wy.
Commerce Rd.
Indian Trail
Bone Hill Rd.
BARNSTABLE
Hyannis Rd.
Braggs Rd.
Mid-Cape Hwy.
Mary Dunn Rd.
Phinneys Ln.
Kidd's Hill Rd.
Willow St.
Bearses Pond
Shallow Pond
Wequaquet Lake
Shootflying Hill Rd.
Iyanough Rd.
Independence Wy.
55
Breed's Hill Rd.
56
Airport Rd.
CENTERVILLE
Phinneys Ln.
Old Post Rd.
Falmouth Rd.
53
54
Barnstable-Hyannis Municipal Airport
Yarmouth Rd.
W. Main St.
Lincoln Rd.
Main St.
17
18
19
Pine St.
Park Ave.
Bearses Wy.
Barnstable Rd.
Main St.
52
51
HYANNIS
Camp St.
Buck Island Rd.
Higgins Crowell Rd.
For nos. 25-50, see pg. 50
Old Craigville Rd.
Straight Wy.
Craigville Beach Rd.
20
21
Scudder Ave.
Old Colony Blvd.
Ocean St.
Bayview Ave.
Centerville Harbor
HYANNISPORT
Sea St.
23
Gosnold St.
24
Kennedy Memorial
Ocean Ave.
22
Squaw Island Rd.
Hyannis Harbor
Lewis Bay
Berry Ave.
S. Sea Ave.
Great Island Rd.

Barnstable

Barnstable County is a study in contrasts. One of the oldest communities on the Cape (it was founded by the parish of English Congregational minister **John Lothrop** in 1639), it's also a nexus of commercial activity—particularly in **Hyannis,** the Cape's transportation hub and unofficial "state capital." Ever since the 60-store **Cape Cod Mall** was built in 1970, strip development has run rampant along routes 132 and 28, while the center of town has slipped into shabbiness. Recently, however, local boosters have teamed up with Barnstable semiretiree **Benjamin Thompson** (the architect who masterminded Boston's Faneuil Hall Marketplace and other urban revitalization projects) to develop the notion of a "Main Street Waterfront District." Thompson had been pushing this plan, to no avail, since the early '60s, and now that the citizenry is paying attention, results are accreting quickly.

Even a few years ago, the waterfront was just a big outdoor waiting room for the up to 900,000 ferry passengers who passed through yearly. Now they can wait in style, tided over with snacks and meals at the dozen or so appealing restaurants that line a newly created harborfront park. The ambience of **Main Street,** the principal thoroughfare, has never been quite as cosmopolitan as **Kennedy** fans expect, and their presence, along with attendant T-shirt shops, only served to drag it down further. A better balance is being struck now: restaurants like **Alberto's** have restored some cachet to an evening on the town, the rose-clustered patio at the **Asa Bearse House** fosters the fine art of people-watching, and several intriguing shops, such as **Plush & Plunder,** reward the determined browser. And even those die-hard Kennedy-peepers now have a healthy outlet: the **John F. Kennedy Museum,** a small but stirring audiovisual display at **Old Town Hall,** shows the human side of the legend that captivated so many.

West of Hyannis is a cluster of seaside communities—full of sleepy, old-money charm—scarcely touched by the relentless commercialism that has infected Route 28. Take a detour into **Cotuit,** so popular among academics since the turn of the century (**Erik Erikson** summered here) that it earned the nickname "Little Harvard"; it's also renowned for its oysters. **Osterville,** bought from Native Americans for two copper kettles and some fencing in 1648 and originally known as "Oysterville," has evolved into the most affluent community on the Cape, harboring such names as **Cabot, Mellon,** and **du Pont:** you won't find a whole lot to do here, except perhaps drool over the real estate (much of it cloistered behind broad gates and long drives) and pretend-shop for your own mythical $2 million mansion. **Centerville,** the site of Christian Camp Meeting Association gatherings since 1872, combines an old-fashioned town with popular (and usually packed) **Craigville Beach,** a.k.a. "Muscle Beach," where the water temperature, warmed by the sound, hovers in the comfortable mid-70s.

Tradition-seekers can head north to the bayside villages of **Barnstable,** a tidy trail of historical sites and B&Bs. Even here, a couple of radical new enterprises, such as the **Pinske Gallery,** have cropped up like colorful wildflowers.

---

1 Cahoon Museum of American Art The 1775 Georgian Colonial farmhouse in which this little museum is located is an artwork in its own right, especially the 1810 stairway stenciling. The top floor, with a flip-up wall, could be converted into a ballroom, handy in the house's tavern days. Bought by *naïf* artists **Ralph** and **Martha Cahoon** in 1945, the house has served as a nonprofit museum since the mid-'80s.

The core collection of the Cahoons' work is, alas, of limited appeal, though apparently of considerable value; it consists of "contemporary primitive" pastiches of Cape Cod icons (mermaids, lighthouses, and the like) rendered in a fashion perhaps better suited to furniture decoration, the craft in which they started out. But the changing exhibits, five or six a year, are much stronger. Some draw on a permanent collection of lesser-known but nonetheless noteworthy American artists, from itinerant portrait painters to impressionists. Contemporary artists are shown as well: a standout exhibit in 1993 featured **Edith Vonnegut's** "domestic goddesses," nude and luminous madonnas struggling to lend some grandeur to the grind of everyday life. **Maureen Twohig's** curatorial notes, posted alongside the artwork, are singularly jargon-free and thought-provoking. ♦ Donation. W-Sa 10AM-4PM; Su 1-4PM. 4676 Falmouth Rd (between Rte 130 and Main St), Cotuit. 428.7581

1 **Isaiah Thomas Books & Prints** How often do you see a 1604 book just sitting on a shelf, open to perusal, or a $1,000 first-edition *Prince and the Pauper* plunked on the counter? **James S. Visbeck,** who in 1991 moved his decades-old Worcester shop (named for the printer who founded the American Antiquarian Society) with its 60,000 tomes to this circa 1850 house, is clearly a book-lover, not just an accumulator. The books *have* tended to pile up, though, forming stalagmites on the floor and even encroaching onto the sofa. No matter—many pleasurable, possibly profitable, hours could be spent poking around among the miniatures, maps, prints, "books on books," and other subspecialties too numerous to list. ♦ M-Sa 10AM-6PM, Su noon-5PM late May to mid-Oct. Tu-Sa 10AM-6PM, Su noon-5PM mid-Oct to late May. 4632 Falmouth Rd/Rte 28 (between Rte 130 and Main St), Cotuit. 428.2752

2 **The Regatta of Cotuit at the Crocker House** ★★★★$$$ **Brantz** and **Wendy Bryan's** branch restaurant has all the allure of their summers-only waterside landmark in Falmouth, plus its own unique charms. Each of the eight *intime* dining rooms in this converted circa 1790 stagecoach inn has a distinctive decor, ranging from delicate florals to clubby burnished wood; you can pick a mood and sink into it. The unifying thread is chef **Martin Murphy's** unsurpassable seasonal fare, supplemented by an astute sprinkling of herbs and garnishes plucked from the kitchen's *potagere.* He might pair sautéed Plymouth rainbow trout, encrusted in pistachios, with orange-cilantro butter sauce, for example, or grilled *poussin* with fresh rosemary and thyme. For all the finesse poured into the preparation and presentation, this is not a stiff, pretentious place—in fact, the dress code is "attractively formal or informal." What could be a hushed gastronomic shrine is instead a joyous convocation of people who appreciate food and its festive potential. ♦ New American ♦ Dinner. Closed Jan-Apr. 4613 Falmouth Rd/Rte 28 (between Rte 130 and Main St), Cotuit. 428.5715

3 **The Samuel B. Dottridge Homestead** There are more exciting historical museums on the Cape, but if you're in the neighborhood, take a quick look around this circa 1790 home, which was occupied in the early 19th century by a carpenter and his family. A barn museum out back, also maintained by the **Historical Society of Santuit & Cotuit,** contains all sorts of odd flotsam from several centuries of domestic and agricultural endeavor. ♦ Tu, Th, Sa-Su 2:30-5PM mid-June to mid-Sept. 1148 Main St (between Pine Ridge Ave and Rushy Marsh Rd), Cotuit. 428.0461

4 **Inn at the Mills** $$ It's hard to imagine a more idyllic spot than this 1780 house (on the **National Register of Historic Places;** illustrated above) overlooking a placid pond complete with swans, geese, and a gazebo. It's a natural for weddings, indeed, for celebrations of any sort. Owner **Bill Henry** used to run the restaurant at the old **Popponessett Inn,** and leftover celebrity photos line a side stairwell off a rustic yet elegant dining area. The front room is a formal parlor with wingback chairs and crystal decanters; it's attached to a wicker-filled sun porch with a white baby grand, off of which is a glimmering pool. Up the semicircular staircase are five rooms with pencil-post, four-poster beds or canopied twins, plus the "hayloft" room, which seems to go on forever. Even with no advertising (not so much as a sign), the inn tends to book up solid through summer, but it's just as lovely and, if possible, even more restful when the greenery's gone and the fireplaces are glowing. ♦ 71 Rte 149, Marstons Mills. 428.2967

5 **Cape Cod Soaring Adventures** If you've ever wondered what it's like to fly like an eagle, here's your chance to find out. Coasting in a glider along the thermal gusts created by Cape Cod's sea breeze front "takes no more training than watching TV," claims pilot **Randy Charlton.** That's because he does the driving. Should you get hooked, he also provides rentals and training (his teenage son already solos). A light plane tows the glider to 3,000 feet, then you ease on down in absolute silence, perhaps performing a few "aerobatics" along the way. You could stay up as long as six to eight hours, but rides generally run 20 to 40 minutes, the fees rising concomitantly. This sleek, white craft is capable of landing on a football field, but as Charlton says, "you only get one shot"; you can't change your mind once you start to descend. Having touched down safely here since 1984, he decided to launch the business in 1989. ♦ Fee. Daily 10AM-5PM Apr-Nov, depending on weather. Marstons Mills Airport (Race Ln, at Rte 149), Marstons Mills. 540.8081, 800/660.4563

6 Johnny Appleseed "Suburban classics" sums up the feminine image evoked here. This relatively small, New England-based chain and mail-order outfit has the well-heeled matron pretty well cased: she wants cotton and florals, in every reasonable combination, and in sizes up to 18 and 20, in case she's not quite the sylph she used to be. ♦ M-Sa 9:30AM-5:30PM; Su noon-5PM. 1374 Main St (between W. Barnstable and Pond Rds), Osterville. 428.6081

6 The Farmhouse **Carolyn** and **Barry Crawford** have set up their antique store to resemble a lived-in house (keeping room, bedroom, parlor)—only with price tags. Over half the stock is here on consignment, which makes for a predominance of treasured objects, not just household surplus. The back room, a barn, holds an intentional mishmash, with stray architectural elements to lend intrigue. ♦ M-Sa 10AM-5PM; Su noon-4PM. 1340 Main St (between W. Barnstable and Pond Rds), Osterville. 420.4200

6 Oak and Ivory This is the only place off-island where you're apt to encounter authentic Nantucket lightship baskets. **Bob Marks,** a Nantucket native, studied with master basketmaker **Bill Sevrens.** Each creation takes from 30 to 45 hours to make, and prices range from about $700 for a simple ice-bucket design to $4,400 for a set of nesting baskets. The store also stocks a few rare antique baskets, as well as compatible home furnishings, such as nubby Kennebec Weavers throws and reproduction Shaker furniture. ♦ M-Sa 10AM-5PM, Su noon-5PM July-Aug; M-Sa 10AM-5PM Sept-July. 1112 Main St (between W. Barnstable and Pond Rds), Osterville. 428.9425

7 Joan Peters The "Joan Peters look," featured in design showrooms from Boston to Dallas, is not so much a look as a world, a pastel-hued, light-drenched landscape where no unpleasantness—much less tastelessness—could ever possibly intrude. Since 1979 her atelier here has produced her signature fabrics and ceramics, and the showroom represents a cohesive portfolio, from throw pillows that resemble sugary little fairy-tale cottages to pale, floral-splashed matching comforters, cushions, tablecloths, and chair covers. You could even commission a complementary sink, for about $1,600. ♦ M-Sa 10AM-5PM. 885 Main St (between Fire Station Rd and Bay St), Osterville. 428.3418

7 Country Store At last: an unspoiled general store that looks, sounds, and even smells as a general store should (a combination of venerable dust and wax). **Charlie Kalas** grew up in this circa 1890 emporium and hasn't seen any need to change it much. Sure, penny candy costs more like 15 cents now, but kids still require their summertime fix of ice cream pops, so he lays in an assortment, including upstart **Ben & Jerry's.** ♦ Daily 7:30AM-8:30PM. 877 Main St (at Bay St), Osterville. 428.2097

8 A. Stanley Wheelock Antiques A semi-retired, Parsons-trained interior designer, Wheelock pretty much buys to suit himself these days, which works out well since his taste is right on target. Among the covetable objects to be found here, unless someone has snapped them up, are a cast-zinc French shop sign of a horse head and a lacquered Regency table, both well under $2,000. Strong suits include Orientalia, silver, and a general mèlange of "very decorative things." ♦ M-Sa 10AM-5PM Apr-Dec; by appointment Jan-Mar. 870 Main St (between Bay St and Wianno Ave), Osterville. 420.3170

8 Eldred Wheeler The company's mission statement—"Handcrafters of Fine 18th Century American Furniture"—may be just a touch oxymoronic, unless they've managed to master time travel, but these reproductions are almost as nice as the real thing, a little less fragile and a whole lot cheaper (80 percent or more). Big modern bodies appreciate a bed in a noncolonial size, like queen or king, and if you're embarrassed to buy new, you can always rough it up a bit and pretend your great-great-great-grandsire was born in it. ♦ M-Sa 10AM-5PM. 866 Main St (between Bay St and Wianno Ave), Osterville. 428.9049

Operating from 1860 to 1923, the West Barnstable Brick Company churned out as many as 100,000 bricks a day. Today, these collectibles fetch up to $35 apiece.

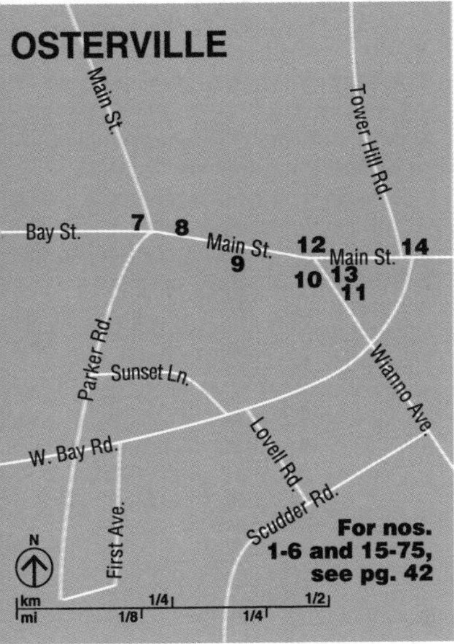

9 Joseph's Restaurant ★★$$ In the ostentatious '80s, this space, with much the same decor, was a postmodern temple of take-out gourmandise. It's even better suited to serve this mannered town as an informal cafe. The bookshelves trailing ivy encourage you to take your time, as do chef **Joe Murray's** hearty Italian dishes. Though he has come up with an ingenious faux Alfredo (using cottage cheese and skim milk) for the faint or sensible of heart, the offerings are mostly peasantlike and plentiful: baked ziti with five cheeses, for example, or roast vegetables *al forno*. Lunch features subs (including grilled chicken pesto with fontina) and custom-built pizzas. ♦ Italian ♦ Breakfast, lunch, and dinner. 825 Main St (between Bay St and Wianno Ave), Osterville. 420.1742

10 Mark, Fore & Strike Purveying to ultra-preps since 1951, this Florida-based chain remains a beacon of unchanging mores. Women can choose among Provençal-print garment bags and traditionalist fashions from designers such as **David Brooks;** meanwhile, men can paw through emblem belts (whales, ducks, and so on) and a rainbow of madras ties. ♦ M-Sa 9AM-5:30PM, Su noon-4PM late May to Dec; M-Sa 9AM-5PM Jan to late May. 21 Wianno Ave (at Main St), Osterville. 428.2270. Also at: 482 Main St, Chatham. 945.0568

11 Talbot's This is the only post for this preppy outfitter on the Cape, and it's perfectly situated in the epicenter of classicism. The company may be owned by a Japanese conglomerate now, but it keeps churning out the most appropriate work and social wear for East Coasters—which is to say, a bit over-formal at times but always in impeccable taste. ♦ M-Sa 9AM-5:30PM, Su noon-5PM May to mid-Oct; M-Sa 9AM-5:30PM mid-Oct to May. 32 Wianno Ave (between Main St and W. Bay Rd), Osterville. 428.2204

12 Natural Image Everything you see is made of natural fibers, but of a rarefied caliber. Designer **Jackie McCoy's** dresses fashioned from antique linen tablecloths fetch in the vicinity of $2,500, and a wedding dress made of handmade lace might go for $5,000—off the rack. Custom work comes dearer. ♦ M-Sa 10AM-5PM. 812 Main St (between Wianno Ave and Tower Hill Rd), Osterville. 428.5729

13 Clothes Encounters What spiffy castoffs these over-moneyed mortals leave! The Cape is full of thrift shops that may do wonders for charity but do little for one's clothes closet. **Ann Marie Ross'** shop brims with women's hand-me-downs, all in impeccable condition and tending to that timeless look that never goes out of fashion. She has two daughters who "never wear anything twice"; they should consider going into the garment business. ♦ Tu-Sa 10AM-4PM Feb-Dec; Sa 10AM-4PM Jan. 805 Main St (between Wianno Ave and W. Bay Rd), Osterville. 428.9265

14 Wimpy's ★$$ This modest and moderately priced restaurant was founded by **Ray Hostetter** to serve workers imported to install water mains in 1938: with only six stools, they had to eat in shifts. After numerous expansions (it now seats 300-plus), it's still owned by the same family and has seen the locals through many a maid's night out. The decor is semicolonial (huge stone fireplace, lots of wood trim, a cheery solarium toward the back), and the menu has kept pace with the times, introducing such dishes as pancetta-wrapped shrimp—a kind of high-class rumaki—and pan-blackened yellowfin tuna with soy sesame butter. For quick snacks, there's the signature jumbo Wimpy's burger or an assortment of whole-wheat pizzas. ♦ American ♦ Breakfast, lunch, and dinner. 752 Main St (at Tower Hill Rd), Osterville. 428.6300

Within Wimpy's:

The Cafe at Wimpy's ★$ Dazzling white, with pale green walls, this cafe serves bountiful breakfasts (try the eggs Nobska: like Bennies, only with lobster), light lunches, and take-out treats, such as old-fashioned latticework pies. ♦ American ♦ Breakfast and lunch. 428.6300

15 Captain John Parker House Serving as the main museum for the ever-growing collections of the **Osterville Historical Society,** this 1824 house exhibits an intriguing array of China trade spoils. There's an especially nice collection of dolls and toys upstairs. Next door, past historically accurate plantings maintained by the **Osterville Garden Club,** is the 1728 **Cammett House,** a "one pile deep narrow house" (only one room straight through), unusual in that it was never expanded; the owners couldn't afford to add on. Rescued when a condominium development threatened it with demolition, it's a valuable repository of early building techniques; down in the cellar, archaeological fragments are displayed. Completing the trio of historic properties is the 19th-century **Herbert F. Crosby Boat Shop,** where owners of antique boats can research their boats' roots and less-nautical types can admire such vessels as a **1922 Catboat Cayuga** and a **Wianno Senior,** favored by **John Fitzgerald Kennedy.** ♦ Nominal admission. Tu, Th, Su 1:30-4:30PM late June to Sept. 155 W. Bay Rd (at Parker Rd), Osterville. 428.5861

16 East Bay Lodge $$ You'd have to pay a lot more than this to secure some prime Osterville real estate, of which this East Bay Lodge is a good example. Unspoiled **Dowses Beach** is just down the lane, and the 18 rooms, set apart from the bustling main building in a separate annex, are thoroughly mainstream and upscale (Chippendale headboards on the beds, richly patterned and trimmed wallpaper, brass lamps). Bunking down for the night here is the next best thing to having friends in the neighborhood. ♦ 199 E. Bay Rd (between S. Main St and Wianno Ave), Osterville. 428.5200, 800/933.2782

Within the East Bay Lodge:

East Bay Lodge Restaurant ★★★$$$$ For years—more than a hundred, to be precise—this was *the* fusty old dining room catering to Osterville's highly conservative gentry. Now it's got a new look (slightly more opened up, but retaining the signature pink-and-green sunporch) and a fresh infusion of talent. **John** and **Arpad Voros** took over the whole place in 1992 and installed a new executive chef, **Alain Di Tommaso,** who's making welcome waves by tossing goat cheese in the spring greens (in port-walnut dressing, yet), grilling jumbo shrimp in red pepper coulis, and, in general, behaving as if food were a substance meant to be enjoyed. Hallelujah, the revolution has come at last. ♦ New American ♦ Dinner; Sunday brunch also May-June. Reservations recommended; jacket requested. 428.5200, 800/933.2782

A single aquifer underlies the entire Cape, serving as its only source of drinking water.

17 Centerville Pastry and Coffee Shop ★$ Pies are the raison d'être of this quaint old diner with a small dining room out back—and not just dessert pies (although there are plenty of those, from ordinary apple to peach, pear, and chocolate pumpkin), but vegetable, chicken, turkey, clam, beef, and even cheeseburger pie. For breakfast, which overlaps lunch for the lazy, this cheerful place—fashioned in incremental stages from an 1876 Methodist church—serves the likes of fruit-stuffed French toast, apple pie oatmeal, and Swedish pancakes made from a family recipe originating in Jönköping, Sweden. Weekend evenings it's transformed into "Christoph's," so that chef-owner **Christopher Bohr** can trot out a quartet of four-course, prix fixe meals (from saltimbocca to Philippine-style pork *adobo*). The deep-pocketed natives just love pinching pennies, and it's worth tracking down this off-the-tourist-trail spot so you can join them. ♦ American ♦ Breakfast and lunch; dinner also Friday and Saturday Apr-Oct. Closed Wednesday Nov-Mar. 23 Park Ave (between Old Stage and Bumps River Rds), Centerville. 775.6023

18 Inn at Fernbrook $$ The Cape is rife with historic inns, but none with quite so checkered a past as this onetime showpiece estate, on the **National Register of Historic Buildings. Howard Marston** of Boston's Parker House had it built in 1881, commissioning renowned landscape architect **Frederick Law Olmsted** to design the sunken sweetheart garden of pink and red roses, pocked with water lily ponds and ringed with exotic trees. After Marston's son, **Shirley,** gambled away his legacy, the house was bought in the '30s by chemist **Dr. Herbert Kalmus,** co-inventor of **Technicolor,** who hosted such notables as **Walt Disney, Cecil B DeMille,** and **Gloria Swanson.** When Kalmus left the property to the Catholic church, it became a summer retreat for **Cardinal Francis Spellman,** who entertained—and advised—both **Nixon** and **Kennedy.** The house had fallen on hard times when **Brian Gallo** and **Sal DiFlorio** (both escapees from the mega-hotel trade) took it on, and they restored it to its Queen Anne grandeur and filled it with period furnishings.

Among the five rooms and suites (there's also a garden cottage), two are knockouts. The Olmsted Suite, on the dormered third floor, has two bedrooms with queen-size brass beds, a living room with fireplace, and at the end of a staircase so steep you practically have to crawl up, a little balcony with a telescope, leading to a private roof deck. The Spellman Room, adapted from a chapel, is atmospheric to say the least, with a private entrance, stained-glass windows, a tile fireplace, and a massive Victorian canopy bed.

It may leave you speechless, but not for long. ♦ 481 Main St (between Bumps River Rd and S. Main St), Centerville. 775.4334

18 Centerville Historical Society Museum Heavily endowed by native son **Charles Lincoln Ayling,** this collection is more extensive than most, running to 14 rooms. Among the treasures: **Reginald Fairfax Bolles'** 1922 portrait of Mrs. Ayling wearing an embroidered, moss velvet Fortuny gown, with the gown itself displayed alongside; some 350 other gowns, plus accessories; perfume bottles dating back to 1760 (including one of a naughty French lady *en deshabille*); carvings of native Cape birds by **Anthony Elmer Crowell;** old currency dating back two centuries, along with some lottery tickets that helped finance the Revolution; many military and marine artifacts; cranberrying and carpentry tools; a great cache of dolls and toys; and a "colonial revival" kitchen as envisioned by Victorians inspired by an exhibit at the 1876 World's Fair. "Of course, in colonial days they never would have had so much *stuff,*" says director/curator **Barbara Friling,** gesturing to the shelves packed with now-rare crockery. There's so much to see, you really do need a guide to make sense of it all, so viewing is by tour only, with the last group leaving at 3:30PM. ♦ Admission. W-Su 1:30-4:30PM mid-June to mid-Sept. 513 Main St (between Bumps River Rd and S. Main St), Centerville. 775.0331

19 Four Seas It's not summer until this classic ice cream parlor—founded in 1934—opens its doors for the season. A former turn-of-the-century smithy and garage, it has seating for only a couple of dozen customers at a time at its blue-and-white counter stools, booths, and bentwood chairs, but on average it serves some 3,000 a day. Fans range from the **Kennedys** (they opened a charge account; owner **Richard Warren** figured they were good for it) to delighted critics from *Food & Wine* magazine and the like. As the authors of *The Best Ice Cream and Where to Find It* wrote: "The Four Seasons is to Cape Cod what the White House is to Washington: every VIP who passes through the area finds time for a brief visit."

The store got its name from the "four seas" that surround the Cape (Buzzards and Cape Cod bays, the Atlantic Ocean, and Nantucket Sound), and it got its reputation from butterfat-packed, super-premium concoctions in scrumptious flavors such as rum butter toffee and cantaloupe. It's all made fresh daily, and once a year Warren whips up a unique variety, Cape Cod beach plum. ♦ Daily 9AM-10:30PM late May to early Sept. 360 S. Main St (at Main St), Centerville. 775.1394

20 Craigville Pizza & Mexican ★$ Other than the heavily laden nachos, don't bother with the Mexican. The tomato sauce is more at home on the regular or whole-wheat pizzas, piled with vegetables, meats, and even whole entrées, such as chicken fajitas. This small, bustling place tends to get packed, even early in the evening. ♦ Italian/Mexican ♦ Lunch and dinner. 618 Craigville Beach Rd (between Marie Ave and Straight Wy), W. Hyannisport. 775.2267. Also at: 4 Barlows Landing Rd, Pocasset. 564.6306

21 Simmons Homestead Inn $$ Animal motifs accentuate and differentiate the 10 rooms at this 1820s captain's house, and though owner **Bill Putman** disavows any responsibility for their presence, you can't help noticing he has a certain Tigger-like quality himself: he positively bounces with enthusiasm—over his inn, over this corner of Cape Cod, over life in general. A former ad man, he sees his new title as covering the role not only of innkeeper but of "purveyor of timely tidbits of information," and he has compiled extraordinarily detailed tipsheet/maps on all there is to do and see and eat in the region. Though he professes to be a terrible cook ("I do card tricks to take their minds off it"), guests—including such assorted notables as **Carly Simon, James Woods, O.J. Simpson,** and **Dinah Shore**—have yet to complain of the blueberry pancakes or the homemade French toast (made with cinnamon bread, no less). As for those animals—stuffed, wooden, needlepointed, painted, every which way but real—you'll probably find them either delightful or *de trop.* ♦ 288 Scudder Ave (between Craigville Beach Rd and W. Main St), Hyannis. 778.4499, 800/637.1649

22 Sea Breeze Inn $ This shingle-sided house (pictured above) has been spiffed up to the hilt, with picket fence, gazebo, picnic tables, and wooden swing. The 14 rooms may not be antique-laden, but they're cheery and fresh, and then there's the sea, which you can not only walk to but see and smell. ♦ 397 Sea St (off Ocean Ave), Hyannis. 771.7213

Restaurants/Clubs: Red **Hotels:** Blue
Shops/ Outdoors: Green **Sights/Culture:** Black

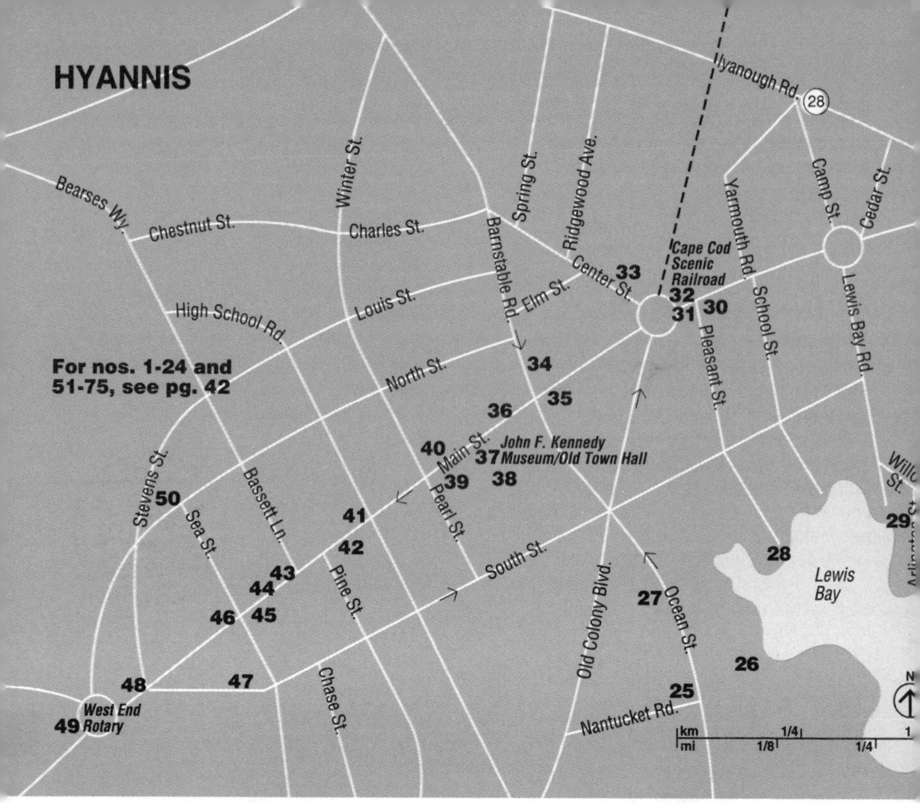

HYANNIS

For nos. 1-24 and 51-75, see pg. 42

Iyanough Rd. 28
Bearses Wy.
Chestnut St.
Winter St.
Charles St.
Barnstable Rd.
Spring St.
Ridgewood Ave.
Center St.
Cape Cod Scenic Railroad
Yarmouth Rd.
School St.
Camp St.
Cedar St.
Lewis Bay Rd.
High School Rd.
Louis St.
Elm St.
Pleasant St.
North St.
Main St.
John F. Kennedy Museum/Old Town Hall
Stevens St.
Sea St.
Bassett Ln.
Pearl St.
South St.
Pine St.
Old Colony Blvd.
Ocean St.
Lewis Bay
Chase St.
West End Rotary
Nantucket Rd.
km 1/4
mi 1/8 1/4
N
23 24 25 26 27 28 29 30 31 32 33 34 35 36 37 38 39 40 41 42 43 44 45 46 47 48 49 50

23 Up the Creek ★★$$ Off the beaten track but worth a short detour, **Jimmy Dow's** marginally anti-mainstream restaurant offers an inviting and affordable alternative to the hurly-burly of downtown Hyannis. The place has a timeless look, with a cream and forest-green color scheme, and encircling the tables are six ample booths. Among the more popular dishes is a seafood strudel served with hollandaise; daily specials are apt to include as ambitious a dish as veal Savoyard, with sun-dried tomatoes, feta, and marsala demi-glaze. Best of all, you feel as if you've left the strip-mall joints of routes 28 and 132 far, far behind. ♦ American/International ♦ Lunch and dinner. Closed for dinner on Sunday May-Oct; closed Tuesday Jan-Apr; closed Nov-Dec. 36 Old Colony Blvd (between Gosnold and Sea Sts), Hyannis. 771.7866

24 Kennedy Memorial "I believe that it is important that this country sail," **President John F. Kennedy** once said, "and not lie still in the harbor." This pretty garden spot, where a stone wall enframes a brass plaque installed in 1966 by the townspeople, invites one to tarry, though. It sits on **Veteran's Beach,** a narrow strip of sand overlooking the placid harbor, where facilities include parking, restrooms, and a children's playground. ♦ Ocean and Gosnold Sts, Hyannis. No phone

On the grounds of Kennedy Memorial:

"La Cuisine Americaine sur la Plage" This unglorified snack bar, where **Patricia** and **James Ruberti** serve such fun fare as fajitas, linguica (Portuguese sausage), fresh-cut fruit, and *pizza fritta* (fried dough), actually merits its admittedly facetious name: "sur la plage" means "on the beach." The chowder's homemade, the sun and jollity *compris.* ♦ Daily 8AM-5PM late May to mid-Oct. No phone

25 Steamers Grill & Bar ★$$ You can't go far wrong with the namesake dish: take a mess of clams, dip in broth, plop in drawn butter, and presto, instant feast. Instant gratification is pretty much the name of the game at this harborside spot catering primarily to the young and carefree, where live bands play weekends in season. The other motif is mesquite grilling: try a slab of swordfish or shrimp stuffed with spinach, garlic, cheese, and pine nuts. At dusk, the deck is packed. ♦ American ♦ Breakfast, lunch, and dinner; call for hours late Dec to Apr. 235 Ocean St (at Nantucket Rd), Hyannis. 778.0818

26 Mooring on the Waterfront ★★$$$ With a captive audience stuck waiting for the Hy-Line, the Mooring could have gotten lazy, but the restaurant goes to such efforts to please that plenty of nonferryers flock here for a waterside feast. The interior is a striking space of skylights and white latticework, with a wood stove front and center to say "welcome." Among the blackboard specials might be pan-seared halibut with fresh basil, tomatoes, scallions, and white wine. For a summer-weight meal, try the grilled *salade niçoise* (a slight misnomer: the salad itself is not grilled, but topped with grilled fish). Lobster turns up in various guises—in seafood pie, sautéed with scallops over linguine, boiled, or baked and stuffed—and it comes from the Mooring's own lobster boat, the F/V *Alyssa and Seth.* ♦ American/ International ♦ Breakfast, lunch, and dinner. Closed Monday; lunch only on Sunday mid-Oct to late May. 230 Ocean St (between Nantucket Rd and South St), Hyannis. 775.4656

26 **Hesperus** It's a classic beauty, this 50-foot **John Alden** sloop, and it can cut along quickly with cooperative winds. Although cruising **Lewis Bay** and the **Hyannisport Harbor** happens to be the only way to cop a discreet peek at the **Kennedy Compound,** your motives for a jaunt don't have to be quite so base: what's wrong with a couple of pleasant hours on the sparkling water? They'll even let you hoist the sails or take the wheel for a while. The *Hesperus* accommodates up to 22 passengers and, in summer, heads out three times during the day, again at sunset, and sometimes under the moonlight, too. ♦ Fee. Four departures late June to early Sept; two departures May to late June, Sept; call for Oct schedule. Pier 16, Ocean St Dock (between Nantucket Rd and South St), Hyannis. 771.7245

27 **The Black Cat** ★★$$$$ A fresh face on the waterfront, this new as of 1993 venue shoots for a more civilized air than the typical fishhouse. It also branches out a bit: about half of the entrées comprise premium steaks (there's a dare-you 22-ounce Porterhouse) and pasta (such as the ultrarich "straw and hay": spinach and egg fettuccine with prosciutto, peas, mushrooms, sausage, cream, and blended cheeses). The decor is upscale but not dauntingly so: there's a handsome mahogany-and-brass bar, pillars painted with flowers, and a row of brocade banquettes, overseen by some pretty silly cat portraits in Elizabethan garb. The daily ferry schedule is thoughtfully posted on a blackboard by the door—or you can just look out and watch them coming in. ♦ New American ♦ Lunch and dinner. 165 Ocean St (between Nantucket Rd and South St), Hyannis. 778.1233

During the 1880s, the Cape averaged a shipwreck every two weeks.

28 **Baxter's Boat House Club and Fish-N-Chips** ★$$ Opened in 1956, Baxter's is so near the water, it's actually over it, atop pilings. This is a something-for-everyone kind of place. Over-21s can hang out in the diner-size lounge, where there's a roving raw bar and usually some good blues piano. The underaged and their families can order great fish and seafood—the fried clams are tops, and the conch fritters toothsome, too—to take out on the deck. Voilà! Everybody's happy. ♦ American/Takeout ♦ Lunch and dinner. Closed Oct-Apr. 177 Pleasant St (off South St), Hyannis. 775.4490

29 **Tugboats** ★$$ Haute it's not, but the food here is fun—especially bar nibbles like spicy Buffalo shrimp or beer-and-corn-batter onion rings—and the two roomy decks are perfect for catching the last precious rays of the sun. Toast a day well spent with "sunset cocktails" packing plenty of ice cream. ♦ American ♦ Breakfast, lunch, and dinner. Closed for breakfast mid-Apr to June, Sept to mid-Nov; closed mid-Nov to mid-Apr. 21 Arlington St (off Willow St), Hyannis. 775.6433

30 **Backside Cafe** ★$$ You practically have to be a local to know this place is here, hidden as it is behind a hardware store. Seek and you will find a cozy tavern (dark green walls, hunting and automotive prints) with a well-priced menu of homey favorites, from onion soup to pizzas and pasta. There's also an even *more* reasonable submenu of "Mom's home cooking": meat loaf, turkey potpie, fishcakes, and more. ♦ American/Takeout ♦ Lunch and dinner. 209 Main St (between Pleasant and School Sts), Hyannis. 771.5505

31 **East End Grill** ★$$ The decor is neo-Victorian, but the pace is much too pumped-up for any pretense of pomp. It's a scene, basically, and if the food is varied and tasty—everything from Cajun fries to "mariner's stew" and shrimp pesto—well, so much the better. ♦ Regional American ♦ Lunch and dinner; Sunday brunch. 247 Main St (between Pleasant St and Old Colony Blvd), Hyannis. 790.2898

32 **Cape Cod Scenic Railroad (CCSR)** Three vintage cars—the **Nobscot, Sconset,** and **Monomoy**—chug the 42-mile round-trip to Buzzards Bay and back in 1¾ hours, with soothing scenery and informative commentary en route. On the "Dinner Train" (★$$$$), which makes the same circuit in three hours with a sunset stopover at the canal, tables of four (or fewer, for an additional fee) partake of a five-course meal

catered by a local restaurant, **D'Olimpio's.** Though not quite "the ultimate dining experience" it bills itself as (the *Boston Globe* was blunt: "lacks in culinary distinction"), it is still romantic and as popular with those planning proposals as those celebrating anniversaries. In addition, CCSR offers occasional "ecology discovery tours," with an on-board naturalist and a half-hour stopover at **Talbots Point Conservation Preserve** in Sandwich for a guided walk through the marsh. ♦ Fee. Sightseeing: three round-trips daily Tu-Su June to late Oct; Sa-Su late Nov to late Dec. Dinner Train: Tu-Su June to mid-Sept; F-Su Mar-May, mid-Sept to Nov; call for Dec and Feb schedule. 252 Main St (at Center St), Hyannis. Reservations and jackets required for Dinner Train. 771.3788

33 Cape Cod Storyland Every putter tells a story? Perhaps they will after playing miniature golf over these two intensively landscaped acres of waterfalls, caves, and miniaturized reproductions of Cape and the Islands landmarks. For a refreshing splash (that's the whole idea), take out a couple of molded-plastic bumper boats and bash one another around. ♦ Admission. Daily 8AM-11PM mid-June to mid-Sept; daily 10AM-closing late Mar to mid-June, mid-Sept to mid-Nov. 70 Center St (between Main St and Ridgewood Ave), Hyannis. 778.4339

34 John's Loft ★$$$ This restaurant looks rather like an Elizabethan cottage turned inside out, with plaster-daubed walls transected by rafters. For a tête-à-tête, ask for one of the barnboard booths. The regular menu tends to stuffy Continental, but the blackboard specials are more adventurous and also more affordable. ♦ Continental/ Takeout ♦ Dinner. 8 Barnstable Rd (off Main St), Hyannis. 775.1111

35 Penguins SeaGrill ★$$$ As **Penguins Go Pasta,** this was once *the* place to get good Italian food in Hyannis, but now that **George Karath** has handed over the reins to stepson **Bobby Gold,** Old Country dishes are in the minority. Wood-grilling is the order of the day, sometimes delightfully (the roasted fresh corn is a treat) and sometimes none too wisely (make what you will of chilled blackened shrimp). The menu's all over the map, with such odd amalgams as wok-fried "Chinatown seafood" with ginger, scallions, and fermented black beans over angelhair pasta. Still, creativity requires experimentation, and if you're patient—or plucky—you could be on the receiving end of a culinary breakthrough. Meanwhile, there's plenty of comfort to be taken in a straightforward dish (syntax notwithstanding) like "garlic mashed baked stuffed potato," and it's a good-looking place One room is sheltered by a giant Roman parasol (shades of Penguins' former life), the other bedecked with chevrons of mirror glass and burnished wood. ♦ International ♦ Lunch and dinner; dinner only on Saturday and Sunday. 331 Main St (at Barnstable Rd), Hyannis. Reservations recommended. 775.2023

36 Ben & Jerry's One of only three Capeside repositories of the post-hippie-phenomenal ice cream, the shop gets steady traffic all day, particularly after dinner. ♦ M-Th 9:30AM-9:30PM; F 9:30AM-11PM; Sa 10AM-10PM; Su noon-9:30PM. 352 Main St (between Barnstable Rd and Winter St), Hyannis. 790.0910. Also at: Rte 6 and Brackett Rd, N. Eastham. 255.2817; Glaceteria, 256 Commercial St, Provincetown. 487.3360

36 Alberto's Ristorante ★★★$$$$ Owner-chef **Felisberto Barreiro** was only 23 when, in 1984, he opened the first incarnation of this delightful restaurant on Ocean Avenue and introduced Cape Codders to the joys of homemade pasta. His reward? Patrons so loyal and plentiful that in 1993 he was able to buy a building on Main Street and expand in style. The new space is contemporarily romantic, with creamy, pale pink walls (echoed in the table linens) and flattering sconces. Though large, seating about 130, the restaurant is broken up into a series of gallerylike rooms, maintaining a sense of intimacy.

The food seduces shamelessly, from an antipasto featuring marinated fresh mozzarella and *ceviche*-like scungilli to veal chops Porto Fino, with morels, porcini, and shiitake mushrooms, in a sauce of shallots, brandy, and cream. The treatments are not of the exquisite, anemic sort, but robust and flavorful; any meal is bound to feel like a celebration. To extend the festive atmosphere right through the off-season (when many towns on the Cape tend to roll up their sidewalks), Barreiro offers celebrants within a set radius free limo service. ♦ Italian ♦ Lunch and dinner. 360 Main St (between Barnstable Rd and Winter St), Hyannis. 778.1770

British forces were all set to land in Hyannis during the War of 1812 but were frightened away by rumors—no doubt fabricated by villagers—that the town was in the throes of a smallpox contagion.

37 John F. Kennedy Museum There is absolutely nothing to see at the **Kennedy Compound** on Irving Street in Hyannisport other than a high wooden fence and lots of hedges. However, with hordes arriving every year hoping to see *something,* the Hyannis Chamber of Commerce finally opened this mini-museum (pictured above) in **Old Town Hall:** in its first six months of operation in 1992, it logged 40,000 visitors. Beyond a 10-minute video narrated by **Walter Cronkite,** it consists mostly of photos from 1934 to 1963—blown-up snapshots exuding charisma. (Among the more telling ones is a shot of two anonymous young boys hawking "Kennedy information 10 cents.") There's an annotated aerial view of the compound to satisfy some of that indefatigable curiosity, but it's the unposed family encounters that really touch the heart. ♦ Nominal admission. M-Sa 10AM-4PM; Su 1-4PM. 397 Main St (between Barnstable Rd and Pearl St), Hyannis. 775.2201

38 Guyer Barn Gallery Initiated by the **Barnstable Arts and Humanities Council** in 1986 and run by volunteer **Chris Green,** this community arts center (pictured above) started out as a "hey, kids" proposition and still enjoys lots of youthful enthusiasm. Green is delighted to give a lot of fledgling artists, some still in their early 20s, their first shows: as he says, "There's a lot of good energy around, and it's good to have a place to put it." (If the quality's uneven, consider your own early output.) The 1865 wood-frame barn was added to the **National Register of Historic Places** in 1988, and if you're wondering about the "action painting" on the floor, it dates from the building's previous tenure as a municipal works warehouse—dozens of lifeguard stands got their yearly coating here. Every August there's a homegrown film and video fest, and Saturday evenings in the summer the gallery is transformed into the "Driftwood Coffeehouse," with an impressive roster of folk musicians drawn from all over the East Coast. ♦ Exhibits free; cover charge for concerts. Gallery: daily (hours vary) June-Oct. Concerts: Sa 8:30PM June to mid-Sept. 230 South St (behind Old Town Hall), Hyannis. 790.6370

39 Asa Bearse House ★$$ This is more of a place to hang out than to chow down, but the food's all right and the surroundings most pleasant. By day, the rose-encircled front patio with its pink and white awnings is the place to take the town's pulse, and perhaps your own. The Sunday jazz brunch is a nice way to cap off a weekend. Inside, the dining room at once spoofs and emulates a more elegant setting, with bamboo chairs and hand-painted golden swags. Appetizers include Texas barbecued shrimp stuffed with bacon-wrapped jalapeño and grilled with "H. Ross Perot's own sauce (honest!)"; entrées run the gamut. All the while, though, one can't help suspecting—correctly—that the real action is in the bar. ♦ American ♦ Lunch, tea, and dinner; Sunday brunch. 415 Main St (at Pearl St), Hyannis. 771.4444

Within the Asa Bearse House:

The Reading Room But for the sound of electric guitars, who would ever suspect that this demure facade sheltered such a peculiar den? It's a warren of Victorian woodwork, with nooks and window seats, meandering bookshelves, a moosehead, Foosball, and a dance floor devoted to "progressive" rock. Popular house bands include the **Underground Cats** and **Cape Fear,** and the demographics cluster in the 25 to 35 range. ♦ M-Th, Sa-Su 6PM-1AM; F 4PM-1AM. 771.4444

40 Caffe e Dolci ★★$ Here's the first harbinger of a revitalized Main Street: a spiffy new (as of 1993) neo-Italianate cafe suffused with light and heady aromas. The coffee's superb (you can load up on arcane paraphernalia, too), and the gelato, granita, and tartuffo—a double-trouble ultra-mousse—are all habit-forming. ♦ Italian ♦ Breakfast, lunch, and dinner. 430 Main St (between Barnstable Rd and Winter St), Hyannis. 790.6900

41 Hyannis Antique Co-op The oldest group shop on the Cape, this is not, unfortunately, among the most distinguished: it's really more like an indoor flea market. Expect to see some pretty shoddy stuff. There's plenty of Depression glass, should you have a set that needs filling out. The few items worth a closer look might include ornately inlaid "ship boxes" (fashioned by bored sailors), going for several thousand apiece. You'll have to hunt to find other quality goods here. ♦ M, W-Su 10AM-5PM. 500 Main St (at High School Rd), Hyannis. 778.0512

42 The Egg & I $ Describing this place as "no frills" would be an understatement, but Hyannis night owls, early birds, and lie-abeds don't mind, as long as they can breakfast all night and past noon. The "Create an Omelet" options span 10 ingredients including linguica, and specials include such Southern rarities as chicken-fried steak with green onion corn bread. As has been true since 1971, the clientele consists largely of collegiate types earning some spending money on the Cape, and if these frugal souls gather here, you know it's a good deal. ♦ American ♦ Breakfast (11PM-1PM). 517 Main St (between High School Rd and Pine St), Hyannis. 771.2558

43 Maggie's Ice Cream It's easy to see why Maggie's, operated by the eight-member **Sweeney** family, is a local fave. It's a cheerful place, white splashed with Kelly green, and the ice cream's made fresh, including some pretty fiendish custom blends. Try a Danish waffle cone brimming with "Cape Cod Mud": coffee ice cream with chocolate chips, smushed Oreos, almonds, and fudge swirls. ♦ Daily 11AM-11PM Apr-Oct; daily 11AM-9PM Nov-Mar. 570 Main St (at Bassett Ln), Hyannis. 775.7540. Also at: Mashpee Commons, Mashpee. 477.6442

44 Fazio's Trattoria ★★$$ This charming hole-in-the-wall has all the classic elements: red-and-white-checked tablecloths, Chianti bottles (there's a very enticing wine list), and old Italian fruit-packing labels as posters. San Francisco transplants **Tom** and **Eileen Fazio** extract such goodies as *foccacia del giorno* (chewy flatbread) and traditional pizzas from their oak-fired oven. The pasta assortment—some incorporating homemade *salsiccia*—is all one could wish for, but the wood grill also yields intriguing specials. To round off a rustic repast try crunchy homemade cannoli or creamy zabaglione. ♦ Italian ♦ Lunch and dinner; dinner only on Sunday. 586 Main St (between Bassett Ln and Sea St), Hyannis. Reservations recommended. 771.7445

44 Tibetan Mandala International Imports With one-stop shopping for that "been there" look, this store sells crafts from around the world. Handwoven Guatemalan parkas make great beach cover-ups, especially after dark, and African trade beads play up a burnished tan, as will all sorts of exotic silver jewelry. Owner **Llakpa Gyadatsang,** who opened this branch of his **Greenwich Village** shop in 1992, says he also does a brisk trade in Tibetan "singing bowls" and cymbals. ♦ Daily 11AM-9PM June-Aug; Sa-Su 11AM-9PM Apr-May, Sept-Dec. 600 Main St (between Bassett Ln and Sea St), Hyannis. 778.4134

45 Pain d'Avignon If it's not quite like any French bread you've ever tasted before, that' because it's Yugoslavian. Don't bother to try your Franglais out (as many customers do) bakers **Vojin Vujosevic** and **Branislav Stamenkovic:** just point and eat. Some of their breads are like fantastical folk sculptures. Here's what's recognizable: skin baguettes strewn with coarse salt, rolls topped with oats, and flatbreads loaded with cheese and caramelized onion. ♦ Bakery ♦ M F 10AM-5PM; Sa-Su 11AM-5PM. Common West Garden Court, 599 Main St (between Pine and Sea Sts), Hyannis. 771.9771

45 Shop Avon Why Shop Avon? Because Cap Cod's breezes don't dispel *all* the bugs (as **Thoreau** said, "I have never been so much troubled by mosquitoes as in such localities" and because Avon's Skin So Soft, available in oil or lotion, makes such an excellent repellent. The oil also apparently works great as a wood polish, paint and stain remover, patent leather shiner, and other uses yet to b deduced. Stop here, and you won't have to wait for a house call. ♦ M-Tu 11AM-6PM; Th Sa 11AM-8PM; Su noon-6PM. Common We Garden Court, 601 Main St (between Pine an Sea Sts), Hyannis. No phone. Also at: 48R Main St, Orleans. 240.0044

45 Plush & Plunder **Ute-Barbara Gardner** ha enough hats to open a museum if she wante to; instead, they plaster the ceiling of her exceptionally well-stocked vintage clothing store. She's been at it since 1981 and must have got while the getting was good: tweed jackets, silk ties, alligator shoes, petticoats, rhinestone-studded cat-glasses, slinky dresses. . . . Everything's in mint condition, and the price tags provide a full gloss. Over the years she has garnered encomia from such disparate celebrities as **Joan Baez** and **Cyndi Lauper. Demi Moore** shops by mail (for those rare occasions requiring clothes) and hubby **Bruce Willis** is another big fan, as you're sure to be, too, the minute you step inside. ♦ M-Sa 10AM-6PM; Su 11AM-6PM. 605 Main St (between Pine and Sea Sts), Hyannis. 775.4467

46 Sweetwaters Grille & Bar ★★$$ Hankering for a Tex-Mex fix? The fajita fixings here are chargrilled over a fruitwood fire and served with sage rice; appetizers include such unusual variations as white chili (made with white beans and chicken), "snakebites" (jalapeños stuffed with cream cheese, then beer-battered and deep-fried), and "painted desert pizza" (like a giant nacho On days when the only remedy for broiling temperatures is a compensatory culinary trial by fire, this cool sage-green eatery will seem an oasis indeed. ♦ Southwestern ♦ Lunch and dinner. 644 Main St (between Sea and Stevens Sts), Hyannis. 775.3323

47 **Roadhouse Cafe** ★★$$$ The decor may say old boys' club—especially the dark and inviting bar, with burgundy banquettes and barstools and an old-fashioned phone booth—but the menu says *paisan.* "Stop and smell the garlic" is owner **Dave Columbo's** rallying cry, and it's hard to resist. The fragrant bud beckons from mussel stew, scampi, cioppino, and from *linguini aglio e olio* dressed up with pignoli, artichoke hearts, and sun-dried tomatoes. The prize dessert, though, gets its inspiration from the Irish: a cheesecake flavored with Bailey's. ♦ American/Italian ♦ Lunch and dinner; Sunday brunch. 488 South St (between Sea St and West End Rotary), Hyannis. 775.2386

48 **Harry's** ★$$ Your basic bar, with a postage-stamp dance floor, Harry's brings a little bit of New Orleans north. Among the specialties are barbecued ribs, blackened fish, and four kinds of Southern-style rice: Hoppin' John (with black-eyed peas), Jambalaya (with andouille), "dirty" (with chicken livers), and red beans and rice slow-cooked with ham hocks and herbs. Seating is at six park-bench booths, and what looks like a Shaker wall of drawers is strictly decorative, though the bartender jokes, "That's where we keep all the money." Evenings, the joint jumps with jazz, blues, rock, or any combination of the above. ♦ Southern/Takeout ♦ Lunch and dinner. 700 Main St (at Stevens St), Hyannis. 778.4188

48 **Cape Cod Brew House** ★$$ With this new but rather nondescript restaurant, Hyannis joins the microbrewery revolution. The fresh-made beer is not just for drinking—it's included in chili, beer-battered fish-and-chips, even chocolate beer cake. ♦ International ♦ Lunch and dinner. 720 Main St (between Stevens St and West End Rotary), Hyannis. 775.4110

49 **The Paddock** ★★★$$$$ The place has a kind of hokey grandeur, with its valet parking, impersonal facade, and heavily paneled interior (the summer-porch room, with a palm court effect, is a little less oppressive). However, no one, least of all the spillover crowds from the **Melody Tent,** complains about the bountiful spread, which stresses Continental standards and derivatives (such as *paupiette of sole Oscar*—a far better conduit for crab than the usual veal). It has been run by the **Zartarian** family since 1970, and they take a proprietary interest in their customers' well-being. ♦ Continental ♦ Lunch and dinner. Closed mid-Nov to Mar. West End Rotary (between W. Main St and Scudder Ave), Hyannis. Reservations recommended; jacket required. 775.7677

49 **Cape Cod Melody Tent** It's a tent, all right, a big blue one, and you'll get as up close and personal to household-name musicians and comedians as you could hope. British actress **Gertrude Lawrence** built her big top in 1950, inspired by America's first summer theater-in-the-round at Lambertville, New Jersey. Today's roster spans a wide range of tastes: from **Steve Lawrence** and **Eydie Gorme** to **Andrew Dice Clay.** There's also a children's theater program Wednesday mornings at 11AM. All proceeds, by the way, are channeled by the nonprofit **South Shore Playhouse Associates** to fund education and the arts on the South Shore and Cape. ♦ Admission. Schedule varies, late June to early Sept. W. Main St and West End Rotary, Hyannis. 775.9100

50 **Eastern Mountain Sports** The only on-Cape outpost of New England's premier outdoor outfitter offers everything you could possibly need to survive—and thrive—in the wild: clothing, gear, and perhaps most important, counsel. You can rent if you're not ready to buy (from tents and sleeping bags to boats and kayaks), and the store offers all sorts of free clinics and guided excursions; call for details. ♦ M-F 10AM-9PM, Sa 10AM-6PM, Su noon-5PM June to mid-Sept; M-W, Sa 10AM-6PM, Th-F 10AM-9PM, Su noon-5PM mid-Sept to May. Village Marketplace, 233 Stevens St (between North St and Bassett Ln), Hyannis. 775.1072

West Barnstable produced one of the Revolution's most fiery orators. In 1761, lawyer James Otis resigned as customs agent to protest the British writs of assistance—search warrants permitting British soldiers to break into the homes of suspected smugglers. "A man's home is his castle," Otis declared at Boston's Old South Meetinghouse, "and whilst he is quiet, he is well guarded as a prince. His right to his life is his liberty, no created being could rightfully contest." But British loyalists believed otherwise, contending that the King had the right to do as he pleased. When Otis made the mistake of stopping in at a Tory tavern in 1769, he was beaten to within an inch of his life. His sanity compromised by a concussion, he burned all his papers and never again preached sedition. But the revolution he helped start rolled on without him.

51 **Play It Again Sports** Surf's up, and you forgot your boogie board? Not to worry, because you can pick up an el-cheapo used one at this secondhand sporting goods franchise. Virtually every pastime is covered, from tennis to rollerblading. And—it being the Cape—golf is especially big: there's always an extensive selection of clubs and bags. Says owner **Buzz Friend,** "Foreigners come and buy the ugliest, most beat-up ones so they can tell Customs, 'Hey, I took this with me.'" ♦ M-Th, Sa 9AM-6PM; F 9AM-5PM; Su noon-5PM. 25 Iyanough Rd (between Main St and Yarmouth Rd), Hyannis. 771.6979

52 **Boxcar Willy's Bar and Grill** ★$ The food—or perhaps grub is a more accurate term—is pretty much an adjunct to the liquor, but it sure is cheap, for those times when filling up takes precedence over fine dining. These two rehabbed train cars are pretty cozy, too, especially the dining car lined with wooden booths, the luggage rack replaced by bookshelves. ♦ American ♦ Lunch and dinner. 165 Yarmouth Rd (at Iyanough Rd), Hyannis. 775.4421

52 **Jammers** An old railroad roundhouse is now the biggest nightclub on the Cape, with a capacity of 1,500; often, another several thousand revelers congregate outside. Among the draws: a state-of-the-art disco with laser-lit dance floors, a sports bar with giant-screen TVs and pool tables, outdoor basketball and volleyball courts, and a pool, plus events ranging from music (mostly) to comedy and, on occasion, boxing and wrestling. The fighting's not always confined to the ring (crowd control has been a problem), so bring along your street smarts or just stand forewarned. ♦ Cover. Daily noon-1AM late May to early Sept; daily 8PM-1AM Mar to late May, early Sept to Nov; Th-Su 8PM-1AM Dec-Feb. 183 Iyanough Rd (between Yarmouth and Barnstable Rds), Hyannis. 775.1115

53 **HyLand American Youth Hostel** $ This hostel has 42 dorm beds, segregated by sex, tucked away in a peaceful pine grove a bracing walk from the center of town. As with all AYH hostels, there's a curfew (11PM) and a "lockout" time (9:30AM to 5:30PM), but for the price ($14 for nonmembers, even less for AYHers), it's hard to beat. And of course, you don't have to be young. ♦ Closed Dec-Feb. 465 Rte 28/Falmouth Rd (between Bearses Wy and Lincoln Rd), Hyannis. 775.2970

54 **Starbuck's** ★★$$ Good wholesome fun in the Friday's vein, this is one of those bars where you'd feel comfortable taking the family—and the children' menu, topping out at $2.97, offers added incentive. Actually, the adult prices are pretty sporting, too, and the scope entertaining. The menu globe-hops from fajitas and pasta to Oriental treats like Thai hot-peppered shrimp. Plenty of people come in just to drink: a 27-ounce margarita ought to do the trick, or, for novices, something silly and sweet like a Frozen Girl Scout Cookie. Kids love the "Prohibition Specials," otherwise known as virgin coladas and fruit daiquiris. Opened in 1985, this is a cavernous barn of a place, with room enough in the rafters for all sorts of flotsam, including an entire Fokker D-7 plane. ♦ International ♦ Lunch and dinner. 645 Iyanough Rd (between Yarmouth and Airport Rds), Hyannis. 778.6767

55 **Cape Cod Potato Chips** Having innovated a "kettle cooking" method designed to impart richer flavor and greater crunch—which it does—Chatham resident **Steve Bernard** started up this company on a $30,000 grubstake in 1980; in 1985, he sold out to **Eagle Snacks Inc.** for a neat $7 million (he's now into croutons). Many people swear by the chips: they're sliced thicker than most and taste more substantial. You can be the judge, since free samples are awarded at the end of your self-guided tour along a glass-walled corridor flanking the assembly line. ♦ M-F 10AM-4PM. Breed's Hill Rd (at Independence Wy), Hyannis. 775.7253

The Pilgrims had only been settled in Plymouth for six months when young John Billingham—the product of what they considered "one of ye profanest families amongst them"—wandered off in the woods. The search party traced him as far as Barnstable Harbor, and from there Chief Iyanough led them to Nauset, where the boy had been happily assimilated into tribal life. Two years later, stirred by Miles Standish's alarums of an "Indian conspiracy," the English herded Iyanough and several other native leaders into a pestilential swamp, where all died, most likely of smallpox. Some settlers regretted the action enough to mark the chief's grave, in Cummaquid. Of Iyanough, Edward Winslow of the *Mayflower* wrote that he was "personable, gentle, courteous, and fair-conditioned; indeed, not like a savage except in his attire."

56 Sam Diego's ★★$$ Papier-mâché toucans and colorful serapes adorn this popular roadside restaurant, and the setting sun casts a warm glow through stained glass onto innumerable hanging plants twinkling with Christmas lights. The fare is fairly standard Americanized Mexican (burritos, enchiladas, chimichangas, quesadillas, fajitas—you know the drill), but it's all done well, and the atmosphere is pleasant and lively. If you haven't come all this way to pretend you're in some other country entirely, try the native cod, either baked under a blanket of *salsa cruda* and cheese or *naranja*-style, with an orange sauce flavored with cilantro, garlic, and Triple Sec. And if you've never tried deep-fried ice cream, it's a must, a real junk-food apotheosis. ♦ Mexican/Southwestern ♦ Lunch and dinner. 950 Iyanough Rd (between Independence Wy and Phinneys Ln), Hyannis. 771.8816

57 West Parish Meetinghouse This fellowship has been meeting nonstop since 1616, when a band of Independent Christians, not yet ready to abandon the Anglican church completely but unable to accept all its precepts, founded the Congregational church in the borough of Southwark, across the bridge from London: standing "in a Ringwise," they "Convenanted togeather to walk in all God's Ways as he had revealed or should make known to them." The semi-renegades had to convene secretly, under threat of death. In 1632, after they had granted "friendly dismissal" to some more extremist members who would become the nucleus of the Baptist church, they were caught at worship by officers of the King, and 42 members were imprisoned, including pastor **John Lothrop.** (While he was in jail, his wife died and his children were reduced to begging on the streets.) Released under pain of exile in 1634, Lothrop led some 30 male followers and their families to the New World, aboard the *Griffin.* (The pewter sacramental vessels they brought with them are still used in the church today.)

After securing a grant from the General Court of **Plymouth Colony,** Lothrop and 22 of his followers left Scituate for the promising territory of "Mattakeese"; the Native American name meant "plowed fields," and indeed the settlers were lucky enough to get land that had already been cleared, near an enormous salt marsh proffering plenty of salt hay as fodder. They named their settlement **Barnstable** (probably for its resemblance to the English harbor of Barnstaple) and erected a meetinghouse in 1646. By 1715, the region was populous enough that the town split into two parishes. The present building went up in 1717-1719 and was "stretched" another 18 feet in 1723, at which time the belltower, with its 5½-foot gilded rooster weathervane from England, was added; in 1806, patriot **Paul Revere** was commissioned to cast the half-ton bell.

In the early days of the nation, there was scant separation of church and state (in fact, Massachusetts towns levied taxes to support local churches until 1834), and so the West Parish Meetinghouse doubled as a town hall until 1849. In 1852, the deteriorating building was subjected to a neoclassical remodeling that totally obscured its plain-spun beauty; what was worse, in the 1880s, someone saw fit to add wallpaper bordered with what parishioners considered "immodest cherubs." It took the lifelong efforts of **Edith Crocker Jenkins** (1874-1956) to restore the church to its original form and intent.

In 1953-1958, drawing on the funds she had been raising since 1922 and a great deal of "architectural sleuthwork," the firm of **Andrews Jones Biscoe & Goodell** revealed, beneath the plaster, the church's original adzed oak framework and curved buttresses, its pine beams and posts; they restored or replicated the extensive woodwork, from high pulpit and "sounding board" to galleries, stairs, and pews. Historical significance aside (it's the oldest public building on the Cape and one of only two surviving "First Period" meetinghouses in New England), the church is quite simply a work of art. To enter it is to be awed. ♦ Service Su 10AM. 1049 Meetinghouse Wy (at Rte 149), W. Barnstable. 362.4445

58 Tern Studio A practitioner of the age-old art of "turning," **A. O. Barbour** has a knack for finding the sculpture hidden in a hunk of wood. For his vases and bowls, which run from $30 to $500 depending on size and complexity, he uses only native woods, whether staples like oak, elm, and maple, or rarer types such as apple, cherry, box elder, and mulberry. He's also working his way through a bumper crop of "bobwood"—the windfall from Hurricane Bob. Each piece is varnished till it shines like polished stone, but the naturally occurring flaws are what lend these works their inimitable beauty; Barbour has no way of knowing, when he starts out, just what forms and innate patterns are going to emerge. ♦ Daily 10AM-4PM. 2454 Meetinghouse Wy (between Church and Main Sts), W. Barnstable. 362.6077

West Barnstable Tables

58 West Barnstable Tables Those centuries-old planks—of pine, oak, and chestnut—that don't find their way into historic renovations may end up here as trestle tables fetching several thousand dollars. You can also find unwanted window frames turned into mirrors. ♦ Daily 9AM-4PM. 2454 Meetinghouse Wy (between Church and Main Sts), W. Barnstable. 362.2676

59 Prince Jenkins Antiques Hitchcock couldn't have invented a more archetypal antiques store. The owner, **Dr. Alfred A. King,** D.F.A., doesn't hesitate to play the eccentric: his card reads "in business since 1773." Another questionable claim of his is that the nucleus of the neighboring house, which he also owns, was the 1626 home of **Governor William Bradford;** King concedes that the shingled front part, with a swan pediment painted with witch silhouettes and no less than seven weathervanes spinning on the captain's walk, more likely dates from 1635 to 1657. In any event, the shop itself offers further puzzles, starting with a skeleton in a coffin and going right on through to a Chinese urn valued at $22,500. Who knows what other mysteries lurk within these murky depths? ♦ Daily 10AM-5PM Mar to mid-Nov. 975 Rte 6A/Main St (at Rte 149), W. Barnstable. No phone

60 Salt & Chestnut Weathervanes Former schoolteacher **Marilyn E. Strauss** admits to being a "frustrated museum director," which is why she doesn't mind a bit if browsers come just to marvel over her extraordinary collection of antique weathervanes—as well as her own replica of the first known weathervane from 48 BC Greece. A fascinating array crowds three rooms and two side gardens. She employs 29 area sculptors either to create their own work or to carry out her own designs, such as copper "lighthouses" to decorate unsightly air vents. The modern work ranges from the understated to the absurd (a zaftig pig tooting a trumpet), and she's just begun to collect elaborate whirligigs as well, such as a shark with a swimmer mid-gulp and a foot-tapping jazz band. She's been at it since 1978, and her collection of antiquities, valued at $200 to $30,000 per piece, accrues daily—not because she's out prowling, but because her reputation is such that "they find me." ♦ Daily 11AM-5PM. 651 Rte 6A/Main St (between Maple and Willow Sts), W. Barnstable. 362.6085

61 Wysteria Antiques etc. Walking into this shop—perhaps *folie* would be a more appropriate term—is like stumbling headfirst into a pirate's treasure chest. The whole place scintillates with scads of vintage costume jewelry, glass, china, and lace. In a word—creator **Ken DiCarlo's**—"glitz," all of it arranged like an incredibly intricate work of folk art. Visitors are greeted by DiCarlo and partner **Clay O'Connor** rattling off a rote spiel about how "if this is not for you, we understand." If it *is* for you (you know who you are), you may wander through, amazed, provided you promise not to touch. ♦ Daily 11AM-5PM, depending on whim. 521 Rte 6A/Main St (between County Rd and Maple St), W. Barnstable. 362.8581

61 Honeysuckle Hill $$ Looking for the grandmother you never had? **Barbara Rosenthal** could fill the bill, with her featherbeds and chocolate chip cookies. Her B&B, in a restored and expanded 1810 farmhouse, has only three rooms, but they're beauties (the Rose Room is especially romantic), and her breakfasts are hard to beat, from turkey sausage soufflés and Havarti omelets to something as simple as strawberries, sour cream, and brown sugar. There's only one possible drawback: if you're put off by hyperactive little dogs, better look elsewhere. Then again, if you've got one, you're welcome to bring it along. ♦ 591 Rte 6A/Main St (between County Rd and Maple St), W. Barnstable. 362.8418, 800/441.8418

61 Black's Weaving Shop You could say that weaving runs in this family. **Bob Black's** parents wove, as do his wife, children, and grandchildren. He started at 14, attended the Rhode Island School of Design, and is currently the only person in the U.S. designing double-sided Jacquard patterns, an all but lost art requiring a mathematician's precision. Working on commission, he'll weave custom designs into each coverlet or panel he makes (one couple celebrating their Cape summers wanted a lawnmower and greenhead flies worked in); with the signature and date, each is a potential future museum piece. The shop also feature's **Gabrielle Black's** colorful throws, shawls, placemats, and ties; the rainbow chenille scarves are especially appealing. ♦ Daily 10AM-5PM. 597 Rte 6A/Main St (between County Rd and Maple St), W. Barnstable. 361.3955

61 West Barnstable Antiques Thomas Slaman's interest span is somewhat staggering, from Shaker implements to '50s kitsch (a select showing). For the most part his stock consists of hard-to-find "primitives," ranging from blanket chests and cupboards, their original paint beautifully scarified, to handsome turned chairs. ♦ Daily 10AM-5PM Apr-Dec; M, F-Su 10AM-5PM Jan-Mar. 625 Rte 6A/Main St (between County Rd and Maple St), W. Barnstable. 362.5120

Restaurants/Clubs: Red **Hotels:** Blue
Shops/ Outdoors: Green **Sights/Culture:** Black

Antiques Ripe for the Picking

First let's dispel any possible illusions: your chances of coming across a priceless 350-year-old heirloom recently retrieved from someone's attic are no better here, in the earliest settled corner of the colonies, than anywhere else. Sophisticated buyers and their networks of professional "pickers" have been prowling the New England countryside for a good 50 years, and the publicity surrounding the rare flea-market find is such that ordinary citizens are keeping a watchful eye on their Flintstone jelly glasses. Still, one can hope and look—which is, after all, half the pleasure.

The antiques market has quieted down a bit since the late-'80s boom erupted when Congoleum floor covering mogul **Eddy Nicholson** purchased a chair and a table for approximately $1 million apiece. Even in the midst of a slump, though, the future value of fine antiques rests relatively assured, as there are only so many to go around. Whereas real estate's three guiding principles are "location, location, location," the value of an antique is established according to its rarity, quality, and desirability. Yet even hardened dealers agree that buying what you like is a better strategy than anticipating that its worth will appreciate. Market tastes are likely to prove more volatile than your own, and even if your acquisitions never shoot up in value, you'll have the pleasure of owning and living with them. As Arts and Crafts avatar **William Morris** once advised: "Have nothing in your homes that you do not know to be useful, or believe to be beautiful." Of course, just what these parameters might include is a matter of individual taste—be it Art Deco accents, or a futuristic 1950s sofa.

What constitutes an antique? The official definition, as acknowledged by U.S. Customs, is anything more than 100 years old. Connoisseurs, however, know that it takes more than mere age to create venerability. The highest-ticket items among domestic antiques are artifacts crafted between 1720, when the graceful Queen Anne style was in vogue, and the 1830s, when mechanized production put fancy furniture within reach of the hoi polloi. Factory-made furniture—especially the whimsical, eclectic creations of the Victorian era—has its aficionados, too. The other primary strains of collectible American furniture derive from human hands: Shaker designs, produced by a sect stressing simplicity, have shot through the roof in popularity and value in recent years (thanks in part to collectors such as **Bill Cosby**), as have the clean-lined creations of a nostalgic consortium of turn-of-the-century artisans, grouped under the "Arts and Crafts" rubric.

Whatever your chosen period, it's wise to be a bit paranoid about provenance, since even reproductions are being reproduced. (It's a dealer's dictum that there are a lot more "antiques" in circulation than were ever made.) The best reassurance is a dealer's reputation—and professional longevity. To allay your fears, some more established merchants may be willing to guarantee a buyback at the original price if you're not satisfied with your purchase. If they've scrutinized their stock carefully, it's a no-risk proposition for them as well, since a high-quality antique can appreciate 30 percent or more annually.

Where to find the treasures you seek? Impecunious antiquers haunt yard sales, church sales, thrift shops, and flea markets; those with more money than time to spare hit the top-notch shops and auctioneers, including **Richard Bourne Co.** (Corporation Road, Hyannis; 775.0797), **Eldred's Auction House** (1483 Route 6A, East Dennis; 385.3116), and **Rafael Osona** (c/o American Legion Hall, 21 Washington Street, Nantucket; 228.3942). For a list of some three dozen thrift shops (most of which are staffed by volunteers and observe limited hours), request a brochure from the **Cape Cod Council of Churches** (394.6361). The **Cape Cod Antique Dealers Association** (255.0191) lists well over a hundred outlets on the Cape alone; for a more selective sampling, **Destinnations** (800/333.4667), a travel-planning company, offers a handy map and guide to the Cape and the Islands' top antiques emporia, already vetted for quality. For information on upcoming events, pick up a copy of *MassBay Antiques* (536.5141); usually offered free at antiques stores, it commands a national readership and publishes prices realized at auction, which may help you develop a feel for the going rates.

62 **Sandy Neck Conservation Area** They make an improbable battleground, these pocky dunes (some up to 100 feet high) covered with eel-grass and low-bush blueberries. But it's here, along a 6½-mile-long barrier beach protecting Barnstable's 4,000-acre **Great Marsh** (the largest on the East Coast), that the endangered piping plover is fighting extinction. Massachusetts' coastline is at the center of the plovers' breeding range, and in the summer of 1992, naturalists recorded that 213 pairs successfully produced 430 offspring; their survivability, though, is far from ensured.

The birds dig a simple depression in which to lay their eggs, and it's up to the hatchlings—"about the size of a half-dollar with wings," according to the *Boston Globe*—to feed themselves, which they do by immediately scooting down to the intertidal zone. Beyond their natural predators, the biggest threat they face is from off-road vehicles, or rather their operators, cruising the dunes. You can park in the lot (for a fee, in summer), walk as far as your curiosity and feet will take you, and hope that the state senate will do the right thing in the battle between bird and machine. ♦ Sandy Neck Rd (off Rte 6A in E. Sandwich), W. Barnstable. 362.8300

63 **Pinske Gallery** You may not like what **Barre Pinske** (born 1963) considers art, but you certainly can't ignore it. The 6,000-square-foot gallery he created from a mattress warehouse on prim-and-pretty Route 6A announces its presence with an oversize mailbox fashioned from an old fuel tank. In 1992, when the gallery and the mailbox were unveiled, local defenders of the status quo worked themselves into a tizzy, claiming the mailbox violated local sign ordinances. However, though signage is carefully controlled along this historic highway, there are no statutes setting limits on mailboxes—or public art, for that matter. So it has remained, along with a towering, slightly skewed "stop" sign in case you missed the message. Definitely do stop in: the dozen or so artists selected by gallery manager **Julie Brooks** (who formerly worked on Boston's Newbury Street) all have interesting things to say and convey—especially **Michael Foley,** whose constructions on the theme of loss, melding old photographs, bloodlike paint, and evocative odds and ends, are strangely stirring. Pinske's own artwork runs the gamut from brash graffiti-style impastos (one entitled "I think with my" contains two murky figures with the cartoonlike caption, "Can we have sex now?") to what he characterizes as "highbrow" chainsaw art. Clearly, he's not the retiring, tortured type.

Although he has attracted such well-heeled patrons as **Barry Manilow** and **Steve Tyler** of **Aerosmith** (now there's a duet), Pinske keeps his output proletarianly priced—so as to sell more. Whatever the marketing strategy, this is a brash, energetic place, much like its namesake, and a very welcome respite from the trite conventions all too prevalent in more "tasteful" venues. P.S.: About a half-mile east of Pinske's, look for some unusual graffiti on a railroad underpass—prototypal "goddesses" painted in her youth by artist **Edith Vonnegut,** so lovely that no one has dared cover them over. ♦ M-Sa 10AM-5PM; Su noon-5PM. 1989 Rte 6A/Main St (between Rte 132 and Scudder Ln), Barnstable. 362.5311

64 **Charles Hinckley House** $$ You practically have to fight your way through the wildflowers—some 100 varieties, all lovingly cultivated by innkeeper **Miya Patrick**—to reach the pilaster-framed front door of this hipped-roof, shipwright-built 1809 Federal house (shown here). It's on the **National Register of Historic Places,** and the interior is furnished accordingly, with hand-picked antiques, but there's nothing posed or formal about the four very individual rooms. From the Library Room, two walls of which consist of well-stocked bookcases, to the summer kitchen turned cathedral-ceilinged sanctum, they all look as if a sensualist had breezed through, adding an inspired touch here and there.

Miya Patrick is that presence, as you'll immediately deduce from her English breakfasts: perhaps poached eggs on crab cakes or French pancakes with homemade raspberry butter and maple syrup. She's an accomplished caterer (neighbors **Ben** and **Jane Thompson,** whose Design Research firm revamped Boston's Faneuil Hall, regularly avail themselves of her services), and her husband, **Les,** is a contractor specializing in period restoration. They started out fixing up houses in Bucks County, Pennsylvania, turned around another Cape B&B, and have put their all into this one since 1983. In summer, the bay beach is an enjoyable stroll down a quiet country lane; in winter, a flickering fire, all those books, and the breakfasts are all one needs. ♦ 8 Scudder Ln (at Rte 6A/Main St), Barnstable. 362.9924

65 **Beechwood** $$ So enveloping is the shade proffered by century-old weeping beech trees that your eyes might need to adjust to take in the sight of this mammoth 1853 Victorian painted butter-yellow and celery-green. It's even cooler and darker inside, past the wraparound porch set with rockers. Several of the six rooms of this B&B are quite extraordinary. Up the tight curl of a brass-handled captain's stairway, "Cottage" features a painted bedroom set in the style of the 1860s, and "Eastlake" embodies that 1880s aesthetic, with **William Morris** wallpaper and a spoon-carved bed and matching marble-topped dresser. In the tin-ceilinged dining room, innkeeper **Ann Livermore** serves blueberry-streusel muffins and apple-puff pancakes. ♦ 2839 Rte 6A/Main St (between Scudder and Old Jail Lns), Barnstable. 362.6618

66 Olde Colonial Courthouse Built in 1772 as Barnstable County's second courthouse, this white clapboard building now houses **Tales of Cape Cod,** an organization founded by **Louis Cataldo** in 1949 to collect and preserve the Cape's folklore and oral history. The organization publishes historical materials and was responsible for acquiring such sites as **Iyanough's Gravesite** in Cummaquid and, for the grand sum of one dollar, the **Trayser Museum and Old Jail.** Tuesday evenings in summer, Tales hosts lectures by experts on Cape Cod arcana and on such subjects of general interest as Cape visitors "from Thoreau to Theroux." Closed to public except for lectures. ♦ Admission for lectures. 3018 Rte 6A/Main St (at Rendezvous Ln), Barnstable. 362.8927

66 Sturgis Library If you think you might have a Pilgrim or two perched in your family tree, here's the easiest place to find out. Ancestor-hunters from across the country flock to consult the outstanding genealogical collection at this library, founded as a bequest of shipping merchant **Captain William Sturgis** (1782-1863). Left with no means of support upon the death of his father, Sturgis, 15 years old and an only son, signed on as a cabin boy aboard the Orient-bound *Caroline;* four years later he returned as master of the ship. To compensate for his lack of formal education, he tackled a Harvard reading list borrowed from his boyhood friend **Lemuel Shaw,** who would later become Chief Justice of Massachusetts. Retiring from the sea in his late 20s after a number of hair-raising adventures (including an attack by Cantonese pirates), Sturgis maneuvered just as cleverly in the tricky waters of entrepreneurship: his Boston-based firm **Sturgis and Bryant** managed to corner about half the China trade.

Though he never again lived in Barnstable, he evidently cared enough about his ancestral home—**Reverend John Lothrop** was an eighth-generation forebear—to buy back his birthplace and leave it to the town as a library, along with a $15,000 endowment. The southeast portion of the building, a 1644 half-house, had in fact been built by the congregation to serve as Lothrop's home and, for two years, pro tem meetinghouse. The Sturgis Library can thus claim two "oldests": oldest surviving building used for worship in North America and the oldest building to house a library. Though the library has been extensively renovated and expanded over the years, the half-house's summer beam and deep window seats are still visible; also showcased in this room is Lothrop's tallow-burned circa 1605 Geneva Bible, which he painstakingly patched up with paper and rewrote from memory.

In addition to its genealogical records (handily cross-indexed over the decades by local volunteers), the Sturgis Library also houses the **Kittredge Maritime History Collection,** begun with a legacy from St. Paul's headmaster **William Crocker Kittredge,** a library trustee and prominent Cape Cod historian. His collection of rare and out-of-print books, along with 1,500 maps and charts, are of intense interest not only to other historians but to shipwreck researchers hoping to score an undiscovered sunken vessel. While all this feverish activity takes place behind the scenes, the townspeople of Barnstable simply enjoy the library as a library, complete with a well-stocked periodicals room and an inviting children's corner. ♦ M, W 10AM-5PM; Tu, Th 1-5PM, 7-9PM; F 1-5PM (hours may vary depending on funding). 3090 Rte 6A/Main St (between Rendezvous Ln and Mill Wy), Barnstable. 362.6636

67 Crocker Tavern Bed and Breakfast $ Built circa 1750, this tavern was a handy stopover on the Boston-Provincetown stagecoach route. It was also favored by attorneys working at the courthouse and, during the Revolution, by Whigs. **Sue** and **Jeff Carlson,** brand-new owners as of 1993, have kept it classically spare; there are no fussy details to distract from the handsome lines of the original paneling and inset window seats. All three bedrooms are big and comfortably appointed within the minimalist aesthetics observed. The back bedroom has the advantage not only of off-road quietude but of a most interesting bathroom fashioned from a colonial pantry. ♦ Closed Monday through Wednesday. 3095 Rte 6A/Main St (between Rendezvous Ln and Hyannis Rd), Barnstable. 362.5115

In 1666, Nicholas Davis, a Quaker, gave the sachem Yanno (a descendant of the Iyanough who had been so helpful to the Pilgrims) £20 and two pairs of pants in exchange for a small parcel of land. Here he built a warehouse for pickling oysters in brine, and around "Yanno's" land grew the town of Hyannis. The tiny hamlet of Wianno was likewise named for the chief.

68 Barnstable Comedy Club Housed in **Village Hall,** a 1910 cedar-shingled building of pleasing proportions, the oldest amateur theater group in the country has adhered to its mission: to "produce good plays . . . and remain amateurs." It has managed to do so since 1922, turning nonprofit in 1975—though, truth be told, profits for many a season totaled in the single digits, even when popular plays brought in everyone's family and friends. "It was founded to keep the locals from getting totally bored in the winter," says resident producer **Henry F. Morlock,** who saw his first "live stage show" here as a high-schooler and was instantly hooked.

In 1993, Morlock and partners **Scott Dalton** and **Janice Nikuta** initiated **Imagine Theatre for Children**—"for, by, and about" would be more accurate. Kids build the sets, usher, and, of course, act, performing eight times a week through the summer. Each year the adult company, including a few members active since the 1950s, puts on four major productions from fall to spring, starting off with a musical in October, plus a workshop, which could be anything from high drama to absurdist farce (one recent example was *Invasion of the Killer Carrots*). A dearth of local talent has never been a problem. Notable alums include **Kurt Vonnegut,** who played in *Tiger at the Gates* (1971), clad in a leopard skin, and had two plays produced in the early '60s. Admittedly sentimental about his early involvement with the Club, Vonnegut has granted the organization blanket permission "to make dramatic use of anything whatsoever of mine throughout all Eternity." ♦ 3171 Rte 6A/Main St (between Old Jail Ln and Hyannis Rd), Barnstable. 362.6333

68 Barnstable Superior Courthouse Barnstable has been the seat of county government since 1685. This 1831-32 granite Greek Revival building, attributed to Bullfinch protégé **Alexander Parris** (who had recently completed Boston's masterful Quincy Market), boasts four fluted Doric columns and a wooden pediment and cornice that convincingly simulate stone; looming over the little village, it sets a suitably pompous tone. The second-story courtroom is imposing, too, with its slightly arched and magnificently stenciled ceiling; two decorative columns, limned in gold, frame the judge. Walk right in and listen to the wrangling—or rather, proceedings. It's justice in action, if not always the most riveting floor show. The cannons on the courthouse lawn, incidentally, were hauled by oxen from Boston to protect the town's saltworks from the British during the **War of 1812.** ♦ M-F 8AM-4:30PM. 3195 Rte 6A/Main St (between Old Jail Ln and Hyannis Rd), Barnstable. 362.2511

69 Barnstable Tavern ★$$ If this early 19th-century tavern hadn't been so exhaustively restored, it might convey a bit more atmosphere. As it is, the back room is more inviting than the modernized barroom, with calico cloths, Oriental rugs, and wide-plank floors. Catch-of-the-day treatments like halibut with herb-lime crumb topping can indeed be a catch, but for the most part the fare never quite makes its own impression. At least it's palatable and well priced. ♦ American/Takeout ♦ Lunch and dinner. 3176 Rte 6A/Main St (between Old Jail Ln and Hyannis Rd), Barnstable. Reservations recommended. 362.2355

70 Mattakeese Wharf ★★$$$ Located right next to the **Hyannis Whale Watcher Cruises** dock, this rambling harborside restaurant has everything you could hope for: broad decks with a sunset view, nautical decor, and bountiful seafood. **Bob** and **Claire Venditti,** owners since 1966, make the most of pasta paired with shellfish, offering fettuccine or linguine heaped with shrimp, mussels, scallops, and clams (singly or all at once), and a variety of sauces ranging from *bianco,* Alfredo, and carbonara to Dijon, marinara, or *fra diavolo.* Fresh slabs of broiled fish can't be beat, and for something a little more elaborate, try sole Florentine, wrapped around spinach and Romano and baked with a Mornay sauce. Or perhaps, with the bay breezes gently riffling, the time has come to crack open a lobster. ♦ American/Italian ♦ Lunch and dinner; Sunday brunch. Closed Nov-May. 271 Mill Wy (at Commerce Rd), Barnstable. 362.4511

Barnstable's West Parish Meetinghouse harbored a school from 1863 to 1883, and in the course of renovations some old papers were discovered behind the plaster, including a composition-on-composition by one Darius Howland. "Composition is something a scholar has to write and puzzle over till he gets a few words put together so as to make sense—or nonsense—which describes the subject he has to write about," he wrote. "The first thing in writing a composition is to think of a subject and then to tell something about it. . . . My stock of knowledge on the composition subject is exhausted so I will close with the truthful lines:

Compositions are hard and tough
I've written these lines and that's enough."

Restaurants/Clubs: Red **Hotels:** Blue
Shops/ Outdoors: Green **Sights/Culture:** Black

71 Unitarian Church The much-younger "twin" of the **West Parish Meetinghouse,** this 1907 building (illustrated above) designed by **Guy Lowell** (right before he took on Boston's Museum of Fine Arts), replaced an 1836 church that had burned, which in turn had replaced the original early-1700s East Precinct meetinghouse. The church became Unitarian in 1825, and Lowell's design is suitably understated. Two small windows are set high in the dove-gray facade, and two Ionic columns flank the recessed doorway. ♦ Service Su 10:30AM. 3330 Rte 6A/Main St (between Mill Wy and Braggs Rd), Barnstable. 362.6381

72 The Trayser Museum Complex Built in 1856 as a customhouse, and used for that purpose for 37 years before serving as a post office from 1913 to 1959, this Italian Renaissance edifice of red-painted brick with white trim, now on the **National Register of Historic Places,** has perhaps found its true calling as a museum for the **Barnstable Historical Commission.** Heralded as the Cape's first fireproof building (fire had already destroyed all the county records once, in 1827), it's also among the grandest, with wrought-iron balustrades, lofty ceilings, and hefty pillars whose leafy crowns conceal heating ducts. From his office on the second floor, the customs collector (the first was Washington-appointee **General Joseph Otis,** brother of famed revolutionary orator **James Otis**) kept tabs on ships entering **Barnstable Harbor** and made sure the government got its due.

The museum housed here today is named for local historian **Donald G. Trayser,** and it contains collections ranging from native and colonial artifacts to China trade booty and children's toys. Among the odds and ends are a fringe-topped wicker baby carriage and a velvet-covered barber's chair. Also on the grounds is a carriage shed housing antique fishing implements, a horse-drawn hearse, and a pair of remarkable bicycles: an 1869 velocipede (with that huge front wheel) and a 1900 bike, seemingly ordinary but for its wood frame. Next door is a circa 1690-1700 wooden jail—the oldest such "gaol" to survive in the United States. Moved hither and yon, and damaged by a 1973 fire, it's undergoing renovations; meanwhile, you can see evidence of inmates' carvings on the cell doors. ♦ Donation. Tu-Sa 1:30-4:30PM July to mid-Oct; call for off-season hours. 3353 Rte 6A/Main St (between Hyannis and Braggs Rds), Barnstable. 362.2092

73 Cape Cod Art Association (CCAA) Founded in Hyannis in 1947, this nonprofit community arts group bounced from site to site before finding a permanent home here in 1972. Local architect **Richard Sears Gallagher,** a CCAA member who had designed the **Parish Hall** addition to the **Unitarian Church** in 1960, came up with the plan for an adjoining pair of catercorner, skylit saltboxes, which not only show off the artwork to best advantage but provide excellent studio facilities. The spaces are so airy and open you have the sense of being on the water, though in fact the complex is well inland. Classes are given year-round, and shows are mounted in season. Though the caliber varies, it's clear that the organization is doing its best to respond to its charter and "promote a high standard of fine art on Cape Cod." ♦ M-Sa 10AM-4PM, Su 1-5PM May-Nov. 3480 Rte 6A/Main St (between Mill Wy and Braggs Rd), Barnstable. 362.2909

74 Ashley Manor $$ This B&B, a 1699 colonial mansion hidden behind a towering privet hedge, has it all: historicity, comfort, and, above all, enchantment. **Donald** and **Fay Bain** (ex-New York lawyer and advertising exec, respectively) have been hosting since 1987 and don't miss a trick. The breakfasts, served in a wainscoted dining room featuring built-in corner cupboards, are especially lavish (quiche, homemade granola, strawberry shortcake), and the two rooms and four suites are charmingly decorated, with spackle-painted, wide-board floors and cheerful, floral-print wallpapers. Some of the more elaborate suites feature working fireplaces and canopied queen-size beds. The living room is at once elegant and comfortable, with midnight-blue velvet couches and a grand piano. The two-acre grounds, redolent with boxwood, encompass a gazebo and a Hart-Tru tennis court. Bikes are available, as is a croquet set. Truly, they've thought of everything. ♦ 3660 Rte 6A/Main St (between Commerce Rd and Indian Tr), Barnstable. 362.8044

75 Owl's Nest Antiques **Nancy** and **David Galloni's** barn is full of stuff you can actually use: complete sets of china, for instance, and a number of nonmuseum quality (but very attractive) quilts. Textiles are a specialty, including clothing and a good selection of vintage wedding dresses. Another strong suit is dolls, and the wardrobes they require. ♦ Daily 10AM-5PM. 4083 Rte 6A/Main St (opposite Bone Hill Rd), Cummaquid. 362.4054

Yarmouth/Dennis

It's in the midsection of the Cape, where Yarmouth and Dennis are ensconced, that the disparity between Route 6A on the bayside of the peninsula and Route 28 near the southern coast is most egregious—almost schizophrenically so. Whereas Route 6A is rich with greenery and history, Route 28 is congested with traffic and tacky buildings; in recent decades, the latter has been strip-developed to a point that's painful to see.

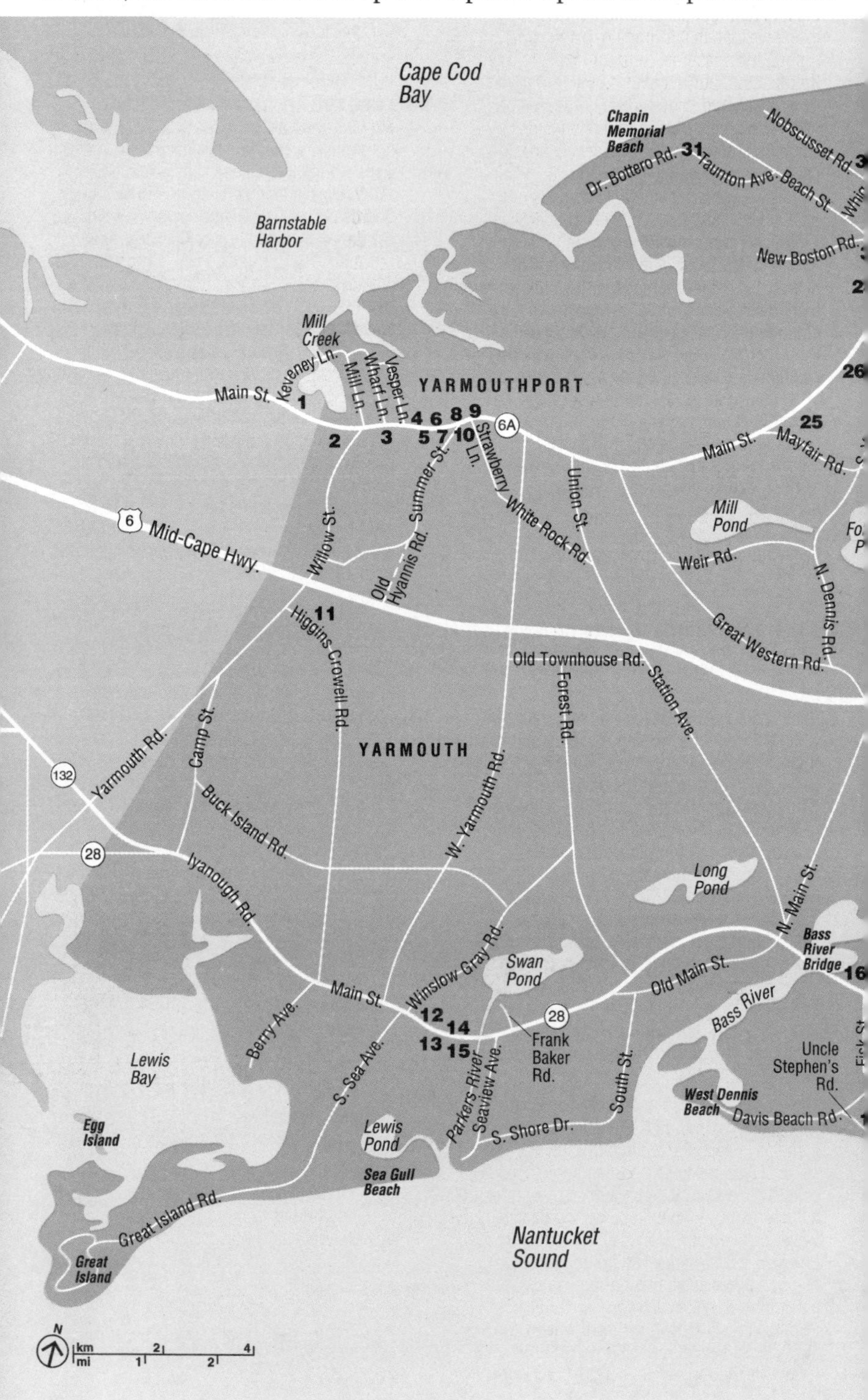

Amid the sprawling "resorts" and restaurants, every so often you'll spot a mouldering showplace with handsome lines that stands out like a tarnished silver brooch among rhinestone gewgaws.

Most discerning travelers will want to plow through Route 28 as fast as possible—wishing, like **Thoreau,** to concentrate only on "those features of the Cape . . . in which it is peculiar or superior" to the mainland. There are, fortunately, a few unspoiled stretches along the southern shore and the odd historical preserve that's well worth a brief detour.

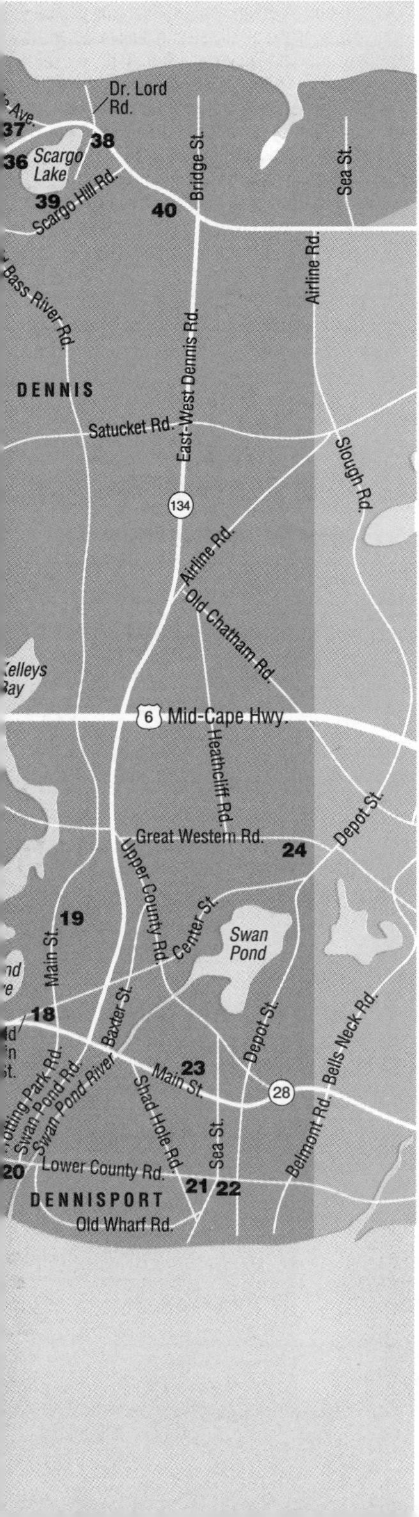

It has been widely claimed, though never proven, that the Vikings, led by **Leif Ericson,** sailed up **Bass River** around the first millennium, and built a camp (now private land) in **Blue Rock Heights** five miles upriver. A number of tribes—including the Wampanoag, Satuit, Mattakee, Nobscusset, Monomoyick, and Cummaquid—were already settled in the area when the first Europeans showed up, but they died by the thousands during the smallpox epidemic of 1770. The first house was built in Yarmouth by **Stephen Hopkins** in 1638; the town (possibly named for the English port **Great Yarmouth,** from which some of the Pilgrims may have sailed) was incorporated the next year. Among its earliest settlers was *Mayflower* passenger **Giles Hopkins.** As with other towns, farming gradually gave way to shipping—at one point, **Yarmouthport's** mile-long "Captains' Row" housed 50 prosperous skippers—and eventually tourism.

Originally part of Yarmouth, Dennis was settled by English cattle farmers. Incorporated in 1793, it was named for **Reverend Josiah Dennis,** who'd served as an area minister for 38 years. Either the early residents had a poor sense of direction, or they let the cows dictate divisions, given that **West Dennis** is southeast of **Dennis** proper, and **East Dennis** is northwest of **South Dennis.** Make no assumptions, and keep your map unfurled.

The native suffix *-set* or *-sett,* applied to innumerable Cape place names, means "by the water."

1 Anthony's Cummaquid Inn ★$$$$ Institution or dinosaur? This plantationlike restaurant is a sibling of the Boston landmark, Anthony's Pier IV, and run by the same family. The main dining room seats 200, the "sunroom," bedecked with giant wooden fish, holds another 120, and Muzak is piped mercilessly into both. Unless you're thrilled at the thought of slurping the same lobster bisque that was served at the inaugurations of **Presidents Reagan** and **Bush,** or of paying more than $30 for a boiled lobster, you'll find few pleasures here. ♦ Continental ♦ Dinner; lunch also on Sunday. Closed Monday through Tuesday Jan-Mar. 2 Main St/Rte 6A (between Keveney and Mill Lns), Yarmouthport. Reservations recommended; jacket requested. 362.4501

2 Abbicci ★★★$$$$ In its previous life as the **Cranberry Moose,** this 1775 house was for many years one of the Cape's quirkiest and most appealing restaurants. Now the interior has turned chic—black steel bar, harsh track lighting, blown-up black-and-white maps of Italy as wall decoration—and what it has gained in modernity, it has lost in charm. All is forgiven, though, once you dip into the oysters Florentine (with spinach, cream, pine nuts, and pancetta), the veal *nocciole* (fork-tender, with toasted hazelnuts and a dash of balsamic vinegar), or the *torta nicolotta* (Tuscan bread-pudding cake with a luscious rum sauce). ♦ Italian ♦ Lunch and dinner; Sunday brunch. 43 Main St/Rte 6A (between Keveney and Mill Lns), Yarmouthport. Reservations recommended. 362.3501

3 Wedgewood Inn $$

C. 1812
Wedgewood Inn
DISTINCTIVE LODGING
OPEN ALL YEAR

Set back from the road on a triple-tiered lawn, this lovely Federal house, built in 1812 for a maritime attorney, was the first in town to be designed by an architect; among the special touches is a beautiful built-in hall clock. Innkeeper **Gerrie Graham** greets you with a tea tray; you'll find a bowl of fresh fruit in your room. The corner rooms are formal, four-poster beauties: the downstairs ones come with both fireplaces and screened-in porches for year-round comfort. But it's the third-floor rooms, tucked at odd angles under the eaves, that are wildly romantic; you're in your own little world. ♦ 83 Main St/Rte 6A (at Wharf Ln), Yarmouthport. 362.5157

Those "Danger, keep off!" signs on dunes are not there just to protect the beach grass; in the early '70s, a 12-year-old boy who paid them no heed was smothered by a sand slide.

TARTUFI'S

4 Tartufi's ★★★$$ Operated by the **Hasson** family (**Alain** cooks, **Beth** hosts, and the teenage children help out), this delightful trattoria is housed in a gingerbread-style 1840s Gothic Revival cottage. Requisite red-and-white-checked tablecloths adorn the intimate rooms, and an impassioned tenor pours his heart out on the stereo (sometimes son **Jean-Yves** can be persuaded to do the same). Tuck into the rustic treats, starting with a dish of roasted garlic cloves in olive oil for dipping the chewy bread. Entrée choices range from *vitello Marsala* to *ravioli Capone* with fresh basil pesto and a dash of cream, and dessert—a goblet of creamy tiramisù or fresh peach gelato—is always rewarding. ♦ Italian ♦ Dinner. Closed Monday mid-Oct to Jan; closed Monday through Wednesday Jan-July. 134 Main St/Rte 6A (between Vesper Ln and Summer St), Yarmouthport. 362.1133

5 Hallet's Nostalgia fans should head straight to this 1889 drugstore, which hasn't changed appreciably since early in the century—though they do rent videos now. **Thacher Taylor Hallet** has long ago ceased dispensing drugs, mail, and justice-of-the-peace services, but today, his granddaughter **Mary Hallet Clark** serves sandwiches from behind the same carved-oak divider, and you can still order a frappé, freeze, float, or ice cream soda from the marble soda fountain. Sit at a stool or in one of the heart-shaped, wrought-iron chairs as a fan whirs beneath the pressed-tin ceiling. ♦ Daily 8AM-9PM Apr to mid-Sept; daily 8AM-5PM mid-Sept to Apr. 139 Main St/Rte 6A (between Vesper Ln and Summer St), Yarmouthport. 362.3362

5 Town Crier Antiques Six dealers share this homey old storefront as well as an interest in dolls. Among the other finds are vintage evening bags, christening dresses of sheerest cotton batiste, and comfortably weathered quilts. ♦ M-Sa 10AM-5PM May to mid-Oct. 153 Main St/Rte 6A (between Vesper Ln and Summer Sts), Yarmouthport. 362.3138

5 Inaho ★★★$$$

Chef/owner **Yuji Watanabe** recently moved his restaurant here from Hyannis and created a tranquil oasis in this plain old clapboard house. Several small dining rooms, separated by ricepaper screens and awash with soothing flute riffs, form a restful, private setting. True aficionados, though, will want to sit center stage—at the sushi bar—to watch Watanabe perform his magic. On the regular menu are "Tails in the Air," tempura shrimp wrapped

Restaurants/Clubs: Red **Hotels:** Blue
Shops/ Outdoors: Green **Sights/Culture:** Black

with avocado and fish roe in rice and seaweed, along with more substantial dishes, such as *shabu-shabu,* but it's hard to break out of a rut in a sushi and sashimi place as good as this one. ♦ Japanese ♦ Dinner. 157 Main St/Rte 6A (between Vesper Ln and Summer St), Yarmouthport. Reservations recommended. 362.5522

5 **Design Works** If you're still searching for the Scandinavian antique pine armoire of your dreams, you may get lucky here. There's an ample selection of linens and crockery as well. ♦ M-Sa 10AM-5PM; Su 1-5PM. 159 Main St/Rte 6A (between Vesper Ln and Summer St), Yarmouthport. 382.9698

5 **Jack's Outback** ★★$ Be prepared: this local landmark, the dominion of **Jack Braginton-Smith** and **Bob O. Edwards,** is not big on hospitality. Their motto is "Great food, lousy service!" and they mean it. You write your own order off the scrawled posters that approximate a menu, then schlep your own plate to the pine-paneled dining room. The menu writer is a believer in creative spelling, whether scrawling out "Roobin on Wry" or "Tappeeyolka Puddin." Prices are rock-bottom, and there's even a children's menu, listed as "For Brats Under 12." ♦ New England ♦ Breakfast, lunch, and dinner; breakfast and lunch only on Monday; Sunday brunch. 161 Main St/Rte 6A (between Vesper Ln and Summer St), Yarmouthport. 362.6690

Nickerson Antiques

6 **Nickerson Antiques** This is one of the few places on the Cape where you can find substantive antiques—so many, in fact, that it's hard to squeeze your way around the jam-packed rooms. If prices seem reasonable, it's because many of the pieces are British transplants (England produced more furniture in the 17th and 18th centuries than the beleaguered colonies ever did). Since the American and British styles are compatible, no one need ever know the true origin of your find. ♦ M-Sa 10AM-5PM; Su noon-5PM. 162 Main St/Rte 6A (between Vesper Ln and Summer St), Yarmouthport. 362.6426

Among the generations of college kids who have spent their summers schlepping tables on the Cape was none other than writer Sylvia Plath, who waitressed at a family resort in 1952, in between her sophomore and junior years. But Plath never felt quite at home among her cohorts, whom she described to her mother as "really wise, drinking flirts" and quit in mid-July, complaining of severe sinusitus.

7 **Peach Tree Designs** From its dramatic showroom on the second floor, where a white bedstead and bold floral prints are accented against black rubberized wallpaper, to its eclectic selection of home furnishings, this store equals excitement. The wide array of merchandise includes everything from false-front books, blankets, and lamps to fanlight mirrors, flowery hats, and even esoteric foods. ♦ M-Sa 9:30AM-5:30PM, Su noon-5PM mid-Jan to mid-Sept; M-Sa 10AM-5PM, Su noon-5PM mid-Sept to mid-Jan. 173 Main St/Rte 6A (between Vesper Ln and Summer Sts), Yarmouthport. 362.8317. Also at: Mashpee Commons, Mashpee. 477.3920

8 **Parnassus Books Ben Muse,** proprietor of this stacked-to-the-gills bookstore—featuring "hand-picked" new, used, and rare books—is just as irascible as his cronies at Jack's Outback. "He may seem dour, but he's really a dear," apologizes assistant **Katherine Warwick.** As for the store's lack of directive signage, there's an explanation for that, too: "He *wants* people to start digging on their own, for the fun of discovery." Muse has been stockpiling books since the '50s and selling since 1960. Specialties include Cape and Islands titles and rare first editions (e.g., **James, Melville**), as well as art, maritime, antiques, and ornithology. Prices start at $1 and can go as high as $5,000 or more, and there's a 24-hour honor-system rack outside if you run out of reading material at bedtime. The building was constructed in 1858 as a combination market/Swedenborgian church; services were held upstairs, where thousands of surplus books now await their turn on the packed shelves below. ♦ M-Sa 9AM-8PM, Su noon-5PM late May to early Sept; M-Sa 9AM-5PM early Sept to late May. 220 Main St/Rte 6A (at Summer St), Yarmouthport. 362.6420

9 **Winslow Crocker House** Of the 33 properties owned and maintained by the **Society for the Preservation of New England Antiquities,** this is the only one located on the Cape. In the 1930s, **Mary Thacher,** a descendant of **Anthony Thacher,** Dennis' first land grantee, bought and moved a magnificent Georgian house built around 1780 by **Winslow Crocker,** a wealthy West Barnstable trader and speculator (and alleged rumrunner) in order to display her growing collection of antiques. Thacher's magnificent furniture ranges from an 1800 tiger-maple case clock to a japanned William and Mary chest-on-chest. Two longtime site administrators, **Sara Porter** and **Jim McGuiness,** can fill you in on the stories

behind the stuff: how Thacher's 1690 family cradle, for instance, is thought to resemble one that **Anthony Thacher** and his wife clung on to when they were shipwrecked in 1635 off what is now Thacher's Island in Rockport, Massachusetts (all four children, alas, were drowned). Mary Thacher spent her life pursuing beauty and distributing largesse. She gave **Corporation Beach** to Dennis and her house to SPNEA one she'd lived out her years here. ♦ Admission. Tu, Th, Sa-Su noon-4PM June to mid-Oct. 250 Main St/Rte 6A (at Summer St), Yarmouthport. 362.4385

9 New Church Swedenborgian fervor swept through Yarmouthport in the early 1800s, instigated by a young Harvard graduate named **Caleb Reed.** The search for a church site culminated in this 1870 building flanking the Village Green. Three small triangular windows, with stained glass in a trefoil pattern, adorn each side; the cloverleaf motif is repeated in the carved and painted roof trusses. A William Clarke tracker organ helps dispel the gloom. ♦ Service Su 10:45AM late May to early Sept. 266 Main St/Rte 6A (opposite Strawberry Ln), Yarmouthport. 362.3364

10 Le Trajet ★★★$$$$ This ambitious French restaurant is housed on the ground floor of the **Yarmouthport Inn,** a pillared Georgian colonial mansion on the **National Register of Historic Places** that is said to be the oldest hostelry on the Cape. It started out in 1696 as the **Wayside Staging Inn.** The Inn's four rooms are dreary; stick to dinner only. Chef **William Hollinger's** menu offers one nouvelle tour de force after another, from smoked salmon, trout, and tuna "pastrami," to roasted lobster infused with champagne beurre blanc, served with basmati risotto. A jazz trio adds aural enhancement Wednesday through Saturday. ♦ French ♦ Dinner. Closed Monday June to mid-Oct; closed Monday and Tuesday mid-Feb to May, mid-Oct to Feb; closed Jan to mid-Feb. 233 Main St/Rte 6A (at Summer St), Yarmouthport. 362.3191, 800/833.5125

10 Hilary Gifford Studio/Boutique Venturing into this former one-room schoolhouse, you'll find the art-to-wear either artful or over-the-edge; there's no middle ground. **Gifford's** hand-painted silk clothing is definitely not for every taste—it veers closer to abstract art than to conventional adornment. ♦ M-Sa 10AM-6PM. 233 Main St/Rte 6A (at Summer St), Yarmouthport. 362.3538

10 Captain Bangs Hallet House This 1840 Greek Revival house, maintained by the **Historical Association of Old Yarmouth,** faces the Village Green but is easier to reach from the back (just drive up behind the post office). Named for the daring China trade captain who lived here from 1863 to 1893, it's decorated with original period pieces, including a Hepplewhite sofa, Sheraton secretary, Chippendale frames, Hitchcock chairs, etc. For all its riches, however, it's more show than soul. Adjoining the property is the two-mile **Yarmouth Nature Trail,** leading to the simple, shingled **Kelley Chapel,** built by a Quaker in 1873 for a daughter left bereft after the loss of a child. ♦ House: Nominal admission. Th-F, Su 1-4PM July-Sept; Su 1-4PM June, Oct. Trail: Donation. Daily dawn-dusk. Chapel: Free. Daily 1-4PM July-Aug. 11 Strawberry Ln (off Rte 6A), Yarmouthport. 362.3021

11 Museum Warehouse Outlet If you spend more time in museum shops than in museums, this outlet is for you. The mail-order fulfillment headquarters for the "Museum Collections" and "Finishing Touches" catalogs, this warehouse is overflowing with surplus and odd lots, from bed linens and bath fixtures to jewelry, needlepoint pillows, and leather luggage. Prices run about half the norm, and there's no telling what treasures you'll uncover. ♦ M-Sa 9AM-5PM; Su 10AM-3PM. 586 Higgins Crowell Rd (between Yarmouth and Buck Island Rds), W. Yarmouth. 775.4643

12 Aqua Circus of Cape Cod The tanks are a little murky and the staff somewhat overtaxed, but the youngsters who visit this place probably won't mind. The centerpiece is a small aquarium with a large tank for sea lion shows (if they're not in a performing mood, you get a raincheck); out back is an extensive petting zoo, with some definite untouchables, including a bobcat and a lion. Though ecological awareness is stressed, the substandard facilities tend to undermine the message. You might want to pass on this attraction. ♦ Admission. Daily 9:30AM-6:30PM July-Aug; daily 9:30AM-5PM mid-Feb to July, Sept to late Nov. 674 Main St/Rte 28 (between Winslow Gray and Frank Baker Rds), W. Yarmouth. 775.8883

13 Lobster Boat ★★$$ Imagine a collision between an enormous lobster boat and a Cape Cod cottage and you have an idea of what this place looks like. Irresistible to tourists, this rambling restaurant (illustrated above) boasts the de rigueur waterside setting (on an inlet), the nautical pastiche of buoys, traps, flags, and nets, and the predictable seafood medley at people-pleasing prices. The place gets mobbed the minute the doors open. "It's a zoo," says the maitre d', affectionately. ♦ American ♦ Dinner. Closed Nov-Apr. 681 Main St/Rte 28 (between S. Sea and Seaview Aves), W. Yarmouth. 775.0486

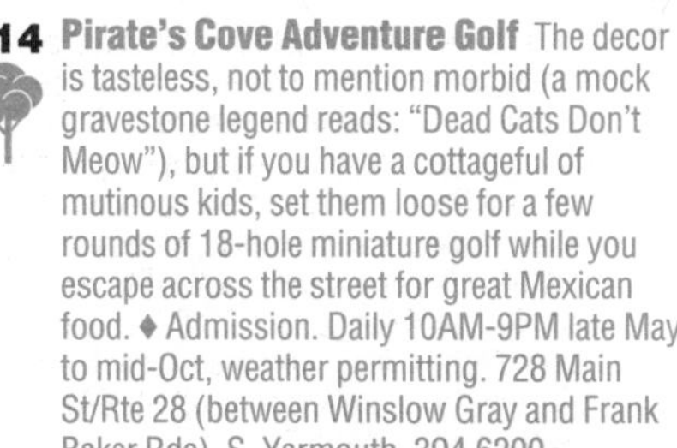

14 Pirate's Cove Adventure Golf The decor is tasteless, not to mention morbid (a mock gravestone legend reads: "Dead Cats Don't Meow"), but if you have a cottageful of mutinous kids, set them loose for a few rounds of 18-hole miniature golf while you escape across the street for great Mexican food. ♦ Admission. Daily 10AM-9PM late May to mid-Oct, weather permitting. 728 Main St/Rte 28 (between Winslow Gray and Frank Baker Rds), S. Yarmouth. 394.6200

15 Fiesta Grande ★★$ Rather than a gringo's version of Mexican food, this cantina serves "the real McCoy," says chef/owner **Sandro Minero,** only recently of Mazatlàn. The restaurant, which opened in 1992, has *serape*-topped tables and stained-glass windows sporting gnomes, a holdover from the house's previous life. Try the *nachos con chorizo* (spicy sausage), *enchiladas de jaiba* (crabmeat), or shrimp fajitas. Die-hard chileheads can breakfast on *chilequiles.* ♦ Mexican ♦ Breakfast, lunch, and dinner. 737 Main St/Rte 28 (between S. Sea and Seaview Aves), S. Yarmouth. 760.2924

16 Water Safaris It's no Zambezi, but the **Bass River** has some pretty interesting wildlife of its own (terns, egrets, herons), and getting out onto the water is a cool way to explore. The *Starfish,* a custom-built 1985 minibarge, accommodates 49 passengers, and captain **Cliff Smith** provides a running commentary on the sights—from windmills to captain's homes—during the 1½-hour cruise. ♦ Fee. Four departures daily mid-June to early Sept; two departures late May to mid-June, early Sept to mid-Oct. Bass River Bridge (at Rte 28), W. Dennis. 362.5555

16 Cape Cod Boats If you'd prefer to paddle your own canoe or self-propel your own motorboat, sailboat, or windsurfer, you can rent by the hour to the week here. Bait, tackle, and licenses can be obtained from the shops in this compact complex. ♦ Bass River Bridge (at Rte 28), W. Dennis. 394. 9268

16 Jacob's Restaurant/Jake's Bakes ★★$$$$ Adorned with buoys and homilies ("I'm sick and tired of being sick and tired"), this place is drowning in quaintness. All the usual seafood is offered here at regular prices, but what sets Jacob's apart is its clambake-to-go. This multicourse feast consists of chowder, barbecued chicken, lobster, steamers, Italian sausage, corn on the cob, red bliss potatoes, steamed onions, and to top it all off—watermelon. Once a summer should suffice. ♦ American ♦ Breakfast, lunch, and dinner. Closed mid-Oct to late Apr. 30 W. Main St (Rte 28 at Bass River Bridge), W. Dennis. 394.0331

17 Lighthouse Inn $$$ The centerpiece of this old-fashioned beachside resort, opened by **Everett Stone** in 1938 and now run by his grandsons, is an 1855 lighthouse (pictured above), decommissioned in 1914 and relit in 1989 in time to celebrate the bicentennial of U.S. lighthouses. Starting with a cluster of cold-water cabins, the Stones expanded their accommodations to 61 homey rooms, suites, and cottages; the complex also includes a pool, tennis and volleyball courts, miniature golf, shuffleboard, horseshoes, and gameroom. If children still cry boredom, enroll them in a structured play program (for an additional fee). The Modified American Plan offers a refreshing nouvelle menu at enticing prices, and after dinner, everyone kicks up their heels at the **Sand Bar** club. Life is pretty carefree here, except for calculating how many pleasures you can cram into one day. ♦ Closed mid-Oct to late May. 4 Lighthouse Rd (off Lower County Rd), W. Dennis. 398.2244

Within the Lighthouse Inn:

Lighthouse Inn Restaurant ★★★$$$ In a barn-size dining room cooled by sea breezes, chef **Roger Bismore** serves everything from smoked chicken and pasta cupped in radicchio to almond-encrusted Norwegian salmon fillet with a mango beurre blanc. ♦ American/Continental ♦ Breakfast, lunch, and dinner. Closed mid-Oct to late May. Reservations requested for dinner. 398.2244

17 The Beach House $ Set in a sleepy community of weathered cottages, this newly renovated seven-room bed and breakfast is a definite sleeper itself: it's right on the beach, and kids are not only welcome, they're catered to, with an elaborate beachside playground. Among the other niceties: a complete kitchen (including two microwaves) for guests who want to cook in, as well as a cookout deck and picnic tables. The rooms are very pretty and have private decks to take advantage of the view. ♦ 61 Uncle Stephen's Rd, W. Dennis. 398.4575

Though in 1602 Bartholomew Gosnold became the first to chart Cape Cod with any degree of detail, Italian explorer Giovanni Verrazzano had mapped a recognizable Cape as early as 1524.

18 Jericho House and Barn Museum This 1801 full Cape was built by **Captain Theophilus Baker,** whose 1834 trainee **Richard Henry Dana** would turn his maritime adventures into *Two Years Before the Mast.* Baker's descendants lived here until 1954. The house was rescued from dereliction by **Virginia Gildersleeve,** former dean of Barnard College. It's filled with period furnishings, including, in the cramped upstairs bedrooms, a child's real fur rocking horse and an assortment of weighty jet-beaded capes. Peek into the musty attic to see the pegged rafters. The 1810 Barn Museum contains a race cart left over from the days when off-duty sea captains were avid fans of harness racing, a miniature model saltworks, extensive carpentry and farm implements (including cranberrying tools), plus a pretend blacksmith shop and country store. The prize, though, is a 20th-century folk-art extravaganza: a 150-creature "driftwood zoo" fashioned in the '50s by retired ad executive **Sherman M. Woodward.** He had not only a good eye for flotsam but a great sense of humor, fashioning everything from King Kong to sea serpents. His imaginative oeuvre is sure to inspire wide-eyed kids to similar creativity. ♦ Donation. W, F 2-4PM July-Aug. Trotting Park Rd (at Old Main St), W. Dennis. 398.6736

19 South Parish Congregational Church Built in 1835 to commemorate 102 sea captains, the chapel is famous for its Sandwich glass chandelier and for its Snetzler rosewood organ; built in London in 1762 and installed here in 1845, it's the oldest pipe organ in the country still in use. ♦ Service Su 10AM. 234 Main St (between Old Main St and Great Western Rd), S. Dennis. 394.5992

20 Swan River Seafood ★★$$ To get fish any fresher, you'd have to head out on a boat with your hibachi. In concert with its on-site fish market, this '50s institution serves fresh-sliced slabs, such as shark steak au poivre or scrod San Sebastian (simmered in garlic broth). The sweeping view takes in a marsh and windmill. ♦ International ♦ Lunch and dinner. Closed Oct to late May. 5 Lower County Rd (at Swan Pond River), Dennisport. 394.4466

21 Woolfie's Home Baking Every beachside community has its favorite doughnut-and-muffin shop, and it's easy to see why Dennisport residents prefer this one. The muffins are humongous and moist, from decadent chip-studded double chocolate to wholesome cranberry-walnut, and the Danish, streudel, and coffee cakes are light and flavorful. ♦ Daily 7AM-6PM May-Sept. 279 Lower County Rd (between Shad Hole Rd and Sea St), Dennisport. 394.3717

Nautical expressions that have crept into common usage since the whaling days include "knowing the ropes" and "seeing if the coast is clear."

22 Sundae School Created in 1976 by **Paul Endres,** a former Milton Academy history teacher, this barn turned ice cream parlor is part museum, with vintage posters and paraphernalia, including a nickelodeon and Belle Epoque marble soda fountain. Choose from traditional flavors or the more exotic Amaretto nut or Kahlua chip. All the usual toppings are on tap, or you could treat yourself to a seasonal sundae smothered in fresh blueberries or raspberries. ♦ Daily 11AM-11PM mid-Apr to mid-Oct. 387 Lower County Rd (at Sea St), Dennisport. 394.9122. Also at: 210 Main St, E. Orleans. 255.5473

22 Bob Briggs' Wee Packet ★★$$ It's tiny all right—a score of lemon-yellow Formica-top tables crammed into a space not much bigger than a garage. But the downhome cooking (all the seafood staples, plus some classic diner fare) has been packing them in since 1949. The homemade desserts don't hurt any either: fudge cake, blueberry shortcake, bread pudding with lemon sauce. ♦ American/Takeout ♦ Breakfast, lunch, and dinner. Closed Oct-May. 79 Depot St (at Lower County Rd), Dennisport. 398.2181

23 Discovery Days Children's Museum & Toy Shop You can't help applauding this venture, a viable alternative to the mind-numbing pastimes typically foisted on vacationing children. Founded by **Kate Clemens** and her husband **Jim Nowack** in 1993, with inspiration from their own toddlers, this is a full-scale, 4,000-square-foot exploratorium with challenges and delights galore for the 12-and-under set. (Actually, adults could have fun with a lot of the stuff, but kids of a certain age are apt to balk at anything "babyish.") Clemens is an award-winning curriculum developer, so it's not surprising her selections are state-of-the-art. Among the sensory treats in store are an "international diner" for pretend food play; a "baby pit" where under-threes can bumble about freely; a puppet theater and music room, with a see-through piano; a shadow room where your outline "freezes" on the wall; games, puzzles, and a cooperative (four-handed) maze; a recycled art corner; and the ever popular "Bubble-ology" lab. If you're planning to be in the area for a while, by all means spring for the family membership: only $50 per annum, grandparents included. ♦ Admission. Daily 9:30AM-7:30PM mid-June to early Sept; M, W-F 10AM-5PM, Sa-Su 11AM-4PM, early Sept to mid-June. 444 Main St (between Baxter and Sea Sts). 398.1600

24 Cape Cod Braided Rug Co. This factory showroom (see above) is operated by the great-grandchildren of **Romeo Paulus,** who in 1910 produced the first machine-made braided rug in the United States. Wool/acrylic blend or rag rugs start at about $20 for throws and go on up for color-coordinated customwork. ♦ M-Sa 10AM-4:30PM. 259 Great Western Rd (between Depot St and Heathcliff Rd), S. Dennis. 398.0089

25 Russ Coppelman In 1969, as a newly minted Harvard grad, **Coppelman** started making "hippie jewelry" and found he had a rare affinity for soft, malleable 22-karat gold, which can be worked into seamless, fluid shapes and beveled settings. He selects gems for their arresting depths of color—e.g., aquamarine, Australian opal, "watermelon" tourmaline—and frames them in illustrious settings. Known for his unusual pearl clasps, Coppelman enjoys reversing expectations with such creations as a "pearl" necklace fashioned of matte black onyx. His work is featured at the best Cape crafts galleries, and has also been shown at the Smithsonian. ♦ M-Sa 10AM-5PM July-Aug; Tu-Sa 10AM-5PM Sept-June. Sunflower Marketplace, 923 Main St/Rte 6A (between Mayfair and S. Yarmouth Rds), Yarmouthport. 362.6108

25 Pewter Crafters of Cape Cod Former computer executive **Barrie Cliff** changed careers in 1977 to delve into the all-but-lost art of pewtermaking. His creations come in two finishes, satiny or shiny, and in two distinct lines: traditional (porringers, tea sets, bowls, and candlesticks, some with a signature scallop-shell motif), and contemporary (especially striking geometric bud vases). ♦ M-Sa 10AM-5PM. 927 Main St/Rte 6A (between Mayfair and S. Yarmouth Rds), Yarmouthport. 362.3407

25 Northside Crafts Gallery **Paulette Cliff,** wife of pewtermaker **Barrie,** runs this contemporary American crafts gallery. A bird-carver herself, she has an eye for exceptional pottery in lush glazes. Also featured are glass, fabric, woodwork, and basketry. ♦ M-Sa 10AM-5PM May-Dec. 933 Main St/Rte 6A (between Mayfair and S. Yarmouth Rds), Yarmouthport. 362.5291

26 Captain Frosty's It's your better-than-average clam shack, with all frying conducted in heart-friendly canola oil. **Mike** and **Pat Henderson,** a naval officer and schoolteacher before they started the business in 1976, are picky about their fish, purchasing hooked cod (not gill-netted) from Chatham, and sea (not bay) scallops and clams. The especially generous lobster roll is refreshingly filler-free. ♦ 219 Main St/Rte 6A (at S. Yarmouth Rd), Dennis. 385.8548

27 Antiques Center of Cape Cod "Dolls to Deco, baskets to Bakelite"—that's just a smidgen of what you'll find at the largest coop shop on the Cape. Founded in 1991, it features more than 135 dealers and their wares, and the pickings are often splendid: everything from primitive blanket chests and colonial shoe buckles to a solid copper bathtub and a 1922 slot machine. The big stuff is upstairs, the small down; depending how acquisitive you're feeling, you might want to allow an hour or more for each. ♦ M-Sa 10AM-5PM, Su 11AM-5PM Mar-Dec; M-Tu, Th-Su 10AM-5PM Jan-Feb. 243 Main St/Rte 6A (at S. Yarmouth Rd), Dennis. 385.6400

28 Ellipse **Fiestaware** fans will come to a screeching halt the minute they spot the front-lawn display. This gaudy '50s dinnerware (yes, the vivid red-orange is marginally radioactive) used to be ubiquitous at flea markets but now fetches $30 or more a plate. **Vince Hinman** and **Richard White's** shop offers other mid-20th century crockery, but the in-your-face Fiestaware steals the show. ♦ Daily 10AM-5PM mid-May to mid-Oct; by chance or appointment mid-Oct to mid-May. 427 Main St/Rte 6A (between S. Yarmouth and New Boston Rds). 385.8626

28 Gingersnaps Stop in at **Ginger Nunez's** cottage bakery to get your daily allotment of Danish, muffins, croissants, fresh-baked breads and pies, "chocolate white-out" devil's food cake—oh, and a big sack of those signature cookies. ♦ Bakery ♦ Tu-Sa 8AM-4PM; Su 8AM-noon. 467 Main St/Rte 6A (between S. Yarmouth and New Boston Rds), Dennis. 385.4200

Among the multitudes of birds that frequent the Atlantic Flyway are occasional "vagrants": birds who took a wrong turn somewhere. In 1983, a brown-chested martin, the first ever seen north of Costa Rica, was spotted living among barn swallows, and a western reef heron, never before sighted in North America, drew bird-watchers from around the country.

29 Grose Gallery If you're leery of art galleries featuring the work of the proprietor, make an exception and check out the exquisite wood engravings of **David T. Grose.** Known for his illustrations of naturalist **John Hay's** trio of Cape Cod studies, *The Run, Nature's Year*, and *The Great Beach,* Grose's take on an image as simple as compass grass (so-called because, when windblown, it draws a circle in the sand) will fill you with wonder. Some works shown in this slaughterhouse-turned-studio (pictured above) are not as skilled, but you won't be sorry you stopped by. Depending on what's lined up that day, you might also be able to watch the printing process. ♦ Daily 10AM-5PM Feb-Dec; by appointment Jan. 524 Main St/Rte 6A (between S. Yarmouth and New Boston Rds), Dennis. 385.3434

30 Old Towne Antiques of Dennis Most of the miscellany here falls into the collectibles rubric, but it's a good selection nonetheless. **Ruth** and **Walt Jensen's** many interests include antique sporting equipment (baseball, golf, fishing), toy soldiers, children's books, and pinups. ♦ Daily 10AM-5PM. 593 Main St/Rte 6A (between S. Yarmouth and New Boston Rds), Dennis. 385.5302

30 Snowgoose Country Cafe ★$ If your traipse down memory lane has left you peckish, this small country-motif eatery can refuel you with homemade soups and breads, well-priced sandwiches, and friendly service. ♦ American/Takeout ♦ Breakfast, lunch, and dinner; breakfast and lunch only on Monday. 605 Main St/Rte 6A (between S. Yarmouth and New Boston Rds), Dennis. 385.7175

31 Gina's by the Sea ★★$$$ Note that it's *by* the sea, not *on*, but it comes close enough. Located a stone's throw from the bay in Dennis' own summer-version of "Little Italy," this white clapboard restaurant has been pleasing locals since 1938; under **Larry Riley's** ownership, the word is beginning to spread. Small, lively, and convivial, Gina's serves the kind of Italian fare that will weather any wave of chic (cannelloni Florentine, for instance), but isn't afraid to dabble in the trendy—smoked mozzarella ravioli, say, with fresh pimiento. A specialty is scampi à la Gina ("garlicized," says Riley, to the max), and for dessert, Mrs. Riley's Chocolate Rum Cake. ♦ Northern Italian ♦ Lunch and dinner; dinner only June to early July, Aug to early Sept. Closed Monday through Wednesday Apr-May, Sept-Nov; closed Dec-Apr. 134 Taunton Ave (at Dr. Bottero Rd), Dennis. 385.3213

32 Isaiah Hall B&B Inn $ The 1857 home of cooper **Isaiah B. Hall,** who patented the original cranberry barrel (his brother, **Henry Hall,** was the first to cultivate the wild fruit), this rambling farmhouse has been an inn since 1948—ever since the **Cape Playhouse** got rolling again after World War II. Over the years, it has served almost as an unofficial dorm annex, hosting a panoply of stars and directors; if you come in summer, you might find several in residence. Innkeeper **Marie Brophy** is a ready-for-anything sort, and the inn reflects her friendly spirit. Breakfast (cranberry breads, banana-nut muffins) is offered farmhand-style, at a massive table-for-12; the cathedral-ceilinged great room in the carriage house makes a comfortable place to socialize come evening. The 11 rooms range from small, pine-paneled, and quite cheap to expansive, beautifully appointed, and still a steal. ♦ Closed mid-Dec to mid-Mar. 152 Whig St (between Nobscusset and Corporation Rds), Dennis. 385.9928, 800/736.0160

33 Josiah Dennis Manse and Old West Schoolhouse **The 1736 saltbox home of the town founder is now a historical museum staffed by friendly docents; you can wander both buckling floors on your own, and they'll volunteer lore. In addition to an unusual step-up borning room (inconceivably small), there's a maritime collection with a beautifully made model of Dennis' Shiverick Shipyard: active in 1849-63, it was the only facility on the Cape large enough to produce clipper ships, sloops, and schooners. The 1770 one-room schoolhouse is sure to summon images of braids dipped in inkwells—of which there's an interesting collection. ♦ Donation. Tu, Th 2-4PM July-Aug. 77 Nobscusset Rd (at Whig St), E. Dennis. 385.2232**

34 Emily Lawrence The women's clothing selections here cleave mostly to the traditional but leave latitude for contemporary flair. There's also a small but astute sampling of personal and home accessories suitable as host/hostess (and child thereof) gifts. ♦ M-F 10AM-7PM, Sa 10AM-5:30PM, Su noon-5PM June-Aug; M-Sa 10AM-5PM, Su noon-5PM Sept-Jan. 710 Main St/Rte 6A (between Nobscusset and Corporation Rds), Dennis. 385.8328. Also at: 1533 Rte 28, Centerville. 771.8898

34 **Ice Cream Smuggler** Yet another very worthy contender in the "finest homemade" category. You'd have to concede bonus points for the Turtleback Sundae (hot fudge *and* hot butterscotch), and for inventive flavors like apple pie. But a tester's work is never done, luckily. ♦ Daily 11AM-11PM late May to early Sept; M-F noon-9PM, Sa-Su noon-10PM Apr to late May, early Sept to Nov. 716 Main St/Rte 6A (between Nobscusset and Corporation Rds), Dennis. 385.5307

34 **Emily's Beach Barn** The bathing-suits-only branch of **Emily Lawrence** has suits by the thousands, plus coverups. Whether you loathe or relish the yearly ritual, this is the fastest, most efficient way to get through it, with the widest range of choices to be found anywhere. ♦ M-F 10AM-7PM; Sa 10AM-5:30PM; Su noon-5PM. Hope Ln (at Rte 6A). 385.8304

34 **Michael Baksa Goldsmith** **Baksa** found his calling early in life: as a teenager, he apprenticed himself to a jeweler, and that was it. Now, some 20 years later, he's enough of a master to keep pushing the limits of the form. The symmetry he finds is not of the mirror-image sort, but something more satisfying: many of his pendants and earrings perform an almost Calder-like balancing act. He's also adept at offsetting colors, comparing the placement of gems against gold to the application of pigment to canvas. To broaden his palette, he's open to trying unconventional stones, such as cobalt calcium crystal (a blazing hot pink) and cool green-gray tourmaline, and he's fond of freshwater pearls in all shapes and hues. If you're contemplating custom work, you couldn't find a more accomplished accomplice. The gallery also features sensuous figurative sculptures in semitranslucent alabaster by his wife, **Laura Baksa.** ♦ M-Sa 10AM-5PM, late May to mid-Sept; Tu-Sa 10AM-5PM mid-Sept to late May. 766 Main St/Rte 6A (at Hope Ln), Dennis. 385.5733

34 **The Mercantile** This is some deli counter (pictured above), offering the likes of avocado, mango, and shrimp salad or chocolate-zucchini cake, along with more traditional staples. It's a great place to piece together a picnic or cobble a cafe meal. You can sit communally at a massive table at the center of the store and catch up on your reading with the complimentary magazines handily stored on a wooden helix. ♦ Daily 7:30AM-7PM July to early Sept; Tu-Sa 7:30AM-5PM, Su 7:30AM-3PM early Sept to July. 766 Main St/Rte 6A (at Mercantile Pl), Dennis. 385.3877

34 **B Mango and Bird** Cape Cod gift shops have a tendency toward triteness, but not this one. Odds are you won't have seen any of this stuff before—not the nubby cotton Steinweinder pillows, hand-painted valises, or drop-dead minimalist **mottura** toiletries, nor the $795 floor-model "pinnacle chime." Kids get some fun stuff, too: giant wooden yo-yos, Velcro sunglasses. About 125 artisans are represented, some local, and if 1993's inaugural season is any omen, this will be a shop to watch. ♦ Daily 9AM-6PM late June to early Sept; M-Sa 10AM-5PM, Su noon-5PM early Sept to late June. 780 Main St/Rte 6A (Mercantile Pl), Dennis. 385.6700

34 **Cape Playhouse** America's oldest continuously operating professional summer theater was founded here in 1927 by Californian **Raymond Moore,** who had come to Provincetown in the early '20s as a painter/playwright and got caught up in the theatrical fervor spawned by the **Provincetown Players.** After producing one barn-theater season in Provincetown, Moore—a young man of vision at age 28—set his sites on the sleepy town of Dennis, where the circa 1838 **Nobscusset (Unitarian) Meetinghouse,** which had already undergone several lives as a livery stable, tin shop, smithy, barn, slaughterhouse, and garage, was up for grabs. He bought it for a couple of hundred dollars, spent another $1,200 for 3½ acres of farmland on which to relocate it, and had up-and-coming architect **Cleon Throckmorton** of New York City renovate, adding a stage, proscenium, and lofty fly gallery.

When the brave new venture opened 4 July 1927, with **Basil Rathbone** performing in *The Guardsman,* the roof leaked, but patrons persisted, popping up umbrellas. The next year they got to see a young **Hank Fonda** perform opposite an ex-usher determined to turn actress, **Bette Davis.** Not every season has been quite so stellar, but an endless roster of luminaries have passed through this "cradle of stars," and to this day it's a place to see the best in the best. Artistic director **Carleton Davis** keeps things lively with a steady influx of fresh material and talent—e.g., in 1993, Tony Award-winner **Maryann Plunkett.** ♦ 36 Hope Ln (off Rte 6A), Dennis. 385.3911

On the Cape Playhouse grounds:

Cape Cinema It looks like a remodeled church, but, in fact it's a copy—**Raymond Moore** asked architect **Alfred Easton Poor** to replicate the exterior of Centerville's **Congregational Church.** The interior is decidedly original, featuring a 6,400-square-foot Art Deco ceiling mural of *Prometheus* designed by **Rockwell Kent** and executed by renowned set designer **Jo Mielziner.** (Kent refused to come work on it himself, because he was still protesting Massachusetts' execution of **Sacco** and **Vanzetti** in 1927; he did, however, show up to sign it.) The collaboration is a marvel of midnight blues, out of which fiery figures loom; Kent also designed the stage curtain as a golden sunburst that folds back like a Japanese fan. Even the seats (of which there are only 92) are out-of-the-ordinary: they're black leather armchairs with white linen antimacassars. Little wonder this luxury cinema, which opened on 1 July 1930, was chosen to host the world premiere of *The Wizard of Oz.* The cinematic fare is still select, hand-picked by well-known Boston art-house booker **George Mansour.** Even the refreshments are recherché: homebaked brownies and cookies, gourmet coffee, esoteric chocolates. And you can experience all this for no more than you'd blow at the local multiplex. ♦ M-Tu, Sa 7:30PM, Su 2PM late May to Oct. 385.4477

Cape Museum of Fine Arts This adjunct to the Playhouse complex, which opened in 1985, hasn't quite caught up with its peers. It has already acquired some 500 permanent works by Cape artists from 1900 to the present, ranging from some bad **Arthur Diehl** (a self-vaunting "speed painter" of the early 20th century, he actually produced some museum-worthy work) to a recent **Paul Resika,** a characteristically understated landscape titled *Long Point and Black Roof* (1988). Unfortunately, selections from the standing collection are mostly displayed in cramped and ill-lit hallways, while the main exhibition space is given over to transient shows, some (contemporary) of a questionable and seemingly cliquish quality. Perhaps it's best to reserve judgment until the institution has had more time to hit its stride. Meanwhile, there are classes, concerts, teas, trips, and film series to enjoy. ♦ Admission. Tu-Th 10AM-5PM, 7-9PM; F-Sa 10AM-5PM; Su 1-5PM. 385.4477

The Playhouse Restaurant ★★$$ A clubby atmosphere prevails here, too: fine if you're "in," a bit alienating if you're a rank newcomer. **Raymond Moore** envisioned this beamed bungalow (pictured above), now painted a soft peach and accented in chintz, as the Sardi's of Cape Cod, and some comparable caveats apply: you can't eat sketches of the stars. At least the menu is agreeably bistrolike and unpretentious, with neo-comfort foods like *Brie en croute* and chicken "pie" served in a carved-out bread bowl. The adjoining bar, presided over by co-managers **Pamela McMurtry** and **Bob Jones,** hosts irregular cabaret, and après-theater "late-nite bites" are served until midnight. ♦ American ♦ Dinner; lunch also on Wednesday and Thursday. Closed Monday, Tuesday, and Sunday Apr to late May, mid-Oct to Jan; closed Jan-Apr. Reservations recommended. 385.8000

35 Scargo Café ★★$$$ This rehabbed sea captain's house doesn't stand on ceremony. The rooms have been opened up into honey-paneled parlors, and there's also a pleasant glassed-in porch. The menu is divided into traditional and "adventurous," convenient for parties of mixed persuasion. The conservative might order baked stuffed sole, or quiche as fluffy and flaky as they come; the trail-blazer, "wildcat chicken" (sautéed with sweet Italian sausage, mushrooms, and raisins in apricot brandy). A fitting finish for both: a Grapenut pudding superb enough to appear in *Bon Appetit.* ♦ American/International ♦ Lunch and dinner. 799 Main St/Rte 6A (between Nobscusset and Corporation Rds), Dennis. 385.8200

36 The Red Pheasant Inn ★★★$$$ Since 1977, this marvelously atmospheric restaurant, an 18th-century ship's chandlery, has managed to remain cutting-edge contemporary. With chef-owner **Bill Atwood, Jr.,** in the kitchen (his father founded the restaurant) and his wife, **Denise,** seeing to the front with unusual grace, customers can relax into a truly extraordinary culinary experience. The decor is simplicity itself: low lighting, white tablecloths, a glassed-in garden room bursting with plants, and two hearths to take the chill off winter. Atwood's menu is inventive yet never overwrought: among the specialties he has evolved are cherrystone and scallop chowder scented with fresh thyme, fried goat cheese ravioli encased in zucchini pasta, and boneless duckling with a sauce of rhubarb, dried cherries, and caramelized ginger. Sensations like these keep customers returning year after year to be amazed anew. ♦ International ♦ Dinner. Closed Monday and Tuesday Jan-Mar. 905 Main St/Rte 6A (at Elm St), Dennis. 385.2133

37 **The Four Chimneys Inn** $ **Russell** and **Kathy Tomasetti** took over this B&B (the 1881 home of **Dr. Samuel Crowell**) in '93 and have rapidly put it to rights. It offered some nice material to work with, including big, airy spaces with 11-foot ceilings. The eight rooms of varying sizes have been spiffed up with stencilwork and wicker; for the location (**Scargo Lake** is across the street, the bay beach a 10-minute walk away), they're very reasonably priced. ♦ Closed Nov-Apr. 946 Main St/Rte 6A (between Elm St and Seaside Ave), Dennis. 385.6317

38 **Scargo Stoneware Pottery and Art Gallery** You'll be blinking in disbelief. Is this Big Sur, circa 1952? No, just **Harry Holl's** woodsy studio, where he's had his hand to the wheel all these years, rearing four daughters to join him in his craft. Their output spills out of the glass-topped showroom and into the bamboo-ringed grove: birdhouses camouflaged as castles, mosques, and basilicas; giant platters and planters; and sculptural pieces in an array of clays and glazes from delicate porcelain to earthy stoneware. Even if you're not in the market, come have a look; their handiwork has a way of restoring one's faith in human usefulness. ♦ Daily 10AM-6PM. 30 Dr. Lord Rd South (off Rte 6A), Dennis. 385.3894

39 **Scargo Tower** From atop this 28-foot stone tower, built on a 160-foot-high hill, you can see the entire sweep of the Cape's "arm," up to the clenched fist that is Provincetown. Constructed as an observatory for the **Nobscusset Hotel,** which was dismantled in the '30s, it was donated to the town as a memorial to the hotel owners. Bring your binoculars, or someone special to horizon-gaze with. Stretched out below is **Scargo Lake,** subject of dueling native legends. One version holds that the giant diety **Maushop** dug it to be remembered by. He piled the earth into a hill, where afterward he sat and smoked his pipe; the smoke created fog, and the ashes and spring rain nurtured nearby pines. A rather more romantic myth holds that an Indian princess received a pair of fish from a brave who was going away on a dangerous mission. When the fish outgrew their hollowed-out pumpkin bowl, she had four of her tribe's strongest braves shoot arrows to delineate the boundaries of a pond, which the squaws then dug out with clamshells. The fish prospered and multiplied, and her beloved returned home safe and sound. The question of origin aside, the lake does support abundant fish, including small-mouth bass and trout. ♦ Daily 6AM-10PM. Off Scargo Hill Rd (between Old Bass River Rd and Rte 6A), Dennis. No phone

Restaurants/Clubs: Red **Hotels:** Blue
Shops/ Outdoors: Green **Sights/Culture:** Black

40 **Webfoot Farm Antiques** This eclectic shop, housed in a 19th-century captain's house, has a wilder assortment than most. It's located right next-door to **Eldred's,** one of the Cape's premier auction houses, but owners **George** and **Diane King** also look farther afield for their plunder: there's quite a vast showing of Orientalia (including some antique kimonos), and among the larger pieces is a striking Spanish colonial desk with bowed, almost froglike legs. With prices ranging from $10 to $25,000, there are ample choices for any budget. Depending on your interests—outdoor accessories are also a forte—you could putter around contentedly for quite some time. ♦ Daily 10AM-5PM mid-June to Oct; M-Tu, Th-Su 10AM-5PM Oct to mid-June. 1475 Rte 6A (between Scargo Hill and East-West Dennis Rds). 385.2334

Bests

Wendy and Brantz Bryan

Owners, The Regatta of Falmouth By-the-Sea and The Regatta of Cotuit at The Crocker House

The secret beauty of Cape Cod lies north and south of routes 28 and 6. Be an adventurer and enjoy the true charm of Cape Cod on the small roads as you head toward the water, sitting on the docks in the harbors of **Falmouth, Woods Hole, Hyannis,** and **Chatham,** watching all the boats and people go by.

If you're staying on the Cape for more than five days, trips to our two sister islands are delightful. If you have to choose between **Martha's Vineyard** and **Nantucket,** by all means choose Nantucket, which has what is probably the quaintest and most beautiful historic downtown area in America (and has many great restaurants). Be sure to fly over early in the morning and fly back in the evening. The flight takes about 15 minutes and is worth every penny.

When it comes to fine restaurants, there are many to choose from throughout the Cape: **Regatta of Falmouth By-the-Sea** and **The Regatta of Cotuit at The Crocker House** in the Falmouth and Cotuit areas; **Alberto's** in Hyannis; **Chillingsworth** in Brewster; and **The Chatham Bars Inn** in Chatham.

Casual, fun eating places near and on the water include the **Popponesset Inn, Baxter's Fish-N-Chips,** the lovely **Thompson's Clam Bar,** the very special **Wharf Restaurant** in Falmouth Heights, and the **Clam Shack** at the Falmouth Harbor entrance.

Razor clams, so named because of their resemblance to old-fashioned straight razors, are technically edible, but no one has found a means of rendering them palatable. These critters also tend to slice tender feet (rather like razors), so take care when wandering the Cape Cod bay at low tide.

BREWSTER/HARWICH/CHATHAM/ORLEANS

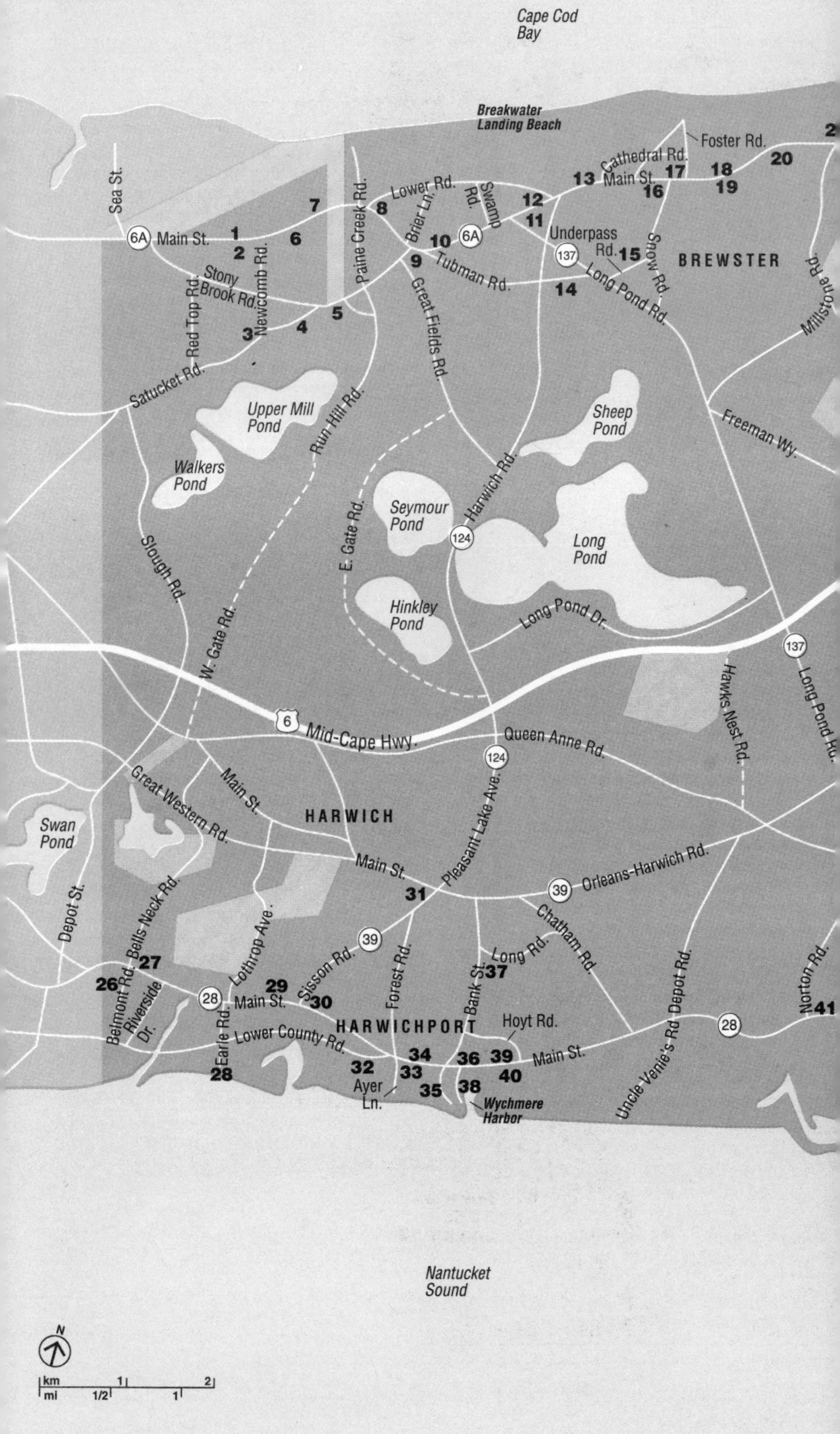

Cape Cod Bay

Breakwater Landing Beach

Foster Rd.

Cathedral Rd.

Main St.

Sea St.

Lower Rd.

Swamp Rd.

Paine Creek Rd.

Brier Ln.

6A Main St.

Underpass Rd.

137

Tubman Rd.

Long Pond Rd.

Snow Rd.

BREWSTER

Millstone Rd.

Stony Brook Rd.

Newcomb Rd.

Red Top Rd.

Great Fields Rd.

Satucket Rd.

Upper Mill Pond

Run Hill Rd.

Sheep Pond

Freeman Wy.

Walkers Pond

E. Gate Rd.

Seymour Pond

Harwich Rd.

124

Long Pond

Slough Rd.

Hinkley Pond

Long Pond Dr.

W. Gate Rd.

Hawks Nest Rd.

Long Pond Rd.

6 Mid-Cape Hwy.

Queen Anne Rd.

Great Western Rd.

Main St.

HARWICH

Pleasant Lake Ave.

Swan Pond

Main St.

Orleans-Harwich Rd.

39

Chatham Rd.

Depot St.

Bells Neck Rd.

Lothrop Ave.

Sisson Rd.

Forest Rd.

Long Rd.

Bank St.

Depot Rd.

Norton Rd.

Belmont Rd.

Riverside Dr.

28 Main St.

HARWICHPORT

Hoyt Rd.

Earle Rd.

Lower County Rd.

Main St.

Uncle Venie's Rd.

Ayer Ln.

Wychmere Harbor

1 2 3 4 5 6 7 8 9 10 11 12 13 14 15 16 17 18 19 20 26 27 28 29 30 31 32 33 34 35 36 37 38 39 40 41

Nantucket Sound

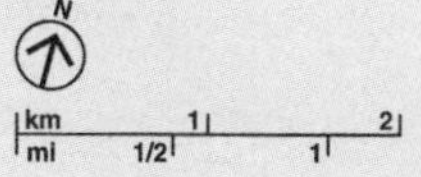

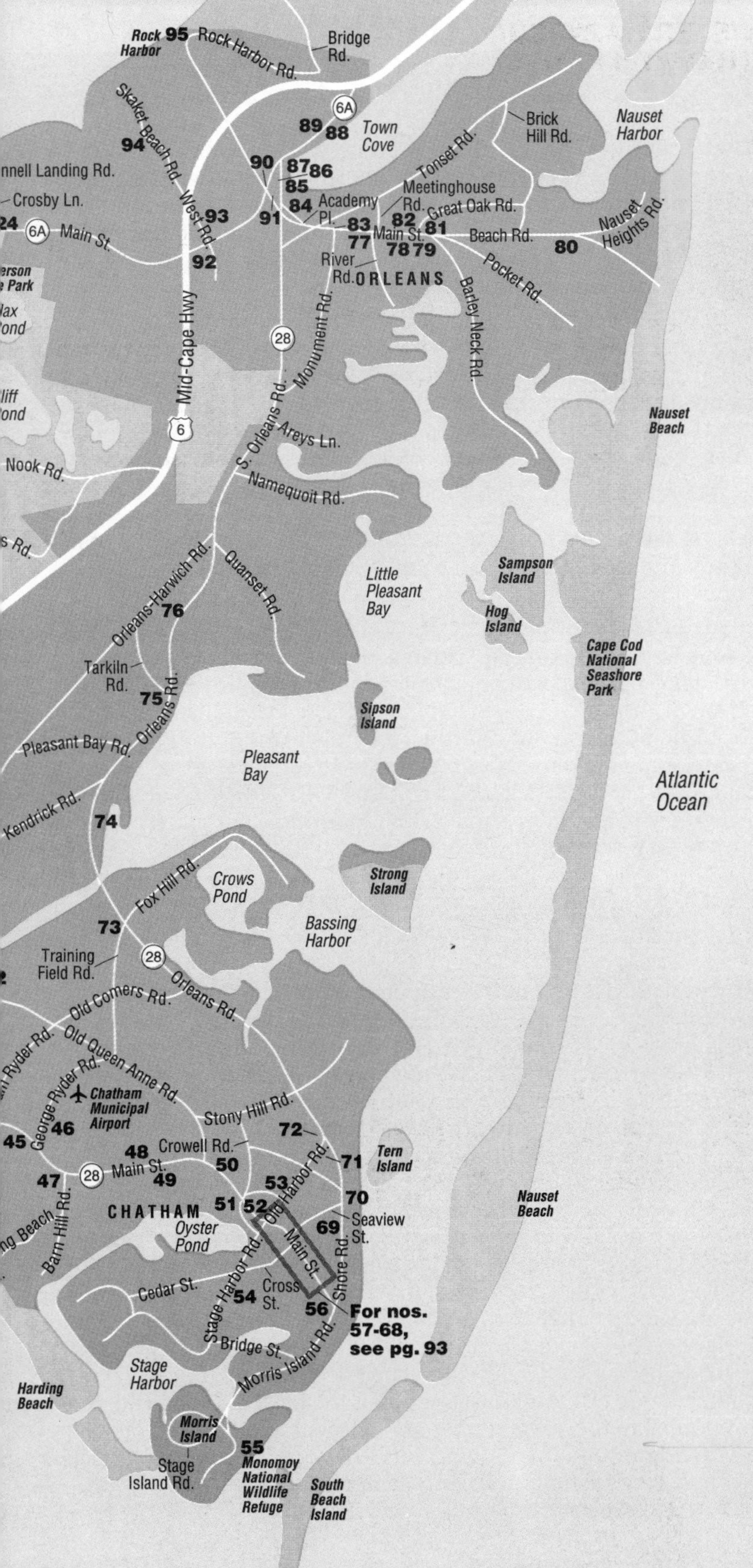
Rock Harbor
95
Rock Harbor Rd.
Bridge Rd.
6A
Town Cove
89 88
Skaket Beach Rd.
94
Brick Hill Rd.
Nauset Harbor
nnell Landing Rd.
Crosby Ln.
90
87 86
85
Tonset Rd.
Meetinghouse Rd.
West Rd.
93
91
84
Academy Pl.
82
Great Oak Rd.
24
6A
Main St.
83
81
Main St.
Beach Rd.
Nauset Heights Rd.
80
77
78 79
92
River Rd.
ORLEANS
Pocket Rd.
Barley Neck Rd.
Mid-Cape Hwy
28
Monument Rd.
6
S. Orleans Rd.
Areys Ln.
Nook Rd.
Namequoit Rd.
Nauset Beach
Little Pleasant Bay
Sampson Island
Hog Island
Orleans-Harwich Rd.
Quanset Rd.
76
Tarkiln Rd.
75
Orleans Rd.
Cape Cod National Seashore Park
Sipson Island
Pleasant Bay Rd.
Pleasant Bay
Atlantic Ocean
Kendrick Rd.
74
Crows Pond
Fox Hill Rd.
Strong Island
Bassing Harbor
73
Training Field Rd.
28
Orleans Rd.
Old Comers Rd.
Old Queen Anne Rd.
George Ryder Rd.
Chatham Municipal Airport
Stony Hill Rd.
72
46
45
48
Crowell Rd.
Tern Island
71
50
47
28
Main St.
49
53
Old Harbor Rd.
70
Nauset Beach
Barn Hill Rd.
CHATHAM
51 52
69
Seaview St.
Oyster Pond
Main St.
Shore Rd.
Stage Harbor Rd.
Cedar St.
Cross St.
54
56
For nos. 57-68, see pg. 93
Bridge St.
Morris Island Rd.
Stage Harbor
Harding Beach
Morris Island
55
Stage Island Rd.
Monomoy National Wildlife Refuge
South Beach Island

Brewster/Harwich/Chatham/ Orleans

The four towns clustered near the elbow of the Cape are among the prettiest summer colonies in the Northeast, each with a unique history and character. **Brewster** (named for *Mayflower* passenger **Elder William Brewster** of the Plymouth Colony) was part of **Harwich** until 1803, when the towns split apart at the instigation of Brewster's prosperous sea captains, who wished to dissociate from their poor neighbors to the south. Harwich went on to pioneer the cranberry industry, however, which took off as the maritime trades began to decline, so the towr fortunes eventually evened out.

Despite the incursion of condominiums (fortunately, hidden from view for the most part) and the proximity of **Nickerson State Park**, Brewster retains i air of calm gentility; its hills and dales and scattering of small ponds make it seem more like open country than a seaside resort. The waters off Brewster's eight bay beaches are shallow and gentle, just right for little kids; at low tide the ocean recedes by as much as two miles, leaving behind a huge salty playground striated with colorful "garnet" sand, so named for its reddish streaks. Harwich, which enjoys the slightly livelier surf of the Sound, has resisted the development that plagues the more westerly stretches of Route 2 and although suffering a bit from post-'80s slump (several tourist enterprises went under), it's well poised to recover gradually and gracefully.

The coast of **Chatham**, known as "the First Stop of the East Wind," was visite by explorer **Samuel de Champlain** in 1606. But **Monomoyick**, as it was the called, did not attract a permanent colony until 1656, when **William Nickerson** of Yarmouth bought land from the sachem chief **Mattaquason**; upon incorporating in 1712, the town took the name of the English earl of Chatham. Perhaps because it's less accessible than the other communities on the Cape, Chatham has remained a cohesive village with a Main Street that's chockablock with attractive shops. This is one of the few places, short of Provincetown, where you'll see throngs out on the street for an evening strol and the band concerts on Friday nights in summer are legendary, drawing crowds of 5,000 or more.

Orleans, the only town on the Cape that does not have an Indian or English name, was settled in 1644. When the hamlet separated from Eastham in 179 the citizens named it for **Louis-Philippe de Bourbon**, duke of Orleans, who had visited that year during his exile; four decades later, he would become king of France. Orleans was targeted by the British during the War of 1812 an again in 1918 by a German sub; it's the only place in the continental United States to have suffered enemy fire in either World War. Today, the skirmishes are of a different sort. As a heavily traveled area (it's here that Routes 6, 6A, and 28S meet), Orleans is half commercial hub and half bourgeois enclave, with no clear identity either way and plenty of p.ressure to topple into the former. Although there are charming restaurants and stores scattered about, they're hard to reach without getting trapped in seemingly inescapable traffi where your chances of executing a left turn are about as good as spotting sno in July. The flow lightens somewhat to the east of town, until you hit **Nauset Beach**, along the southernmost part of the **Cape Cod National Seashore** (a 40-mile preserve that extends along the entire outer length of the Cape's "forearm"). There are other, less populated stretches of sand farther up the coast, but because Nauset is the closest, it is the most crowded and as such th most appealing to those who *want* to mingle with their peers. You guessed it: teenagers and twentysomethings, as far as the eye can see, with just a few families and elders permitted among them.

1 The Spectrum Two **Rhode Island School of Design** grads started this enterprise in a country schoolhouse in 1966 and quickly developed it into a premier purveyor of crafts, with shops as far-flung as Palm Beach. The split-level store is very late-'60s, with its sculpture gardens and expanses of plate glass. The stock is accessible and appealing, from **Josh Simpson's** glass-marble "planets" to **Thomas Mann's** totemic "techno-romantic" jewelry, old-fashioned charms gone awry. ♦ Daily 9:30AM-5:30PM July-Aug; M-Sa 10AM-5:30PM, Su 12:30-5:30PM Sept to mid-Oct, May-June; M-Sa 10AM-5PM, Su 12:30-5:30PM mid-Oct to Jan; M-Sa 10AM-5PM Jan-Apr. 369 Main St/Rte 6A (between Stony Brook and Newcomb Rds), W. Brewster. 385.3322, 800/221.2472. Also at: 342 Main St, Hyannis. 771.4554; 26 Main St, Nantucket. 228.4606

2 Kingsland Manor Antiques There's only one thing to be said about **Doris** and **Norman Schepp's** ivy-cloaked antiques shop, which offers an array of goods from tin to Tiffany: it won't leave you neutral. This place is over the top, with Oriental carpets layered several deep, and oddities as varied as matching baby elephant foot ashtrays ($350 a pair) and an antique medical exam table (slightly shy of $3,000). You can even buy a carved Victorian bar—for a mere $20,000. Mixed in with the outrageous items are some impressive big pieces with equally big price tags. ♦ Daily 9AM-5PM. 440 Main St/Rte 6A (between Stony Brook and Newcomb Rds), W. Brewster. 385.9741

3 Underground Gallery In this amazingly light and airy studio/bunker, 10 massive tree trunks support 200 tons of earth, plus a sprinkling of wildflowers. **Karen North Wells** creates realistic watercolors and lithographs of local sights; underground architect/avatar **Malcolm Wells** fills mail orders for his enormously successful books (from 1977's bestselling *Underground Design* to his delightful booklet *Sandcastles*) and executes impressionistic landscapes in plain latex house paint. His paintings sell for $40 to $1,000, but occasionally he puts a "free" tag on, "just to lighten things up a bit." ♦ Daily noon-5PM. 673 Satucket Rd (at Newcomb Rd), W. Brewster. 896.6850

4 High Brewster $$$ This 1738 homestead on 3½ acres shows its history in its intimate, low-ceilinged rooms. There's limited common space beyond the dining rooms (and the rock garden overlooking placid **Lower Mill Pond**), so you might want to consider staying over purely as a post-prandial treat—unless you reserve one of the three roomy cottages, which are full-scale country retreats. The four rooms in the inn itself are a steep hike upstairs, and, although charmingly decorated, they are far from spacious and a bit pricey for the square footage. However, inn guests do get to indulge in the rather spectacular breakfasts. ♦ Closed Jan. 964 Satucket Rd (between Newcomb and Stony Brook Rds), W. Brewster. 896.3636

Within High Brewster:

High Brewster Restaurant ★★★$$$$ The five-course, prix fixe dinner changes every other week to take advantage of seasonal offerings, but chef **Elizabeth White's** creations are invariably bold and robustly flavored. In early summer, for instance, you might partake of pan-seared duck breast with a pear demi-glace and buttermilk spaetzle, accompanied by local greens tossed with sweet marjoram vinaigrette and garnished with pea tendrils and chive flowers. You'll marvel at the variety. The three small dining rooms, with ladderback chairs, antique paneling, ceilings close enough to touch, and glowing candlelight are romance incarnate. ♦ New American ♦ Dinner. Closed Monday and Tuesday Feb to mid-May, mid-Sept to Jan; closed Jan. Reservations recommended. 896.3636

5 Stony Brook Grist Mill and Museum The 1663 original, the oldest water-powered mill in America, is long gone, and this circa 1873 model, built of saltworks salvage, started grinding corn only after it had exhausted its usefulness in the manufacture of overalls and ice cream. In other words, the building is not especially venerable, but it is one of the few vestiges of the **Factory Village** that thrived here in the 19th century. Also, the volunteer grinders are so enthusiastic, and so good at involving young children in the process ("You could run this place!" they're often told), that families might want to make a special stop. Upstairs is a pleasantly musty, eclectic museum featuring everything from a five-inch quartz arrowhead (tools dating back 10 millennia have been unearthed nearby) to a monumental 100-year-old loom; you might catch a weaving demo in progress. There's a pretty walkway around the millpond, and in spring, thousands of alewife herrings can be seen leaping the natural rock ladder to spawn. ♦ Free. Th-Sa 2-5PM July-Aug. 830 Stony Brook Rd (between Newcomb and Paine Creek Rds), W. Brewster. No phone

> "On the beach there is a ceaseless activity, always something going on, in storm and in calm, winter and summer, night and day."
>
> **Henry David Thoreau,** ***Cape Cod***

6 Punkhorn Bookshop Unlike most of its ilk, **David L. Luebke's** rare and used bookstore is extremely tidy and well organized. Instead of languishing in dusty piles, his stock sits upright on ample shelving, grouped by the Dewey Decimal system and wrapped in protective translucent covers by his wife, **Irene,** a bookbinder. Specialties include natural history and New England regional titles; there's also a section featuring decorative bindings, and an intriguing selection of prints. ♦ M-Sa 10AM-5PM late May to mid-Oct; by appointment mid-Oct to late May. 672 Main St/Rte 6A (between Newcomb and Paine Creek Rds), Brewster. 896.2114

6 Brewster Farmhouse Inn $$ **Robert Messina** and **Joseph Zelich** took over this small, luxurious inn in 1992 and have polished it up even further. The Greek Revival facade, with its striped awnings, may look a trifle stodgy, but step inside and you'll feel as if you've been transported to California—the space is awash with light and inviting down-filled sofas in soft neutral tones; a pool and hot tub beckon from beyond the expansive wooden deck. The five rooms share the same restful color scheme and center on dramatic canopied or hand-carved beds. Breakfasts are a feast, featuring such delicacies as homemade croissants and cheese blintzes with raspberry puree and fresh figs; teatime summons a fresh parade of treats, such as nectarine *clafouti.* The only difficulty will be tearing yourself away to enjoy some sightseeing. ♦ 716 Main St/Rte 6A (between Newcomb and Paine Creek Rds), Brewster. 896.3910, 800/892.3910

7 Harris-Black House and Higgins Farm Windmill That an entire family fit in this 1795 one-room half-Cape house, only 16 feet square, is amazing enough; then consider the fact that barber/blacksmith **Nathan Black** managed to raise 10 children here. The 30-foot-tall octagonal windmill, also built in 1795, is remarkable not only for its smocklike silhouette (popular in England when the Pilgrims set sail) but for its unusual boat-shaped cap, curved like a ship's hull. Knowledgeable members of the **Brewster Historical Society** are on hand to answer your questions. ♦ Donation. Tu-F 1-4PM July-Aug; Sa-Su 1-4PM May-June, Sept-Oct. 785 Main St/Rte 6A (between Newcomb and Paine Creek Rds), Brewster. 896.9521

7 Cape Cod Museum of Natural History Founded in 1954 by naturalist writer **John Hay,** this marvelous museum has long been in the vanguard of interactive exhibits. Children and adults alike will be fascinated by the "live hive" (a see-through working beehive) and the "window on the marsh," where myriad birds come to feed. For an even more active experience, venture out to the museum's 82 acres, transected by three trails: the 1/4-mile **North Trail** crosses a salt marsh; the 1/2-mile **South Trail** wanders through cattails, cranberries, and beech trees; and the 1.3-mile **John Wing Trail** (named for the town founder) leads to an untouched bay beach. In addition to permanent exhibits (the whale display is especially strong, enlivened with a tape of leviathan vocalizations), the museum schedules numerous special events, including children's and family programs, lectures, concerts, "eco-treks," and cruises of **Nauset Marsh** and the **Monomoy Islands;** there's even a sleepover at a Monomoy lighthouse, billed as "the ultimate Cape Cod experience." ♦ Admission. M-Sa 9:30AM-4:30PM, Su 12:30-4:30PM mid-Apr to mid-Oct; Tu-Sa 9:30AM-4:30PM, Su 12:30-4:30PM mid-Oct to mid-Apr. 869 Main St/Rte 6A (between Newcomb and Paine Creek Rds), Brewster. 896.3867, 800/479.3867

8 The Cook Shop If it has anything to do with food, you're likely to find it here: picnic hampers, cookbooks, professional-caliber pots and pans, blocks of French sink soap, weighty Italian pottery, tortilla warmers—no culinary tool is too exotic for inclusion. There's also an extensive and tempting array of gourmet staples. ♦ M-Sa 10AM-5:30PM; Su noon-5:30PM. 1091 Main St/Rte 6A (between Paine Creek Rd and Brier Ln), Brewster. 896.7689

8 Pranzo ★★$ For a delicious light lunch, grab a *panino* at this charming little deli/cafe run by chef/owner **Virginia Reiser.** The unusual sandwiches, offered on fresh-baked rolls, range from grilled eggplant and prosciutto to roast chicken with sliced apples and chutney. The mix-and-match salads are even more enticing: the lemon-dill potato salad is substantial yet lyrical, the cold Thai noodles in spicy satay sauce surprisingly cooling. Photos of Italian scenes adorn the walls, and postcards have been slipped under the glass tabletops; one visitor added the scribbled comment *"proprio elegante,"* which perfectly describes this exceptional fast food. ♦ Deli ♦ M-Sa 10AM-5:30PM, Su 9AM-4:30PM Apr-Oct. 1097 Main St/Rte 6A (between Paine Creek Rd and Brier Ln), Brewster. 896.9350

Restaurants/Clubs: Red | **Hotels:** Blue
Shops/ Outdoors: Green | **Sights/Culture:** Black

9 **Beechcroft Inn** $ **Linda** and **Richard Hoffman** took over this venerable inn in 1993. The building was the town's original 1828 Universalist meetinghouse; after being moved and having its steeple lopped off, it became an inn in 1852. The decor was in dire need of freshening when the Hoffmans arrived, but they have the project well in hand. The 10 rooms, all named for native wildflowers, are adorned with wicker and stenciling, and the whole place now enjoys the advantage of affable hosts. ♦ Closed Jan. 1360 Main St/Rte 6A (at Tubman Rd), Brewster. 896.9534

Within the Beechcroft Inn:

Beechcroft Inn Restaurant ★★$$$$ **Richard Hoffman** is putting his Cordon Bleu training to good use in an ambitious, classically influenced menu featuring oysters sabayon (warmed with champagne sauce) and grilled sea scallops with cranberry beurre blanc. If the decor does not yet live up to the cuisine, it surely will in time. ♦ French ♦ Dinner. Closed Monday mid-May to mid-Sept; closed Monday through Wednesday mid-Sept to Jan, Feb to mid-May. Reservations recommended. 896.9534

10 **New England Fire & History Museum** There's an endearingly homespun quality to the exhibits here, from the mannequins representing firefighters through the ages (since 226 BC) to a diorama of the Chicago Fire of 1871. In addition to the 30-odd antique fire engines and the late Boston Pops maestro **Arthur Fiedler's** helmet collection, there are a few unrelated exhibits such as a reproduction smithy and apothecary shop. Adults not interested in the topic may find themselves underwhelmed, but children invariably lap it up. The gift shop features, not too surprisingly, fire chief hats and toy engines. ♦ Admission. M-Sa 10AM-4PM, Su noon-4PM late May to mid-Oct. 1429 Main St/Rte 6A (between Brier Ln and Swamp Rd), Brewster. 896.5711

11 **Brewster Ladies' Library** Stirred to action by two public-spirited 17-year-olds, **Augusta Mayo** and **Mary Louise Cobb,** a dozen Brewster ladies established a "library"—rather, a shelf of books available for loan—in Miss Mayo's home in 1852. With financial assistance from local sea captains, they were able to move the growing collection into this picturesque yellow Victorian (see above) in 1868. The building has since expanded several times, but the two original front parlors, each with a fireplace, stenciled stained glass, and enveloping armchairs, are still good places to sit out a storm with a riveting book. You might also inquire about lectures and story hours. ♦ Tu-W 9AM-1PM, 6-9PM, Th-Sa 9AM-1PM late June to early Sept; Tu-W noon-8PM, Th-F 10AM-4PM, Sa 10AM-2PM early Sept to late June. 1822 Main St/Rte 6A (between Rtes 137 and 124), Brewster. 896.3913

12 **The Old Manse Inn** $ Built for **Captain Winslow Lewis Knowles** in the early 1800s, this imposing house enjoyed a checkered career as an **Underground Railroad** stopover and a Lutheran chapel before becoming an inn in 1945. **Sugar** and **Doug Manchester** took over in 1980 and turned it into a top-notch, nine-room B&B, with traditional decor and a superlative restaurant. Breakfast may be savory, but dinner is a must. ♦ Closed Jan to mid-Apr. 1861 Main St/Rte 6A (between Rtes 137 and 124), Brewster. 896.3149

Within The Old Manse Inn:

The Old Manse Inn Restaurant ★★★$$$$ The executive chef is the proprietors' daughter-in-law, **Ruth Manchester,** whose own restaurant is at **The Bramble Inn,** just up the road. The acting chef is her daughter, **Sue Johnson,** who trained at the Culinary Institute of America and favors the cuisine of the Mediterranean. You might start with grilled shrimp wrapped in prosciutto, accompanied by melon and fig *romescu,* then move on to lobster Milano (an elaborate preparation involving risotto and porcini duxelle, plus sautéed foie gras) or refreshing grilled lamb Mechoui (marinated in mint, lemon, garlic, cumin, and orange zest) with roasted eggplant-pepper jam. If possible, opt to eat on the screened sunporch, surrounded by fragrant perennials. ♦ New American ♦ Dinner. Closed Monday and Sunday; closed mid-May to mid-Oct; closed Monday through Thursday and Sunday mid-Oct to Jan; closed Jan to mid-May. Reservations recommended. 896.3149

13 **The Brewster Store** This genial general store started out as an 1852 Universalist church, which was sold in 1858 because of declining membership. In 1866, proprietor **W.W. Knowles** removed the top of the tower and extended the front corners to make it look more storelike, but luckily he didn't touch the magnificent arched windows on the second floor. Today, the ambience is rather hokey but jolly; kids go nuts here (a lot of the touristic gewgaws fit their budgets), and thrown in among the Cape Cod mementos are some fairly useful kitchen gadgets and beach gear. Drop a dime in the "Nickelodeon," a

piano-less player-piano machine, and peruse your reserved newspaper in one of the church pews arranged out front. ♦ Daily 6AM-10PM July-Aug; daily 7AM-5PM Sept-June. 1935 Main St/Rte 6A (at Rte 124), Brewster. 896.3744

13 The Captain Freeman Inn $$$ If you tend to associate B&Bs with penury (no TV, minimal privacy), you owe it to yourself to try one of the three suites at this 12-bedroom, circa 1866 Victorian mansion. Innkeeper **Carol Covitz,** a former computer exec, has thought of everything: each suite comes with a canopied queen-size four-poster; loveseat; cable television with VCR and a long list of movies; mini-fridge stocked with soda; and, on an enclosed balcony, a clover-shaped whirlpool bath. "People often come for a week or more," she says, and it's no wonder.

Covitz is serious about food and attended the Grand Master Chefs program to prepare for her new vocation. The upshot is a lavish yet lowfat breakfast—served in summer on a screened porch overlooking the pool—that runs from eggs Brewster (smoked salmon and poached eggs on a cranberry English muffin with orange hollandaise) to fresh corn pancakes and sausage-and-pepper quiche. During winter, guest chefs conduct cooking-school weekends, where participants feast on their own handiwork. **Captain William Freeman,** a prosperous clipper shipmaster whose command included the *Kingfisher* (hence the inn's logo), designed the striking herringbone-pattern floors in the parlor. The second-story rooms have the unusual feature of windows that start at the floor, which render the spaces wonderfully cozy. On the third floor, you'll find smaller rooms tucked under the eaves, but they have a pared-down charm of their own, and beautiful views; available only in summer, they're very reasonably priced. **Breakwater Beach,** whence packet boats used to ply the bay to Boston, is a bucolic stroll away. ♦ 15 Breakwater Rd (at Rte 6A), Brewster. 896.7481, 800/843.4664

On 12 July 1918, a German submarine surfaced three miles off Nauset Inlet, sinking four barges and a tug before sending several shells toward town (one struck land). Though most of the Chatham Naval Air Station crew was engaged in a baseball game in Provincetown that particular day, two seaplanes managed to drop four retaliatory bombs that missed their mark but scared the sub away.

13 First Parish Church This 1834 white clapboard church, a mixture of Greek and Gothic Revival styles, is the second replacement for the 1700 original built for fiery preacher **Nathaniel Stone.** The pews are marked with prominent captains' names, and the burial ground out back contains many a notable headstone, including that of **Captain David Nickerson** and one **"Rene Rousseau."** Folklore has it that Nickerson was presented with an infant during the French Revolution and asked to raise him; it was rumored that the child was the lost *dauphin,* son of **Louis XVI** and **Marie Antoinette.** Rousseau became a captain himself and was lost at sea; his name is carved on the back of Nickerson's gravestone, as was the custom. Now a Unitarian Universalist church, First Parish hosts two popular traditions in July and August: traditional chowder suppers Wednesday evenings at 6PM, and Mimsy puppet shows for children Thursday mornings at 10AM. ♦ Services Su 9AM, 11AM. 1969 Main St/Rte 6A (between Rte 124 and Cathedral Rd), Brewster. 896.5577

13 The Bramble Inn $$ Twelve rooms and a suite are housed in three buildings (shown above) dating from 1861, 1849, and 1792. The rooms come in "all shapes and sizes," says innkeeper **Cliff Manchester,** who opened the Bramble in 1985, following his parents' lead at the **Old Manse.** The two "younger" houses are decorated in a country mode, with brass beds and wicker; the Federal house gets the full formal treatment, with elegant wallpapers and four-posters with crochet canopies. The equestrian-motif suite takes the prize, though, with exposed beams and horsey paraphernalia. Overnight guests are the beneficiaries of **Ruth Manchester's** considerable skill in the kitchen: morning repasts might include apple pancakes or chèvre-Roquefort tart. ♦ Closed mid-Jan to mid-Mar. 2019 Main St/Rte 6A (between Rte 124 and Cathedral Rd), Brewster. 896.7644

Within The Bramble Inn:

The Bramble Inn Restaurant

★★★$$$$ Every antique table setting is unique, as is the decor in each of five small dining rooms, from a pink-striped sunporch to a wood-paneled tack room and a formal parlor with pheasant motif. The personal attention that informs the setting also infuses the food. Chef **Ruth Manchester** has an exploratory bent, and her menu has evolved over the years from inventive nouvelle to daring world-beat. The four-course prix fixe menu, which changes monthly, typically offers a half-dozen appetizers and as many entrées, ranging from chilled white gazpacho to grilled Gulf shrimp with jalapeño glaze or a house variation on bouillabaisse with a tomato saffron *fumé*. The dessert selection is exquisite: make sure at least one person in your party orders the signature white chocolate *coeur à la crème* so you can all sample. ♦ New American ♦ Dinner. Closed Monday mid-Sept to mid-Oct; closed Monday through Wednesday mid-Oct to Dec, mid-Apr to mid-May; closed Monday through Thursday and Sunday Dec; closed Jan to mid-Apr. Reservations required. 896.7644

14 **Bassett Wild Animal Farm** Opened in the early '60s and owned by **Gail Smithson** since 1978, this mini-zoo located in a 20-acre oak grove has the comfortable look and feel of a backyard enterprise. Peacocks (including some white ones) wander around in full display, and an African lion and a mountain cougar pace menacingly behind a chainlink fence. There's an enclosed petting area where goats roam free, looking for a handout, and patient ponies plod in a circle. Little kids will take it all in with wonder; slightly older kids might question whether these "natural surroundings" are really fair to the animals. ♦ Admission. Daily 10AM-5PM mid-May to mid-Sept. 620 Tubman Rd (off Rte 124), Brewster. 896.3224

15 **Rail Trail Bike Shop** One of the better-stocked shops along the trail, this store has all the basics, maintained at top condition, plus child carriers and trailers in snazzy neon green and pink. "We get people from all over the world," says manager **Daniel Poitras.** One reason why may be the ample free parking; another the propinquity of **Mano's.** ♦ Daily 8AM-6PM Apr-Oct. 302 Underpass Rd (at Snow Rd), Brewster. 896.8200

15 **Mano's Pizza & More** ★$ The "more" includes grinders and gyros, pastitsio and spinach pie, tacos and nachos; there's even pasta, for pre-marathon carbo-loading. And for bringing that blood sugar backup: honey-suffused baklava. ♦ International ♦ Lunch and dinner. 302 Underpass Rd (at Snow Rd), Brewster. 896.8600

16 **Brewster Fish House** ★★★$$$ It's roadside-ordinary on the outside, small and nautically neat on the inside, with a minuscule bar that seats five and a handful of hunter-green tables encircled by burnished Windsor chairs. It's not until you get your hands on the menu that the restaurant's self-characterization as "nonconforming" becomes clear. There aren't very many places on the Cape where you can sample fried artichokes or barbecued squid with garlic-and-ginger ketchup, say, or a mixed grill (swordfish, shrimp, scallops, and Andouille sausage) with a dipping sauce of soy, sesame, and molasses. For a jazzy dessert, try the chocolate espresso torte. ♦ New American ♦ Lunch and dinner. Closed Monday through Wednesday Apr-May, mid-Oct to Dec; closed Dec-Mar. 2208 Main St/Rte 6A (between Point of Rocks and Snow Rds), Brewster. 896.7867

17 **Chillingsworth** $$ Three Ralph Lauren-accoutered rooms are available in this 1689 homestead reputedly built by a *Mayflower* passenger, but the main draw is indisputably the restaurant. If you're looking forward to being temporarily immobilized by the feast of a lifetime, these chambers, with their eclectic antiques, make a pleasant and convenient place to crash. ♦ Closed late Nov to late May. 2449 Main St/Rte 6A (between Snow and Foster Rds), Brewster. 896.3640

Within Chillingsworth:

Chillingsworth Restaurant ★★★★$$$$ Supremely elegant and agreeably eccentric, Chillingsworth has long been the Cape's premier restaurant. The seven-course prix fixe dinner unfolds at two seatings in a warren of candlelit, salonlike dining rooms appointed with antiques (some as early as Louis XV). Chef-owner **Robert Rabin** revises the menu daily to make the most of market offerings, and he stands ready to produce any of a dozen appetizers and as many entrées, along with soup, salad, sorbet, and pre-dessert amusements. Narrowing down the menu can be torment: for starters, should you try the snails with tomatoes, hazelnuts, garlic, sage, and brandied green peppercorn sauce, or a foie gras, *haricots verts,* jicama, and arugula salad with warm truffle vinaigrette? Remember to pace yourself for the main course (veal loin with saffron risotto and garlic custard, perhaps, or venison with celery-root puree and sun-dried cranberries) and the assorted killer desserts, the deadliest of which is Chocolate Nemesis drizzled with *crème anglaise.* If eating were a competitive sport (one sometimes wonders), this would qualify as the Olympics, with all due pomp and circumstance. ♦ French ♦ Lunch and dinner. Closed Monday July-Aug; closed Friday through Sunday late May to July, Sept to late Nov; closed late Nov to late May. Jacket requested at dinner; reservations required. 896.3640

Le Bistrot For a lighter repast, grab some goodies to go or a complete take-home meal at this retail counter, which also offers an intriguing assortment of antiques. Or stop in just to preview the desserts: raspberry crème brûlée, fresh plum cobbler, chocolate Bavarian cream pie. . . . It's hard to leave empty-handed. ♦ M 9:30AM-5:30PM, Tu-Su 9:30AM-noon July-Aug; Sa-Su 9:30AM-11PM late May to July, Sept to late Nov. 896.3640

18 **Old Sea Pines Inn** $$ This 1907 shingle-style mansion (pictured above) on 3½ acres was originally the **Sea Pines School of Charm and Personality for Young Women**, and owners **Michele** and **Steve Rowan** have hosted some nostalgiac graduates. Mostly, though, the clientele consists of urban escapees seeking a respite from modern-day stress. The main house is preserved at its 1930s apogee, with green cane rockers set out on the wraparound porch; the rooms here range from spacious to rather cramped and are priced accordingly. The guesthouse annex is wheelchair-accessible and more contemporary in decor, featuring cheery floral prints and (why not?) pink TVs. ♦ Closed Jan-Mar. 2553 Main St/Rte 6A (between Foster and Millstone Rds), Brewster. 896.6114

Within the Old Sea Pines Inn:

Old Sea Pines Inn Restaurant ★★$$$ "It's not trendy, not nouvelle, not anything," says innkeeper **Steve Rowan,** who doubles as chef. The closest he'll come to characterizing his cuisine is "Grandmother's Sunday best." That means standbys such as clam chowder, scrod, and scallops, with nothing fancier for dessert than strawberry shortcake or profiteroles. With '20s and '30s tapes playing on the stereo, many diners will indeed be reminded of weekends at Grandma's. ♦ American ♦ Dinner. Closed early Sept to July. Reservations recommended. 896.6114

18 **The Tower House Restaurant** ★★$$ The menu is middle-of-the-road, but the prices are reasonable, the staff pleasant, and the setting handsome, with dramatic wrought-iron chandeliers and French-blue napery. In summer, everyone competes for porch space. If you crave straightforward fish—baked, poached,

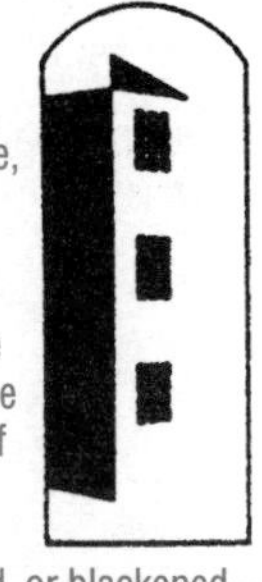

sautéed, broiled, charbroiled, or blackened—that hankering will be well met here. They also do a nice job with mussels, tossing them with garlic, butter, wine, and pesto over spinach fettuccine. ♦ American ♦ Breakfast, lunch, and dinner. 2671 Main St/Rte 6A (between Foster and Millstone Rds), Brewster. 896.2671

19 **Great Cape Cod Herb, Spice & Tea Co.** Herbalist **Stephan Brown's** "natural apothecary" dates back only to 1991, but native Cape dwellers who died out or were driven off hundreds of years ago would recognize here some of their favored natural remedies such as burdock and sassafras. The store stocks more than 140 herbs, some incorporated in Brown's custom-blended teas, ranging from Monomoy Morning to Wellfleetian Whispers. This rustic shed also serves, perforce, as a New Age nexus. It's open on occasion as an all-natural coffeehouse, and Brown conducts regular classes as well as "weed walks" Saturdays at 10AM June through September. ♦ M-Sa 9AM-5:30PM; Su 10AM-5:30PM. 2628 Main St/Rte 6A (between Snow and Millstone Rds), Brewster. 896.5900

20 **Ocean Edge** $$$ This 380-acre resort-and-condo complex—plus the 1,700-acre **Nickerson State Park** to the east—is all that's left of the vast **Roland C. Nickerson** estate. **Samuel Mayo Nickerson,** a Chatham native, headed west in 1847 as a young man with no money to his name; within 16 years, he helped found the **First National Bank of Chicago.** In 1890, he built a magnificent shingle-and-stone mansion, **Fieldstone Hall,** for his only son, Roland; boasting a nine-hole golf course, a game preserve, and its own horse-powered electric plant, it was a magnet for nobs throughout New England. The mansion burned to the ground in 1906 and Roland died two weeks later. In 1908, his widow, **Addie,** started rebuilding—this time with fireproof steel-reinforced concrete covered with stucco, in a mix of Renaissance Revival and Gothic styles.

The 400-foot-long house, with its overscale rooms and intricately carved oak trim, remained in the family until 1942, when it was sold to the **LaSalette Fathers** for use as a seminary. It was bought by **Corocoran, Mullins, Jennison, Inc.** in 1980 and converted to its present use as a conference center. While this Gilded Age relic has been preserved, it's been hemmed in by characterless condos. Those clustered oppressively around the mansion, with a matching color scheme of dun walls and red tarpaper roofs, resemble a Caribbean resort, with a 1,000-foot private beach, five Har-Tru tennis courts, and a fitness center. Across Route 6A and west a bit is the rest of the complex: a championship golf course, six "all-weather" (i.e., asphalt) tennis courts, an assortment of indoor and outdoor pools, and condos, condos, condos—17 "villages" in all.

They're attractive enough, but so, no doubt, was this land before it was developed. ♦ 2660 Main St/Rte 6A (between Snow and Millstone Rds), Brewster. 896.9000, 800/343.6074

Within Ocean Edge:

Mulligans Restaurant ★★$$$ The glassed-in architecture is light and airy, the green-and-rose chintz accents pretty, but if you're at all uncomfortable crashing a country club where you don't belong, this might not be the best place to go. The restaurant operates independently of the resort, and chef/owner **Jake Jacobus** turns out interesting dishes, such as smoked duck spring roll, and almond-crusted sole with grapefruit, scallions, and beurre blanc. Still, unless you're captivated by a view of hearty golfers puttering about in their carts, it's hard to overlook the venue for the menu. ♦ New American ♦ Lunch and dinner; Sunday brunch. Closed Monday and Tuesday mid-Mar to late May, early Sept to Dec; closed Monday through Thursday Nov-Dec; closed Jan to mid-Mar. 832 Villages Dr (off Rte 6A or 137), Brewster. Reservations recommended. 896.8521

21 **Cobie's** ★$ If this silver-shingled clam shack looks like a classic, that's because it is one, dating back to 1948. Regulars have been known to drive long distances for the fried clams, and **Rail Trail** cyclists hardly have to break stride to enjoy a snack at the picnic tables on the porch. ♦ American ♦ Lunch and dinner. Closed mid-Sept to late May. 3260 Main St/Rte 6A (between Millstone and Linnell Landing Rds), E. Brewster. 896.7021

22 **Brewster Historical Society Museum** This small but touching collection, housed in an 1840 homestead, features snippets of the past: an 1884 barbershop, the old **East Brewster Post Office,** an assortment of dolls and toys, and a doll-size reproduction of the town's oldest dwelling, the 1660 **Dillingham House.** It's worth a brief look around before you head off on the **Spruce Hill Trail,** a 1/4-mile nature walk over the dunes to the bay. The wide grassy path was once a carriage road and, it is rumored, a conduit for bootleggers during Prohibition. ♦ Free. Museum: Tu-Su 1-4PM July-Aug; Sa-Su 1-4PM May-June, Sept-Oct. Trail: daily sunrise-sunset. 3341 Main St/Rte 6A (between Millstone and Linnell Landing Rds), E. Brewster. 896.9521

23 **Cape Rep Outdoor Theatre** Come summer, the peripatetic Cape Rep gets an outdoor home of its own—a rustic amphitheater on the old **Crosby Estate.** The summer fare is straight Shakespeare (typically, two plays, alternating weeks). Don't forget to bring the bug spray. ♦ Admission. Tu-Sa 8:30PM early July to early September. Closed early Sept; call for schedule and sites early Sept to early July. 3379 Main St/Rte 6A (between Linnell Landing Rd and Crosby Ln), E. Brewster. 896.6140

23 **Shirley Walker Antiques** This carriage-house shop is set up like an art gallery, with items carefully isolated so that you can contemplate each *objet* as a work of art, from a giant copper kettle ($300) to a four-foot New Bedford ship model (about $3,300). Children's homespun dresses become hanging sculptures, and an 1865 "bonecrusher" bicycle could one-up a **Giacometti.** An adjoining garden room is devoted to fanciful wicker. ♦ Daily 11AM-5PM June-Sept; by appointment Nov-May. 3425 Main St/Rte 6A (at Crosby Ln), E. Brewster. 896.6570

24 **William M. Baxter Antiques** Much of **William Baxter's** holdings belong by rights in a museum, and they'll probably get there eventually, but meanwhile private buyers can take advantage of his "gradual liquidation sale." After more than three decades in this spot (he moved here from Boston's antiquarian alley, Charles Street), he's ready to retire but has barns full of goods to unload. Among the treasures up for grabs is a 1740 bonnet-top highboy, appraised at $55,000; he discovered it gathering dust in a suburban attic. Other odds and ends start as low as $100. ♦ M-Sa 10AM-5PM late May to late Nov. 3439 Main St/Rte 6A (between Crosby Ln and Mitchell Rd), E. Brewster. 896.3998

25 **Nickerson State Park** Donated by **Addie Nickerson** (widow of **Roland**) in 1934 to commemorate her son who died during the flu epidemic of 1918, this 2,000-acre retreat is Massachusetts' fourth-largest state park. It contains 88,000 white pine, hemlock, and spruce trees introduced by the **Civilian Conservation Corps,** eight miles of bike paths (which hook up to the **Rail Trail**), and eight kettle ponds, the largest of which, **Cliff Pond,** is surrounded by "glacial erratics," huge boulders transported from the mainland by advancing glaciers. The park offers 420 campsites (usually booked solid in summer) and, although it may seem overrun in parts, is doing its best to protect its natural resources while enabling people to enjoy them. ♦ Free admission; fee for camping. Daily 8AM-8PM. Rte 6A and Crosby Ln, E. Brewster. 896.3491

Within Nickerson State Park:

Jack's Boat Rentals Choose from Hobiecats, Sunfish, sailboards, kayaks, canoes, aquabikes, and even pedalboats at this shop on **Flax Pond.** You don't have to be a certified jock to get out on the water. ♦ Daily 9AM-6PM late June to early Sept. 896.8556. Also at: Gull Pond, Wellfleet. 349.7553; Beach Point Rd, N. Truro. 487.1686

26 **Lion's Head Inn** $$ Tucked away in a quiet neighborhood, this attractive B&B fashioned from an 1810 sea captain's house has it all: comfortable common rooms with a collection of maritime artifacts and a library of related titles (games, too, for the leisure-minded), six comfortable bedrooms, plus two cottages that rent by the week, and a screened sunroom overlooking a 40-foot pool. It's here that delectable breakfasts are served—maybe apple-and-cheese quiche one day, "Heavenly French Toast" (sweet Portuguese bread flavored with almond extract) the next. ♦ 186 Belmont Rd (off Rte 28), W. Harwich. 432.7766, 800/321.3155

27 **Bishop's Terrace** ★★$$ This centuries-old captain's house (shown above) has been a popular local spot since 1942. The same somewhat conservative fare is served in the terrace room with mint-green tablecloths as in the formal dining room with Queen Anne chairs and an impressive scrimshaw collection. The dishes may not dazzle, but neither will the prices dismay. At night there's dancing to jazz in the barn-turned-bar. ♦ American ♦ Lunch and dinner; Sunday brunch. Closed Jan-Feb. 108 Main St/Rte 28 (between Bells Neck Rd and Riverside Dr), W. Harwich. Reservations requested. 432.0253

28 **The Commodore Inn** $$ New owners **Bill** and **Jayne Condon** have taken a basic motel and spiffed up the rooms with wicker and white cotton bedspreads; they're tasteful and inviting, and only 300 pastoral yards from the beach, or steps from a large heated pool. ♦ 30 Earle Rd (off Rte 28), W. Harwich. 432.3103

Within The Commodore Inn:

Raspberries ★★★$$$$ Chef **Ralph Binder** comes from the Culinary Institute of America by way of **Chillingsworth** and **Ocean Edge,** so his spreads are hardly standard motel fare. Breakfast is an all-you-can-eat buffet; lunch might consist of grilled duck quesadillas with roast peppers and cilantro demi-glace; dinner, an Italian specialty such as stuffed shells Florentine; dessert, a strawberry Grand Marnier cheesecake. ♦ New American ♦ Breakfast, lunch, and dinner. Closed mid-Oct to late May. Reservations recommended. 432.1180

29 **Trampoline Center** Only two rules apply: no shoes and no flips. The 12 in-ground trampolines are in such constant motion throughout the summer, they could be harnessed as an alternative energy source. The sound track? "Mom, Dad, watch this!" ♦ Fee. Daily 9AM-11PM mid-June to early Sept; Sa-Su 9AM-11PM May. 296 Main St/Rte 28 (between Lothrop Ave and Sisson Rd), W. Harwich. 432.8717

29 **Seafood Sam's** ★$ When the kids are through bouncing their brains out, duck next door for some well-priced, no-frills seafood, from lobster bisque to deep-fried popcorn shrimp. ♦ American ♦ Lunch and dinner. Closed Nov to mid-Mar. 302 Main St/Rte 28 (between Lothrop Ave and Sisson Rd), W. Harwich. 432.1422. Also at: Coast Guard Rd, Sandwich. 888.4629; Palmer Ave, Falmouth. 540.7877; 1006 Rte 28, S. Yarmouth. 394.3504

30 **Bud's Go-Karts** Drivers as young as eight can solo at this busy track (maximum speed: 15mph); younger speedsters can ride on their parents' laps. No helmets are provided, so you might want to bring your own for this not-exactly-cheap thrill. ♦ Fee. M-Sa 9AM-11PM, Su 1-11PM late May to early Sept; Sa 9AM-11PM, Su 1-11PM late Apr to late May, early to mid-Sept, weather permitting. 364 Sisson Rd (at Rte 28), Harwichport. 432.4964

31 **Brooks Academy Museum** This former navigation school (the first in the U.S., built by **Sidney Brooks** in 1844 and pictured above) now houses the collections of the **Harwich Historical Society** commemorating high points in town history. An entire room is given over to cranberry harvesting: **Captain Alvin Cahoon** of Harwich was the first commercial grower, starting his bogs in 1846. Other displays include Native American and maritime artifacts, such as a sample "Frosty," the bathtub-size sailboat that serves as a starter raft for many an amateur salt. Among the domestic goods are lace, wedding gowns, dolls, and games. There's also a display on local celeb **Caleb Chase,** who co-founded **Chase & Sanborn** coffee in 1878; volunteer historian **Patrica Ellis Buck** made headlines herself in 1993 when she pointed out that the founders' likenesses had been switched on the label—how many years back, even the 91-year-old company archivist couldn't say. The gents have at long last been restored to rights. Also on the grounds are a powderhouse used during the Revolutionary War and a restored 1872 outhouse. ♦ Free. Th-Su 1-4PM mid-June to mid-Oct. 80 Parallel St (off Sisson Rd), Harwich Center. 432.8089

32 Goucho's Mexican Restaurant and Bar ★★$$ This suburban house, yellow with green shutters, doesn't look especially south-of-the-border, and the spelling's a bit unsettling, but step inside and you'll be sufficiently convinced: the walls are daubed in plaster, with archways crudely limned in blue, serapes are draped here and there, and way back on a stone mantelpiece hearth sits the requisite O'Keeffian cow skull. The menu blends classics with some curious hybrids: the "Mayan Pupu Platter" is an hors d'oeuvre sampler, the "Philly burrito" consists of steak, onions, and cheese enfolded in a flour tortilla, and "Margarita Pie" is a piquant variant on Key lime. If the lineup suggests more frivolity that serious cross-cultural exchange, that's the general idea. In July and August, there's live entertainment Wednesday through Sunday, culminating in a free midnight Mexican feast. ♦ Mexican ♦ Lunch and dinner. Closed mid-Oct to mid-June. 403 Lower County Rd (between Earle and Forest Rds), Harwichport. 432.7768

33 The Mews at Harwichport There's scarcely enough stuff in this small saltbox (pictured above) to furnish a room, but it's a good place to find decorative touches to finish one. The five dealers have complementary fortes, from stoneware and majolica to baskets, jugs, and antique chocolate molds. ♦ M-Sa 10AM-5PM, Su noon-5PM, May-Nov. 517 Main St/Rte 28 (at Ayer Ln), Harwichport. 432.6397

33 Amazing Lace **Donna Burns** used to have a vintage clothing shop at Peacock Alley in Orleans, and aficionados dedicatedly track her down here. The selection is excellent, with a special focus on cotton batiste (there's nothing lighter, or prettier) and ever-classic linen. Thrown in among the body adornments are kitschy home accessories such as chenille bedspreads and '30s block-print tablecloths. ♦ Daily 10AM-8PM July-Aug; Th-Sa 10AM-4PM, Su noon-4PM Apr-June, Sept-Dec. 521 Main St/Rte 28 (at Ayer Ln), Harwichport. 430.1909

AUGUSTUS SNOW HOUSE

34 Augustus Snow House $$ Victoriana fans will flip over this green-shingled 1901 Princess Anne mansion with gabled dormers and a wraparound veranda. Owner **Anne Geuss** claims she furnished the lavish guest rooms to match the bathrooms, and these are indeed inspiring, featuring marble and brass sinks and fixtures and retrofitted whirlpool baths. The breakfast (included) is sumptuous, as are the afternoon hors d'oeuvres. The pleasures of town—a small, sleepy one with a summery insouciance—are right outside the door, and a private beach is a country block away. ♦ Closed Mar. 528 Main St/Rte 28 (between Forest Rd and Bank St), Harwichport, 430.0528, 800/339.0528

Within the Augustus Snow House:

Augustus Snow House Restaurant ★★★$$$$ It's no wonder that the ladies who lunch, brunch, and take tea in these parts tend to descend here in force. Not only is the decor conducive to pleasant repartee, but chef **Burt Jennison's** menu is well-calibrated to lighter appetites, which might tend to lobster and corn chowder, or grilled tiger shrimp with bell pepper relish, cilantro, and lime over angel-hair pasta. Dinners are more elaborate, featuring such preliminaries as a phyllo tulip of sea scallops with vermouth chive sauce, and main events on the order of filet mignon with roasted shallot Pinot Noir sauce. Of the dozen or so entrées offered, at least half are heart-healthy; and all is not lost with dessert, since patissier **Ken Rose,** a very talented grad of Cape Tech, whips seasonal fruits into treats that are relatively light yet satisfying, such as raspberry and blackberry pâté and daiquiri cheesecake. If you feel like throwing caution to the wind, try his irresistible white-chocolate "ravioli" stuffed with chocolate mousse. ♦ Creative American ♦ Breakfast, lunch, tea, and dinner; Sunday brunch. Closed Mar. Reservations required. 430.0528

34 Monahan **Michael O'Neill Monahan's** great-great-great-grandfather founded this store in 1848, and there's never been a need to change the name. In addition to lots of old photographs, there's varied stock ranging from Cape Cod charms as low as $10 to $175,000 diamond necklaces. Monahan makes a lot of custom wedding rings. It's one-stop shopping; he's also a justice of the peace. ♦ Daily 10AM-5PM May-Dec. 540 Main St/Rte 28 (between Forest Rd and Bank St), Harwichport. 432.3302

Restaurants/Clubs: Red **Hotels:** Blue
Shops/ Outdoors: Green **Sights/Culture:** Black

35 **Beach House Inn** $$ **Gregg Winston** and **David Plunkett's** inn is a perfect blend of nostalgia and modern comfort. The 12 rooms may have homey pine paneling and chenille bedspreads, but they also come equipped with their own fridges, color TVs, and air conditioning—not that you'll much need the latter, since the place is right on the Sound, where cooling breezes accompany the gently pounding surf. ♦ 4 Braddock Ln (off Bank St), Harwichport. 432.4444, 800/870.4405

35 **Sandpiper Beach Inn** $$ **Bill** and **Jayne Condon** bought and revamped this place just as they did the **Commodore,** and what used to be a humdrum motel now sparkles. The layout is U-shaped, with a courtyard facing the beach, so the end rooms have the best views, but even with the lower-priced units you're guaranteed to get your fill of sun and sand. ♦ 16 Bank St (off Rte 28), Harwichport. 432.0485

36 **Nick and Dick's Restaurant & Ice Cream** ★$$ The bill of fare is what you might find in a roadside stand (fried fish platters, lobster roll, etc.), but the decor is much nicer for the price: lace-curtained windows with pastel rainbow swags, tulip-shaped chandeliers. Many stop in just for the ice cream parlor, a glistening green-and-pink tile sanctum that serves such delectables as a "Pie in a Dish" sundae with pralines and caramel. ♦ American ♦ Breakfast, lunch, and dinner. Closed mid-Oct to late May. 594 Main St/Rte 28 (at Bank St), Harwichport. 430.1239

37 **The Barn at Windsong** It's a bit off the beaten track (which is to say, inland), but this antiques shop is worth seeking out. The five dealers are always well stocked with silver, wicker, prints, toys, and an exceptionally broad textile selection, from quilts to samplers to embroidered tablecloths and bed linens. Occasionally you might come across a nice piece of "primitive" furniture, dressed in its original, wonderfully worn paint. ♦ M-Sa 10AM-5PM, Su noon-5PM May-Oct; Sa 10AM-5PM, Su noon-5PM Apr, Nov-Dec. 245 Bank St (between Hoyt and Long Rds), Harwich. 432.8281

38 **Thompson's Clam Bar** ★★★$$$$ Even before it was dazzlingly renovated in 1991, Thompson's was one of those must-visit places—a status enjoyed since 1949. It could be the wall of windows overlooking **Wychmere Harbor** (a former pond around which captains raced horses), or the nautical ambience generated by the wooden tables and boat chairs. In any case, it's a good place to chow down on the basics: a seafood platter of fried everything, for instance, and cholesterol be damned. The desserts will take you back a couple of decades: they include Indian pudding, apple crisp, and fresh fruit pie à la mode. ♦ American ♦ Lunch and dinner. Closed Monday; closed mid-Sept to mid-June 23 Snow Inn Rd (on Wychmere Harbor), Harwichport. No reservations. 432.3595

Within Thompson's Clam Bar:

The HarborWatch Room ★★★$$$$ This second-story space is far more formal but has the same sea views. The decor is a clubby blend of dark woods and deep greens, and a pianist is on hand to lend atmosphere. Although the waiters sport tuxes, you can dress as casually as you want. Executive chef **Al Hynes'** menu is more hearty than precious, but does contain such delicacies as fresh lobster ravioli with tomato-vodka sauce and pecan-crusted rack of lamb. ♦ New American ♦ Dinner. Closed Monday; closed mid-Sept to mid-June. Reservations recommended. 432.3595

39 **Melrose** Pro **Tom Avery,** a contributor to *Tennis* magazine, manages this two-part complex, which consists of six Har-Tru courts here and three all-weather courts closer to town (next to **Nick and Dick's**). The public is welcome to take lessons or just play, and the pro shop also stocks running and rollerblading gear. ♦ Fee. Daily 9AM-6PM early May-Oct. 792 Main St/Rte 28 (between Bank St and Hoyt Rd), Harwichport. 430.7012

40 **L'Alouette** ★★★$$$ You have only to smell the stock simmering to know this is *real* French food. Chef **Louis Bastres,** who came from Biarritz in 1986, brings his native expertise to bear on sautéed frogs' legs *niçoise,* bouillabaisse, filet mignon au poivre with brandy demi-glace, and Chateaubriand *bouquetière.* The decor could dupe you into thinking you were on the southern coast of France. ♦ French ♦ Dinner; Sunday brunch. Closed Monday. 787 Main St/Rte 28 (between Bank St and Hoyt Rd), Harwichport. 430.0405

40 **Cape Cod Ski, Bike, and Scuba** In addition to rentals and sales of related sporting equipment, this shop offers swimming lessons for all ages and scuba instruction (12 years and up) in a heated pool. They also conduct shipwreck dive charters out of Harwichport and Provincetown. ♦ M-Sa 9AM-6PM, Su 9AM-5PM July-Aug; M, W-Sa 9AM-6PM, Su 9AM-5PM late Mar to July, Sept-Nov. 815 Main St/Rte 28 (between Bank St and Hoyt Rd), Harwichport. 432.9035, 800/348.4641. Also at: 269 Barnstable Rd, Hyannis. 775.3301; 6 Nells Wy, Orleans. 255.7547

41 **Chatham Pottery** **Gill Wilson** and **Margaret Wilson-Grey** have about a half-century's experience between them, and it shows in their line of thick, sturdy stoneware, mostly in deep blues against off-white. Motifs from floral to piscine are applied to the bowls and lamp bases, sinks and tiles, hanging planters and pitcher-shaped fountains. Depending on the workload, you're welcome to tour the studio out back. ♦ Daily 10AM-5:30PM. 2568 Main St/Rte 28 (between Norton Rd and Rte 137), S. Chatham. 430.1543

42 **Cape Cod Cooperage** The scent of sawdust is heady with possibilities. You can't imagine how many wooden things you really *need* until you start wandering around this rambling barn: windowboxes, clothes racks, painted chests, Adirondack chairs, bookshelves, birdhouses . . . all for about half what you'd pay elsewhere, and the majority made on the premises. Fish and cranberry barrels have been made here since the late 1800s, and now the company is the only remaining cooperage in Massachusetts. There's also an on-site blacksmith, **Robert S. Jordan,** who gives demonstrations every Saturday from 1PM to 4PM in July and August. His handiwork ranges in scale from kitchen utensils to ornamental fences, and in style from early American to contemporary. ♦ M-Sa 9AM-5PM; Su 11AM-5PM. 1150 Old Queen Anne Rd (between Rte 137 and Old Comers Rd), Harwich. 432.0788

43 **The Seafarer of Chatham** $$ When is a motel not a motel? When you get the same pretty surroundings (fluffy coverlets, colonial-style wall stenciling, extensive garden) and concierge-quality referrals (from innkeeper **John Houhoulis**) as you would at a fancy B&B. The only "downside" is that instead of having to tiptoe around and chat with other guests, you have no choice at the end of the day but to return to your spacious room and hit the voluminous bed with your travel companion and/or 44 channels of cable. ♦ 2079 Main St/Rte 28 (between Rte 137 and Ridgevale Rd), W. Chatham. 432.1739

44 **Marion's Pie Shop** The Cape used to be loaded with these summertime larders, so handy when guests show up unannounced or when you'd rather bake in the sun than over a hot stove. Marion's has been around since 1951, and the lemon meringue pies are as lofty as ever, the chicken and clam pie just as sustaining, and the cinnamon rolls and fruit breads (cranberry-nut, zucchini-pineapple) eternally yummy. ♦ M-Sa 7AM-7PM, Su 7AM-2PM July-Aug; Tu-Sa 7AM-7PM, Su 7AM-2PM Sept-June. 2022 Main St/Rte 28 (between Ridgevale and Sam Ryder Rds), W. Chatham. 432.9439

45 **1736 House Antiques** **John Miller's** full Cape is packed with odd treasures, from mule-ear rockers to ancient hooked rugs. He also shows the landscapes of Chatham-based painter **Linda George**—definitely worth a lingering look. ♦ M-Tu, Th-Su 10AM-5PM May-Nov; by appointment Dec-Apr. 1731 Main St/Rte 28 (between Sam Ryder and George Ryder Rds), W. Chatham. 945.5690

45 **Blue Moon Delicatessen-Bistro** ★★$ **Patti** and **Dave Schuman** pack a lot of energy into this compact eatery, painted like a deep-twilight skyscape, with glitter-stars hanging from the rafters. The menu is a nosher's delight, with nibbles ranging from "Greek" burgers (with spinach and feta) to *fra diavolo* pizza and oversize Heath Bar cookies. Breakfast (featuring homemade bagels, latkes, and myriad other choices) is available all day. You can eat in, take out, or have whatever you like delivered. ♦ International ♦ Breakfast, lunch, and dinner. Closed for dinner Monday through Friday Jan-Mar. 1715 Main St/Rte 28 (at George Ryder Rd), W. Chatham. 945.5555

46 **Cape Cod Flying Circus** Ready to execute some rolls, loops, and inversions in an open-cockpit, 1927-model biplane? Pilot **Jim McDevitt** promises a smooth, graceful flight in his 1978 Great Lakes 2T1A-2, but for the slightly less daring, for whom a faceful of wind is thrill enough, he's just as glad to offer straight sightseeing. Go take a look at Chatham's famous "breach," where a cross-beach current that started as a trickle in 1987 became a full-scale breakthrough that turned South Beach into an island and several prime chunks of Chatham real estate into driftwood. ♦ Fee. By appointment May to mid-Sept. Chatham Municipal Airport (George Ryder Rd), W. Chatham. 362.9452

46 **Crosswind Landing** ★★$ Scarcely bigger than a cockpit, this tiny restaurant overlooking the airstrip turns out a fabulous breakfast (try the "Frequent Flyer": deep-dish quiche, bacon, and homefries) and a savory assortment of soups and sandwiches, such as the CBLT, which is a BLT with herbed cheese, served on a croissant. All the pastries (from muffins and crumbcakes to cookies and tarts) are baked right here, and creative customers can contribute to the tabletop collages of postcards, doodles, and tabloid headlines. ♦ International ♦ Breakfast and lunch. Closed mid-Oct to mid-May. Chatham Municipal Airport (George Ryder Rd), W. Chatham. 945.5955

47 Christian's Commissary Although **Christian Schultz** owns one of the hottest restaurants in town—**Christian's**—his culinary fervor required yet another outlet, so he opened this fun food and provisions shop. The imported inventory is top of the line, and the dishes fresh from the kitchen deserve export. Takeouts include esoteric entrées and salads, and desserts that may not make it home, such as little Key lime puddings and fresh cannoli filled to order. ♦ M-Sa 10AM-6PM; Su noon-5PM. 1603 Main St/Rte 28 (between George Ryder and Barn Hill Rds), W. Chatham. 945.5223

48 Chatham Glass **James Holmes** blows the glass, and **Deborah Doane** helps design it, a collaborative effort that has earned many an award and a regular place in such upscale emporia as **Henri Bendel's** and **Barney's, Gump's,** and **Neiman Marcus.** The line is constantly evolving, but one trademark is the unconventional use of color, or rather colors, some 70 in all, usually paired unpredictably. Their signature candlestick, for example, a clean-lined column transected by chubby rings, might stack up in lavender, lime, and aqua. Some of the pieces are more organic in shape, resembling strange gourds or warped fruit. Observe all this and more in the making in the sunny, wide-open studio/showroom. ♦ M-Sa 10AM-5PM. 17 Balfour Ln (off Rte 28), W. Chatham. 945.5547

49 The Picnic Basket If you're not in the habit of buying your meals at a liquor store, make an exception and check out chef/owner **Barbara Obrig's** offerings at this upscale deli counter. As a summer visitor, she couldn't understand why it was impossible to find high-quality food at good prices, so she decided to abandon her career in banking and provide it herself. The sandwiches on home-made bread are superb (don't miss the cut-rate but top-notch shrimp salad), as is the changing array of cold dishes, such as ripe plum tomatoes with slivered Spanish onion and fresh mozzarella. The refrigerator case is likely to yield the likes of peach cobbler or "mudballs"—mounds of chocolate mousse encased in drizzled chocolate. ♦ M-Sa 8:30AM-11PM late May to early Sept; M-Th 8:30AM-9PM, F-Sa 8:30AM-10PM early Sept to late May. 1221 Main St/Rte 28 (between Barn Hill and Old Queen Anne Rds), W. Chatham. 945.0501

Orleans native son Isaac Snow, whose house—with a plaque—still stands on Brick Hill Road, was so keen to enlist for the War of Independence that he walked to Boston, wearing out his shoes en route. After participating in the siege of Dorchester Heights (where he filled barrels with clay and stone to roll down on British soldiers), he returned home "strongly in love with my country's cause" and promptly reenlisted.

50 Munson Gallery In operation since 1955, the Munson Gallery numbers among Cape Cod's oldest; it is also one of the finest. Housed in a 1920s horse barn (one room still contains stalls, which make for a nicely compartmentalized display space), the gallery shows some 20 established artists (such as colorist **Wolf Kahn**) while regularly making room for promising newcomers. ♦ M-Sa 9:30AM-5PM mid-June to mid-Oct. 880 Main St/Rte 28 (between Old Queen Anne and Crowell Rds), Chatham. 945.9851

51 Queen Anne Inn $$$$ Part of the **Romantik Hotels** network, this 1840s house—built by a sea captain for his daughter—has been an inn since 1874. The 30 rooms vary widely in size, furnishings, and price; some feature fireplaces, whirlpools, and balconies overlooking the garden. All guests enjoy access to the three Har-Tru tennis courts and to resident pro **Sandy Dobbrow,** who runs three-day refresher clinics. Innkeeper **Guenther Weinkopf** can arrange or skipper (schedule permitting) day cruises and dives. ♦ Closed Jan to mid-Feb. 70 Queen Anne Rd (off Rte 28), Chatham. 945.0394, 800/545.4667

Within the Queen Anne Inn:

Cafe at the Queen Anne Inn ★★★$$$$ In previous years, the restaurant never quite lived up to its billing, but now that it's leased by **Chillingsworth** (a four-star restaurant in Brewster), quality is assured. The decor is nowhere near as grand as that of the Brewster institution, and the menu is more bistro-level than *gastronomique,* but each dish is beautifully presented, from duck mousse to crispy salmon with lemon chive butter. ♦ International ♦ Dinner. Closed Tuesday; closed Nov to late-May. Reservations recommended. 945.0394

52 Monomoy Theatre The Cape's second-oldest surviving stage, this former toy factory became an Equity theater in the 1930s. In 1957, it was taken over by the **Ohio University Players** (the university president was a longtime Chatham summerer), and now a mix of students from across the country and returning alums, some with impressive credits under their belts, put on a play a week every summer, starting with a musical and ending with Shakespeare, and usually managing to work in something provocative (in '93, it was **Athol Fugard's** *A Lesson from*

Aloes) among the crowd-pleasers. They take one break in late July, when the critically acclaimed **Monomoy Chamber Ensemble** mounts a series of popular concerts, including a free morning performance for children. This charming theater seats only 276 patrons, all of whom enjoy excellent sightlines. ♦ Tu-W, F, Su 8:30PM, Th, Sa 2PM, 8:30PM late June to Sept. 776 Main St/Rte 28 (between Crowell and Old Harbor Rds), Chatham. 945.1589

53 Railroad Museum What a pleasure it must have been to ride the rails, with buildings like this 1887 Victorian beauty as a destination. This "Railroad Gothic" station, buttercup yellow with sepia trim, was decommissioned in 1937 and, fortunately, bought for the town by a generous donor in 1951 and restored as a museum in 1960. With its shingled "candlesnuffer" turret and Cheerio-like decorations spaced beneath the eave brackets, it's a welcome sight still, even if the trains beside it (including a 1918 New York Central caboose) are permanently parked—all the better to climb aboard. The station is full of models, relics, and photos, and the background tape of wheels and whistles helps conjure up aural memories. If you've got a young train buff along, leave plenty of free time for the **Play-a-round** park across the street. Built by townspeople in 1990, it's one of the largest **Robert Leathers**-designed playgrounds in the Northeast, a fantastical, vaguely medieval-looking conglomeration of chutes, slides, bridges, and parapets. ♦ Donation. Tu-Sa 10AM-4PM mid-June to mid-Sept. 153 Depot Rd (between Crowell and Old Harbor Rds), Chatham. 945.0342

54 The Old Atwood House and Museums This gambrel-roofed 1752 house has been a repository for the **Chatham Historical Society** since 1926, and they've collected well. In addition to the usual colonial accoutrements, plus the memorabilia of prolific Cape writer **Joseph C. Lincoln,** they've saved portraits of sea captains and local characters captured in a straight-on yet painterly fashion by **Frederick Stallknecht Wight** (1901-86). However, it was his mother, **Alice Stallknecht Wight** (1880-1973), who received most of the attention during their shared lifetime, as well as after (there's an entire barn devoted to her murals). Although her work may have seemed fauve and bold in the 1930s, today it looks more cartoonish and crude, like overcalculated folk art; she worked local citizens into tableaux depicting a modern Last Supper and gained considerable notoriety for depicting Christ as a modern-day fisherman.

Among the museum's odder acquisitions is a 1947 fishing camp—a shanty that would otherwise have been washed out to sea after the 1987 break. It may seem a bit premature to preserve a type of cottage that's still quite common, but perhaps a half-century from now it will have proved a shrewd save. ♦ Admission. W-Sa 2-5PM June-Sept. 347 Stage Harbor Rd (between Cross and Bridge Sts), Chatham. 945.2493

55 Monomoy National Wildlife Refuge This stretch of land has been through quite a few changes since it was declared a refuge in 1944. First, a 1958 storm turned what had been **Monomoy Point** into **Monomoy Island,** and then a 1978 blizzard sliced that island in two. Monomoy, along with Provincetown, is the only area of the Cape that's actually growing, so perhaps in the future this currently 2,750-acre property, overseen by the **U.S. Fish and Wildlife Service,** will shelter even more animal life. Right now it harbors every species of bird native to New England, some 285 in all, including piping plovers, heron, and egrets; a prime resting spot along the Atlantic Flyway, it's frequented by birds from as far away as the Arctic and Brazil. Deer wander among the 175 species of plants, ranging from red cedar to orchids and sundews. Thousands of harbor and grey seals winter here; in fact, grey pups born here in 1990 heralded the establishment of the first grey seal colony in Massachusetts. The one species you won't see much of is Homo sapiens.

About 40 acres on **Morris Island** are accessible by car, then foot (there's a ¾-mile trail, closed during high tide), but the islands are uninhabited. You can visit them as part of a naturalist-guided tour conducted by either the **Cape Cod Museum of Natural History** (896.3867) or the **Wellfleet Bay Wildlife Sanctuary** (349.2615). ♦ Daily dawn-dusk. Morris Island Rd (off Main St), Chatham. 945.0594

56 Chatham Light & Coast Guard Station Built in 1828 and rebuilt in 1876, this 24,000-candlepower beacon is visible 15 miles out to sea. The tower isn't open to the public, but the parking area is a popular spot from which to watch the sunrise or to observe the famous "break" that is altering Chatham's shoreline. Some take comfort in the fact that an 1846 break patched itself up, and in fact South Beach has already reattached itself to the mainland, adding a brand-new sandy peninsula to town. ♦ Main St (between Bridge St and Shore Rd), Chatham. 945.3830

56 Inn Among Friends $$ This 14-bedroom inn is perfectly situated to take advantage of Chatham's newest beach. It's a cluster of unprepossessing gray-shingled houses with a surprisingly stylish common room dominated by a pair of pale blue tattersall chaise lounges. The bedrooms are decorated with unstuffy antiques, and the place is as relaxing and welcoming as a real friend's house. ♦ Closed Jan-May. 207 Main St (between Bridge St and Shore Rd), Chatham. 945.0792

Within the Inn Among Friends:

The Break-away Cafe ★★$$ The place is plain and cozy, with calico tablecloths. Breakfast might consist of chef **David Bruce's** cranberry pancakes; lunch, a pizza; dinner, an enticing and well-priced assortment of blackboard specials, and homey desserts like double-chocolate layer cake. ♦ American ♦ Breakfast, lunch, and dinner. Closed for dinner on Monday and Sunday July to early Sept; closed for dinner and closed Tuesday early Sept to Jan, May-June; closed Jan-May. 945.5288

57 **The Cranberry Inn at Chatham** $$ An inn since the 1830s (it was known as the "Traveler's Home"), this rambling old place (shown above) got a total overhaul when **Richard Morris** and **Peggy DeHan** took it over in 1988. They've managed to create 18 rooms that could be categorized as a "Traveler's Dream": all feature four-poster, brass, or canopy beds (some so high that you practically have to pole-vault into them), with quilted coverlets and a lavishing of fabrics and decorative touches, often antique. What's most striking about these rooms is their sheer spaciousness; the second-floor units, in particular, boast beamed cathedral ceilings and, as often as not, a working fireplace. It's as if every room were poised to serve as a honeymoon suite. The common rooms include a neo-colonial green-paneled tavern—unusual for a B&B but a thoughtful addition for those who like to enjoy a quiet brandy by the fire after an active, blustery day. The inn is located midway between the shore (two blocks away) and Chatham's highly civilized shopping district. ♦ Closed Jan to mid-Mar. 359 Main St (between School St and Homestead Ln), Chatham. 945.9232, 800/332.4667

58 **Christian's Restaurant** ★★★$$$$ Chef/owner **Christian Schultz** was quite young when he opened this restaurant in 1980, but clearly he knew what he was about: it was an immediate success, and remains one of the best restaurants in the region. The 1818 house lost a lot of its interior walls to create a bistrolike, see-and-be-seen ambience; the terrace room, with its brick floors, woven tablecloths, and striped shades, is especially inviting. Like many a chef of late, Schultz has caught southwestern fever, but his hybrids are inspired—Brie wrapped in a flour tortilla, for instance, with Vidalia onions, mango, and cilantro, served warm with fruit salsa. Fish, of course, is featured prominently, and well treated, but his rack of lamb is like no other; grilled in a crust of goat cheese, rosemary, and pumpernickel. ♦ New American ♦ Dinner. Closed mid-Oct to mid-May. 443 Main St (between Homestead Ln and Mill Pond Rd), Chatham. Reservations recommended. 945.3362

Within Christian's Restaurant:

Upstairs at Christian's ★★★$$ Same kitchen, lighter fare, lower prices—a winning combo all around, and all the more in a setting guaranteed to evoke instant nostalgia, if only the secondhand, cinematic kind. The furnishings would have suited Teddy Roosevelt: oak bar, mahogany paneling, scruffy leather couches and armchairs, with a sprinkling of hunting prints, caricatures, and movie posters. The menu items, including drinks, are all named for movies—a little gimmicky, perhaps, but it makes for entertaining reading, and nibbling, too. "Great Balls of Fire" are spicy crab and corn fritters, "Prizzi's Honor" is a pesto pizza, and "Monkey Business" is Absolut Citron with crème de banana and tropical fruit juice—you get the picture. In summer, the trellised deck is the place to be, in town but slightly above it all. ♦ New American ♦ Lunch and dinner. Closed Tuesday Jan-Feb. 945.3362

58 **Mildred Georges Antiques** Georges has been in business since 1956, and her accumulated acquisitions make for rich and varied pickings. Poke through and you'll find just about everything you could possibly seek. Personal adornments are especially strong, from tortoiseshell combs and painted porcelain buttons to jewelry of every era. ♦ Daily 10AM-6:30PM June-Sept; daily 10AM-5PM Oct; daily 10AM-4PM May. 447 Main St (between Homestead Ln and Mill Pond Rd), Chatham. 945.1939

59 **Midsummer Nights** Here's a store to delight die-hard sensualists and even to convert the ascetically inclined. The stock spans extravagant bodycare products (from natural sponges to antique manicure sets), modernist lingerie, and imaginative home accessories. ♦ M-Sa 10AM-5PM, Su noon-5PM June-Aug; M-Sa 10AM-5PM Sept-May. 471 Main St (between Mill Pond Rd and Cross St), Chatham. 945.5562

Henry David Thoreau wrote of Brewster, "This town has more mates and masters of vessels than any other town in the country."

That hulk of a boat visible from the bay sides of Brewster and Eastham is the USS *James Longstreet*, used for military target practice in the years 1943-70.

60 Impudent Oyster ★★★$$$$ Main Street strollers might overlook this popular spot, but not so the locals, who know to venture around the corner for outstanding seafood in a variety of international guises. Oysters Sardinia, for instance, are baked on the half-shell with spinach pesto and prosciutto; Scandinavian-style scallops Kristiansund are broiled, then topped with slivers of smoked salmon and a dilled lemon-butter sauce and served over wild rice. For dessert, try the native blueberry pie. The decor is late-1970s artsy-craftsy with a cathedral ceiling sporting exposed beams and skylights, plus a bit of stained glass. Even when jammed (which is often), it's a civilized place, with a bar fit for grownups and food that consistently surprises. ♦ International ♦ Lunch and dinner. 15 Chatham Bars Ave (off Main St), Chatham. Reservations recommended. 945.3545

61 Chatham Candy Manor **Naomi Turner's** mother started this business in the 1940s, and the quality hasn't slipped a bit, nor has the demand for premium, hand-dipped chocolates. Just walking in the door is a treat: take a deep whiff, then peruse the wooden cases of molded chocolate scallop shells, dipped strawberries, "turtles" of every stripe. The shop maintains an open kitchen policy, which means you're welcome to wander in and see what's cooking. During the holiday season, children and adults press their noses against the front window to watch candy canes evolve out of a big copper pot. Mail order is available for those who depart with appetites permanently whetted. ♦ Daily 9AM-10PM late June to early Sept; daily 9AM-6PM early Sept to late June. 484 Main St (between Chatham Bars Ave and Blackberry Ln), Chatham. 945.0825, 800/221.6497

62 Kate Gould Park The brass-band concerts held here have long been a genteel summer tradition; now drawing crowds of up to 6,000, they're approaching rock-concert proportions. Part of their popularity is no doubt attributable to octagenarian conductor **Whitney W. Tileston,** who cheerfully whips the 40-member band of locals to its musical best; the repertoire ranges from the bunny hop to waltzes and big-band numbers, and spontaneous sing-alongs are common. If you've found yourself wondering whatever happened to family values, just take a look around and join in. ♦ F 8PM July to early Sept. Off Main St (between Chatham Bars Ave and Blackberry Ln), Chatham. 945.0342

63 The Children's Shop Future fixtures on best-dressed lists will owe their start to **Ginny Nickerson Carter's** excellent selection of kids' clothes. From sunhats to polar fleece snowsuits, this stuff is the best, and for all its emphasis on traditional tastefulness, there's plenty of room for playfulness, too—check out the hot-pink boas. ♦ M-F 9AM-9PM, Sa 9AM-5:30PM, Su noon-5PM July-Aug; M-Sa 9:30AM-5PM Sept-Feb, Apr-June. 515 Main St (between Mill Pond Rd and Cross St), Chatham. 945.0234. Also at: 27 Wianno Ave, Osterville. 428.9458

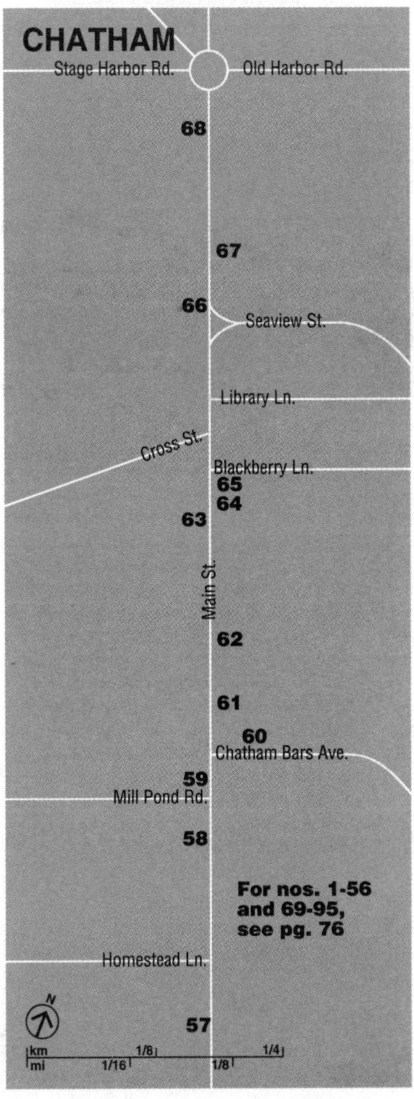

64 Chatham Cookware Opened by **Vera Champlain** in 1979, this shop features stylish and functional wares for the well-dressed kitchen, as well as the output from one very accomplished one: hers. From ready-to-heat hors d'oeuvres and entrées (spinach-feta borreks, smoked salmon-and-dill quiche) to coffeecakes, tortes, and sugar cookies, everything tastes as good as it looks. There's a tiny lunchroom in back, wallpapered in a vine pattern, if you can't wait to get home to start snacking. ♦ Daily 6AM-6PM July-Aug; daily 7AM-5PM Sept-Dec, Feb-June. 524 Main St (between Chatham Bars Ave and Blackberry Ln), Chatham. 945.1550

65 Mayo House This diminutive yellow 1818 three-quarter Cape, maintained and occupied by the **Chatham Conservation Foundation,** has no outstanding historical significance, but it's right there, and gratis, so why not look around? You might enjoy deciphering the homiletic sampler of **Catherine Mayo,** executed in 1829, or climbing the steep stairs to view the minuscule bedrooms. Friendly volunteers are on hand to field questions. ♦ Free. Tu-Th 11AM-4PM mid-June to Oct. 540 Main St (at Blackberry Ln), Chatham. 945.4084

66 Vining's Bistro ★★★$$$ Housed on the upper floor of a well-camouflaged mini-mall, this wood-grill proves that Chatham, though sedate, still has room for spice; indeed, there's plenty of it in the "pasta from hell" with banana-guava catsup, and in the Thai beef salad drenched in Panang vinaigrette with a satay dipping sauce. Cooler options are offered, too, including a vegetarian hazelnut and wild mushroom lasagna. If you've had it with same old same old, head to this loft, where **Kurt Hedmark's** murals hint at denizens with pastimes possibly racier than chowder suppers. ♦ International ♦ Lunch and dinner. Closed for lunch on Tuesday late May to mid-Oct; closed mid-Jan to Apr. 595 Main St (at Seaview St), Chatham. 945.5033

67 The Trading Company Somehow, the sculptural, earth-toned couture of **Armani** and **Joseph Abboud** seems at home in this barnboard interior. Country living needn't mean giving up all the finer things, and city-sophisticated women will find appropriate crossover dressing here. ♦ Daily 10AM-5PM mid-Apr to Jan; Tu-Sa 10AM-5PM Jan to mid-Apr. 614 Main St (between Seaview St and Old Harbor Rd), Chatham. 945.9191

67 The Spyglass Even if you're not in the market, you've got to see the 16th-century armada coffers **Dan Vaughan** has collected since opening this shop in 1981; some are studded with mermaids and sea serpents. His main stock in trade is antique telescopes, but anything nautical or optical is fair game, from barometers to opera glasses, sextants to captain's desks. ♦ M-Sa 9AM-5PM, Su 1-4PM Jun-Sept; M-Sa 9AM-5PM Oct-May. 618 Ma St (between Seaview St and Old Harbor Rd), Chatham. 945.9686

68 The Dead Zone This is the kind of shop you'd least expect in somewhat stuffy Chatham, and it's pretty hidden away, in a basement space around back, but the **Grateful Dead** merchandise and incense, tie-dyes, Native American prints, and beads are selling as if it were 1968. ♦ M-Sa 9AM-10PM, Su 10AM-9PM late May to early Sept; call for off-season hours. 647 Main St (between Cross St and Stage Harbor Rd), Chatham. 945.5853

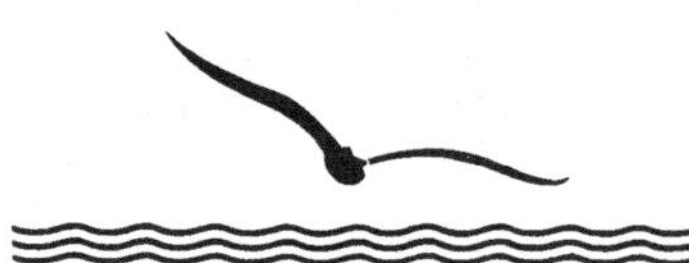

69 Chatham Bars Inn $$$$ Built as a hunting lodge in 1914, and designed by Boston architect **Harvey Bailey Alden,** this 44-room shingled inn, with 103 more rooms in cottages along the shore, is a living reminder of an opulent age. To the credit of **William Langelier** and **Alan Green,** who took over in 1988, the property is probably grander now than ever before, yet still retains its relaxed, gracious air. There are plenty of facilities to explore on its 80 acres (a nine-hole golf course, five tennis courts, shuffleboard, croquet, volleyball, fitness room, heated outdoor pool, private beach) and along the surf of the Outer Bar (a complementary launch ride away), but it's tempting just to sit on one's private balcony—nearly all the rooms have one—and take in this lovely shore.

The rooms are deliberately underdone, sticking to a breezy summerhouse scheme, with cheery fabrics and prints, and plenty of wicker. The lobby and hallways, in shades of beige, cream, and green, seem to stretch on forever; staffers joke that it reminds them of *The Shining.* Malevolence is the last thing th comes to mind, though, as you sip cocktails on the veranda, reminiscing to the smooth riffs of jazz pianist **Dave McKenna.** Children are offered supervised recreation morning, afternoon, and evening so that parents can enjoy some couple time. The off-season is spiced with themed weekend packages; one the most popular, tellingly, is "Let's Do Nothing!" ♦ Shore Rd (at Seaview St), Chatham. 945.0096, 800/527.4884

Within the Chatham Bars Inn:

The Main Dining Room ★★★★$$$$ The vast dining room is painted palest peach, the color of sand at sunset; as the sea views deepen into dusk, copper lanterns are lit, casting a romantic glow. Chef **Robert Trainor's** cuisine is as exquisite as the setting. The four-course à la carte menu will more than satisfy most palates, but if you're seriou about food, treat yourself to a *menu degustation,* a delicately portioned hit parade of 6 to 10 courses. Among the standouts are the pan-seared foie gras in Armagnac with fresh figs and shallots, and the roast saddle of lamb with grilled vegetable lasagna and a trio of garlics—crisped, roasted, and stewed. Desserts, including a rare chocolate and chestnut *gateau,* are just as lavish. ♦ New American ♦ Dinner. Reservations required; jacket requested. 945.0096, 800/527.4884

The Tavern at the Inner Bar ★★★$$$ Although less ambitious in scope, the cuisine in this clubby enclave is just as skilled, from the wild mushroom wontons with chive sauce to Chatham lobster Alfredo with fresh tarragon. The don't-miss dessert is banana and chocolate pudding with brioche. ♦ New American ♦ Lunch and dinner; Sunday brunch. 945.0096

Beach House Grill ★★$ Beach potatoes too sun-besotted to make the trek up to the main inn can sustain themselves on mussels steamed in white wine and garlic, upscale fried clams (with remoulade sauce in lieu of tartar), and summery salads and sandwiches. Evening events include lobster/clam bakes and barbecues. ♦ American ♦ Breakfast and lunch; dinner also on Monday and Wednesday. Closed early Sept to early July. 945.0096, 800/527.4884

70 Fish Pier From midafternoon on, you can watch Chatham's 60-boat fleet bringing in the day's catch: mostly haddock, cod, and flounder, some pretty sizable. (Toward dusk, the sand fleas get vicious, so come foreslathered.) A wooden observation deck provides a good vantage point, and a postage-stamp park with an impressive sculpture by **Sig Purwin,** *The Provider,* was added in 1992. ♦ Free. Shore Rd (between Seaview St and Barcliff Ave), Chatham. 945.3114

At the Fish Pier:

The Water Taxi **John W. McGrath, Jr.,** represents the third generation to run this family business, in operation since 1944. What it consists of is "cabs" to remote beaches or wherever you want to go—on a seal watch, perhaps, or a sunset cruise. "We run on demand," says McGrath. "You make the schedule." ♦ Fee. By appointment. 430.2346

As you indulge in yet another bounteous B&B breakfast, consider the feast that confronted Henry David Thoreau when he took shelter with a Wellfleet farming family: eels, buttermilk cake, cold bread, green beans, doughnuts, and tea.

71 Moses Nickerson House $$ This 1839 captain's house exemplifies Jeffersonian classicism at its height, and innkeeper **Elsie Piccola's** interior decoration lives up to the exterior. The living room, with its impractical white sofa and needlepoint rug, hints at the extravagances in store: the seven rooms are decorated in a spectrum from ultrafeminine (lace, tussy-mussies, and such) to ruggedly masculine (hunting prints, Ralph Lauren bedding). Pick a theme and sink into it—particularly if you've opted for a room with a feather bed. Breakfasts of homemade baked goods are served in a cheerful solarium surrounded by an especially exuberant garden. ♦ 364 Old Harbor Rd (between Shore Rd and Barcliff Ave), Chatham. 945.5859, 800/628.6972

72 The Captain's House Inn of Chatham $$$ The house, an 1839 Greek Revival mansion, is grand, and the spacious rooms (there are 16, including the cottage and carriage house) are country-palatial. Expect four-posters with crochet canopies, lush Oriental rugs, wingbacks, a blazing fire (if you wish), and breakfast and tea served on fine linens in a glassed-in garden room. ♦ Closed Dec-Jan. 371 Old Harbor Rd (between Orleans Rd and Barcliff Ave), Chatham. 945.0127

73 Pleasant Bay Village Resort Motel $$$$ This 58-room motel has something of a split personality: the breakfast room, with its kilims and antique cupboards, wants to belong to a China Trade-era B&B, and the six-acre grounds, intensively landscaped with Japanese plantings and a waterfall-fed koi pool, look lifted from a botanical garden. All these extras have been added over the past quarter-century by owner/gardener **Howard Gamsey,** who admits to having spent $1 million on improvements in just the past 10 years. He obviously loves the place, as do his loyal guests. The motel, you might want to note, is not right *on* the bay but a reasonable walk away. ♦ Closed Nov to mid-May. 1191 Orleans Rd/Rte 28 (at Training Field Rd), Chathamport. 945.1153, 800/547.1011

74 Wequassett Inn $$$$ The Native American name for this lovely setting cupped by **Pleasant Bay** means "crescent on the water." The inn started out in the early 1940s as a pair of transplanted 18th-century homesteads, but soon nearly a score of cottages sprouted up around it, covering 22 acres. So well assimilated are these outbuildings into the leafy landscape that you feel as if you've landed in a particularly nice village, not a full-scale resort. With 104 rooms, newly redecorated in an elegant country motif, Wequassett *is* large, though, with amenities to match. These include five all-weather "plexi-pave" tennis

Restaurants/Clubs: Red **Hotels:** Blue
Shops/ Outdoors: Green **Sights/Culture:** Black

courts, with three pros in attendance, and a fleet of sailboards, Sunfish, Daysailers, and Hobie Cats for rent—again, with instruction if needed. (Clinic packages are sometimes offered in both sports.) The 68-foot heated pool sits at the neck of **Clam Point,** a little promontory perfect for strolling or calm-water swimming. If you yearn for surf, the inn's launch can ferry you over to the unspoiled southerly stretches of **Nauset Beach;** sightseers can hop a seaplane for a scenic tour or a quick jog to Boston or the Islands. It's awfully tempting, though, just to stay put, kick off your shoes, and feel your accumulated stresses subside. ♦ Closed Nov-May. 173 Rte 28 (at Kendrick Rd), Chatham. 432.5400, 800/225.7125

Within the Wequassett Inn:

Eben Ryder House ★★★★$$$$ Appended to a late 18th-century Brewster house once known to locals as "Square Top," the dining room enjoys sweeping views and chef **Frank McMullen's** contemporary artistry. The place may look staid, but he's up on all the new world-beat moves, such as melon salsa to accompany plump Wellfleet oysters, and the searing spices that yield a Jamaican mixed grill. However, it's his classicist cuisine that's apt to convert you into an instant conservative: the Nantucket scallop and saffron bisque, for example, or Gulf shrimp stuffed with crabmeat, ricotta, and spinach, baked in puff pastry, and served in a sea of sun-dried tomato beurre blanc. Desserts fully measure up, especially the white chocolate cranberry mousse on a delicate cookie "doily." ♦ New American ♦ Dinner. Closed Nov-May. Reservations recommended; jacket requested. 432.5400, 800/225.7125

75 Hillbourne House $ Located in a quiet pocket between Chatham and Orleans, this B&B inn with a motel extension has a superb view of **Pleasant Bay** and its own private beach and dock (you're welcome to bring your own boat). Built in 1798, it served as a stop on the **Underground Railroad** (escaped slaves hid in a stone pit beneath a trap door) and weathered the age when the bay was a favored rendezvous for pirates. The five in-house rooms have more character (one has a water view via a well-placed toile chaise), but the three motel units are quite nice, too—very unboxy, with beamed ceilings. **Barbara Hayes,** a schoolteacher, makes a scrumptious breakfast—Dutch oven pancakes, perhaps, with homemade cinnamon syrup. ♦ Closed Nov to late Apr. 654 Orleans Rd/Rte 28 (at Tarkiln Rd), S. Orleans. 255.0780

Early on, colonists got in the habit of using corn as currency, paying for services with it and even purchasing land.

76 Pleasant Bay Antiques Although **Steve Tyng's** house and barn are far off the beaten path of Route 6A, the finest antiques on the Cape have a way of falling into his hands—perhaps because sellers know they'll be appreciated. Buyers flock here, too, looking for goods that are fresh on the market. As a result, some of his most coveted inventory—$28,000 Queen Anne chest on chest, for instance—might enjoy a 15-minute turnaround. Because the prices aren't jacked up by serial trading, it's possible to find relative deals. It's also a very instructive place just to look. ♦ Daily 9AM-5PM. 540 Orleans Rd/Rte 28 (between Tarkiln and Quanset Rds), S. Orleans. 255.0930

77 The Meeting House Museum This 1833 Greek Revival Universalist church now houses the collections of the **Orleans Historical Society:** clothing, photographs, marine artifacts, farm implements, a cast-iron artillery shell from the War of 1812. The amalgam, alas, is less than riveting unless you have a special interest in town history. ♦ M-F 11AM-2PM July-Aug. 3 River Rd (at Main St), Orleans. 255.1386

78 Fancy's Farm It may be rustic, with dried herbs and flowers slung from rough-hewn rafters, but this farmstand has city smarts. In addition to top-grade produce, exotic as well as domestic, you can buy fresh gazpacho, fruit smoothies, jellybeans by the scoop, and all sorts of home-baked treats from pies to tea cakes. ♦ Daily 7AM-7PM late June to early Sept; daily 7AM-6PM early Sept to late June. 199 Main St (between Meetinghouse and Great Oak Rds), E. Orleans. 255.1949. Also at: The Cornfield, 1291 Rte 28, W. Chatham. 945.1949

79 Countryside Antiques As you meander through this large shop, the eight rooms unfold like a maze; jokes owner **Deborah Rita,** "I offer people breadcrumbs at the door." It's a good place to get lost in, with a great assortment of English, Irish, and Scandinavian antique pieces in pine, mahogany, and fruitwood, mixed in with reproductions and contemporary accessories. Rita has a knack for arranging the groupings so that each item's singularity stands out, and for all the investment-level furniture, there are plenty of affordable knickknacks, such as flattering silverplate picture frames. If you find your way out, take a look at the barn—it's full of stuff waiting for a slot in the big house. ♦ M-Tu, Th-Sa 10AM-5PM, Su noon-4PM June-Aug; M, Th-Sa 10AM-5PM, Su noon-4PM Sept-May. 6 Lewis Rd (off Main St), E. Orleans. 240.0525

80 Nauset House Inn $ This circa 1810 dormered farmhouse is full of lovely eccentricities, starting with a turn-of-the-century conservatory filled with intoxicating camellias and welcoming wicker settees. The brick-floored dining room features a rustic hearth and plank table where **Diane Johnson's** delectable breakfasts are laid out. The meal is optional, for a nominal charge, but who would want to sleep through ginger pancakes with lemon sauce, or oatmeal butterscotch muffins? The 14 rooms vary in size and splendor (those in the carriage house are the most spacious), but all partake of the bucolic grounds, and **Nauset Beach** is a breezy 10-minute walk away. ♦ Closed Nov-Apr. 143 Beach Rd (between Brick Hill and Nauset Heights Rds), E. Orleans. 255.2195

81 Nauset Beach Club ★★★$$$ This pint-size roadside restaurant (a former duck-hunting cottage) packs a surprisingly sophisticated punch. Chef **Jack Salemi** keeps tinkering with the menu, but you're likely to encounter a luscious lobster tarte with warm citrus vinaigrette or classic osso buco on a bed of polenta. The terracotta-hued dining room is an intimate retreat; sociable sorts can sit out on the patio and watch the beachgoers buzz by. ♦ Northern Italian ♦ Dinner. Closed Monday late Nov to May. 222 Main St (between Barley Neck and Great Oak Rds), E. Orleans. 255.8547

81 Kadee's Gray Elephant $$ Owner **Chris Cavanaugh** is not afraid of color; she loads it on, with hand-decorated furniture, layers of bright quilts, and purple-painted wicker. These studio apartments, which rent by the night or by the week, are so busy and bright, you might not mind an occasional gray day. ♦ 212 Main St (between Barley Neck and Great Oak Rds), E. Orleans. 255.7608

On the grounds:

Kadee's Lobster & Clam Bar ★★$$$ The same bouncy energy extends to this dolled-up sea shack, with floral umbrellas for fine weather, tarps and a blue-striped awning when the sea air turns cold and wet. The creamy seafood stews—oyster, crab, lobster—are modeled after those served at the **Oyster Bar** in New York's **Grand Central Station.** Try a "seabob" (marinated swordfish and shrimp skewered and grilled), or the "seafood simmer"—shrimp, scallops, and lobster sautéed with sherry, butter, lemon, parsley, and sweet basil. ♦ American/Takeout ♦ Lunch and dinner. Closed Monday through Friday late May to mid-June, early Sept to mid-Oct; closed mid-Oct to late May. 255.6184

Apple Grove Mini Golf Perhaps not the world's most challenging course, it's certainly picturesque, with miniature houses and a lighthouse; in any case, it's a good way to pass the time while waiting for a take-out order. ♦ Daily 10:30AM-9PM. 255.6184

81 East Orleans Art & Antiques Owner **Katherine Fox** does her best to keep prices low, and as a result, many of her customers are dealers themselves. Specialties include estate jewelry, kilims (new as well as old), and whatever country furniture she can find; as an example of her nongouging approach, consider a corner cupboard for only $3,200. She also represents a few local artists, including Brewster watercolorist **Karen North Wells.** ♦ Tu-Sa 10:30AM-5PM June-Sept; Th-Sa 10:30AM-5PM Oct-Dec. 204 Main St (at Great Oak Rd), E. Orleans. 255.7799

82 The Parsonage Inn $ English innkeepers lend a civilized lilt to this eight-bedroom B&B, fashioned from an extended circa 1770 full Cape. **Elizabeth Brown,** a piano teacher who grew up in Kenya, might play a little Liszt or Chopin during the evening in the moss-green paneled living room, and breakfast might consist of scones with Devonshire cream. Among the more dramatic rooms is "The Barn," with a daubed ceiling and fencepost bed. ♦ 202 Main St (at Great Oak Rd), E. Orleans. 255.8217

83 Academy Playhouse Orleans outgrew its 1873 town hall in 1949, but the former forum for town meetings turned out to be an excellent setting for an arena stage. The **Academy of Performing Arts** mounts performances here year-round; typically, fluffy stuff (mostly musicals) in summer, and more substance for the locals during off-season, plus concerts, dance, and poetry readings. ♦ Tu-Su 8:30PM July to mid-Sept; F-Su mid-Sept to July. 120 Main St (at Monument Rd), Orleans. 255.1963

> In the summer of 1944, alarmed at the growing popularity of halter-tops and shorts in their town, Harwich police handed out several hundred cards requesting that, in future, the recipient stick to "conventional dress."

Restaurants/Clubs: Red **Hotels:** Blue
Shops/ Outdoors: Green **Sights/Culture:** Black

Local Bounty Then and Now

Confronted with a landscape that bore no relation to the tamed and tidy English countryside, the Pilgrims immediately set about exercising their Yankee ingenuity to adapt to the new terrain. The early settlers and their descendants to this day are known for maximizing every conceivable yield.

A Salty Tale

The Pilgrims' first order of business, in a pre-refrigeration age, was to preserve the seasonal windfalls that came their way, in order to survive the cruel winters. All along the Cape and coast, for instance, "aloofes" (*Pomolobus pseudo-harengus,* a herring relative that eventually came to be known as "alewife herring") arrived in great numbers every spring to spawn; the settlers could literally step into a stream and pick their fill. Salted, this fish, as well as the plentiful cod, could serve as a year-round staple, and also as a valuable trading commodity. Salt, however, was prohibitively expensive and impossible to obtain, what with the embargos imposed by the British during the Revolutionary War. Noting that they were, in fact, surrounded by salt, **Captain John Sears** of Dennis attempted to extract it from seawater by means of solar evaporation. Though skeptics called his scheme "Sears' Folly," because initially it took 350 gallons of water to produce one bushel of salt, he devised a wind-powered pump that facilitated the process. By the War of 1812, the wooden "saltworks"—house-size repositories with movable roofs to keep out the rain—were deemed so vital an asset, they were often the target of bombardment, or at the very least extortion. **Captain Richard Raggett** of the HMS *Spencer* exacted $4,000 from the town of Brewster for sparing their works; in Barnstable, he upped the ante to $6,000 but was fended off by two cannons hastily fetched from Boston. (The townspeople of Brewster, incidentally, have a long memory—they petitioned **Queen Elizabeth** for restitution in 1976, but their request has thus far been ignored.) By the 1830s, some 450 saltworks were scattered about the Cape, producing more than half a million bushels a year. When tariffs and thus import prices declined after 1840, so did this homegrown industry. By the time of **Henry David Thoreau's** visit in 1849, all the sprawling "turtlelike" sheds lay idle.

Bitter Berries, Sweet Success

By the mid-19th century, Cape Codders had discovered a new foodstuff to exploit. The cranberry—officially, *Vaccinium macrocarpon*—got its common name from Dutch settlers who thought the vines' pinkish-white flowers resembled the head and beak of a crane; it's a stretch, but *kraanbere* stuck. The Narragansett Indians, who called the berries *sassamanesh*—"bitter berries"—had long used them not only as food (typically, either sweetened with maple sap or pounded together with venison and fat to make trail-food cakes called "pemmican"), but as a dye and a poultice for wounds. Once instructed in its uses, the colonists quickly embraced this new fruit. According to *New-Englands Rarities Discovered* by **John Josselyn** (published in London in 1672), the cranberry, or bear berry, was found to have "a sower, astringent taste," yet "the Indians and English use them much, boyling them with Sugar for Sauce to eat with their Meat. . . . They are excellent against the Scurvy . . . also good to allay the Fervour of hot Diseases." Knowing nothing of the connection between vitamin deficiency and scurvy, the whalers always packed along a barrel of vitamin-C-laden cranberries in water when heading off for distant ports.

A low-growing evergreen vine, cranberries flourish in bogs that dry up during the growing season, and also do better when lightly covered with blowing sand—characteristics noted by **Henry Hall** of Dennis, who in 1816 replanted some wild vines and became the first cultivator of the fruit. In the early 1840s, **Alvin Cahoon** of Harwich was the first person to clear bogs in which to grow cranberries commercially, and the crop achieved profitability by 1880. Today, they're the state's primary agricultural product, bringing in revenues of $200 million a year. Massachusetts is, concomitantly, the largest cranberry producer in the world, encompassing some 12,200 acres of cranberry bogs, half in the town of Carver (west of Plymouth), the rest on the Cape and Nantucket. Since every acre must be surrounded by four times that area of supporting wetlands (harvesting is achieved through flooding: the threshed berries float to the surface), cranberry cultivation has ensured the preservation of vast tracts that not only shelter rare and endangered wildlife but are lovely to look at—especially in fall, when the leaves turn a deep crimson.

Harvesting the Sea

Not always the sought-after delicacy they are today, lobsters during the Pilgrim's time were considered "hard rations" (to be resorted to only in desperation). So plentiful were the crustaceans in 1860 that a whole boatload sold for as little as a penny and prisoners were known to riot when served one too many lobster dinners. Instead they were used as fertilizer, bait, and pig fodder. Now, no summer is complete without at least one bib-and-pliers feast. If you happen to be an experienced SCUBA diver with a $40 permit from the state Marine Fisheries, you can pluck your own. Otherwise, you're at the whim of market prices.

The Pilgrims were equally contemptuous of clams, present on the Cape in three guises. Soft-shell clams (also called longnecks), the kind served as "steamers," are a messy but delicious proposition: you must pry open the shell, pull out the clam, and strip off the often gritty covering, then dunk it first in broth (for cleaning), then butter (for flavor). Quahogs (pronounced "CO-hogs") are hard-shell clams; when still small- or medium-size, they're called cherrystones and littlenecks, respectively, and make a briny treat served raw on the half-shell. Full-grown quahogs are flavorful but tough; they're best minced, and presented in a breading or used for pies and chowders. Giant sea clams, measuring five or six inches across, are good only for chowder.

Another one-time throwaway food, the lowly mussel is a more recent addition to fine menus. Belatedly following the European lead, restaurants began featuring them only within the past few decades. The oval, black shells yield a crustacean of tender texture, buttery taste, and occasionally the surprise dividend of a small black pearl—worthless but pretty nonetheless.

Scallops have been treasured all along—so much so that unscrupulous vendors sometimes substituted sliced skate, or soaked the real thing in soda to make them swell and sell for more. Such practices have long been outlawed, as has the taking of any scallop showing no rings on the shell (each ring marks a year and about an inch's worth of growth: a full-grown scallop will attain three rings). Ironically, though, all these years restaurants have been throwing away most of the scallop and serving only the adductor muscle. Many of the better restaurants are now taking advantage of locally cultivated scallops and serving them whole.

Wellfleet's oysters have been garnering raves since 1601, when explorer **Samuel de Champlain** named their home base "Porte aux huîtres." Rivaled only by their cousins in Cotuit, Wellfleet oysters are best consumed within moments of shucking; by the time they're arrayed prettily on ice and brought to the table, they're likely to have lost some of their delicate bouquet. True aficionados frequent raw bars, where the pricey bivalves race straight from the shucker's hands to your lips.

Potent Potables

Like their fellow Englishmen, the Pilgrims—men, women, and children alike—drank beer rather than water; the water back home was too polluted, and the New World's water, unless in a fermented brew, too risky. Popular regional variations evolved, including spruce beer and birch beer, sometimes doctored with maple sap or parings from pumpkins and apples (the colonists were disinclined to let anything go to waste). A precursor to sodas was a "beverige" consisting of spring water, molasses, and ginger; the sailors' version, "switchel," came spiked with rum and vinegar.

Whereas the settlers produced fruit or herb wine on a small scale for their own use, several start-up enterprises have been founded in recent decades on the premise that this unlikely clime might actually lend itself to commercial-scale wine production. The warmer-than-normal temperatures are all to the good, as is the quick-draining sandy soil. As for the results, you'll have to judge for yourself. Some might find the cranberry blends at the **Plymouth Colony Winery** (Pinewood Road, Plymouth, 747.3334) or the fruit, flower, and berry concoctions of the **Chatham Winery** (Route 28, Chatham, 945.0300) more than a mite too sweet. Established in 1986, the **Nantucket Vineyard** (Bartlett Farm Road, Nantucket, 228.9235) sticks strictly to grapes (some homegrown), but the output is still somewhat erratic. The front-runner remains **Chicama Vineyards** (Stoney Hill Road, West Tisbury, Martha's Vineyard, 693.0309), started way back in 1971; all that prescient early effort has begun to pay off in Chardonnays, Cabernets, Rieslings, Pinot Noirs, and the island's first appellation Merlot.

Josef Berger's *Cape Cod Pilot,* written under the aegis of the WPA in 1937, contains the following instructions for a traditional clambake: "You will require a good supply of stones as big as your two fists. You must have enough of these to fill in a circle, six feet in diameter, of two layers. On top of your stones build a fire of driftwood and race it for an hour, covering all the stones. *You* do the direction, and let the others in your party bring piles of wet seaweed, washed as clean as possible of sand. Rake the embers off your hot stones and pile the wood on to a depth of 18 inches. Spread your clams over the weed, with your lobsters, potatoes, corn, or anything else you want to bake. Keep everything well away from the edge, and bunched towards the center. Then cover with more weed, to a depth of three feet. Then batten all down with an old piece of sailcloth, tucking in the edges all round, to retain the steam, and on top of this pile plenty of sand. Your work is finished now, except for the hardest chore of all—to keep everybody else away from the bake for at least 45 minutes, and to argue down those in the party who insist that half an hour is long enough, and they know because they tried it once on Long Island. Tell them this is Cape Cod. Explain that they do everything wrong here. That's why the baked clams taste so good."

84 The Wheel Haus Kaffee Cafe ★$$ Like many a retired schooner captain before him, **Uli Pruesse** came to the Cape to set up a small business—several of them, in fact. This tiny, stylish cafe is a good start. Indoors or out in the garden, you can lunch on light sandwiches like the Little Mermaid (crab salad with fresh shrimp) or sup on platters such as the October Fest: roast smoked pork with homemade cinnamon applesauce, barrel-cured sauerkraut, and fried potatoes. The desserts are so elegant—bombes and tortes, imported from New York and the Continent—that it's tempting to follow European tradition and make no pretense of eating anything wholesome at all. ♦ International ♦ Breakfast, lunch, and dinner. Closed for dinner Sunday through Thursday Nov-May. 2 Academy Pl (at Main St), Orleans. 240.1585

On the grounds:

The Wheel Haus Guest House $ The four rooms are pretty and neat, if not especially atmospheric; the location, central; the price, right. ♦ 240.1585

Wheel Haus Nautiques & Gifts Pruesse knows this equipment firsthand, so if you want an explanation to go with your ship model, sextant, chart (old or new), or scrimshaw, you have only to ask. ♦ Daily noon-3PM, 6-10PM June-Dec; call for off-season hours. 240.1585

85 French Cable Station Museum From 1891 to 1941, this office was a key communications link between America and Europe. Before the wireless and the radio rendered the practice obsolete, stock reports and news were transmitted daily across the ocean to Brest (originally via Newfoundland, and by 1898 direct) by means of a hefty cable. It was here that word of **Lindbergh's** successful 1927 New York-Paris flight first reached the United States, as well as the announcement of the German invasion of France. The station was decommissioned in 1959, and in 1971 nine local **French Telegraph Cable Co.** employees bought the building. The **Smithsonian** helped prepare the displays; the contents are rather complex and can be confusing to the uninitiated, so if you're interested, ask for the full tour, or just view it as a house-size fax machine. ♦ Admission. M-Sa 10AM-4PM June to early Sept. 41 S. Orleans Rd/Rte 28 (between Main St and Rte 6A), Orleans. 255.1386

Restaurants/Clubs: Red | **Hotels:** Blue
Shops/ Outdoors: Green | **Sights/Culture:** Black

85 Peacock Alley Antiques Two dealers share this funky shop: **Jerry Kibbe** with his Art Deco and '50s artifacts, and **Jane Merrill** with her vintage fashions, accessories, and jewelry, from beaded bags to Bakelite bracelets. The customer profile? Those nostalgic for the modern furniture they grew up with a few short decades ago, and clothes lovers convinced you're never too old to play dress-up. ♦ M-Sa 10AM-4:30PM, Su noon-4:30PM mid-May to Jan; M, Th-Sa 10AM-4:30PM, Su noon-4:30PM Jan to mid-May. 35 S. Orleans Rd/Rte 28 (between Main St and Rte 6A), Orleans. 240.1804

85 New Horizons This 19th-century captain's house was once the studio of artist **Peter Hunt,** who started a fad in the 1940s and 1950s for furniture painted with folk motifs. A few of his creations can be found in the antiques section of this rambling shop. For the most part, though, the stock is brand-new: an astute selection of top-quality crafts from around the country, chosen by shop owners **Nancy Norton** and **Sandy Bockman.** Among the distinguished locals represented here are **Chatham Pottery** and **Pewter Crafters of Cape Cod.** ♦ M-F 9:30AM-9PM, Sa 9:30AM-5:30PM, Su 11AM-5PM July-Aug; M-Sa 10AM-5PM, Su noon-5PM Sept-June. Peacock Alley, 35 S. Orleans Rd/Rte 28 (between Main St and Rte 6A), Orleans. 255.8766

85 Yellow House **Lucille Danneman's** antiques are on the pricey side, but perfectly picked to dress up any setting. She's a designer, too, so the showroom is pleasingly laid out. Cupboards, bureaus, tables—it's all very practical stuff, just unusually good-looking. ♦ Daily 10AM-5PM May-Oct; by appointment Nov-Apr. 21 S. Orleans Rd/Rte 28 (between Main St and Rte 6A), Orleans. 255.9686

86 The Arbor Restaurant ★★$$$ Who needs a floor show when you've got decor this entertaining? It looks as if a flea market hit the fan. You're greeted by a barber's chair and a crib converted into a settee. Every square inch is plastered with tchotchkes, and not a single plate matches another. The menu is on the quirky side, too: mussels baked in mushroom caps with port and garlic butter, veal in a Harvey's Bristol Cream sauce with capers and leeks—there's even Cajun pasta. It's all rather rich, if not haute, and you won't lack for conversation pieces. ♦ American/Continental ♦ Dinner. 20 S. Orleans Rd/Rte 28 (between Main St and Rte 6A), Orleans. 255.4847

Within The Arbor Restaurant:

Binnacle Tavern ★★$ The funhouse atmosphere continues here, and the place is usually packed. The draw: family-friendly prices, and what some consider the best pizza on the Cape, in odd topping combos like chopped apples and shrimp, or currants and Gorgonzola (they're not all so bizarre). ♦ International ♦ Dinner. 255.7901

87 **The Cove** $$ This is one very handsome motel, painted a muted green and overlooking its namesake. The rooms have condo-style furnishings (not dazzling, but nice enough), and most have decks with views of the heated pool and waterside gazebo. Guests are offered a complimentary "FloteBote" ride around **Town Cove.** ♦ 13 S. Orleans Rd/Rte 28 (between Main St and Rte 6A), Orleans. 343.2233, 800/343.2233

87 **Continuum** Old-house owners seeking just the right vintage lighting fixtures have a friend in **Dan Johnson,** who keeps more than 300 in stock, from Victorian to Deco. The selection's so good, you'll have to forgive the lightbulb jokes in his "Light Reading" newsletter. ♦ M-Sa 11AM-5PM, Su noon-5PM early July to Aug; M, Th-Su 10:30AM-5PM Oct to early July. Closed Sunday in summer if sunny. 7 S. Orleans Rd/Rte 28 (between Main St and Rte 6A), Orleans. 255.8513

87 **Cottage St. Bakery** **JoAnna Keeley's** concoctions are outstanding, from all sorts of healthy breads (dill-cheese, carrot-onion-oatmeal, and such) to insidiously delicious desserts. For a brunch party, take home one of her pizza-size mega-Danishes. ♦ Bakery ♦ Daily 7AM-9PM. Cottage St (off Rte 6A), Orleans. 255.2821

88 **Oceana** **Carol Wright's** shop is like a small-scale **Nature Company** with hand-picked gifts of the sort you might actually want to give someone (or keep for yourself)—nature-related books, tapes, and puzzles; silver and gold jewelry; broad-brimmed straw hats. It's a peaceful place and a pleasure to browse. ♦ M-Sa 9AM-9PM, Su 10:30AM-6PM late June to early Sept; M-Sa 9AM-5:30PM early Sept to Jan; Th-Sa 9AM-5:30PM Jan-Mar; M-Sa 9AM-5:30PM Apr to late June. 37 Rte 6A (between Rtes 28 and 6), Orleans. 240.1414

88 **Spindrift Pottery** **Mahala Bishop** has been spinning her wheel here since 1980, and she's unflaggingly friendly, happy to chat as she throws. Her plates, bowls, and casseroles (all oven-, microwave-, and dishwasher-safe), are durable as well as beautiful. She favors glazes the color of sea and sand and imprints some pieces with scallop shells. ♦ Daily 10AM-6PM late May to mid-Oct, Dec; W-Su 10AM-5PM mid-Oct to Dec, Apr to late May. 37 Rte 6A, Orleans. 255.1404

88 **Jonathan Young Windmill** Built circa 1720 in Orleans, later moved here and there (millers typically took their tools along when relocating), and eventually returned to the town in 1938, this mill unfortunately is no longer in operation: when the **Orleans Historical Society** took it over, they had to choose between preserving its architectural integrity or functionality. You'll be glad that aesthetics won out when you peer up into the intricate wooden gears. The helpful docents are well versed in their milling lore, pointing out, for instance, that the phrase "keeping one's nose to the grindstone" was necessitated by the grain's tendency to go up in flames, and the mill along with it. ♦ Daily 11AM-4PM July-Aug. Town Cove Park (between Rtes 28 and 6), Orleans. 255.1386

88 **The Goose Hummock Shop** This long-established shop spans two buildings. The one up by the road features every conceivable wrinkle in fishing gear, with advice thrown in for free. **Goose Hummock Marine,** behind it, stocks general sporting goods, such as bikes, canoes, kayaks, and, for the masochistically inclined, a towable canvas-covered tube called the Bump-R-Ride. ♦ M-Sa 8AM-8PM, Su 8AM-3PM July-Aug; M-Sa 8AM-5:30PM, Su 8AM-3PM mid-Apr to July, Sept-Nov; M-Sa 8AM-5:30PM Dec to mid-Apr. 15 Rte 6A, Orleans. 255.0455. Also at: 2 Rte 28, Yarmouth. 778.0877

88 **Kemp Pottery** One of the Cape's most prominent potters, **Steve Kemp** is just as comfortable producing functional pieces as he is creating one-of-a-kind artworks. The former category includes affordable crockery, mirrors, lamps, and sinks; the latter, well-crafted busts and torsos; and in between, some fanciful, elaborately decorated tureens and garden statuary. He doesn't mind being watched as he works, and, given a curious young crowd, he'll expound entertainingly on the history of ceramics. ♦ M-Sa 10AM-5PM; Su 11AM-4PM. 9 Rte 6A (between Rtes 28 and 6), Orleans. 255.5853

88 **The Pump House** Cape surfers are a small but hardy bunch. Even if you don't plan to join their ranks (Wellfleet's beaches are said to be the best for beginners, and you can start out, prone, on a bodyboard), stop here if only to update your wardrobe. The wetsuits and boards come used or new, and the baggy flannels and cool shades require no prior dude experience. ♦ M-Sa 9AM-7PM, Su 10AM-7PM May-Sept; Sa 9AM-7PM, Su 2-7PM Oct-Jan. 9 Rte 6A (between Rtes 28 and 6), Orleans. 255.5832

89 Bird Watcher's General Store It's no secret that Cape Codders are bird-crazy, but until hobbyist **Mike O'Connor** opened his shop in 1983, no one could have gauged their numbers and fervor. After less than a decade in business, this store had to relocate to larger quarters, and now moves almost a ton of birdseed a day. Among the hundreds of avian items sold in the barn-size emporium is an O'Connor invention, the **Avarium,** a windowsill birdfeeder with a one-way mirror; elegant granite birdbaths ($300-$650); and telescopes (up to $1,600). Most of the stuff is a lot less expensive and, in some cases, sillier: bird giftwrap, puzzles, sound tracks, socks. ♦ Daily 9AM-9PM July-Aug; daily 9AM-6PM Sept-Oct, May-June; daily 9AM-5PM Nov-Apr. 36 Rte 6A (between Rtes 28 and 6), Orleans. 255.6974, 800/562.1512

90 The Artful Hand Gallery **Joseph** and **Mary Pocari** founded this crafts shop in the early 1980s and have since attracted some 500 artisans and opened branches in Chatham and in Boston's upscale **Copley Place.** Their guidelines, as far as can be deduced, are the lush and the offbeat, sometimes both. Glassware and glass jewelry are strong suits. A lot of the goods have a humorous touch (a da Vincian jellybean mill) but stop just short of dreaded "whimsy." ♦ M-Th, Sa 10AM-7PM, F 10AM-9PM, Su noon-5PM July to early Sept; M-F 10AM-5PM, Sa 10AM-5:30PM. Main St Sq (off Main St, between Rte 6A and Locust Rd), Orleans. 255.2969. Also at: 459 Main St, Chatham. 945.4933

90 Off-The-Bay Cafe ★★★$$$$ **Steve Hickock's** place, in a rehabbed century-old Main Street shop, is the spiffiest eatery in town, with lots of gleaming brass and burnished pine wainscoting, a tin ceiling, revolving fans, and flowered tablecloths. The cuisine is as varied and skilled as you'll find in these parts, ranging from grilled crab cakes with red pepper and papaya hollandaise to spit-roasted duckling with beach plum and cranberry compote. Come back for brunch: lobster omelets accompanied by jazz. ♦ New American ♦ Breakfast, lunch, and dinner; Sunday brunch. Closed for breakfast Monday through Friday Sept-June. 28 Main St (between Rte 6A and Locust Rd), Orleans. 255.5505

91 Head & Foot Shop If you're escorting teenagers who insist on having the right labels (**Esprit, Levi, Champion,** et al) before they'll consent to appear in public, stop here for a great selection, all of it slightly knocked down in price. ♦ M-Sa 9AM-9PM, Su noon-5PM late May to early Sept; M-Sa 9AM-5:30PM, Su noon-5PM early Sept to late May. 42 Main St (between Rtes 6A and 28), Orleans. 255.1281. Also at: 578 Main St, Chatham. 945.9019; 193 Commercial St, Provincetown. 487.3683

91 Land Ho! ★★$$ You'd have to be a local just to figure out that this nondescript white clapboard building harbors a restaurant. Owner **John Murphy** has been so busy keeping hordes of regulars happy for the past quarter-century that he certainly doesn't need to solicit the tourist trade. It's basically a pub with wood walls plastered with business ads. There's not much to the menu, although the kale soup recipe did make the pages of *Gourmet.* ♦ American/International ♦ Lunch and dinner. 38 Main St (at Rte 6A), Orleans. 255.5165

92 Charles Moore Arena Families can skate away the rainy-day blues at this cavernous public rink, which offers lessons, rentals, and space just to kick loose. In summer, it's given over to rollerskating or blading; the rest of the year it's under ice. Whatever the season, Friday is "Roller Rock-Nite," a DJ'd, strobe-lit party reserved exclusively for kids nine to 15. ♦ Admission. Rainy days 2-4PM, W 7-9PM, F 8-10PM mid-June to early Sept; Tu-W, F 11AM-1PM, Th 3:30-5PM, Sa 7-9PM, Su 2-4PM early Sept to late Nov; Tu-W, F 11AM-1PM, Th 3:30-5PM, Su 2-4PM late Nov to mid-Apr; call for spring hours. O'Connor Wy (off Eldridge Park Wy), Orleans. 255.2972

93 Old Jailhouse Tavern ★★$$ How many bars are housed in a hoosegow? This rubble-stone building was actually constable **Henry Perry's** home a century ago, but he did put up a few surplus miscreants from time to time, so owner **Lynee Hirst** and architect **Anthony E. Ferragamo** ran with the motif. A massive iron gate separates the bar from the dining room proper, which opens out into a greenhouse. The menu is nothing out of the ordinary, except for its prison-talk nomenclature, but there are some tasty snacks available at any time of day. The toast Nelson—French bread topped with bacon, onion, crabmeat, shrimp, scallops, hollandaise, and Parmesan—sure beats bread and water. ♦ International ♦ Lunch and dinner; Sunday brunch. 28 West Rd (off Rte 6A), Orleans. 255.5245

94 Captain Linnell House ★★★$$$$ With its neoclassic Ionic columns, **Captain Eben Linnell's** 1854 mansion is often compared to the fictional Tara, but in fact he copied it from from a seagoing colleague's Marseilles villa; planning to retire here with his wife and three daughters, he took one final—and, as it turned out, fatal—voyage. Although long-term renovations are under way, some of the interior choices detract from the overall elegance: the metal chairs, for instance, would seem much more at home in a function room.

Chef/owner **William Conway's** work in the kitchen is above complaint. His bourbon-splashed lobster bisque is a front-runner for best of the Cape, and his innovative approach to fish is exemplified in a baked scrod wrapped in parchment with lemon-lime vermouth sauce. Of the three dining rooms, the prettiest is the one overlooking the garden with its mossy brick wall, gazebo, and voluminous catalpa; it's an ideal spot for brunch. ♦ New American ♦ Dinner; Sunday brunch. 137 Skaket Beach Rd (off West Rd), Orleans. Reservations requested. 255.3400

95 Rock Harbor Charter Fishing Fleet

Serious recreational fishers (no oxymoron there) make a beeline for this lineup of 15 boats, the Cape's largest for-hire fishing fleet. You can walk along the pier and see which appeals: perhaps the 39-foot *Empress,* whose captain, **Stu Finlay,** has as many years' experience tracking down bluefish, bass, haddock, cod, flounder, and, with any luck in late summer, tuna. Each boat accommodates up to six people for half- or full-day excursions. ♦ Fee. By reservation June to mid-Oct. Rock Harbor (off Rock Harbor Rd), Orleans. 255.9757, 800/287.1771

95 Capt. Cass Rock Harbor Seafood

★★$$ This buoy-strewn, shingled cottage is picturesque to the hilt, and authentic, too—it hasn't changed a whit since the '50s. The tables are covered with oilcloth, the menu is scrawled on posterboard, and the fare is simple but ample: all the usual bounty, plus she-crab stew, and, for a splurge (twice the price of most items on the menu), a shore dinner centered on a hefty two-pound lobster. ♦ American ♦ Lunch and dinner. Closed mid-Oct to late May. 117 Rock Harbor Rd (between Main St and Bridge Rd), Orleans. No phone

Bests

Eleanor Lawrence (Steindler)
Flutist/Artistic Director of the Monomoy Chamber Ensemble

The sound of the birds, the wind in the trees, the gentle climate—cool nights—and fog, sun, sand, wind, and water, both fresh and salt. Going to the **Outer Beach** to see the surf during or after a big storm is awesome, as are beach walks at sunset after the sun-worshiping crowds have gone home.

Favorite towns: **Chatham** for the unspoiled main street (great tourist shopping), **Wellfleet** for gallery browsing, and **Provincetown** for the whale watches and the people-watching. "P-town" is especially charming after the summer season.

Favorite things to do:

The **Monomoy Theatre,** which presents a new play each week for two months. The fare is more substantial than at many summer theaters, offering thoughtful dramas as well as entertaining comedies and musicals. In the last week of July, the **Monomoy Chamber Ensemble** appears in the theater, presenting fine classical music played by renowned professional musicians, which I take great pleasure in producing.

The **Cape Cod Bike Trail**—enter from Route 137 in Brewster. Turn left toward Harwich. After several miles of biking, buy a sandwich at the country grocery store; on the return trip, swim in the freshwater pond you pass alongside the trail. The other way takes you to **Nickerson State Park,** and the ride from the **National Seashore Headquarters** in Eastham to the Outer Beach is especially beautiful.

The **Outer Beach** may be reached by car at several public access points, but the real way to do it is to sail across Chatham's **Pleasant Bay.** (A motorboat runs across for hire.) Because there is no land access, the beach is very natural and relatively unpeopled, especially during the week. Here you can experience the wild freedom of a vast expanse of ocean beach. For a greater appreciation of this experience, read **Henry Beston's** *The Outermost House,* available at local bookstores.

Cape Cod Baseball League—baseball like it used to be—free, small-town, promising college players, low-key.

Audubon Society Swamp, Eastham—lovely for a nature walk.

Gingerbread House, Harwich—high tea, English-style scones, etc.

Mark Zanger (pen name **Robert Nadeau**)
Restaurant Critic, *The Boston Phoenix*

Heritage Plantation, Sandwich—in June, one of the world's great collections of rhododendrons.

Wellfleet Flea Market—endless amusement.

Pilgrim Monument—exercise kids on rainy days.

Low-tide sandbar, **East Dennis,** Bayside—vast expanse of sand.

Cypress Forest, Marconi Wildlife area—chartreuse-lit tropical microclimate.

Picking berries and beach plums.

Broiled bluefish with green peppercorns.

Commercial Street in Provincetown by night.

Bicycling the **Provincetown** dunes.

Body-boarding.

Eastham/Wellfleet/Truro

In **Eastham** in 1620, a *Mayflower* scouting party led by **Myles Standish** met the Nauset Indians at what is now called **First Encounter Beach.** The tribe attacked the would-be settlers with bows and arrows, and in doing so, ensured that they would pretty much have the area to themselves until 1644, when a group of **Plymouth Colony** malcontents showed up seeking larger land grants and more fertile turf. They hit agricultural pay dirt: even as the colonists set about deforesting their new home, they extracted two bumper crops from the sandy soil: asparagus and turnips. In the early 1800s, Eastham became a locus of revivalist fervor: thousands of Methodists gathered here each summer to soak up sermons by as many as 150 ministers-in-residence. (They soon packed up their tents, however, and headed for more scenic **Craigville** and **Oak Bluffs.**) Today, Eastham fans like the town for what it's *not:* not too crowded, not very developed, and not offering a lot to do, except hit the beach and maybe grab a bite somewhere before heading back to your cottage or motel. The bayside beaches are shallow and placid, with a broad intertidal zone that's great for shell-seeking and kite-flying; invigorating surf churns at the base of the spectacular oceanside bluffs, a protectorate of the **Cape Cod National Seashore.**

Wellfleet—a classic New England town most likely named for Wallfleet, England, equally renowned for its oysters—possesses the cultural attractions absent in Eastham. The galleries are easily as lively as those in **Provincetown** (without the attendant commercialization), and several stores and restaurants warrant a leisurely visit. Women in search of affordable and au courant designer clothing will be particularly well served at shops such as **Karol Richardson** and **Hannah.** There's even challenging drama to take in at the **Wellfleet Harbor Actors' Theater (WHAT)**, and for those who prefer to play the philistine while on vacation, nothing beats a trashy double feature at the **Wellfleet Drive-In.**

In **Truro**, there's *really* "no there, there"—just a general store (upscale, admittedly), a post office, and a facetious sign heralding "Downtown Truro." Originally part of Eastham (it separated in 1790), Truro started out as a Native American village called **Payomet**, or **Pamet**, named for the resident tribe. Its 18th-century settlers called it **Dangerfield,** alluding to the treacherous waters flanking it (the region lost so many of its citizens at sea that it was known as "the town of empty graves"); later, residents fearing bad PR rechristened it after an English town in Cornwall that it resembled. Truro once rivaled Provincetown as a fishing port, but in the 1800s, **Pamet Harbor** started filling up with sand; the fishing vessels went elsewhere, and the town dozed for a century or so. With a year-round population of 1,400 (spread over 42 square miles), Truro still qualifies as the Cape's sleepiest community. **Thoreau** wrote in *Cape Cod,* "In the north part of town there is no house from shore to shore for several miles, and it is wild and solitary as the Western Prairies used to be." Quite a few more houses are now tucked in the woods and along the shore, but the feeling of space and isolation remains. **Truro Center** is the favored summer retreat of writers and psychiatrists, while **North Truro** is more of a working-class suburb of Provincetown, its bay side plastered with cute if chockablock cottages.

---

1 Mid-Cape American Youth Hostel $ Yet another great **AYH** deal: eight tiny barn-red cabins sleeping six to eight apiece surround a common room with a screened-in porch. On the down side, you're locked out from 9:30AM to 5:30PM, there aren't many places to take refuge during those hours when the weather's nasty (as the staff can be to anyone attempting to talk to them "off the clock"), and it's bring-your-own-food. However, there are picnic tables and a pair of outdoor grills, as well as a communal kitchen. Those who are

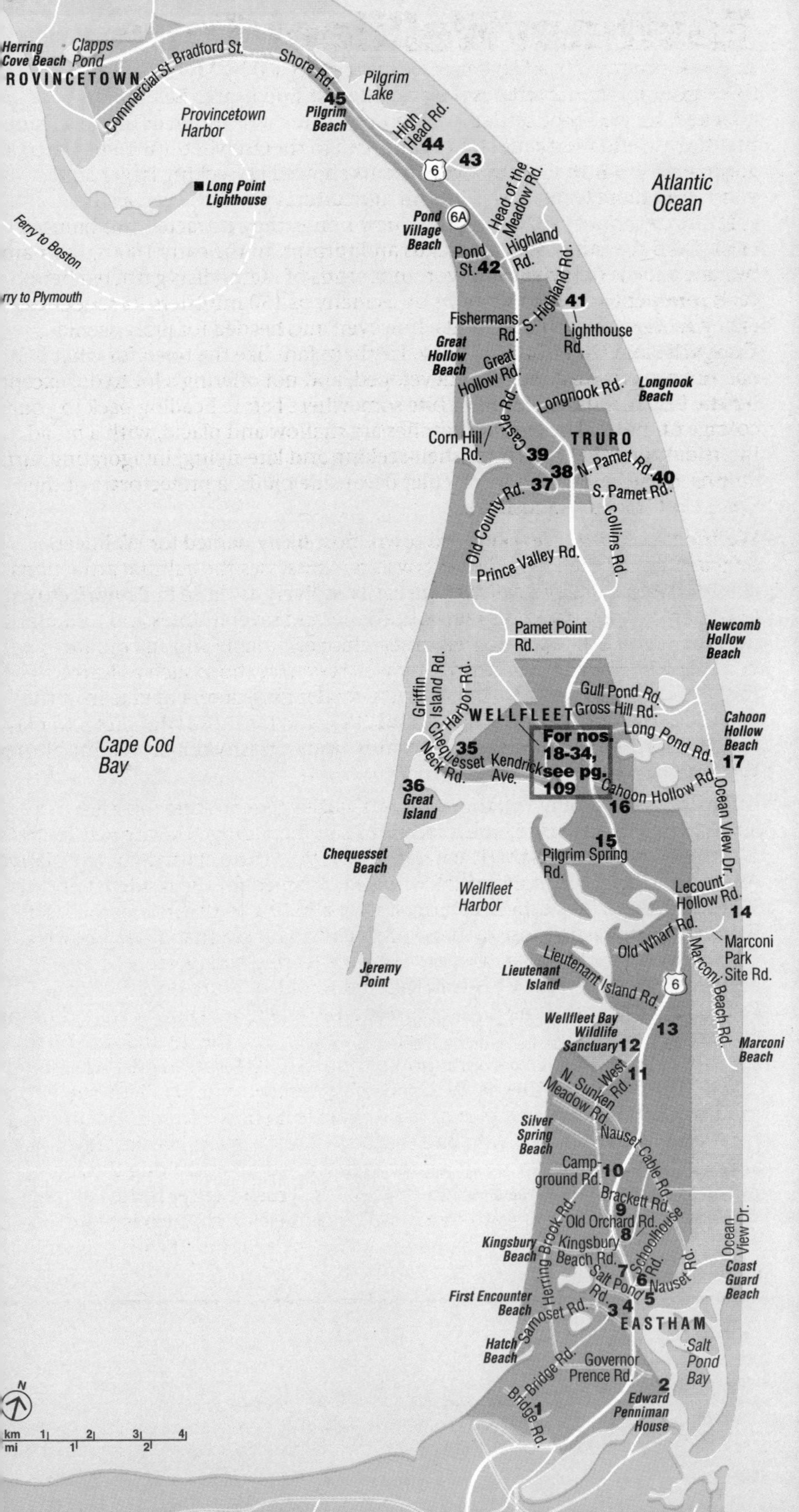

Herring Cove Beach
Clapps Pond
ROVINCETOWN
Commercial St.
Bradford St.
Shore Rd.
Pilgrim Lake
Provincetown Harbor
45 Pilgrim Beach
High Head Rd.
44
43
6
Long Point Lighthouse
Atlantic Ocean
Head of the Meadow Rd.
Ferry to Boston
rry to Plymouth
Pond Village Beach
6A
Pond St.
42
Highland Rd.
S. Highland Rd.
41
Lighthouse Rd.
Fishermans Rd.
Great Hollow Beach
Great Hollow Rd.
Longnook Rd.
Longnook Beach
Castle Rd.
Corn Hill Rd.
TRURO
39
38
N. Pamet Rd.
40
37
S. Pamet Rd.
Old County Rd.
Collins Rd.
Prince Valley Rd.
Pamet Point Rd.
Newcomb Hollow Beach
Griffin Island Rd.
Harbor Rd.
Gull Pond Rd.
WELLFLEET
Gross Hill Rd.
Cahoon Hollow Beach
Chequesset Neck Rd.
35
Kendrick Ave.
For nos. 18-34, see pg. 109
Long Pond Rd.
17
Cape Cod Bay
36 Great Island
Cahoon Hollow Rd.
16
Ocean View Dr.
15
Pilgrim Spring Rd.
Chequesset Beach
Wellfleet Harbor
Lecount Hollow Rd.
14
Old Wharf Rd.
Marconi Park Site Rd.
Jeremy Point
Lieutenant Island
Lieutenant Island Rd.
6
Marconi Beach Rd.
Wellfleet Bay Wildlife Sanctuary
12
13
Marconi Beach
West Rd.
11
N. Sunken Meadow Rd.
Silver Spring Beach
Nauset Cable Rd.
Campground Rd.
10
Brackett Rd.
9
Old Orchard Rd.
Schoolhouse Rd.
Ocean View Dr.
Kingsbury Beach
Herring Brook Rd.
8
Kingsbury Beach Rd.
7
6
Nauset Rd.
Coast Guard Beach
Salt Pond Rd.
5
First Encounter Beach
Samoset Rd.
3
4
EASTHAM
Hatch Beach
Salt Pond Bay
Bridge Rd.
Governor Prence Rd.
2
Edward Penniman House
1
N
km 1 2 3 4
mi 1 2

accustomed to hostel life will appreciate the setting, on three wooded acres just a brisk 15-minute walk from the bay and close to the 20-mile **Rail Trail.** ♦ Closed mid-Sept to mid-May. 75 Goody Hallet Dr (off Bridge Rd), Eastham. 255.2785

1 Whalewalk Inn $$ This 1830s Greek Revival captain's house was converted to an inn in 1953, but it took the ministrations of **Dick** and **Carolyn Smith,** who bought it in 1990, to make it shine. The seven rooms and five suites, plus a saltbox cottage, are decorated in a country mode: lots of honey-toned antiques, accented by crisp new comforters and curtains in a color scheme of pale blue, peach, and pink. Breakfast, served on a terraced garden in summer, is well worth waking up for: Grand Marnier French toast, for instance, is a great way to start the day. ♦ Closed mid-Dec to Mar. 220 Bridge Rd (between Goody Hallet and Bayview Rds), Eastham. 255.0617

2 Edward Penniman House Prosperous whaler **Edward Penniman** had this Second Empire mansion constructed in 1868 while he and his wife and two children were off to sea. Painted yellow, with a two-tone red mansard roof, it's a veritable dictionary of decorative detail, from its lantern cupola and upstairs windows sheltered by wedding-cake pediments down to the ground floor's faux masonry quoins and elaborate portico supported by Corinthian columns. To date it's more of a drive-by (or, better, walk-by) attraction. Although restoration is under way, there are as yet no furnishings, save a Victorian bedroom set and a few interesting turn-of-the-century photographs by daughter **Bessie.** Mother **Betsy's** 1864-68 whaling journal, illustrated with sketches, is on display at the **Salt Pond Visitor Center,** and the **Cape Cod National Seashore (CCNS)** offers tours of the house, should you be interested in hearing some tales. A two-mile loop comprising two CCNS trails, the Fort Hill and Red Maple Swamp trails, passes right by the yard, guarded by a gate of lichen-encrusted whale bones. ♦ Fort Hill Rd (off Rte 6), Eastham. 255.3421

Writer and naturalist Henry Beston saw more like a painter. "Late in the afternoon," he wrote of the Eastham coast in *The Outermost House,* "there descends upon the beach and the bordering sea a delicate overtone of faintest violet. There is no harshness here in the landscape line, no hard Northern brightness or brusque revelation; there is always reserve and mystery, always something beyond, on earth and sea something which nature, honouring, conceals."

3 First Encounter Coffee House Many folk music legends—including Wellfleet resident **Patty Larkin** and Vineyard import **Livingston Taylor**—have played for intimate crowds at this sweet yellow clapboard 1899 Chapel in the Pines, ever since the Unitarian-Universalist church opened its doors to a music-based ministry in 1974. Concerts are held every Saturday evening in summer, and on the third Saturday of the month in winter. Fewer than 100 rapt listeners can crowd into the small room decorated with Gothic stained-glass windows. ♦ Admission. Closed May, Sept. 220 Samoset Rd (between Rte 6 and Great Pond Rd), Eastham. 255.5438

4 Beach Plum Motor Lodge $ Behind her house, **Gloria Moll** tends to a handful of pine-paneled cabin rooms that each year turn into "a little United Nations." The international visitors are no doubt drawn by the tiny kidney-shaped pool, the thousands of flowers she plants every year, the banana bread and lemon cake she bakes for breakfast, the pasta dinners her Italian mother prepares on request, and by some of the lowest rates on the Cape. ♦ Closed mid-Oct to mid-May. 2555 Rte 6 (between Samoset and Salt Pond Rds), Eastham. 255.7668

5 Salt Pond Visitor Center This modern complex, which overlooks a tidal pond and serves as an educational gateway to the 44,000-acre **Cape Cod National Seashore,** offers newcomers an excellent introduction to the ecology of the Cape. A 10-minute video screened hourly provides an overview of the area's natural history, while other films go into more detail on a variety of related topics. A diorama illustrates the vagaries of the ocean floor, and the small museum has fascinating exhibits on local history, architecture, industry and flora and fauna. Special events in summer include band concerts, slide-show presentations, and classic movies such as *Moby-Dick* and *Captains Courageous.* The center is a hub for several nature trails, including **Buttonbush Trail for the Blind,** a 1/4-mile path marked with descriptive plaques in large type and Braille. Other, longer hikes lead to **Nauset Light Beach** and **Coast Guard Beach,** popular with harbor seals in winter and human swimmers in summer.

The cottage where **Henry Beston** wrote *The Outermost House* was washed away in the Great Blizzard of 1978, but an informative sign marks its location. Further erosion in 1990 revealed to an amateur archaeologist what appeared to be an ancient hearth; rushing to excavate before more storms intervened, the **U.S. Park Service** uncovered the oldest undisturbed archaeological site found in New England to date. It contains evidence of several eras of habitation dating as far back as the Early Archaic Culture 11,000 years ago, when the site was a good five miles from the sea. ♦ Daily 9AM-5PM and occasional evenings. Salt Pond Rd (off Rte 6), Eastham. 255.3421

6 The 1869 Schoolhouse Museum This yellow clapboard was the town's one-room schoolhouse from 1869 to 1936. It's now the headquarters of the **Eastham Historical Society,** whose displays range from Native American artifacts to exhibits of farming and nautical implements. The most interesting array concerns author **Henry Beston,** who spent a year at nearby **Coast Guard Beach** writing the conservation classic *The Outermost House* (published in 1928 and still in print). The Historical Society also maintains the **1741 Swift-Daley House and Tool Museum** on Route 6, which in the mid-19th century was home to future mega-meatpacker **Gustavus Swift,** but its contents are not especially distinguished. ♦ Free. M-F 1:30-4:30PM July-Aug. Nauset and Schoolhouse Rds, Eastham. 255.0788

7 Over Look Inn $$ This 1869 Queen Anne Victorian (pictured above) is as colorful inside as out—a tough act to follow when you're talking about a creamy yellow behemoth trimmed in avocado, rust, and lilac. The Winston Churchill Library is dominated by a green leather couch, the mustard-and-emerald Ernest Hemingway Billiard Room by game trophies, and the Sarah Chipman Parlor by a life-size doll commemorating the original owner. If you venture that the place is unusual, Scottish innkeeper **Nan Aitchison** will tell you, "Eccentric is more like it." The 11 bedrooms tend toward the same overdoneness—there's one in mauve with a cathedral ceiling, fireplace, clawfoot tub, and brass bed—and amenable visitors will revel in the unsubtlety of it all. You might be in for an "eccentric" breakfast as well: a native kedgeree sauté of smoked cod, rice, onion, chopped egg, and raisins, with mango chutney. ♦ 3085 Rte 6 (between Salt Pond and Kingsbury Beach Rds), Eastham. 255.1886, 800/356.1121

8 Arnold's ★$$ This casual eatery offers all the usual deep-fried munchies, plus some mussels steamed in white wine and garlic that give white-tablecloth restaurants a run for their money. Eat in a beer garden decked out in the traditional nets and traps, or take your tray to picnic tables in the pine grove for a less populous repast. The brewski in tall plastic cups hits the spot, but don't fall for the fancy coolers—the prefab mixes taste like Pez. ♦ American/Takeout ♦ Lunch and dinner. Closed mid-Sept to mid-May. 3580 Rte 6 (at Old Orchard Rd), Eastham. 255.2575

9 Eastham Lobster Pool ★★$$$ With cement floors and VFW-style seating, this sit-down restaurant is far from fancy. And yet it is a place to revel in fish—in so many permutations (fried, grilled, broiled, baked with crumbs, stuffed with lobster sauce, or poached in a fat-free, lemon-herb court bouillon) that the menu employs a chart to list them all. The daily specials can be quite sophisticated: grilled halibut with champagne-shallot butter, for instance, or lobster with tomato-basil cream over linguine. The fresh peach daiquiris are sublime, and desserts include killer ice cream pies. Come straight from the beach, before the place is packed to its buoy-strewn rafters. ♦ American/Takeout ♦ Lunch and dinner. Closed Dec-Mar. 4360 Rte 6 (between Old Orchard and Brackett Rds), N. Eastham. 255.9706

10 The Penny House Bed & Breakfast $$ A full breakfast (featuring such delicious jump-starters as *strata*) is served in the beamed dining room of the circa 1751 main house; 11 nicely appointed rooms, of varying sizes and prices, fill the more recent addition. There's not much by way of a common sitting area, but, on the plus side, you can come and go as you please, with no fuss; **Margaret Keith,** who hails from Australia, is a friendly but unobtrusive host. The inn is set back behind a high hedge, so you'll forget you're on teeming Route 6. ♦ 4885 Rte 6 (between Brackett and Nauset Cable Rds), N. Eastham. 255.6632, 800/554.1751

THE PENNY HOUSE Bed & Breakfast 1751

11 Wellfleet Drive-In Built in 1957, this indispensable institution is the last of its breed on the Cape; luckily, loyal patrons fully appreciate the treasure and show up practically every time the program changes (typically, three times a week). Long the province of teenagers on the make, drive-ins are also great family entertainment: take along some pillows and blankets in case younger viewers conk out. Until they do, they'll enjoy the little tot lot behind the well-stocked concession stand. ♦ Daily dusk-closing late-May to mid-Sept. Rte 6 (between Aspinet and West Rds), S. Wellfleet. 349.2520, 800/696.3532

Within the Wellfleet Drive-In:

Wellfleet Flea Market Seconds dealers and wholesalers pushing everything from vacuum cleaners to "designer" T-shirts outnumber the *antiquaires* by a heavy margin, but it's still worth a look around. Among the 300 or so booths, you might find something as useful as a pair of used Rollerblades or a vintage brass Victrola. ♦ Nominal admission. W-Th, Sa-Su 8AM-4PM July-Aug; Sa-Su 8AM-4PM mid-Apr to July, Sept-Oct. 349.2520, 800/696.3532

12 Wellfleet Bay Wildlife Sanctuary Wandering through the **Massachusetts Audubon Society's** 710-acre preserve, it's hard to imagine that 100 years ago this area was a virtually treeless turnip and asparagus farm. Now it's a lively patchwork of salt marsh, moors, and piney woods, laced with five miles of hiking trails and capped in '93 by a $1.6 million visitor center designed by **Gerard Ives** of Boston. The low-slung, modestly shingled building suits its site environmentally as well as aesthetically. Its "Green Design" incorporates superinsulation, natural light combined with passive solar heating, and even composting toilets; program coordinator **Chris Brothers** figures the latter aspect alone will conserve some 100,000 gallons of water a year as the projected 40,000 visitors file through. The water will go to nurture indoor banks of petunias, lobelia, marigolds, and geraniums. Swirls of wavelike blue-green walls demarcate exhibits, a gift shop, and a lecture hall. All sorts of workshops and guided walks are offered, such as "Living Lighter on the Land" and "Birding for Beginners"; there are special activities for children, plus canoeing, snorkeling, whale-watching, and cruises along the bay, **Nauset Marsh,** and **Monomoy Island.** ♦ Admission. Trails: daily 8AM-8PM. Building: daily 8:30AM-5PM. Off West Rd (near Rte 6), S. Wellfleet. 349.2615

13 Finely JP's ★★$$ It doesn't look like much from the road, and the pine-paneled interior is more suited to a rec room than a restaurant, but the beauty lies in chef-owner **John Pontius'** ambitious yet unaggressively priced menu. Choosing from the likes of warm spinach and scallop salad with balsamic vinegar, or sautéed medaillons of pork with green apples and goat cheese, diners get to feel they've made a real discovery. ♦ New American ♦ Dinner. Rte 6 (between West and Lieutenant Island Rds), S. Wellfleet. 349.7500

13 Even Tide Motel $ This mid-'60s motel is set back in the woods; behind it, hiking trails lead to the sea, about 3/4 mile away. If it's raining, or you're lazy, you can make do with the 60-foot heated indoor pool. Some of the smaller rooms are rather snug, but for not much more you can snag a two-room suite or kitchen-equipped studio apartment. The owners, **Dick** and **Grace Filliman,** don't care for standard-issue motel furniture, so everything's handmade of blond oak, including the back-coddling platform beds. ♦ Rte 6 (between West and Lieutenant Island Rds), S. Wellfleet. 349.3410, 800/368.0007

14 Marconi Wireless Station **Guglielmo Marconi** started fooling around with wireless communication as a teenager in Italy; at 16, he fashioned a working model out of tin plates in his father's garden. Perusing the sketches of the station built here in 1902 (it was dismantled in 1920 as the surf encroached and successive inventions took the fore), it's clear that the project was the work of either a visionary or a maniac: 25,000 volts were required to activate the four 210-foot towers, secured with a cat's cradle of cables. Amazingly enough, this Rube Goldbergian device did the job. On 18 January 1903, **King Edward VII** received "most cordial greetings" in Poldhu, Wales, from **President "Theadore" Roosevelt** (the system still had a few bugs). Marconi's technology, leapfrogging on the work of Serbian-American inventor **Nikola Tesla,** suddenly shrank the world; the global communications now taken for granted began at this desolate outpost.

Virtually no traces remain beyond some concrete foundations and sand anchors, but the observation deck, with its interpretive plaques and dioramas, induces contemplation. Shore access has been closed off because of erosion, but nearby **Marconi Beach** is flanked by dramatic dunes. Also close at hand is the fascinating **Atlantic White Cedar Swamp Trail,** where the species so prized by the settlers for its light weight, workability, and pale color maintains a dwindling toehold (red maples are taking over). The 1 1/4-mile path has boardwalks over the mucky stuff (peat bogs seven feet deep), but trekkers have to cross a 1/2 mile of soft sand. If you take the trail in August, you can sustain yourself on wild highbush blueberries. ♦ Marconi Park Site Rd (off Rte 6), Wellfleet. 349.3785

To protect the productivity of the community's farms, unmarried Eastham men in 1695 had to kill six blackbirds or three crows before they were allowed to wed.

15 Olivers Clay Tennis Courts Seven clay courts and one Truflex are hidden away in an oak grove. The clubhouse is about the size of a kid's, but here lessons and matches are arranged and racquets restrung. It's a treat to play in so pastoral a setting. ♦ Daily 7AM-7:30PM May to mid-Oct. Rte 6 (between Pilgrim Spring and Cahoon Hollow Rds), Wellfleet. 349.3330

16 Cahoon Hollow Bed & Breakfast $ It has only two suites, but they're beauties, as is this secluded 1842 house. **Baily Ruckert** has decided flair, and, lounging in her elegant ivory-hued living room or feasting on her gourmet breakfasts (sherried eggs and ham, perhaps, or Dutch babies with rhubarb-orange compote), you'll feel as if you've landed in the home of an especially stylish friend. Take off on a loaner bike, and you'll hit salt water two miles in either direction. ♦ Cahoon Hollow Rd (off Rte 6), Wellfleet. 349.6372

17 The Beachcomber Raise a glass to the Surfmen who once lived at this 1897 Coast Guard station—they're said to have saved some 100,000 lives. The twentysomethings who frequent the "Comber" (or, alternately, "Coma") clearly live for today, and who could blame them, with wild **Cahoon Hollow Beach** right at the doorstep and the best bands on the Cape competing with the surf? The **Incredible Casuals** have a lock on Sundays; the rest of the week usually fills up with stellar reggae and blues acts. ♦ Cover. F 8PM-closing, Sa-Su 4PM-closing late May to late June; M-F 8PM-closing, Sa-Su 4PM-closing late June to mid-Sept. Old Cahoon Hollow Rd (off Ocean View Dr), Wellfleet. 349.6055

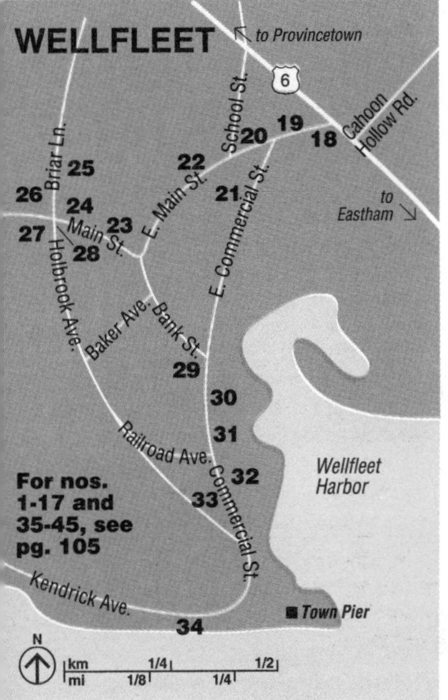

18 Cielo ★★★$$$ This century-old saltbox overlooking a marsh is tiny: there's just enough room for a little gallery featuring the color photographs of **Nancy Shieferstein** and a handful of tables. The menu's small, too—a four-course prix fixe, served at two seatings. **Mitch Rosenbaum** was a chef at the Good Housekeeping Institute, and his fare is worthy indeed. Try baked littlenecks with arugula, pancetta, and Parmesan; roast rib eye of veal stuffed with spinach and Gorgonzola; baked sea scallops with pine nuts, basil, plum tomatoes, and polenta; and, the kicker, date and walnut *dacquoise.* On Monday and Tuesday evenings, he and his partner, **Laxmi Venkateshwaran,** prepare an authentic Indian buffet. ♦ International ♦ Dinner. Closed Dec-Mar. E. Main St (between Rte 6 and E. Commercial St), Wellfleet. 349.2108

19 The Wellfleet Oyster House ★★$$ This ramshackle 1750 structure (shown here) makes a fine plain setting for homespun foods from around the world, from bouillabaisse to paella to "Jamaican mystery cake" made with bananas, walnuts, Kahlua, and Cointreau. The approach is not haute, just comfortable. ♦ International ♦ Dinner. Closed Monday through Friday late May to mid-June, early Sept to Nov; closed Nov-May. E. Main St (between Rte 6 and School St), Wellfleet. 349.2134

19 Inn at Duck Creeke $ Quarters in this 1810 captain's house (illustrated above), converted into an inn in the 1940s, are a bit cramped—adequate, though, and a bargain for the location and price. The five wooded acres overlook a salt marsh, but traffic noise from Route 6 can be a problem if you're the sensitive sort. ♦ Closed mid-Oct to mid-May. E. Main St (between Rte 6 and School St), Wellfleet. 349.9333

Within the Inn at Duck Creeke:

Sweet Seasons Restaurant ★★$$$ The look is spare yet inviting, with splashes of floral prints, and you get the full benefit of the view. Chef/owner **Judith Pihl** has worked up some very appealing signature dishes, such as shrimp sautéed with tomatoes, garlic, ouzo, and feta, and roast lobster with bourbon brown butter. ♦ New American ♦ Dinner. Closed Oct to late June. Reservations recommended. 349.6535

The Tavern Room Restaurant ★$$ Check out the bar, made from antique doors. The food here is simple (pizza, pasta, assorted fish) but comes with a musical accompaniment of jazz, folk, pop, and what-have-you. ♦ International ♦ Dinner. Closed Monday and mid-Oct to late May. 349.7369

20 First Congregational Church of the United Church of Christ If the proportions look a little odd, it's because this 1850 Greek Revival (illustrated here) lost its original tapering steeple to a storm in 1879. Someone thought a bell-shaped cupola on columns might prove more wind-resistant; and so it has. The **Town Clock,** installed in 1952, is the only one in the world to strike ship's time, a complicated system of one to four bells. On Sundays at 8PM in July and August, concerts are given on the 738-pipe 1873 **Hook and Hastings** organ; it's a good chance to get a look at the church's rare stained-glass window showing a ship of the *Mayflower* era. ♦ Services Su 9:30AM mid-June to mid-Sept; Su 10AM mid-Sept to mid-June. E. Main St (at School St), Wellfleet. 349.6877

21 Cherry Stone Gallery This gallery is abou the size of its namesake. It's also among the Cape's most distinguished, having shown such giants as **Motherwell** and **Rauschenberg** since opening in 1972. Curat **Sally Nerber** is equally proud of having give emerging artists such as **Helen Miranda Wilson** (who does small oil landscapes of astonishing depth and impact) their first shows, a stepping-stone to New York and beyond. Very few works are on view at any given time (seven exhibits, with SRO alternate-Tuesday-evening openings, typical span the summer), but the gallery has the works of two dozen artists in stock, includin the above-mentioned, as well as those of **Berenice Abbott, Eugene Atget, Jasper Johns,** and others who no doubt warrant attention, given the company they keep. ♦ Tu Sa noon-6PM mid-June to mid-Sept; by appointment mid-Sept to mid-June. E. Commercial St (between E. Main and Bank Sts), Wellfleet. 349.3026

22 Swansborough Gallery The artwork may not grab you (the focus is largely on semiabstract landscapes), but the interior alone is a must-see. Architect **Richard Hall** bought a crumbling 1830 barn in 1980 and essentially turned it inside out. The worm-eaten beams are things of beauty, the shingled ceiling a low-key Surrealist joke, and great bright spaces with polished floors spin out from a spiraling central staircase. ♦ M, Su 1-6PM, Tu-Sa 11AM-6PM late May to mid-Sept; Th-Sa 11AM-6PM, Su 1-6PM mid-Sept to mid-Oct. E. Main and School Sts, Wellfleet. 349.1883

22 Hannah Since 1982, **Susan Hannah** has been designing clean-lined "new classics" fo women, and this frame house showcases he own and other designers' works (the **Angelhearts** reversible rayons are especially popular). Fabrics are mostly, but not strictly, natural, and the overall look is stylish but never stiff. The balance between comfort and chic is struck so skillfully, often you'll find your fellow shoppers hail from either New York or Paris. ♦ M-Sa 10AM-6PM, Su noon-4:30PM (when rainy) late May to mid-Sept. E. Main St (between School and Bank Sts), Wellfleet. 349.9884. Also at: 47 Main St, Orleans. 255.8324

The sea was an unwitting abettor in the War of Independence. Though occasional small skirmishes broke out along the coast, the most vivid "victory" occurred in November 1778 when the British man-of-war *Somerset* struck some shoals off North Truro and sank. The 480 survivors who washed ashore were promptly captured and marched to Boston.

22 Wellfleet Historical Society Museum "Anything that 'might come in handy some day' found its way into the Cape Codder's attic," wrote **Josef Berger** in his personable WPA guide, *Cape Cod Pilot* (1937), "and for most of the gimcracks thus disposed of, 'some day' has not yet arrived." In the intervening decades, a lot of these anythings have found their way into historical collections of this sort, gallimaufries of anything remotely town-related. The holdings have been roughly sorted into topics (e.g., Marconi, oystering), so it's possible to pursue a special interest. The atticlike upstairs is especially worthwhile for its toys (such as felt "ten pins") and two sketches by early **Provincetown Arts Association** member **Ann Wells Munger,** an artist apparently overdue for resurrection. ♦ Admission. M, W-Th, Sa 2-5PM; Tu, F 10AM-noon, 2-5PM mid-June to early Sept. E. Main St (between School and Bank Sts), Wellfleet. 349.9157

23 Hatch's Fish Market/Hatch's Produce A fish shack since the 1950s, this shingled cottage behind Town Hall is the local variant on **Dean & DeLuca,** serving nothing but the best. **Rob McClellan** stocks not only the freshest fish but tasty take-homes like smoked mussel pâté and sea-clam pie; **Lauren McClellan's** fruits, vegetables, herbs, and flowers are luscious. ♦ M-Th 9AM-6PM, F-Su 9AM-7PM late May to late Sept. Main St (between Bank St and Holbrook Ave), Wellfleet. 349.2810

23 Aesop's Tables ★★★$$$$ **Brian Dunne's** festive restaurant is just the right mix of special occasion (this white-clapboard house was once the summer home of a Massachusetts governor) and come-as-you-are. Each intimate dining room has a slightly different feel; the unifying motif is playful yet elegant paper art by Dunne's wife, **Kim Kettler.** The extensive menu celebrates the region: the exotic edible flowers that go into "Monet's Garden Salad," for instance, come from the restaurant's own farm, and the "Midsummer Night's Scallops"—sautéed whole with garlic, shallots, spinach, and basil, and plumped on saffron spaeztle—tarry no more than three hours en route from bay to plate. Among the delectable desserts is "La Petite Isadora," an evanescent cheesecake topped with native raspberry-blueberry sauce. For many regular summerers, no season would be complete without at least one celebratory visit. ♦ New American ♦ Tea and dinner; Sunday brunch; dinner also on Sunday mid-May to July, Sept to mid-Oct. Closed mid-Oct to mid-May. Main St (between Bank St and Holbrook Ave), Wellfleet. Reservations recommended. 349.6450

Within Aesop's Tables:

Upstairs Bar at Aesop's Tables This raftered attic *boîte* looms over Main Street like a glassed-in, life-size dollhouse. Inside, it's a sensual mix of rose velvet armchairs and Victorian divans, where, to the mellow accompaniment of local jazz musicians, one can sup lightly, indulge in desserts, or just drink in style. The Tea Isadora, an Earl Grey/apricot blend steeped with apricot and Wild Turkey liqueurs, is a bracing aperitif for a blustery day. ♦ Daily 5:30PM-closing July-Aug; M, Th-Su mid-May to July, Sept to mid-Oct. 349.6450

24 Off Center Owner/buyer **Gail MacGibbon** favors the kind of clothes that could easily make the transition from sleepy beach town to Soho: slinky rayons and ready-to-rumple cottons and linens in earth tones and muted colors. ♦ Daily 9:30AM-6PM late June to early Sept; daily 10AM-5PM May, early Sept to mid-Oct; Sa-Su 10AM-5PM Apr, mid-Oct to Jan. Main St (between Bank St and Holbrook Ave), Wellfleet. 349.3634

25 Box Lunch So popular are the "rollwiches"—rolled pita sandwiches—prepared here that franchises have sprung up all over the Cape; there's even one in Portland, Maine. Some of the combos are pretty clever (such as the "Humpty Dumpty," a deviled egg salad with bacon), but if you like things simple, there's always the "Boring": melted cheese, period. There's a kid's menu (the "Piglet" is a mini ham and cheese) and roll-up breakfasts to go at selected stores. ♦ Daily 6AM-9PM July-Aug; call for off-season hours. Briar Ln (between Main St and Rte 6), Wellfleet. 349.2178. Also at: 357 Main St, Hyannis. 790.5855; Underpass Rd, Brewster. 896.6682; 353 Commercial St, Provincetown. 487.6026

26 Flying Fish Cafe ★★$$$ The tourist throngs that mob Main Street have not yet discovered this quiet and convivial cafe, and with any luck they never will. You can actually conduct an intelligent, leisurely conversation over a breakfast of "green eggs and ham" (vegetables provide coloration), a lunch of "risky pizza" (chef's choice), or a dinner of "lobster *romantique*" (steamed, with grilled leeks and tomatoes, on black pepper fettuccine with a ginger-cinnamon beurre blanc). The rustic breads and fine pastries are made in-house. ♦ New American ♦ Breakfast, lunch, tea, and dinner; tea and dinner only on Monday; Sunday brunch. Closed Nov-Mar. Briar Ln (between Main St and Rte 6), Wellfleet. 349.3100

27 Karol Richardson A London born and trained clothing designer of extraordinary talent, Richardson gave up her thriving Tribeca-based business to live in the country. She showed a few clothes in Wellfleet's cooperative **Hopkins Gallery** and quickly built an avid local following. Richardson scours Europe for the finest fabrics—velours in jewel tones, nubby linens, ribbed cotton knits. Although many of her designs celebrate the body, she's also skilled at devising looser silhouettes to flatter the "less than perfect" shape. This new shop, with its sidelines of comfortable/trendy shoes and statement jewelry (including some beautiful pieces featuring Baltic amber by **Josef Bajanowski**), satisfies style-conscious teenagers and dowagers alike. ♦ M-W 9:30AM-6PM; Th-Sa 9:30AM-9PM; Su 11AM-5PM May to mid-Oct. W. Main St (at Holbrook Ave), Wellfleet. 349.6378. Also at: 47 Main St, Orleans. 349.6378

28 Hopkins Gallery Founded by three local artists in 1983, this accessible gallery (illustrated at right) is a great place to see what the up-and-comers have been up to: **Karin Rosenthal** with her sensuous photographs of nudes, for instance, or **Donald Beal** with his vaguely menacing interior landscapes. The summer season usually includes a painting show, then photography, and a small selection of crafts. ♦ Daily 9:30AM-6PM May-Jan. Main St and Holbrook Ave, Wellfleet. 349.7264

Talk about South Sea adventures: In 1858, Captain Josiah Knowles of Eastham was bound from San Francisco to South America when he wrecked the *Wild Wave* on a coral reef. While the crew took shelter on a tiny island, he and a mate rowed to Pitcairn Island, presumed to be inhabited by mutineers from the *Bounty*. They'd departed, leaving some livestock behind, so Knowles killed and dressed it, fashioned a boat from abandoned lumber, with clothes for sails, and set off for Tahiti, 1,500 miles away. The captain was lucky enough to run into a "sloop of war" somewhat short of there, and they returned to rescue the crew, who'd subsisted for six months on crabs and coconuts. Knowles finally made it home, to be surprised by a baby he hadn't known his wife had been expecting.

Restaurants/Clubs: Red **Hotels:** Blue
Shops/ Outdoors: Green **Sights/Culture:** Black

29 Upper Crust Pizza ★$ Duck into this listir barn if a 15-inch pizza will hit the spot—thin-crusted, so a four-topping maximum is encouraged. Salads, juices, and sodas complete the no-frills menu. ♦ Pizza ♦ Dinne Closed Monday through Wednesday early Sept to mid-June. Commercial and Bank Sts, Wellfleet. 349.9562

29 Buenos Nachos ★$ It's little bigger than a countertop, but serves big-value tacos, enchiladas, and burritos—including a region clam-tender burrito. Fresh-fruit smoothies maintain the tropical mood. ♦ Mexican ♦ Dinner. Closed Monday through Wednesda early Sept to mid-June. Commercial and Ban Sts, Wellfleet. 349.0200

30 Cove Gallery Larry Biron and **Liane Schneider-Biron's** stable is a lively bunch, including master engraver **Leonard Baskin,** painters **Judith Shahn** and **Larry Horowitz,** photographer **Alan Nyiri,** and two dozen oth accomplished artists. The gallery also offers fine framing and has a sculpture garden set beside Duck Creek. ♦ Daily 10AM-6PM late May-Aug; daily 10AM-5PM Sept to mid-Oct; Sa-Su 10AM-5PM mid-Oct to Jan. Commercial St (between Bank St and Railroa Ave), Wellfleet. 349.2530

30 Left Bank Gallery This 1933 **American Legion Hall** has served splendidly as a galler since 1971. What's on the walls is not quite a impressive as the space itself, however; the art, much of it hyperrealistic, seems mainly commercially motivated. The crafts, particularly a Shaker-influenced cherry musi stand by **S.L. Macintosh,** fare somewhat better. Toward the back is "The Potter's Room," featuring all sorts of table-ready war ♦ Daily 10AM-6PM Apr-Oct; M, Th-Su 10AM 6PM Oct-Nov; Sa-Su 10AM-6PM Dec-Mar. Commercial St (between Bank St and Railroa Ave), Wellfleet. 349.9451

31 Celeste's Depot Cafe ★$ It wasn't *really* depot, but it sort of looks the part, and the railroad *used* to run by. . . . At least the food i duplicity-free, starting with French toast layered with ham and cheese for breakfast, continuing with custom sandwiches for lunc (including a caponata pocket), and on throug dinner specials such as lemon-thyme pan-fried hake. ♦ International ♦ Breakfast, lunch and dinner; breakfast and lunch only on Sunday. Closed Nov-Mar. Commercial St (between Bank St and Railroad Ave), Wellflee 349.9533

'he Celestial Cape: Second łome to the Stars

ıpe Codders and the Islanders have had more an a century to get used to celebrities in their idst. The first well-known personality to vacation the environs was **Grover Cleveland,** whose ansion **Gray Gables** in Bourne became the first ;ummer White House." By 1993, it seemed the cals really had the routine down, mouthing such ıntiments as "They're just people like the rest of ;," or as one Martha's Vineyard resident put it, Ve think we're *all* pretty important." Then **resident Bill Clinton** and his family picked the ineyard for an impromptu summer holiday, and 'eryone basically went celebrity crazy—thronging ıe streets, wharves, and golf courses in hopes of st a glimpse. All the brouhaha reminded some ılookers of that summer day in 1960 when 25,000 ell-wishers turned out in Hyannis to greet a young enator just back from the Democratic Convention: **ɔhn F. Kennedy** was on his way to the White ouse and his family's summer place on its way to ecoming something of a national shrine.

ɔseph P. and **Rose Kennedy** of Boston first rented ıe **Malcolm Cottage** in Hyannisport in 1926; they ought the rambling clapboard house three years ter and hired the original architect, **Frank Paine** of oston, to remodel it, doubling its size to 14 ɔoms, and adding a motion picture theater (New ngland's first private screening room) in the asement. In 1956, John F. Kennedy, by then a enator, bought the adjacent house, and other ımily members followed suit, ultimately forming ıe "Kennedy Compound." Tourists who go the trouble of tracking it down are in for a sappointment; it's all fenced in, and there's othing much to see. They would do better to atisfy their curiosity at the **John F. Kennedy luseum** in nearby Hyannis and to honor the entiment the President once voiced: "The Cape is ıe one place I can think and be alone"—a entiment no doubt shared by his extended family.

he Upper Cape harbors celebrities of a quieter ripe: in Wellfleet, for instance, writers such as **nnie Dillard, Marge Piercy, E.J. Kahn,** and **leanor Munro** of the *New Yorker.* They have no eed to evade autograph hunters, and in fact can be ɔund giving readings and workshops at the **Castle rts Center** in Truro and downing lobster rolls at **ainter's Lunch.** Provincetown is not quite the ultural hot spot it was when the dune shacks ttracted such squatters as **Eugene O'Neill** and **ack Kerouac,** but the community's most notorious ummer resident, **Norman Mailer,** can be regularly potted on his morning stroll to get the paper. Such ; his clout as a local "big fish" that in the summer of 1993, his doodles were accorded a show at the prestigious **Berta Walker Gallery.**

Celebrities, of course, attract celebrities, a thesis borne out on the Vineyard, which over the past 50 years has hosted such notables as **Thomas Hart Benton, Dashiell Hammett, Lillian Hellman, Somerset Maugham, Jimmy Cagney, Paul Robeson, Thornton Wilder, Martin Luther King, Jr., Garson Kanin,** and **Ruth Gordon.** More recently, the roster spans **Jackie Onassis, Carly Simon** and **James Taylor** (both summered here as children), **Walter Cronkite, Mike Wallace, William Styron, Art Buchwald, Katherine Graham** (owner of the *Washington Post*), **Beverly Sills, Patricia Neal, Christopher Reeve, Tracy Pollan** and **Michael J. Fox, Dan Aykroyd, Spike Lee,** and newcomers **Billy Joel** and **Christie Brinkley.** All they have to do is invite a few friends over, and the list will continue to grow. As for the island's particular appeal, in *On the Vineyard II,* a collection of essays published by photographer **Peter Simon** (yes, he's Carly's brother), writer **Jib Ellis** posits that the celebs are attracted "by a sizable moat and qualifying prices." A prime waterfront rental can easily fetch $5,000 a week; Carly Simon's Menemsha cottage was put on the market in 1993 for $850,000. Many of the local stars ensure a trickle-down effect by participating in the "Possible Dreams" auction held every summer to benefit **Martha's Vineyard Community Services,** with Art Buchwald as emcee. Year after year, Simon tops her own records. In 1988, she raised $52,000 by promising the two winning bidders "a song and a peanut butter sandwich"; in 1993, a couple paid $81,000 for just a tune, sans snacks. While Vineyard residents are for the most part blasé about the stellar presences in their midst, they made an exception when the Clintons blew into town; not only did the hoi polloi line the roadsides, higher stakes intensified the usual jockeying for position on the upper-echelon cocktail-party circuit.

But, in general, discretion reigns. Nantucket's reserve is typical of what celebrities can expect. When **Eleanor Roosevelt** visited the **Wauwinet House,** a grand old hotel on the island, in 1950, the owner gave strict instructions that there was to be no gawking and no autographs. Word has gotten around that the same rules still apply when the exalted ones are in residence. Every so often, you'll hear belatedly of a visitation—most recently, for instance, **Michelle Pfeiffer** at the **White Elephant**—but even a star as well known as Pfeiffer can get a taste of privacy in this last bastion of New England confidentiality.

32 Bayside Lobster Hutt ★★$$ This 1857 oyster shack (shown here), its roof sporting a yellow-slickered fisherman in a dory hauling in a lobster twice his size, is so quintessential a lobster joint that its praises have been sung in such polar periodicals as *Glamour* and *Outside*. What you get is self-service, picnic-style feasting at communal tables cloaked in red-and-white-checked oilcloth; better hope your nearest neighbors know how to dismantle a slippery arthropod. You can bring your own bottle, but "no neckties, please." ♦ American ♦ Lunch and dinner; dinner only late May to July, Sept. Closed Oct to late May. Commercial St (between Railroad and Holbrook Aves), Wellfleet. 349.6333

32 Just Desserts Like Chinese food, shore dinners don't usually rate much by way of sweet endings, but this patio overlooking the cove aims to make up for that lack, with mile-high apple pie, marble cheesecake, "chocolate outrage," strawberry shortcake, and such. ♦ Daily 5-10:30PM late June to early Sept. Commercial St (between Railroad and Holbrook Aves), Wellfleet. No phone

33 The Holden Inn $ **Captain Richard Freeman's** 1840 manse was converted into an inn in 1924, and has been in the same family ever since. The breeze-swept rooms are timeless (braided rugs, iron bedsteads, flounced curtains), and the prices are a throwback as well; the monthly rates are mighty tempting. ♦ Closed Nov to mid-Apr. Commercial St (between Railroad and Holbrook Aves), Wellfleet. 349.3450

34 Painter's Lunch ★★$ **Katherine Painter** has cooked at some of the fanciest venues on both coasts (**Stars** in San Francisco, Boston's **Biba,** and **Chillingsworth** in Brewster). But when she decided to open a place of her own in 1992, her bent was decidedly downscale. "Simple food in a funky place" is what she had in mind, and thus, although the walls of this ramshackle lunchroom were never completely painted, you might find her between customers working on a canvas of her own. The daughter of accomplished writers, **Pamela Painter** and **Robie Macauley,** the easygoing proprietor has created a kind of clubhouse for local literati, as well as for low-budget aspirants her own age. And the food is not always that "simple": her "Rockin' Lobster Roll," for instance, is state of the art, with hand-picked chunks and lemon-soaked red onion slivers for extra zing. Specials might include a white bean soup with sour cream, baked ziti with snowpeas, zucchini, corn, an provolone. Lingering is encouraged, althoug the doors close for the night when the WHA curtain goes up. ♦ New American ♦ Lunch and dinner; lunch only on Monday. Closed early Sept to late May. Kendrick Ave (near Town Pier), Wellfleet. No phone

34 Wellfleet Harbor Actors' Theater (WHAT) This modest black-box theater, founded in 1985 by **Jeff Zinn** and **Gip Hoppe** is the clearest heir apparent to the mantle of the **Provincetown Players.** The output can a times be jejune, but it's never dull, and the repertoire of six plays per summer usually includes some bold choices and an original work or two. ♦ Admission. Daily 8PM July to early Sept; Th-Su 8PM mid-May to July, mid Sept to mid-Oct. Kendrick Ave (near Town Pier), Wellfleet. 349.6835

35 The Colony of Wellfleet $$$$ Establish as a private club in 1949 by architect and ar patron **Ned Saltonstall** (one of the founders of Boston's **Institute for Contemporary Arts** this cluster of cottages on 10 piney acres is rare and marvelous Bauhaus preserve. The smallish, squarish living-room/bedrooms clearly serve their intended function of spilli occupants outdoors to enjoy the wooded setting, and the original furnishings—designed by **Charles** and **Ray Eames,** amon others—have counterparts in the collection of the **Museum of Modern Art.** For all its artfulness, and a guest roster that spans so notable names, the atmosphere is far from formal: says **Eleanor Stefani,** who has overseen the colony since the early '60s, "if you want to change your clothes three times day and parade around, this is not the place. There are no TVs (books are regarded as mo than adequate entertainment); however, the is an on-site "Casserole Kitchen" so you can order dinner in. Cottages usually rent by the week or more, but you might be lucky enoug to find one for a night or two. ♦ Closed Oct-Apr. Chequesset Neck Rd (between Kendric Ave and Harbor Rd), Wellfleet. 349.3761

In his yearlong sojourn on the dunes of Eastham in the 1920s, Henry Beston, author of the classic *The Outermost House,* found a transcendental awareness thrust on him by the diurnal rhythms of the dunes: "In that hollow of space and brightness, in that ceaseless travail of wind and sand and ocean, the world one sees is still the world unharrassed of man, a place of the instancy and eternity of creation. . . ." He only meant to stay a fortnight but found himself lingering on: "As the year lengthened into autumn, the beauty and mystery of this earth and outer sea so possessed and held me that I could not go."

36 Great Island Rated the most difficult among the **Cape Cod National Seashore's** nine self-guided trails, this 8.4-mile loop consists primarily of soft sand, leading from woods through meadow to a remote beach at Chequesset Neck. This is where in 1970 archaeologists from the **National Park Service** and **Plimoth Plantation** excavated the remains of **Smith Tavern,** a 1690-1740 whalers' haunt. The finds included not only the usual shards but a 1724 farthing and a huge whale vertebra that had evidently been used as a chopping block. ♦ Daily dawn-dusk. Off Chequesset Neck and Griffin Island Rds, Wellfleet. 349.3785

37 Jams Vacationing New York psychiatrists get their deli fix at this gourmet grocery; in fact, they're honored with a namesake sandwich, "The Shrink"—nova and cream cheese with sliced onion. The pizzas are pretty special, made with fresh tomatoes and herbs, and appearing in such exotic guises as *niçoise* and pupu. The French "wall of fire" rotisserie is busy searing chickens, ducks, and ribs, leaving them coated with caramelized juices. And the pastry case displays such delectables as peach-strawberry cobbler and ricotta tart. Day in and out, there's the sumptuous aroma of baking, from baguettes to peanut butter chocolate-chip cookies. Look longing enough, and maybe one of the congenial staffers will slip you a nibble straight from the oven. ♦ Daily 7:30AM-closing late May to early Sept. Off Rte 6, Truro Center. 349.1616

38 The Blacksmith Shop ★★$$$ A local favorite (actually, it's the only restaurant "downtown"), this unassuming spot packs surprising charm; the interior is decorated with dollhouses and a folk-art rocking horse. Chef/owner **Warren Falkenburg** is appreciated for such homey dishes as shepherd's pie, as well as for fancier fare like roast duck with apricot, Amaretto, and almond sauce. His signature entrée is haddock broiled in sour cream. ♦ International ♦ Dinner. Closed Monday through Wednesday mid-Oct to late May. Off Rte 6, Truro Center. 349.6554

39 Truro Center for the Arts at Castle Hill This converted 1880s horse barn (the windmill, once used to draw water for the animals, now houses administrative offices) is a hotbed of artistic activity all summer long: **Donald Beal** teaches basic painting, **Michael Mazur** leads a print-making class, **Joel Meyerowitz** offers a bring-your-camera "photographic exploration," potter **Harry Holl** teaches "The Natural Way to Throw," architect **Malcolm Wells** gives a free sand-castle course at Corn Hill Beach, **Pamela Painter** and **Anne Bernays** conduct fiction exercises based on their book *What If?*, **E.J. Kahn, Jr.,** teaches nonfiction techniques, Pulitzer Prize winner **Alan Dugan** heads an informal poetry group. This is just a small sampling of the scores of classes and workshops offered, according to director **Mary Stackhouse,** in 10 disciplines in six rooms and on the beach. ♦ Office: daily 9:30AM-5PM July-Aug. Castle and Meetinghouse Rds, Truro. 349.7511

40 Little America AYH-Hostel $ This beautifully bleak former Coast Guard station near **Ballston Beach** is straight out of an Edward Hopper painting. There are 42 beds, the ocean's a few hundred yards away, and the only drawback—common to all **American Youth Hostels**—is a curfew (10:30PM). With such glorious countryside to explore, the 9:30AM-5PM lockout is no punishment at all. ♦ Closed mid-Sept to mid-June. N. Pamet Rd (off Rte 6), Truro. 349.3889

Though known, of course, for its shores, Cape Cod contains 400 ponds—proportionately, eight times as many ponds per square mile as Minnesota has lakes. About 300 are kettle ponds, left over from the Ice Age. When the last glaciers retreated north 12,000 to 14,000 years ago, they left behind huge chunks, or "teeth," of ice, which formed depressions, then melted, creating "kettle ponds" with steep banks and extreme depths (some up to 85 feet at the center). Naturally acidic (long before acid rain), kettle ponds are typically crystal-clear with sandy bottoms, and surrounded by plants that have adapted to their varying shorelines; the level each year depends on the amount of spring rainfall. Among the hitherto-hardy flora is the endangered Plymouth gentian.

41 **Truro Historical Museum** The **Highland House,** a semidecrepit turn-of-the-century inn, makes an optimal home for the holdings of the **Truro Historical Society,** which run the gamut from shipwreck detritus (including a pirate's chest) to farming tools to old tourist postcards—and a whole lot more. The tiny rooms upstairs contain odd little tableaux. ♦ Admission. Daily 10AM-5PM mid-June to mid-Sept. Lighthouse Rd (off S. Highland Rd), N. Truro. 487.3397

41 **Highland Links** This public course is the oldest on the Cape (established in 1892), and, with its straight-out-to-sea views, it's assured of maintaining its status as the most scenic. The nine holes (one of which is shown here) skirt the bluffs like a restless sandpiper. ♦ Daily 6AM-5:30PM June-Sept. Lighthouse Rd (off S. Highland Rd), N. Truro. 487.9201

41 **Highland Light** The original—built in 1797 and powered by whale oil—was the first lighthouse on Cape Cod; during his celebrated travels, **Henry David Thoreau** boarded briefly at this 1853 replacement, capped by a 65-foot tower of whitewashed brick. The light was the last to be automated (in 1986) and remains the brightest beacon on the New England coast, at 620,000 candlepower. Its future may be dim, though: its 10-acre spread has been whittled down to four, and at the current rate of erosion, the prognosis is that it may have as little as five years before tumbling down the 120-foot cliff on which it stands. The **Committee to Save the Cape Cod Light,** an offshoot of the **Truro Historical Society** formed in 1990, has been working feverishly to raise the several million dollars needed to move it back from the brink, and visitors will be encouraged by volunteer staffers to join the crusade.

That intriguing parapet visible to the south received just such an eleventh-hour rescue: called the **Jenny Lind Tower,** it's part of Boston's old **Fitchburg Railroad Depot.** It was from this tower, in 1850, that the "Swedish nightingale" trilled gratis for a mob of fans who'd been flimflammed by her overbooking promoter, **P.T. Barnum.** In 1927, when the station was slated for demolition, a Boston attorney moved it here for safekeeping. It's not open to the public, and profuse poison ivy guards it as effectively as the thickets around Sleeping Beauty's castle. But plans f making it a public attraction have been bandied about. ♦ Closed to the public. Lighthouse Rd (off S. Highland Rd), N. Truro 968.6300

42 **Terra Luna** ★★$$ Formerly home to **Adrian's,** this modest pine-paneled space is known for breakfasts fit for champions. The **Stefani** siblings are now in charge, and they start the day right with such exotica as a breakfast burrito (scrambled eggs wrapped i a whole-wheat tortilla, with all the traditional trimmings) or South American pancakes (topped with bananas and drizzled with a thir chocolate syrup). An array of *nuova cucina* pizzas and pastas fill out the dinner menu, along with fish, chicken, steak, and—at the lighter end of the cholesterol spectrum—vegetable tofu in "baskets" fashioned from puff pastry. ♦ New American/Italian ♦ Breakfast and dinner. Closed mid-Oct to la May. Shore Rd (between Rte 6 and Pond St), N. Truro. 487.1019

43 **Pilgrim Heights** This easy-to-moderate hiking loop, part of the **Cape Cod National Seashore,** links two 3/4-mile trails. The **Pilgrim Spring Trail** leads to where the newcomers found their first fresh water (wrote a witness: "We . . . sat us downe and drunke our first New England water with as much delight as ever we drunke drinke in all our lives"). The **Small Swamp Trail** is name not for its size but for farmer **Thomas Small,** who grew corn and asparagus here, and planted apple and plum trees, starting in 1860; so fruitless were the latter efforts, though, that the farm was left unclaimed afte his death in 1922. ♦ Daily dawn-dusk. Off Rt 6 (between Head of the Meadow and High Head Rds), N. Truro. 349.3785

44 **Outer Reach Motel** $$ The bay views fror atop these dunes are spectacular, but this 54 room complex is such a blight on the landscape, it's hard not to feel exploitive enjoying it. The rooms are nothing special, b a very good deal for the price. Guests have access to the facilities (pool, beach, and, mos precious of all, parking) at the **Provincetown Inn,** a sprawling resort that makes this barrackslike infestation look downright dainty ♦ Closed mid-Oct to late May. Rte 6 (betweer Head of the Meadow and High Head Rds), N. Truro. 487.9090, 800/942.5388

Within the Outer Reach Motel:.

Adrian's ★★★$$ Independently operated by **Adrian** and **Annette Salcedo Cyr,** Adrian's shares vistas with the Outer Reach, but brought its own ambience along when it made the move in 1993 from less visible Route 6A. The motif is mellow house party, with jazz wafting through the barnlike space, potted herbs on the tables, and Peroni Italian beer to take the edge off. The various antipasti, *insalate,* and pasta are quite inviting, but it's hard to hold off on the pizza, in such irresistible renditions as "Greco" (with lamb and feta) or layered potatoes and pesto; another unbeatable combo is *scampi e carciofi* (shrimp and artichokes) on a crunchy cornmeal crust. Breakfasts are just as adventurous, ranging from the delicate cranberry pancakes with orange butter to the robust frittata with zucchini, provolone, and Romano. No wonder Provincetown residents flee the hustle of their home turf to graze at this peaceful aerie. ♦ Italian/Takeout ♦ Breakfast and dinner. Closed Tuesday mid-May to July, Sept to mid-Oct; closed mid-Oct to mid-May. 487.4360

45 **Kalmar Village** $$ Most of the boxy cottages that line the bay look like cookie-cutter Monopoly houses. Not so these white-shingled, black-shuttered cottages set amid green lawns on a 400-foot stretch of private beach. This family oasis has been in **Don Prelack's** family since the early 1940s, and certain eternal verities prevail: plenty of kids striking up instant friendships around the pool, relaxed parents tending the hibachi at dusk, and tuck-ins in the pine-paneled bedrooms promising even more sun, sand, and salt tomorrow. Cottages go for the week in July and August, but if you book well enough ahead, you might be able to secure an efficiency or motel room. This is definitely not a place to get away from it all, but parents who appreciate the value of plentiful playmates find it most congenial. ♦ Closed mid-Oct to late May. Shore Rd (between High Head Rd and Commercial St), N. Truro. 487.0585

Bests

Helen Miranda Wilson
Painter/Artist

In Wellfleet:

Bayside Lobster Hutt—owned by a native of Wellfleet whose father is an oysterman. This is the best place for seafood I know; very informal.

Great Island—sticks out for miles into Wellfleet Harbor. No houses. Much beauty. Empty beaches. No cars.

Flying Fish Cafe—great breakfasts and lunches.

Cielo—wonderful fancy food. A small, special restaurant.

Wellfleet Public Library—a major treat. What you always dreamed a library could be.

Justin Kaplan
Writer/Biographer

Canoeing and kayaking: **Herring River** (Wellfleet), **Pamet River** (Truro), **Cape Cod Bay,** any of the Wellfleet/Truro ponds.

Swimming: with the incoming or outgoing tide in the **Pamet River,** between Truro Harbor and Castle Hill.

Clam flats: a local secret.

Route 6: stay off it whenever possible.

Anne Bernays
Novelist/Teacher

PJ's on Route 6 in Wellfleet. You place and pick up your own order. A favorite with the natives, and the best fried clams on the Outer Cape.

Ballston Beach in Truro. Fine, pale sand for miles along Cape Cod's outer spine. Impressive waves. But the world's smallest parking lot, shrunk even further during the big storm of '93.

Commercial Street in Provincetown, where camera-toting tourists, leathery year-rounders, artists, and a summertime gay/lesbian population converge harmoniously. In the West End are some dazzling examples of 18th- and 19th-century domestic architecture—all beautifully maintained.

Provincetown light is justly world-famous—a kind of silvery sheen.

> "Cape Cod is anchored to the heavens, as it were, by myriad little cables of beach-grass, and, if they should fail, would become a total wreck, and erelong go to the bottom."
>
> **Henry David Thoreau,** *Cape Cod*

Provincetown

Visitors expecting prim shingled cottages and sedate New England greens are in for a considerable shock when they arrive in Provincetown, which is as far out, both literally and figuratively, as Cape Cod gets. While it's surrounded by peaceful dunes under the protectorate of the **Cape Cod National Seashore**, the core of this long, narrow, harbor-hugging hamlet is a three-mile stretch of restaurants, galleries, and shops. In summer, the population swells from about 4,000 to more than 40,000, and it's easy to believe they're all strolling **Commercial Street** (the main drag) from morning 'til after midnight.

Of course, this once-upon-a-time outpost of civilization does have historical significance—it is, after all, the spot where the Pilgrims first set foot in the New World in 1620 (though **Plymouth Rock** gets the credit in most history books). The town's venerable roots, however, have been all but obscured by the showy growth that has sprung up since the turn of the century in response to the blossoming tourist trade. It was presidents **Teddy Roosevelt** and **William Howard Taft** who put this remote fishing village on the map, when, in 1907 and 1910, respectively, they yachted up the coast to celebrate first the cornerstone and then the completion of the **Pilgrim Monument.** In the 'teens and '20s, the Greenwich Village intelligentsia migrated north, establishing an artistic enclave. This bohemian crowd was impressed not only by the low rents and cheap food (all that fish!) but by the town's tolerance of nonconformity—a trait that today's gay and lesbian tourists treasure as well.

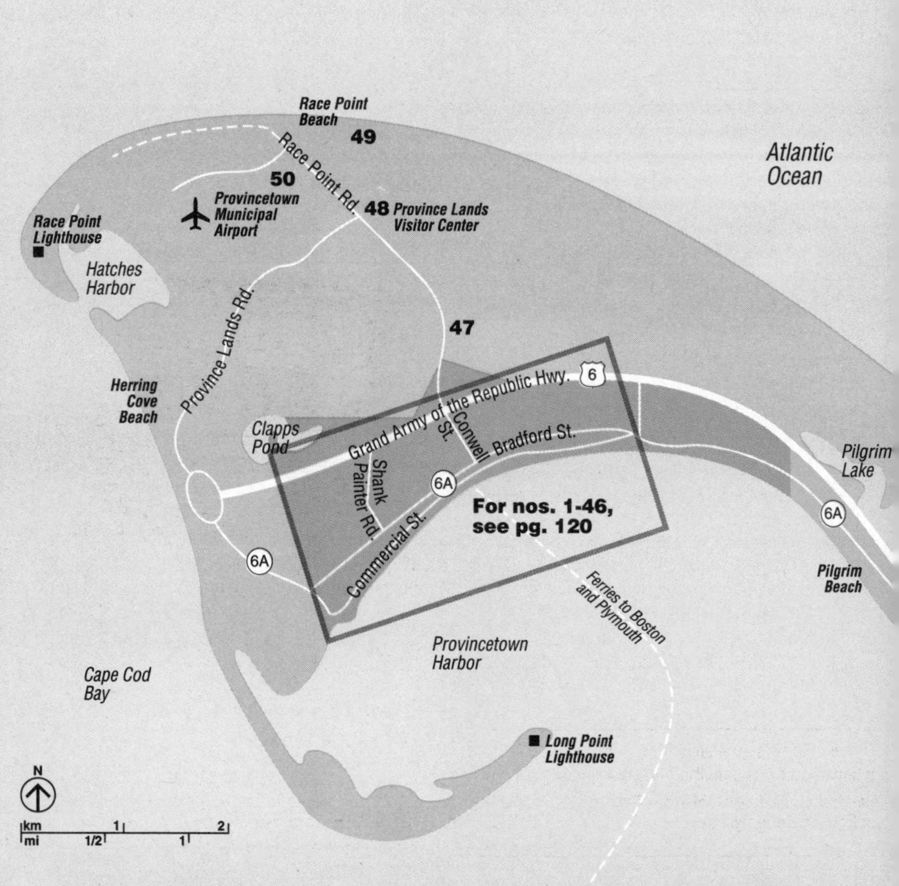

1 Watermark Inn $$$ Harvard-educated architect **Kevin Shea** is responsible for the clean lines that characterize this light-filled contemporary inn in the quiet East End, and his wife and partner, graphic designer **Judy Richland,** modestly accepts credit for the decor—bold splashes of color against whitewashed walls and sea-blue views. Ten suites featuring (variously) sleeping lofts, mini-kitchens, fireplaces, and private decks make the most of the hotel's little stretch of beach. The ambience is kick-your-shoes-off casual, yet every aesthetic detail is resolved; the combination is immensely relaxing. ♦ 603 Commercial St (between Allertown and Snow Sts). 487.0165, 800/734.0165

2 Provincetown Group Gallery Founded in 1964, this cooperative gallery is the oldest one in continuous operation in Provincetown. Some of its 16 members, like **Sal del Deo,** are comfortably ensconced in a style all their own, while others, like **Nick Lawrence** (who has gone from dreamy landscapes to Rorschach-like monotypes), are still experimenting. Typically, five shows are mounted in the course of the summer, so it's hard to predict what you'll see. ♦ M-Sa noon-4PM, 7-10PM, Su noon-10PM late June to mid-Sept. 286 Bradford St (between Snow and Conway Sts). 487.0275

3 Windamar House $ Catering mainly to women, this six-room, mid-1800s guesthouse is peaceful and cheery. The standout room is The Studio, with a cathedral ceiling and a glass wall overlooking the spacious garden, where guests are encouraged to unwind. Also designed for that purpose is the common room, with TV, VCR, fridge, and microwave. A Continental breakfast of fresh muffins and loaves is served. ♦ 568 Commercial St (between Conway and Kendall Sts). 487.0599

4 White Horse Inn $ **Frank Schaefer** bought this rambling late 18th-century captain's house in 1963 and set about transforming it with the help of his artist friends. Their work not only adorns the walls but informs the architecture; the six studios are artful assemblages of salvaged materials including stained-glass windows said to have come from **Eugene O'Neill's** cottage. The 12 guest rooms are a bit plainer, with hooked rugs and heavily daubed plaster (a necessary measure when the house's original horsehair walls gave out); Schaefer has democratically distributed his extensive art collection, however, so you're assured of something interesting to contemplate. ♦ 500 Commercial St (at Howland St). 487.1790

Provincetown's earliest schools were funded with a fishery tax. It is said that the least successful fisher in town each year was assigned to schoolmaster duty.

Restaurants/Clubs: Red **Hotels:** Blue
Shops/ Outdoors: Green **Sights/Culture:** Black

5 Rising Tide Gallery Downstairs from the legendary **Long Point Gallery** (they share a rehabbed 1844 schoolhouse), this 16-artist co-op features emerging and midcareer artists, among them **Noa Hall,** whose colorist landscapes are growing ever more abstract. Members have a solo show every other year, and the season starts and ends with a group sampling. ♦ Daily 11AM-4PM, 8-10PM mid-June to mid-Sept. 494 Commercial St (at Howland St). 487.4037

5 Long Point Gallery In light of its long association with such luminaries as **Robert Motherwell** and **Paul Resika,** this gallery is generally viewed as Provincetown's most prestigious. Shows usually pair a painter with a sculptor, and a "Summer's Work" exhibit at the end of the season gives you a chance to see what everyone's been up to. Keep an eye out for **Gilbert Franklin's** faceless bronze figures, eloquent in pose and posture. ♦ Daily 11AM-3PM, 8-10PM mid-June to mid-Sept. 492 Commercial St (at Howland St). 487.1795

6 Berta Walker Gallery This space, though off the beaten path on Provincetown's "back" street, is hardly retiring—splashy is more like it. Walker is not afraid of the limelight: why else mount a solo show of **Norman Mailer's** doodles, as she did in '93? In pursuit of "Provincetown artists, past, present, and future," she has assembled a fine cache of works that appeal to collectors of varied tastes, from landscapes by **Paul Resika** and **Wolf Kahn** to the early output of Provincetown's pioneer artist, **Charles W. Hawthorne.** ♦ Daily 11AM-4PM, 7-10PM late May to Oct; F-Sa 11AM-4PM or by appointment Nov to late May. 208 Bradford St (between Howland and Cook Sts). 487.6411

7 Asheton House $ A circa 1840 captain's residence fronted by a white Nantucket fence, this guesthouse (see above) has only three rooms, but they're among the most elegant in town. The Captain's Room, with a four-poster bed and Queen Anne armchairs, looks out on an English garden and the **Pilgrim Monument;** the Suite, furnished with French antiques, boasts a dressing room, fireplace, and bay view; and the Safari Room features an assortment of bamboo and wicker. This is about as close as you can get to downtown without sacrificing peace and quiet. ♦ 3 Cook St (between Commercial and Bradford Sts). 487.9966

8 Provincetown Art Association & Museum Founded in 1914 by a handful of established artists and the local bank president, this organization continues to uphold its stated mission: "To promote education of the public in the arts, and social intercourse between artists and laymen." One notable benefit of its longevity is an extensive and ever-growing collection of works created in the region. **Charles Hawthorne** and four other co-founders kicked in a painting apiece at the outset, and around that nucleus a mighty body of work has accrued, as a Who's Who of 20th-century artists traipsed through town; the collection now stands at 1,700 pieces. Some of the older works are in need of a conservator's intercession—hence the institution of the innovative "Adopt a Painting" program, in which patrons select a favorite piece and underwrite its restoration. Schoolchildren are brought into the dialogue, too: several winter shows consist of their picks from the permanent collection. The juried shows of members' work tend, alas, to be less than impressive, to the extent that one wonders at the criteria for inclusion; on the other hand, many of the fledgling artists are as yet unrepresented, so there's discovery potential, at rock-bottom prices. A year-round array of classes, lectures, readings, and concerts round out the outreach program. ♦ Admission. Daily noon-5PM, 7-10PM late May to early Sept; call for off-season hours. 460 Commercial St (between Cook and Bangs Sts). 487.1750

9 Flagship Restaurant ★★$$$ Provincetown's oldest eatery (opened in 1933) was on the skids when it was taken over by **Napi Van Dereck,** whose other restaurant, **Napi's,** has been one of the town's most agreeably eccentric establishments for two decades. The old sail loft has now been restored to rights, complete with its Dory Bar created from a halved Grand Banks fishing boat. Naturally, seafood is the focus of the menu, with dishes from Portugal, Italy, Asia—you name it. Adjoining the Flagship, incidentally, is the ramshackle **Beachcomber's Club,** which has served as an informal gathering place for a self-select group of artists since **Charles Hawthorne's** day. ♦ International ♦ Dinner. 463 Commercial St (at Bangs St). 487.4200

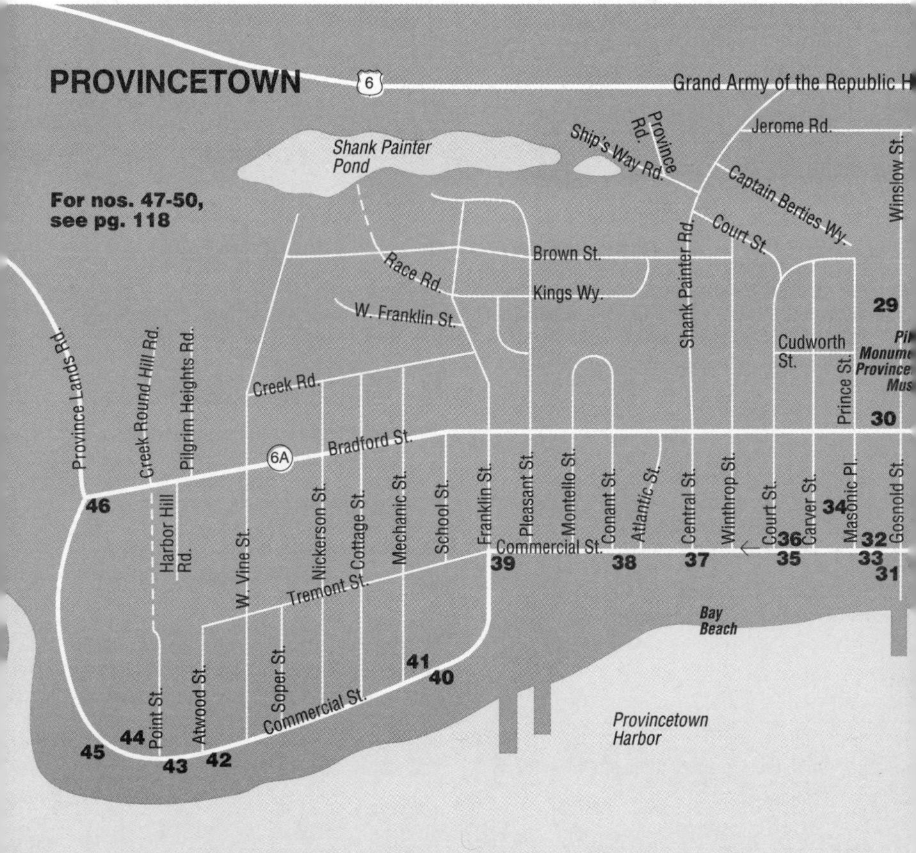

PROVINCETOWN

For nos. 47-50, see pg. 118

6
Grand Army of the Republic H
Shank Painter Pond
Province Rd.
Ship's Way Rd.
Jerome Rd.
Captain Berties Wy.
Winslow St.
Court St.
Brown St.
Race Rd.
Kings Wy.
W. Franklin St.
Shank Painter Rd.
29
Cudworth St.
Prince St.
Province Lands Rd.
Creek Round Hill Rd.
Pilgrim Heights Rd.
Creek Rd.
6A
Bradford St.
30
46
Harbor Hill Rd.
W. Vine St.
Nickerson St.
Cottage St.
Mechanic St.
School St.
Franklin St.
Pleasant St.
Montello St.
Conant St.
Atlantic St.
Central St.
Winthrop St.
Court St.
Carver St.
Masonic Pl.
Gosnold St.
34
Commercial St.
39
38
37
36
35
32
33
31
Tremont St.
Bay Beach
41
40
Soper St.
Atwood St.
Point St.
Commercial St.
44
45
43
42
Provincetown Harbor

10 **James R. Bakker Gallery** In 1993, the well-regarded arts auctioneer from Cambridge opened a small branch in Provincetown to traffic in vintage local wares. Given his unerring eye, this should be a space to watch. ♦ Daily 11AM-4PM, 7-10PM late May to mid-Oct. 432 Commercial St (at Kiley Ct). 487.4032

10 **Tiffany Lamp Studio** In a small atelier on a tree-shaded alley, **Stephen Donnelly** pieces together Tiffany lamps—both authentic models and his own adaptations, some fetching $5,000. Removed from their usual fern bar habitat, and distinct from cheap reproductions, they're singularly beautiful objects, and it's fascinating to see patterns emerge from vivid chunks of glass. ♦ Daily 9AM-10:30PM July-Aug; daily 9AM-5PM Sept-June. 432 Commercial St (at Kiley Ct). 487.1101

11 **Ciro & Sal's** ★★★$$$ This semi-subterranean trattoria, awash with Chianti bottles and operatic arias, started out as an artists' coffeehouse in 1951 and soon evolved into a local institution. The specialties include hand-cut veal in seven regional guises and five types of pasta with luscious sauces. The menu trails on at great length; among the don't-misses are *ostriche al Giannini*—broiled Wellfleets with pesto and Parmesan—and, to finish, a rich zabaglione. ♦ Italian ♦ Dinner. 4 Kiley Ct (at Commercial St). Reservations recommended. 487.0049

12 **The Mews** ★★★$$$ Step down to an understated, sand-hued restaurant that blends effortlessly into the beach. Lest you forget where you are, the waiters' nautical uniforms will remind you. The menu includes some culinary innovations, such as shrimp beignets served with apricot and guava puree, a scorching Thai salad garnished with rare filet mignon, and lobster wonton dumplings in a tomato and basil cream sauce. ♦ International ♦ Lunch and dinner; weekend brunch. Closed Monday through Wednesday and for lunch Monday through Friday mid-Feb to late June, early Sept to mid-Dec; closed mid-Dec to mid-Feb. 429 Commercial St (between Kiley Ct and Lovetts Ln). Reservations recommended. 487.1500

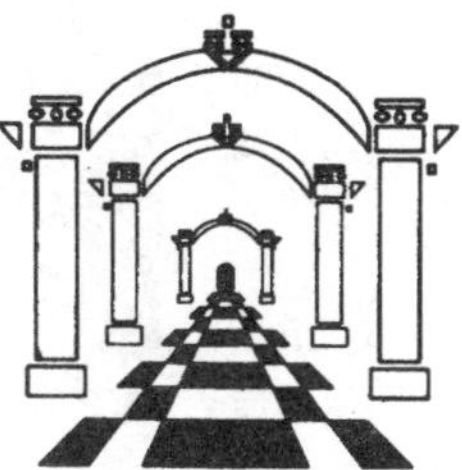

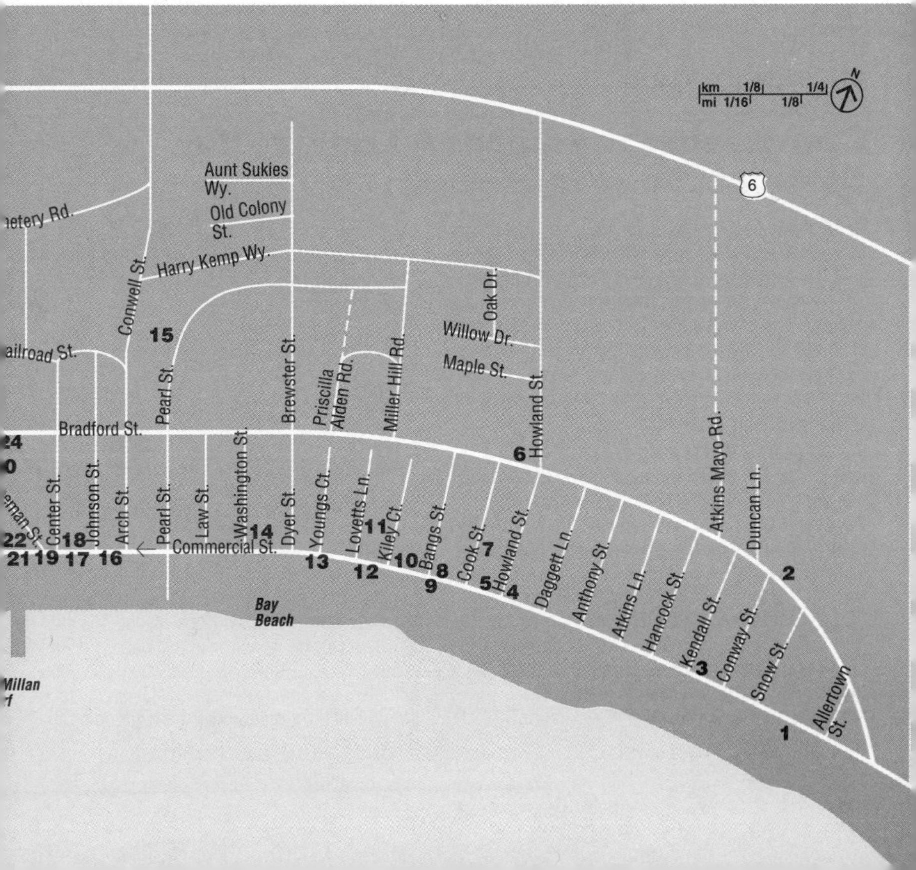
km 1/8 1/4
mi 1/16 1/8
N
6
Aunt Sukies Wy.
Old Colony St.
Harry Kemp Wy.
Conwell St.
Railroad St.
Pearl St.
Brewster St.
Priscilla Alden Rd.
Miller Hill Rd.
Oak Dr.
Willow Dr.
Maple St.
Howland St.
Bradford St.
Atkins Mayo Rd.
Duncan Ln.
Center St.
Johnson St.
Arch St.
Law St.
Washington St.
Dyer St.
Youngs Ct.
Lovetts Ln.
Kiley Ct.
Bangs St.
Cook St.
Daggett Ln.
Anthony St.
Atkins Ln.
Hancock St.
Kendall St.
Conway St.
Snow St.
Allertown St.
Commercial St.
Bay Beach
15
6
14
11
7
2
22
18
21
19
17
16
13
12
10
8
9
5
4
3
1

Within The Mews:

Café Mews ★★$$ Step upstairs and the pace is a bit brisker, but it's the same kitchen turning out the same salads and appetizers, plus pasta and pizza, Gorgonzola or garden burgers (the latter is a tasty vegetarian impostor), and some relatively simple entrées. ♦ International ♦ Lunch and dinner; weekend brunch. Closed Monday through Wednesday and for lunch Monday through Friday mid-Feb to late June, early Sept to mid-Dec; closed mid-Dec to mid-Feb. 487.1500

13 Giardelli/Antonelli Studio Showroom Local designer **Jerry Giardelli** makes dramatic, sculptural clothing for women, with fabrics that change in response to the season: a rainbow of dolman-sleeved cotton jersey shirts, for instance, might give way to styles in sueded rayon for the fall. **Diana Antonelli** contributes the stylish silver jewelry. ♦ Daily 11AM-6PM, 8-10PM late May to early Sept; daily 11AM-6PM early Sept to Jan; Sa-Su 11AM-6PM Jan to late May. 417 Commercial St (at Youngs Ct). 487.3016

14 The Landmark ★★$$$ The exterior is certainly grand enough—an 1840s neoclassical mansion replete with columns—but the real draw, according to a regular, is "the chance to be fussed over by queens." (Not the blue-blood variety.) The decor is modified bordello, the menu not particularly distinguished. The staff is what gives the experience spice; "it's the original dinner theater," says one fan. ♦ Continental ♦ Dinner. Closed Nov-Mar. 402 Commercial St (between Dyer and Washington Sts). 487.9319

15 Fine Arts Work Center (FAWC) Housed in the former **Day's Lumber Yard,** a source of patron-subsidized lodging for artists since early in the century, this fellowship program hosts 10 writers and as many visual artists from fall through spring—a period long enough for them to forge strong bonds among themselves and with the community. That's precisely what the founders (including such influential figures as **Robert Motherwell** and **Stanley Kunitz**) had in mind when they initiated the program in 1968; they wanted to ensure that their artistic successors would be inspired and supported by Provincetown as they had been. To this end, FAWC sponsors regular seminars, workshops, exhibits, and readings; call for information. ♦ 24 Pearl St (between Bradford and Brewster Sts). 487.9960

16 Silk & Feathers "Gourmet lingerie" describes this collection of upscale underwear, some of it on the demure side of kinky. Hats and accessories round out the look, which is not, of course, strictly limited to the boudoir. ♦ Daily 10AM-11PM Apr-Sept; daily noon-6PM Oct-Mar. 377 Commercial St (at Arch St). 487.2057

Canvassing the Cape: A Look at the State of the Arts

Henry James once called Cape Cod "the Italy of Massachusetts." Like its continental counterpart, the area has long exerted a Circe-like allure for artists. The numbers that have gravitated here over the past century were drawn partly by the light (diffracted by sand and sea so that it seems to scintillate), partly by the promise of *la dolce vita,* and largely—until the tourist camp-followers arrived to jack up prices—by the low rents.

Painter **Charles Webster Hawthorne** is widely credited for having led the avant-garde to the tip of this remote peninsula. The **Cape Cod School of Painting (CCSP),** which he founded in 1899 and ran until 1929 (it still exists, directed by the protégée of a protégé), attracted art students from across the country. As an advocate of the *premier coup* (literally, "first stroke") method, Hawthorne was intent on getting his students to work outdoors—a fairly radical notion in those days. As he noted in the manual *Hawthorne on Painting* (published posthumously by his widow and still in print):

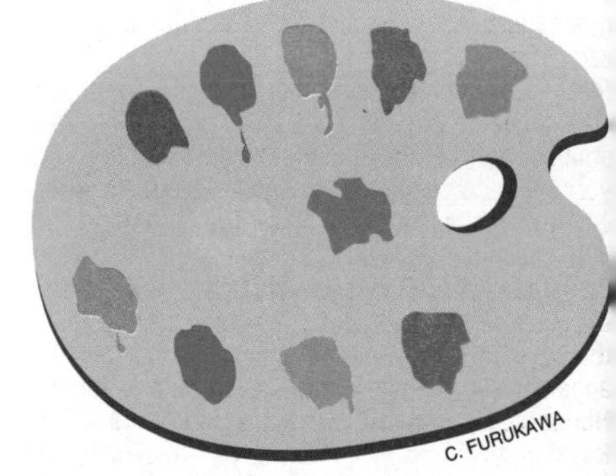

"Painting is a matter of impulse, it is a matter of getting out to nature and having some joy in registering it. . . . Go out like a savage," he exhorted his students, "as if paint had just been invented." To inspire them, he'd give dramatic demonstrations, completing a huge canvas, *en plein air,* in just one session as his awestruck students gazed on.

Among Hawthorne's acolytes was the painter **Edwin Dickinson,** who came to study with him in 1912 at the age of 20, stayed on three more years as his assistant, and three more as his friend. In the heady pre-World War I years, the two lived side by side, at 48 and 46 Pearl Street, in what was then **Day's Lumberyard** (the building now houses the **Fine Arts Work Center,** dedicated to introducing emerging artists to the town, and vice versa). Provincetown at that time, according to **Jacob Getlar** in *Edwin Dickinson—American Mystic,* was the antithesis of what you see here today, and a shadow, even, of its seafaring 18th-century self: Getlar describes a desolate landscape characterized by "deserted beaches, aimless alleys . . . creaking piers . . . paintless weather-beaten shacks"—all offering, as Hawthorne cheerfully put it in a CCSP brochure, "an endless number of subjects for the student painter." In an oral history published by **Columbia University** in 1975, Dickinson recalled: "I lived in my studio and painted in it, slept in it, and cooked in it." Even though the cold in his uninsulated cabin was such that he sometimes had to resort to wrapping up in one of his giant canvasses to make it through the night, "emotionally," he remembered fondly, "I lived more luxuriously than J.P. Morgan ever thought of."

Dickinson was not alone, ecstatically roughing it in the boondocks; he soon had plenty of illustrious company. In 1914, thanks in large part to Hawthorne's tireless promotion, Greenwich Village unofficially elected Provincetown its summer place, and a steady stream of artists, playwrights, painters, poets, protestors, and patrons made the pilgrimage to its rustic shores. By 1916, the town was supporting no fewer than six art schools.

At the same time, a revolution was underway in the arts. The notorious **Armory Show** of 1913 sent out a clarion statement that the "rules" no longer applied. By the time the **Provincetown Art Association & Museum (PAAM),** founded in 1914, had acquired sufficient exhibition space to mount shows; the modernists and traditionalists were so inimical, each camp insisted on having its own wall (canvasses crammed every square inch). The space wars raged on through the '20s, a golden age when studios could still be found for as little as $50 a year. (Among the new arrivals was **Edward Hopper,** who would spend every summer from 1920 to 1967 in the neighboring town of Truro.) By the late '30s, the traditionalists had regained their ascendancy in the battle for PAAM, but they had also, clearly, lost the war. When Hawthorne died in 1930, his heir apparent was German abstract expressionist **Hans Hofmann,** who started giving classes in 1935 in Hawthorne's old studio on Miller Hill Road. Informal links with the **Art Students League** in New York (where Hawthorne himself had studied) ensured that the colony kept up-to-date with metropolitan trends, and abstract expressionism reigned supreme in Provincetown well into the '50s and beyond, attracting such luminaries as **Franz Kline, Mark Rothko, Helen Frankenthaler, Robert Motherwell,** and **Jackson Pollock (Thomas Hart Benton's** renegade protégé, who took up residence in one of the Province Lands dune shacks, home over the years to such other notable misfits as **Eugene O'Neill, Jack Kerouac, Tennessee Williams,** and **Norman Mailer**).

In recent decades, the arts scene has pretty much mirrored the international zeitgeist. There is no longer a recognized "school" of Provincetown painting, but there are still plenty of places throughout the Cape and the Islands where you can see brilliant examples of past work, as well as art history in the making. These include:

Barnstable Not for fans of primitive art only, the **Cahoon Museum of American Art** (428.7581) in Cotuit mounts interesting contemporary shows. The **Pinske Gallery** (362.5311) is young, bold, and brash, and a breath of fresh air, so forgive the artists their aesthetic trespasses.

Chatham Contemporary though rarely outré, the **Munson Gallery** (945.9851), housed in a former horse barn, has a stellar track record.

Dennis The new shows may disappoint, but be sure to prowl the hallways of the **Cape Museum of Fine Arts** (385.4477) to rout out some seminal works.

Falmouth **Edith Bruce's** carefully tended stable at the **Woods Hole Gallery** (548.7594) is worth keeping an eye on.

Martha's Vineyard If you're in the market for lesser-known Old Masters, browse through the art gallery in the lobby of the **Charlotte Inn** (627.4751). **The Granary Gallery** (693.0455) at the Red Barn Emporium warrants a visit for its exquisite photography, including prints by **Alfred Eisenstaedt;** stop at **The Field Gallery** (693.5595) to wander among **Tom Maley's** fanciful statues. And **On the Vineyard Gallery** (693.1338) will give you a glimpse of indigenous creativity few tourists get to see.

Nantucket Too-pretty pastels predominate on this enchanted isle, but the **Main Street Gallery** (228.2252) offers more substantial work to savor. **The Gallery at Four India Street** (228.8509) caters to big budgets and traditional tastes.

Provincetown The good galleries are too numerous to list, but among the must-visits are the **Provincetown Group Gallery** (487.0275), the **Long Point Gallery** (487.1795), the **Berta Walker Gallery** (487.6411), the **Provincetown Art Association & Museum** (487.1750), and the **Julie Heller Gallery** (487.2169).

Sandwich The art museum at the **Heritage Plantation** (888.3300) has a wonderful collection of folk art, from samplers to endearingly primitive portraits.

Wellfleet From here north you're getting into serious art territory, starting—and culminating with—the roster of the famous and about-to-be-famous at the **Cherry Stone Gallery** (349.3026). The **Hopkins Gallery** (349.7264) is a good place to spot up-and-comers.

16 Pepe's Wharf ★★$$$$ A black-and-white awning stretches toward the bay, and oversize bamboo chairs add a tropical touch. The seafood goes native in any number of directions (Portuguese, Japanese, French), and in summer **Jim Wetherbee**—who winters at the **Copley Plaza** in Boston—regales bar patrons with Gershwin and Porter tunes. ♦ International ♦ Breakfast, lunch, and dinner; call for May-June, Sept-Oct hours. Closed Nov-Apr. 371-373 Commercial St (between Arch and Johnson Sts). 487.0670

16 Halcyon Gallery This roundup of hand-crafted women's clothing and adornments melds practicality with fun at agreeable prices. Among the nicer items are **Cynthia Krause's** chenille tunics in gently graded hues, and **Maralyce Ferree's** fleece parkas and shredded denim jackets. ♦ Daily 10AM-11PM mid-May to mid-Sept; Sa-Su noon-6PM mid-Sept to mid-May. 371 Commercial St (between Arch and Johnson Sts). 487.9415

17 Northern Lights Hammock Shop Every conceivable kind of suspended seating is available here, from cozy Mexican slings to a cypress-wood stand that resembles an abbreviated boat. Best of all, the staff encourages you to sample the wares—a delightful respite from the tour-de-foot of Commercial Street. ♦ Daily 11AM-11PM June-Aug; daily 10AM-8PM May, Sept-Oct. 361 Commercial St (between Johnson and Center Sts). 487.9376

17 Small Pleasures After more than two decades of handling estate jewelry, **Virginia McKenna** doesn't have to shop around; the top dealers (many from England) come to her. Her scintillating stock is particularly strong on 1920s accessories for men, but women are well served, too, with exquisite Victorian emeralds and opals, along with intricate clusters of garnets. ♦ Daily 11AM-11PM late May to early Sept; daily 11AM-6PM early Sept to late Oct, Apr to late May; Sa-Su 11AM-6PM Nov-Mar (call for additional holiday hours). 359 Commercial St (between Johnson and Center Sts). 487.3712

18 Mad Hatter Enhance your fantasy life with one of these instant identities. The stock ranges from velvet cloches to straw boaters, with some fantastic creations that defy categorization. There's an in-depth selection of cowboy/girl hats, some adorned with feathers, and assorted jackets, vests, and shirts to amplify that particular wardrobe. ♦ Daily 10AM-11PM June-Sept; daily 10AM-6PM Oct, May; Sa-Su 11AM-5PM Nov-Dec, mid-Feb to May. 360 Commercial St (between Johnson and Center Sts). 487.3040

18 Provincetown Heritage Museum Established by the community in 1976 and housed in a former church, this museum is a bouillabaisse of eclectic elements. Dominating the collection is a half-scale model of the fishing schooner *Rose Dorothea,* which rises from the second floor seemingly into the rafters. The ground floor is given over to various period rooms inhabited by "lifelike" wax figures; the effect is more than a little hokey. The main reason to visit is to see the artworks documenting the changing face of Provincetown. Here the homespun quality of the galleries detracts not in the least from the sprinkling of gems, among them a semi-abstract study of Truro's Back Beach by **Edwin Dickinson.** ♦ Admission. Daily 10AM-6PM mid-June to mid-Oct. 356 Commercial St (at Center St). 487.0666

19 Soul to Soul Euro-rock wafts through the chicly sparse racks, featuring a laid-back collection of *au courant* clothes: linen skimmers and Doc Martens footwear. The sunglasses selection is the best in town. ♦ M-F, Su 10AM-11PM, Sa 10AM-midnight late May to early Sept; daily 10AM-8PM early Sept to Jan, mid-Apr to late May. 349 Commercial St (between Center and Freeman Sts). 487.0311

20 Napi's ★★$$$ Since 1973, **Napi** and **Helen Van Dereck's** flamboyant restaurant has served as a haven for artists and others burned out on the hurly-burly of Commercial Street; in fact, a lot of local talents were roped in for the construction, which involved salvage elements and outtakes from the Van Derecks' antiques business. The kitchen covers the world: lobster Alfredo is available alongside Chinese potstickers or falafel. Home-baked wholewheat bread accompanies every meal, and the finale of choice is Double Fudge Madness, a chocolate-glazed rum custard cake. ♦ International ♦ Lunch and dinner. Closed for lunch Oct-May. 7 Freeman St (at Bradford St). 487.1145

The "Surfmen" of the U.S. Life Saving Service (in operation on Cape Cod from 1872 to 1915) trained by day and walked the beaches by night, in hopes of spotting a ship in distress. Their creed: "You have to go out, but you don't have to come back."

21 Cafe Edwige/Bubala's Restaurant ★★★$$$$ Mornings, in its Edwige guise, this cathedral-ceilinged space serves a bountiful, natural-foods breakfast: fresh OJ, homemade granola, fritattas—the works. Evenings, tiny lights twinkle on the deck, and Deco lamps cast a romantic glow indoors. Bubala's playful menu caters to the oddest of cravings: Southwestern fried squid with chipotle remoulade, say, or homemade pesto ravioli in walnut-flecked vermouth cream sauce. This is one of the few places along this stretch of the strip where you can duck the tourist hordes—a fact not lost on the locals, so expect a wait. ♦ International ♦ Breakfast and dinner; call for dinner schedule Apr to late May, early Sept to Jan. Closed Jan-Mar. 333 Commercial St (at Freeman St). 487.2008

CAFÉ BLASÉ

22 Café Blasé ★★$ People-watching is the main reason to frequent this highly visible cafe, a festive convocation of tasseled umbrellas and giant Japanese lanterns at the epicenter of the shopping/shmoozing quarter. The prices are gauged just right for grazing, and among the more inviting delectables are Terrine Oceanus (a pâté of seafood, leeks, pimiento, and saffron) and a classic *salade niçoise.* Sandwiches, pizzas, quiches, quesadillas, and more fill out the bill, or you might just want to sip an arcane Italian aperitif and look ineffably cool. ♦ International ♦ Breakfast, lunch, and dinner. Closed for breakfast late May, early to mid-Sept. 328 Commercial St (between Freeman and Standish Sts). 487.9465

23 Governor Bradford This beer-steeped old bar has made no concessions to the yuppie crowd. Year-rounders play chess in the window tables, and blues-lovers flock here for headliners like **Luther "Guitar Jr." Johnson, Roomful of Blues,** and the home-grown **Provincetown Jug Band.** ♦ Daily 11AM-1PM; live entertainment M, Th. 312 Commercial St (at Standish St). 487.9618

23 Art's Dune Tours To get a look at the humble dune shacks that sheltered such luminaries as **Eugene O'Neill, Jack Kerouac, Tennessee Williams,** and **Jackson Pollock,** hop a ride in a GMC Suburban with **Art Costa,** who has been covering this territory since 1946. These driftwood hovels may not look like much (the park service wanted to raze them as eyesores), but after years of intense crusading they've at last been granted **National Historic Landmark** status, solely for the quality of the tenants they attracted. ♦ Fee. By reservation only. Closed Nov-Mar. Commercial and Standish Sts. 487.1950

≋FRANCO'S≋

24 Franco's by the Sea ★★★$$$ When **Franco Palumbo** moved his operation here from the East End in 1992, the decor came with him: lock, stock, streamlined lamps, and Fiesta Ware (some of the stuff is for sale, should you share his mania). The dimly lit Art Deco interior fairly shouts style, as does the more-sophisticated-than-thou staff. Palumbo considers his cuisine a mix of "comfort food" and "passion food"; it's mostly Italian, with a smattering of New Orleans and other influences. Try the Cajun corn chowder with andouille, or stick to the tried-and-true shrimp Luigi, tossed with garlic, lemon, and roasted peppers. ♦ Italian/International ♦ Dinner. Closed Dec-Mar. 133 Bradford St (at Standish St). Reservations recommended. 487.3178

Above Franco's by the Sea:

Luigi's ★★★$$ The upstairs cafe/bar is more classically Italian, with a menu to match. Some of the entrées overlap, like Hideaway Pasta (named for Palumbo's original 1984 restaurant, it's tossed with olive oil, garlic, pine nuts, raisins, and cheese), and others, such as a chef's choice *foccacia del giorno,* are conceived to suit a grazer's picky appetite. The bar offers a dramatic view of the Pilgrim Monument. ♦ Italian ♦ Dinner. Closed Dec-Mar. Reservations recommended. 487.4723

Bodysurfers might try testing naturalist Henry Beston's theory of threes. "On Celtic coasts," he wrote in *The Outermost House* (1928), "it is the seventh wave that is seen coming like a king out of the grey, cold sea. The Cape tradition, however, is no half-real, half-mystical fancy. Great waves do indeed approach this beach by threes . . . Coast guard crews are all well aware of this triple rhythm and take advantage of the lull that follows the last wave to launch their boats."

Pilgrims' Progress

The Puritans (so-called because they wanted to "purify" the Anglican church) were Protestants—mostly farmers and craftsmen—who bridled at what they perceived as the corruption endemic to the Church of England. They viewed the established hierarchy, with its elaborate ceremonies and trappings, and the intermingling of religious and secular power, as scarce improvement over Catholicism. After convening secretly in Scrooby, England (under threat of imprisonment) in 1606, the Puritans emigrated to Leyden in the Netherlands in 1607 and 1608, but never fully adjusted to life in exile. The Dutch, though tolerant, were even more worldly than their English peers, and not only did the Puritans experience extreme difficulty securing work, they despaired at the thought of their children growing up in a foreign culture.

Naturally, they leapt at the proposal made by the **Merchant Adventurers,** a company of speculators who offered New World colonists financial backing in exchange for the natural riches sure to be found overseas. A contingent of Puritans (or "separatists," as they were called by less rebellious Protestants) sailed for England aboard the *Speedwell,* there to link up with the *Mayflower* and head overseas. On 6 September 1620, 102 passengers (including 34 children) crowded onto the 90-foot *Mayflower.* Of the adults, about half were "saints" (that is, Puritans) seeking religious freedom, the other half "strangers" merely seeking economic betterment. Collectively, they would come to be known as Pilgrims, for their long and arduous journey. The 66-day crossing, undertaken in what is now recognized as hurricane season, was indeed horrendous. Aiming for the mouth of the Hudson River (then part of the Virginia colonies), the *Mayflower* was blown off-course, at length dropping anchor off the tip of Cape Cod at sunrise on 11 November. The Pilgrims put off debarking because insurrection was brewing among their ranks. The indentured servants aboard, no longer bound for the households of an established colony, insisted that they be granted their freedom if they were to participate in the risks and rewards of settlement; mutiny seemed likely if their status was not spelled out. Before going ashore, the Pilgrims drafted the **Mayflower Compact,** a precursor to the U.S. Constitution, which asserted their belief in self-rule as a "body politick" and made the servants full citizens. By mapping out their own deeply held beliefs, the Pilgrims helped set the course for the colonies' ultimate independence.

Meanwhile, the group faced more pressing needs. The day after their arrival, while the women washed clothes in salt water, the men went ashore to collect firewood and reconnoiter. What they found was utte desolation. Wrote **William Bradford** in *Of Plimoth Plantation:* "Being thus passed the vast ocean . . . they had no friend to welcome them, no inns to entertain them or refresh their weatherbeaten bodies; no houses, or much less towns to repair to, to seek for succour." One lucky scouting party, led by the group's military officer, **Captain Miles Standish,** found a cache of Indian seed corn at the site now known as **Corn Hill** in Truro. They helped themselves to 10 bushels, without which they might never have survived the next season. Pressing on in search of a hospitable place to settle, they met a band of hostile natives at what is now called **First Encounter Beach** in Eastham. Distrustful of such interlopers after an encounter with one **Captain Thomas Hunt** in 1614 (while participating in **Captair John Smith's** mapping expedition, Hunt had captured two dozen Wampanoags and sold them into slavery in Spain), the natives attacked the scouting party with arrows; the Pilgrims retaliated with musket fire. No lives were lost, but the Pilgrims had second thoughts about the neighborhood.

Within five weeks of landing, increasingly harsh weather impelled the settlers to cross the bay in search of a more protected port. On 20 December 1620, they landed in Plymouth, where, providentially, they found a plot already cleared, ready and waiting, at a relatively safe, high location near freshwater springs. The Indians who had cleared the land had been decimated by plague during the preceding year and were nowhere to be seen. Of the handful remaining, one astounded the Pilgrims several months later, on 16 March 1621, by walking into their compound and addressing them in their own language: "Welcome!" This was **Samoset,** who had picked up a bit of English from cod fishers and would be of great help as the Pilgrims adapted to their strange new world. Six days later he returned with another invaluable aide, **Squanto**—one of the very men, ironically, kidnapped by Hunt in 1614.

Squanto's first encounter with Western civilization had occurred in 1605, when he voluntarily boarded a ship bound for London; after nine years as a sideshow attraction, he was finally allowed to return home; on the final leg of his journey, however, he had the misfortune of running into Hunt. Shipped to Spain, he appealed to two friars who managed to get him to London. After three years of working as a servant, he was able to book passage again in 1619, and returned home just in time to find his entire clan wiped out by plague. Although some settlers complained of his penchant for peddling favors, Squanto was a paragon of forgiveness and a literal lifesaver. For the Pilgrims, wrote Bradford, he "was a spetiall instrument sent of God for their good beyond their expectation. He directed them how to set their corne, wher to take fish and to procure other commodoties and was their pilott to bring them to unknowne places for their profitt, and never left them till he dyed." Squanto succumbed to a fever in 1622, Bradford records, "desiring ye Govr to pray for him, that he might goe to ye Englishmens God in heaven." The peace treaties he helped to secure between **Governor John Carver** and **Chief Massasoit** lasted for half a century. As **Edward Winslow** noted, the mutual goodwill was such that the Pilgrims could "walk as safely in the woods as on the highways of England."

The Pilgrims needed every possible advantage. That first winter half of them died from scurvy, pneumonia, and other diseases. Come spring, the Indians helped the survivors plant crops. A three-day harvest celebration was held that fall in mid-October; 90 natives attended, far outnumbering the colonists. They feasted on wild turkeys, geese, duck, lobsters, clams, oysters, fish, and eels, accompanied by fruit tarts and beer. The natives brought along five deer, as well as corn and popcorn.

Such bounty notwithstanding, the New World never yielded the riches anticipated by the Merchant Adventurers. The Pilgrims dutifully sent all they could gather to England—principally, pelts and oak staves for barrels—but their backers, who had initially invested $34,000, were inclined to end the venture. The Pilgrims, for their part, were ready to cut loose: in 1627, eight Plymouth leaders, fed up with the managers' attempts to foist an Established Church minister on them, and with being forced to borrow money at 60 percent interest, purchased the Londoners' share in the company for $9,000. They were officially on their own.

Three years later, 1,000 more Puritans on 11 ships landed at Salem during the "Great Migration," and soon worked their way southward to Boston to take advantage of its well-protected harbor, teeming with fish. By 1636, another 12,000 immigrants arrived. In just 16 years, the colonists had secured their foothold in the New World.

25 Aqua Ventures Parasailing What better way to get a good look at the environs than from a parachute? Tethered by a long rope (your choice of 300 or 600 feet), you rise serenely behind **Jack Ferreira's** $70,000 parasailing boat, never even getting your feet wet. Ascents and descents couldn't be easier (you're reeled out and in) and no particular physical prowess is required, just a certain degree of daring. ♦ Fee. Daily 9AM-6PM June-Sept, weather permitting. MacMillan Wharf (off Commercial St). Reservations required. 487.6386, 800/300.3787

26 Provincetown Portuguese Bakery This venerable bakery has been turning out savories and sweets since the turn of the century. In summer, the demand is so high that they bake around the clock. The meat pies and linguica rolls are on the heavy, greasy side; you might opt for an unusual pastry, such as an orange-soaked torta or a plain, refreshing flan. ♦ Bakery ♦ Daily 7:30AM-11PM late June to early Sept; call for hours early Mar to late June, early Sept to Nov. 299 Commercial St (between MacMillan Wharf and Ryder St Extension). 487.1803

27 Rambling Rose Carriage Co. Horse-and-buggy jaunts through town are offered at surprisingly reasonable rates ($15 and up per couple). Afterwards, you can reward your conveyor with a carrot. ♦ Fee. Daily 11AM-11PM June-Aug; daily 10AM-4PM May, Sept-Oct. Town Hall (Commercial and Ryder Sts). 487.4246

27 **Provincetown Trolley, Inc.** For a brief, nontaxing local history lesson (not to mention chauffeured transport), try this 40-minute tour that meanders past the Monument, out to the **Province Lands Visitor Center** in the dunes, and back into town via the East End. There are five spots where you can hop off and look around for a half-hour or more before reboarding, and it's worth momentarily exposing yourself as a tourist to avoid the hassle of maneuvering a car through Provincetown's congested, virtually unparkable streets. ♦ Fee. Departures daily every half-hour 10AM-4PM and hourly 5-8PM May-Oct. Town Hall (Commercial and Ryder Sts). 487.9483

27 **Provincetown Town Hall** Built in 1878, this grand old heap still serves its original function while doubling as a 600-seat performance space. Up a massive horseshoe staircase, the auditorium has seen such headliners as **Odetta, Shawn Colvin,** and the **Klezmer Conservatory Band** perform under the **Muse Series** banner since 1982. En route, don't miss **Ross Moffett's** neoclassical WPA-era murals: farming women on the right, fishing men on the left. Wander the halls to turn up *Fish Cleaners,* a portrait by Provincetown's pioneer painter **Charles Hawthorne,** and many other intriguing works, such as **Henry Hensche's** *His Breakfast.* The lighting is woefully inadequate—possibly a boon for the aging artwork but a real detriment for viewers. ♦ For concert schedule, call 487.0955. Building: daily 8:30AM-5PM. 260 Commercial St (at Ryder St). 487.7000

Dawn may not be quite early enough to catch the launching of the fleet. Provincetown fishing boats head out between 2AM and 5AM and return around 5PM to have their catch shipped overnight to major metropolitan markets.

One of the Cape's more fleeting get-rich-quick schemes was the manufacture of faux pearls from fish scales. French chemist Edward I. Petow came up with a formula during World War I and moved to Hyannis to set up a factory. Business boomed, with revenues peaking at $50 million a year. The Depression, along with Japan's introduction of synthetic pearls, knocked the bottom out of the market, and the product—guaranteed to last five years—definitely didn't last much longer before starting to discolor and flake.

Restaurants/Clubs: Red **Hotels:** Blue
Shops/ Outdoors: Green **Sights/Culture:** Black

27 **Euro Island Grill** ★★$$ A thatched tiki bar plunked on a deck above teeming Commercial Street, the Euro does a convincing job of lulling you into an island frame of mind. Sip a Red Stripe beer while slurping conch chowder, then move on to grilled fish in lively Caribbean mumbo sauce or go the Sicilian route and order pasta or a thin-crusted pizza. Either way, time comes to a standstill as you regroup to resume the stroll or wind down at day's end. ♦ Caribbean ♦ Lunch and dinner; breakfast also on Saturday and Sunday. Closed Nov-Apr. 258 Commercial St (between Ryder and Gosnold Sts). 487.2505

Within the Euro Island Grill:

Club Euro A cavernous space that was once an 1843 Congregational Church now sports an oceanic dreamscape mural (complete with 3-D mermaid) and welcomes world-music bands on summer weekends. **Taj Mahal** and **Buckwheat Zydeco** are among the draws of recent seasons. The schedule is sporadic, so check newspaper listings or call for an update. ♦ Cover. 487.2505

28 **Pilgrim Monument & Provincetown Museum** The Pilgrims may have slighted Provincetown by moving on to greener pastures in Plymouth, but the **Cape Cod Pilgrim Memorial Association,** a civic group founded in 1892, was determined that their historic stopover not be overlooked. Hence the construction of this 253-foot-high neo-Renaissance memorial. Modeled after the **Torre del Mangia** in Sienna, it's the tallest granite structure in the country. A flight of 116 steps leads to the gargoyle-guarded heights, where on a clear day it's possible to scan all of the Cape's curving "arm" and even make out the Boston skyline 42 miles away. A museum was added in 1962, and its catch-all collection of maritime artifacts and artistic mementos was greatly enhanced by **Barry Clifford's** 1984 discovery of the pirate ship *Whydah* off Wellfleet. An entire room pays tribute to this unprecedented haul, and at the center, in a Plexiglas-enclosed lab, you can watch technicians process the sand-encrusted booty. ♦ Admission. Daily 9AM-7PM July-Sept; daily 9AM-5PM Apr-June, Oct-Nov; daily 9AM-4PM Dec-Mar. Last admission 45 minutes before closing. High Pole Hill Rd (off Winslow St). 487.1310

29 Outermost Hostel $ The starving artists of O'Neill's day would be tickled to find an honorable tradition upheld. This privately operated hostel offers 30 bunk beds in five cabins (one with a kitchen) for the rock-bottom price of $14 per person a night. Depending on the housekeeping skills of the other guests, conditions may resemble a documentary on the plight of migrant workers. Then again, this laudable enterprise renders the pleasures of Provincetown accessible to those young and spirited enough (albeit impecunious) to take full advantage. ♦ Closed Oct to late May. Registration: daily 8-9:30AM, 6-9:30PM at 30A Winslow St. 28 Winslow St (between Bradford St and Jerome Rd). 487.43768

30 The Fairbanks Inn $ Bradford Street's B&Bs tend to be slightly less expensive than those right on Commercial Street, and this 1776 captain's house (shown above) is surprisingly affordable, especially given its status as one of Provincetown's oldest buildings. (The very oldest, the **Seth Nickerson House,** a 1746 full Cape at 72 Commercial Street, is a private home.) All the expected niceties are accounted for: broad planked floors, Oriental rugs, four-posters, and, in some of the 16 rooms, fireplaces to chase away the chill. Continental breakfast is served in summer in a wicker-filled porch overlooking a patio, with private parking (a rarity in these parts) just beyond. ♦ 90 Bradford St (at Webster Pl). 487.0386

30 6 Webster Place $ Tucked behind the Fairbanks Inn, 6 Webster—a five-bedroom B&B—is even older (circa 1750); indoor plumbing wasn't introduced until 1986. Today, guests can enjoy all the modern amenities, plus the peace of a paneled library and a country-style decor that's tastefully restrained. The breakfasts are country-bountiful, featuring fresh muffins or homemade quiche. ♦ 6 Webster Pl (off Bradford St). 487.2266

31 Julie Heller Gallery As a child, **Julie Heller** was entranced by the works of early Provincetown artists and started acquiring examples as soon as she was able. Today, she displays such groundbreakers as **Charles Hawthorne** and **Milton Avery** and a select group of contemporary artists she feels continue the regional tradition. This fishing-shack-turned-gallery contains museum-quality pieces as well as prints and photos priced right for start-up collectors. Especially noteworthy are the white-line lithographs of **Blanche Lazzell,** who pioneered the style. ♦ Daily 10AM-11PM June to early Sept; daily noon-4PM early Sept to June (call ahead to confirm). 2 Gosnold St (off Commercial St). 487.2169

32 Keely's Kites The unobstructed beaches of the Back Side are a great place to launch a kite. This shop has the goods, including some competitive models that go for more than $200. You're welcome to pick up a more modest assemblage, though, and send it skyward. ♦ Daily 9:30AM-11PM late June to early Sept; daily 10AM-7PM June to Oct; daily 10AM-6PM mid-Apr to June, Oct. 240 Commercial St (between Gosnold St and Masonic Pl). 487.6499, 800/487.5483

32 Universalist Meetinghouse This handsome 1851 Greek Revival edifice (see above), on the **National Register of Historic Places,** has near-mythic origins: it is said that in 1820, *Mayflower* descendants **Sylvia** and **Elizabeth Freeman** came upon a waterlogged book on a beach, *The Life of the Rev. John Murray: Preacher of Universal Salvation.* The salvaged tome was passed around the community; within nine years, a meeting was organized. The church the Universalists eventually constructed was a repository for all the architectural and decorative glories of its day. The mahogany-trimmed pine pews are graced with scrimshaw medallions, the chandelier is a product of the Sandwich Glass factory, and the Holbrook tracker organ, installed in 1854, is the oldest instrument of its kind still in use on Cape Cod. The trompe l'oeil murals are the work of Swiss artist **Carl Wendte,** who in 1844 had dressed up Nantucket's Unitarian Universalist Church in a similar manner. ♦ Service Su 11AM. 236 Commercial St (between Gosnold St and Masonic Pl). 487.9344

32 Cortland Jessup Gallery It's actually three galleries, clustered around a pretty courtyard: one for painting and sculpture, another for photography, and a third that's more of a store. Owner **Cortland Jessup** likes to mix it up, evidenced in such 1993 exhibits as "Blinks," featuring **Mary Rhinelander's** manipulations of **Elsa Dorfman's** oversize Polaroid portraits, or a display of tattoo art by the notorious **Spider Webb.** Between the Saturday salons and Friday evening opening receptions, there's always something interesting going on. ♦ Daily noon-4PM, 7-11PM late May to early Sept; F-Su noon-4PM, 7-11PM Apr-June; F-Sa noon-10PM, Su noon-8PM early Sept to mid-Oct; call for hours mid-Oct to Jan. 234 Commercial St (between Gosnold St and Masonic Pl). 487.4479

32 Front Street Restaurant ★★★$$$$ Front Street was one of the first restaurants to spark the culinary awakening of the late 1970s, and it's still a delightful place. Located in the brick-walled cellar of a Victorian mansion, a few steps down from street level, it can be a bit cramped and noisy, but the hubbub just adds to the sense of excitement generated by such dishes as curried apple carrot bisque, plum barbecued lamb spareribs, and nectarine croustade with hurricane sauce. The menu changes weekly. If you'd like to get a glimpse of the "real" Provincetown, this may be your best shot. ♦ New American ♦ Dinner. Closed Monday through Wednesday Nov-Dec; closed Jan-Mar. 230 Commercial St (between Gosnold St and Masonic Pl). Reservations recommended. 487.9715

> Explorer Bartholomew Gosnold landed near Provincetown on 23 March 1602, seeking gold and finding cod instead. Wrote a crewman: "We came to anchor in fifteen fadome, where wee tooke great store of codfish for which we altered the name and called it Cape Cod."

33 Marine Specialties Since 1961, this hangar-size space has offered an Army-Navy type jumble sale, with the displays—virtually indistinguishable from the heaps of goods—growing ever more convoluted and bizarre. You'll find everything from grungewear to camping equipment, with all sorts of odd lots thrown in. ♦ Daily 10AM-midnight July-Aug; call for reduced hours daily Sept-Dec, mid-Feb to July; Sa-Su noon-5PM Jan to mid-Feb. 235 Commercial St (between Gosnold St and Masonic Pl). 487.1730

33 Clifford-Williams Antiques At the risk of a possibly snooty reception (the staff could benefit from a refresher course in public relations), head up the outdoor staircase for the only antiques shop in Provincetown worth a serious once-over. It's packed with English pine and oak, porcelains, and works by Provincetown artists, such as the late Pulitzer Prize-winning *Life* photographer **John Gregory.** ♦ Daily 11AM-11PM July-Aug; daily 11AM-5PM or by appointment Sept-June. 22[illegible] Commercial St (at Masonic Pl). 487.4174

34 Atlantic House Judging from the leather-trussed contenders lounging outside, this must be the place: Provincetown's premier gay bar, and one of the best known in the nation. Of course, if you came looking for it, you already knew that. ♦ Daily 4PM-closing. 4-6 Masonic Pl (between Commercial and Bradford Sts). 487.3821

35 Cafe Heaven ★★$ A plain and boxy storefront spiffed up with splashy paintings, this stylish cafe dishes out yummy custom omelets until 3PM—helpful should you make a dazed late start on the day. The home fries are state of the art, and you can wash them down with fresh-squeezed OJ or GJ (grapefruit juice) by the pitcher. Chilled salads and sandwiches on **Provincetown Portugues[e] Bakery** bread fill out the lunchtime slot, and a[t] night, patrons are treated to a taste of hamburger heaven: choices include a garlic burger, a Brie-topped French burger, and eve[n] a vegetarian garden burger. Don't overlook the inspired desserts, such as a fresh plum *clafoutis.* ♦ American ♦ Breakfast, lunch, and dinner. Closed for dinner May, early Sept to Nov; closed Nov-Apr. 199 Commercial St (between Carver and Court Sts). 487.9639. Takeout branch at: 338 Commercial St. 487.3314

35 **Pied Piper** There's not much to it—a triangular dance space with a bayside deck for cooling off—but no less an authority than *Time* called it the best women's bar in the country. Give it 'til about 10PM for the dancing to heat up. ♦ Daily 5PM-closing July-Aug; F-Sa mid-Apr to July, Sept-Oct. 193A Commercial St (at Court St). 487.1527

36 **Spiritus** ★★$ Between 1AM, when the bars close, and 2AM, when this glorified pizza parlor locks its doors, as many as 1,000 people have been known to crowd around, still cruising. If all you want is a pizza, you can get a good one here, with various toppings, including garlic and linguica. Or come back for a morning pastry when there's hardly anyone around, except for the cherubs and gargoyles frolicking in a mural above the massive stoves. ♦ Pizza ♦ Breakfast, lunch, and dinner. Closed late Oct to Mar. 190 Commercial St (between Carver and Court Sts). 487.2808. Also at: 500 Main St, Hyannis. 775.2955

37 **The Boatslip Beach Club** $$ This modern 45-room hotel is more of a permanent party than merely a place to stay. Certainly the waterfront footage and views, as well as the sun deck and pool, are pluses, but the main reason to hang around is the built-in social life. It's here that Provincetown's gay summer season is officially launched in late June with a drag "debutante ball," and guests stay in the social swim by attending afternoon "tea dances" or nightly DJ'd sessions alternating ballroom dancing with two-stepping. Although the clientele is mostly male, females will not be made to feel *de trop;* in fact, a special **Women's Weekend** is an annual event. ♦ Closed Nov to early Apr. 161 Commercial St (at Central St). 487.1669

Within The Boatslip Beach Club:

Soufflé Factory Restaurant ★★$$$$ Chef **Lea Forant** is as fluent with French classics (e.g., lobster *à l'Américaine,* conveniently de-shelled) as she is with Caribbean chicken or Far Eastern duck breast marinated in ginger, scallions, lemon, and turmeric. You can come as you are and—foregoing high-ticket items like the bouillabaisse—leave with your wallet not too egregiously lightened. ♦ International ♦ Breakfast, lunch, and dinner. Closed Nov to early Apr. Reservations recommended. 487.2509

MARTIN HOUSE

38 **Martin House** ★★$$$ This circa 1750 captain's house is a warren of low-slung, fire-lit dining rooms, and the garden terrace is a particularly pleasant spot for brunch. The "regional New England fare" ranges as far afield as Mexico (for the seafood burritos) and Thailand (red curry shrimp); still, the indigenous entrées are treated well, as when cod wears a pistachio crust and a cloaking of Chardonnay beurre blanc. ♦ Regional New England ♦ Breakfast and dinner. Closed Jan-Mar. 157 Commercial St (at Atlantic St). 487.1327

38 **Rick's** ★$$$ Food plays second fiddle to the entertainment at this simple, commodious *boîte.* Owner **Rick Weinstock,** a former Off-Broadway music director, plays show tunes nightly. When it comes to guest artists, the bill is eclectic, ranging from classic cabaret acts to the **Lesbian Lounge Lizards.** Comestibles are somewhat less ambitious, spanning chowder and other seafood staples, but can include—if the occasion demands—full-scale entrées such as sirloin doused with green peppercorns, cream, and cognac. ♦ International ♦ Breakfast and dinner. Closed mid-Oct to mid-May. 149 Commercial St (between Atlantic and Conant Sts). 487.6409

39 **Gallerani's Cafe** ★★★$$$ This bistro-style restaurant, with three walls of windows surrounding a grid of booths, buzzes with that hum of well-being that ensures success. Mornings start off promisingly with such brunch treats as eggs Benedict Imperiale (with smoked salmon and caviar) and zucchini latkes; dinner might be swordfish marinated in raspberry vinaigrette or cold sesame noodles with peanut sauce and grilled shrimp. It's one of the few restaurants to offer parking *and* stay open year-round, so it's no wonder that visitors and residents have taken to it like a charm. ♦ International ♦ Breakfast and dinner; dinner only on Wednesday. Closed for breakfast Monday and Tuesday Oct to mid-May. 133 Commercial St (between Pleasant and Franklin Sts). 487.4433

Commercial and Bradford streets in Provincetown didn't even exist until the early 19th century. The only streets in town were those that ran up from the harbor, and anyone wanting to cross to the other side of town had to go along the beach.

SAL'S PLACE

40 Sal's Place ★★★$$$ If it's a timeless quality you're seeking, you'll want to put in a relaxed evening here. Like the original Sal's across town, this wharfside trattoria is strewn with Chianti bottles and serenaded with opera. The difference is an expansive vine-covered deck that transports you straight to Sorrento. The strictly traditional menu abounds in inimitable staples, from *spaghettini puttanesca* to *vitello saltimbocca.* The Friday *piatto di giorno* is squid stuffed with pignoli, and any day of the week, the *tiramisù* is a superlative dessert. ♦ Italian ♦ Dinner. Closed Monday through Thursday May to mid-June, Oct; closed Nov-Apr. 99 Commercial St (between Franklin and Mechanic Sts). Reservations recommended. 487.1279

41 Captain Lysander Inn $ This 1850s captain's house, with fancy fanlight, stands at the end of an inviting walkway lined with flowers. The 13 handsome traditional rooms enjoy the advantage of a quiet West End setting, and the very modest price includes a Continental breakfast. ♦ 96 Commercial St (between Franklin and Mechanic Sts). 487.2253

42 Center for Coastal Studies (CCS) Marine biologist **Dr. Charles "Stormy" Mayo,** whose work inspired the whole whale-watching mania (and subsequent industry), wrote: "It seems likely that the future of the seas and of the earth system as a whole will be assured only if we can win a race with technical development, and know our environment before the system, the whales, and we ourselves are overcome." His nonprofit CCS is a step in that direction, and offers the public nature walks, lectures, and other educational programs; call for details. ♦ 59 Commercial St (between W. Vine and Atwood Sts). 487.3622

"The man who ventures a trip on a trawler," wrote George H. Proctor in *The Fisheries and Fishery Industries of the United States* (1887), "finds . . . little of romance. He must rise early and work late in order to visit his trawls, remove his fish, rebait and reset the lines, and take care of the day's catch. A moment of carelessness or inattention, or a slight miscalculation may cost him his life. And at any time fog could leave him afloat in a measureless void."

43 The Masthead $$$ A cluster of 21 antiqu appointed rooms, cottages, and apartments interlaced with brick walkways, this rose-covered colony hasn't changed much since 1959, except to get prettier and more desirable. A 450-foot private beach lies righ outside the ample picture windows, and the staff is known for spoiling—like the time the provided **Billy Joel** and **Christie Brinkley** wi a shuttle to their yacht. ♦ 31-41 Commercia St (between Atwood and Point Sts). 487.0523, 800/395.5095

44 Lands End Inn $$ For two decades clinica psychologist **David Schoolman** has been filling up this 1907 Gull Hill bungalow with A Deco and Nouveau furnishings. The result is B&B, set amid two terraced acres, that's *sui generis:* each of the 16 rooms is packed with collectors' items that will strike the visitor as either oppressive or exquisite, depending on one's decorative bent. (In other words, Bauhaus buffs beware.) Those susceptible t this kind of fantasy environment will certainl be swept away, and no one can resist the 36 degree view of town and the dunes beyond, optimally captured in the Octagon Room, the latest addition to this unabashedly outré dwelling. ♦ 22 Commercial St (between Poi St and Province Lands Rd). 487.0706

45 Red Inn $$ When this 1805 Federalist hous first opened as an inn in 1905, guests delighted in diving into the sea from the fron porch at high tide. A more proper decorum prevails now, befitting a historic dwelling located at the very spot where the Pilgrims landed. Innkeepers **Bob Kulesza** and **Mike Clifford** took over the inn in 1992 and have shaken off the cobwebs of middle-brow mediocrity by rejuvenating the restaurant an playing up the inn's homespun charms. The sitting room is dominated by a crazily patterned chimney, like a work of folk art, an painted chairs by **Peter Hunt.** The four doub rooms, plus an apartment, feature antiques, original oils, and enviable bay views. ♦ 15 Commercial St (at Province Lands Rd). 487.0050

Within the Red Inn:

Red Inn Restaurant ★★★$$$$ Each of the three intimate dining rooms holds fewer than two dozen people, so everyone's assure of a peaceful atmosphere as well as a water view. The fare is mostly traditional New England, with a few twists—rice-stuffed duc for instance, with an orange-lychee nut glaze (the treatment varies nightly). Within the straight-and-narrow choices, there's ample opportunity to go overboard: tackling a 1½-pound stuffed lobster for brunch, for instance, or enjoying clam and corn chowder, giant native sea scallops in orange cream sauce, and cappuccino cheesecake for dinner, as the streaky light of the evening sky is superseded by the glow of oil lamps on linen tablecloths. ♦ New England ♦ Brunch and dinner. Closed Monday and Tuesday May, Oct; closed Monday through Wednesday Nov-Apr. Reservations recommended. 487.0050

46 The Moors ★★$$ **Maline Costa** built his atmospheric restaurant out of nautical wreckage in 1939. It looks like the kind of place Long John Silver would have favored; the contemporary clientele has included **Tennessee Williams** and **Norman Mailer.** Pianist/comedian **Lenny Grandchamps** holds forth in the briglike bar, and the bustling, dimly lit restaurant serves classic Azorean cuisine, including kale soup, *porco empau* (marinated pork cubes), and Portuguese wedding cake. ♦ Portuguese/American ♦ Lunch and dinner. Closed Monday through Friday Apr, mid-Oct to late Nov; closed late Nov to Apr. 5 Bradford St Extension (at Province Lands Rd). Reservations recommended. 487.0840

47 Nelson's Riding Stable What could be more relaxing than exploring the dunes by horseback? Guided western-style tours are offered along three **National Seashore** trails, each lasting about an hour; for experienced riders there's a two-hour beach trek where you'll get up some speed. The minimum age is 13, and riding helmets are provided. ♦ Fee. Daily noon-dusk Mar-Nov. 43 Race Point Rd (between Rte 6A and Province Lands Rd). 487.1112

48 Province Lands Visitor Center If you plan to bike the swooping dune trails, you might want to stop here first to get your bearings: the 360-degree observation deck can be very helpful in that regard, and it's beautiful, besides. The trails, which include a one-mile self-guided nature walk, can be accessed at five points; here, the parking is free. There's a worthwhile exhibit of local flora in the lobby, and the rangers arrange activities, such as a children's discovery hour and sunset campfires with storytelling. ♦ Daily 9AM-6PM July-Aug; daily 9AM-4:30PM early Apr to July, Sept-Nov. Race Point Rd (at Province Lands Rd). 487.1256

49 Life Saving Museum Now operated by the **Cape Cod National Seashore,** this shingled building was once the Chatham outpost of the short-lived but valiant **United States Life Saving Service** (established in 1872, it was folded into the U.S. Coast Guard in 1915, after the **Cape Cod Canal** was completed). Hoping to stem the tide of disastrous shipwrecks along the Cape's Atlantic shore, Congress funded nine life-saving stations, each manned by a crew of six "Surfmen." They patrolled the beaches in all kinds of weather (holding wooden shingles in front of their faces during sandstorms), on the lookout for ships in distress. Spotting one, they'd light a flare and the team would either launch a surfboat or, if the surf was unnavigable, send a line over by shooting a Lyle gun (a small cannon) and rig up a "breeches buoy"—like a pair of roomy canvas shorts attached to a ring buoy. In this laborious way they'd haul the victims in, one at a time.

The Life Saving Museum not only houses their original equipment but mounts dramatic demonstrations every Thursday at 10AM. This is the very beach, incidentally, of which **Thoreau** wrote: "Here a man can stand and put all America behind him." **Stellwagen Bank** is straight out, and if you take along binoculars, you might spot a whale. With its western orientation, this is a popular spot to catch a psychedelic sunset; dazzled audiences have been known to break out in spontaneous applause. ♦ Beach entrance fee. Daily 10AM-4PM July-Aug; Sa-Su 10AM-4PM June, Sept. Race Point Beach (off Race Point Rd). 487.1256

50 Cape Air Sightseeing Rides Before you head back to the mainland, consider a helicopter jaunt or a barnstormer flight aboard a 1930 **Stinson Detroiter** airliner for one last thrilling overview. ♦ Fee; two-person minimum. Daily 10AM-6PM July-Aug; Sa-Su 10AM-6PM May-June, Sept-Oct. Provincetown Municipal Airport (off Race Point Rd). 487.0240

Though Cape Cod's historic windmills may seem plentiful, they're but a tiny fraction of the original number. As Josef Berger wrote in *Cape Cod Pilot* (a 1937 WPA project): "Wealthy summer residents began to buy the old mills as adornments for their estates, and many of them had the machinery removed and junked, using the empty tower for storage of lawnmowers, bridge tables, children and other impedimenta; so that now, with a large premium attaching to any mill that works, many an owner can stand in the hollow tower and regret the day he stripped her of her drive-shaft, her wheels and spindle, and followed the fashion of setting the millstone down for his doorstep."

Martha's Vineyard

Native American mythology held that the god Maushop, discomfited by sand in his moccasins, flung them out to sea, where they formed the islands of Martha's Vineyard and Nantucket. Geologically, both were once connected to the Cape and were shaped by glacial activity. According to another legend, when explorer **Bartholomew Gosnold** happened upon New England's largest island (100 square miles) in 1602, he named it for one of his young daughters and for its abundance of wild grapes. To this day, the land of Martha's Vineyard is remarkably fertile. Great chunks of the westward "up-island" are still farmland; wander far enough from the lively towns of down-island and you'll swear you've somehow ended up in Vermont.

Blessed with protected harbors and only seven miles from the mainland (a 45-minute ferry ride), the Vineyard's down-island attracted the first droves of settlers in 1642, starting with **Thomas Mayhew, Jr.**, who converted 1,600 natives to Christianity within a few years of his arrival. His father, a Watertown, Massachusetts, entrepreneur, had bought Martha's Vineyard, Nantucket, and the Elizabeth Islands from an English nobleman who had no use for them. The purchase price: 40 pounds.

Mayhew, Jr., established **Edgartown**, naming it for England's heir apparent, the young son of the Duke of York (who had died a month before this honor was conferred, unbeknownst to the colonists). Edgartown, which benefited

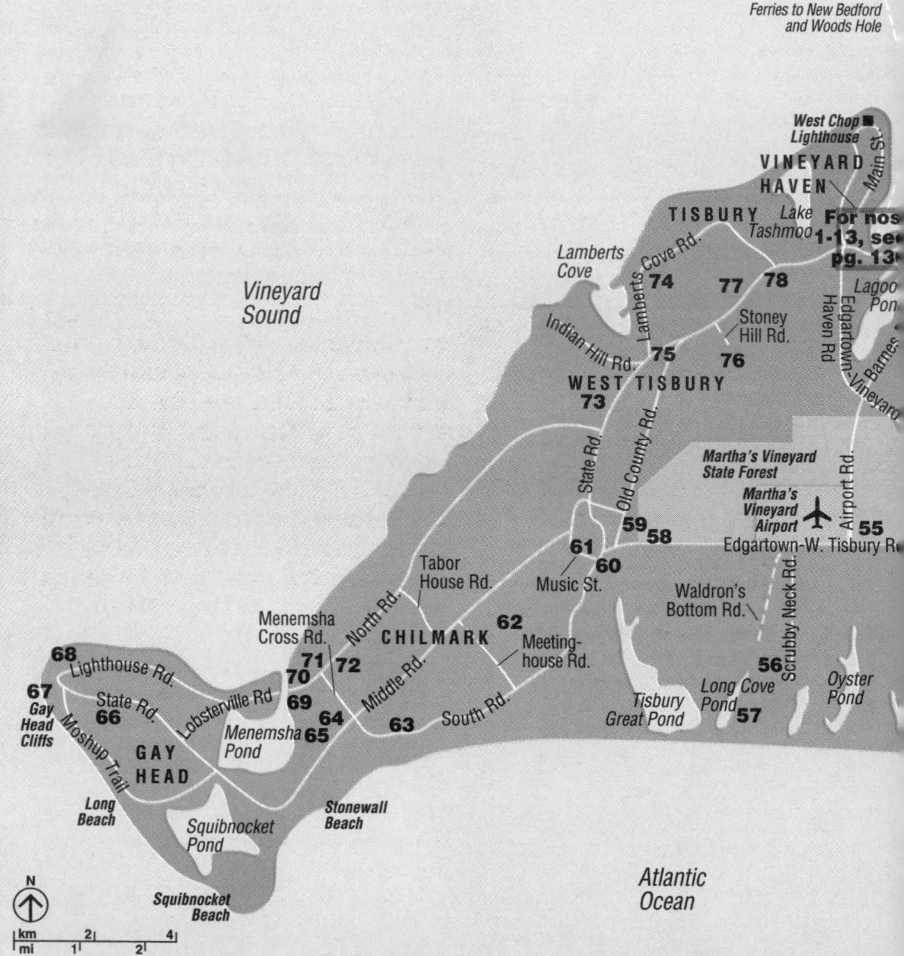

from the great whaling boom, remains an extraordinary repository of black-trimmed, white clapboard Greek Revival captain's houses. Because this summer colony isn't served directly by any ferry (visitors can bike the six miles from **Oak Bluffs**, take a cab, or hop a shuttle bus), it's able to maintain an upscale ambience. There are plenty of pricey shops for browsing, but nary a T-shirt stand in sight.

Vineyard Haven is the island's second-oldest town as well as its primary port and year-round commercial center. Vineyard Haven's residents, who tend to be more liberal counterparts of Edgartown's landed gentry, take pride in the town's proletarian image. As resident **William Styron** writes in *On the Vineyard II,* a collection of essays edited by photographer **Peter Simon**, Vineyard Haven "thrives on a kind of forthright frowsiness." It has pockets of beauty, though, such as **William Street** lined with National Register houses or pretty little **Owen Park**, overlooking the harbor.

To a large extent, Oak Bluffs is the materialization of Methodist camp meetings that began here in 1835 and gained popularity as the century advanced. It survives today as a vast grid of elaborately decorated and painted gingerbread cottages, whose basic shape resembles that of a canvas tent. The original structures clustered around the **Trinity Park Tabernacle**, subsequent spokes of what was then called "Cottage City," represent one of the earliest examples of urban planning in the United States. With its atmosphere of religious fervor and refreshing sea air, Oak Bluffs was an enormously popular beach resort in Victorian times. One of the few vacation communities to welcome visitors of color in those days, it has reigned for some four generations as a "black Newport," attracting such high-profile summer sojourners as **Adam Clayton Powell** and, more recently, **Spike Lee.** A prevailing sense of interracial ease enhances the pleasure of strolling the town's charming lanes.

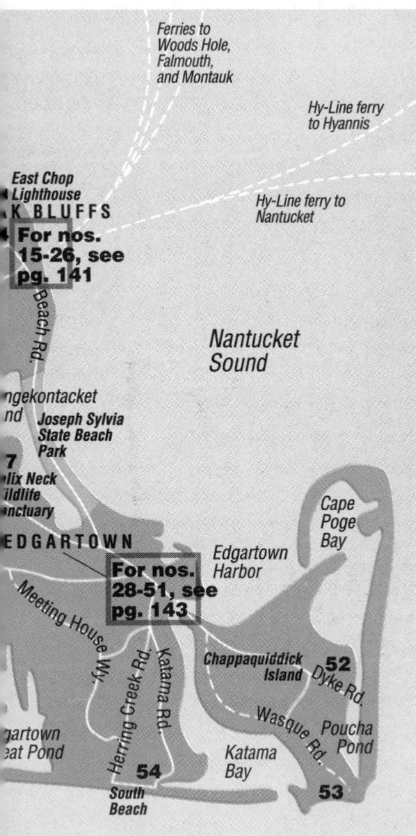

The up-island towns are mere villages by comparison: **West Tisbury**, with its landmark **Alley's General Store** and Saturday-morning farmers' market (the social event of the summer season); the agrarian community of **Chilmark**, whose **Beetlebung Crossing** is named for its grove of tupelo trees that provided the material to make both beetles and bungs—that is, mallets and cask stoppers; the Wampanoag settlement of **Gay Head**; and the picturesque fishing port of **Menemsha**, where the sunsets are unforgettable. So diverse is this landscape, and so entrancing, it's little wonder that residents of Martha's Vineyard begrudge any business that calls them to the mainland—a journey they refer to, sighing, as "going to America."

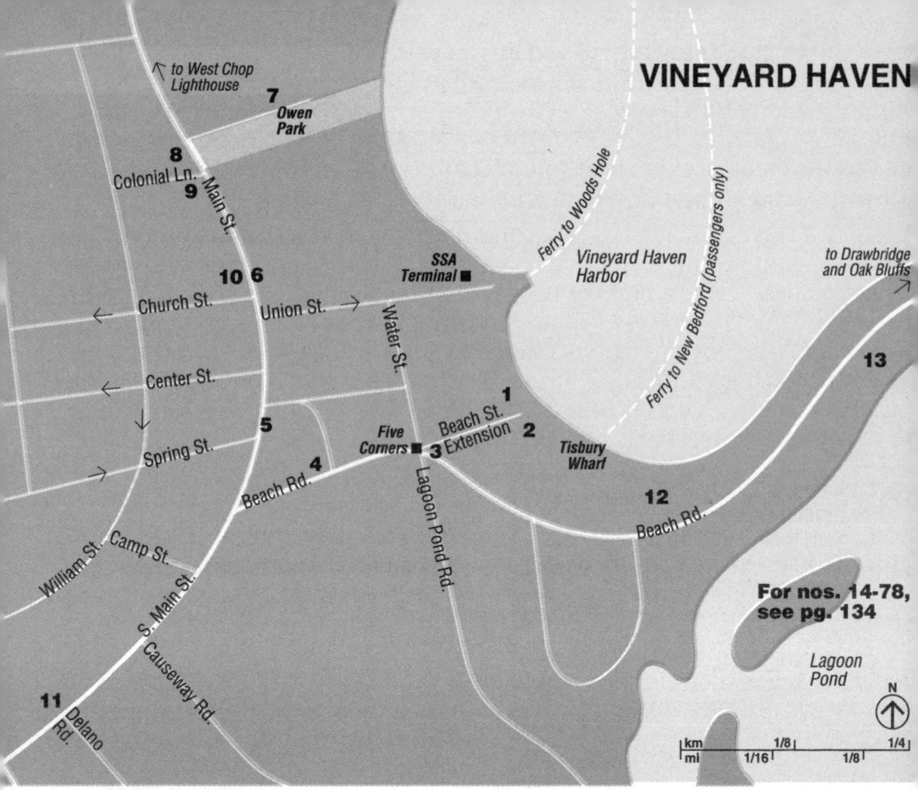

VINEYARD HAVEN

to West Chop Lighthouse
7 Owen Park
8 Colonial Ln.
9 Main St.
10 6
Church St.
Union St.
Center St.
Spring St.
5
Water St.
SSA Terminal
Ferry to Woods Hole
Ferry to New Bedford (passengers only)
Vineyard Haven Harbor
to Drawbridge and Oak Bluffs
13
1 Beach St. Extension 2
Five Corners 3
4 Beach Rd.
Tisbury Wharf
12 Beach Rd.
Lagoon Pond Rd.
William St.
Camp St.
S. Main St.
Causeway Rd.
11 Delano Rd.
For nos. 14-78, see pg. 134
Lagoon Pond
N
km 1/8 1/4
mi 1/16 1/8

1 **Black Dog Tavern** ★★★$$$$ For many (possibly too many), this shingled saltbox overlooking the harbor represents the essence of the Vineyard. The establishment's once-secret charm became common knowledge long ago; in fact, now there's an entire mail-order catalog (with everything from boxer shorts to *biscotti*) emblazoned with the logo of a "Martha's Vineyard whitefoot," an imaginary breed conceived by co-owner **Charlene Douglas.** The enterprise was sparked in 1971, when her husband, **Robert Douglas,** sailed into the Vineyard Haven harbor and wondered why no one had thought to open a restaurant there.

Though it has since ballooned into a 100-person operation, the tavern has preserved its simplicity and personal scale: with its bare plank floors and close-packed tables it looks like the kind of place Melville might have frequented. The inventive main courses include grilled swordfish with banana, basil, and lime, and bluefish with mustard soufflé. ♦ New England ♦ Breakfast, lunch, and dinner; Sunday brunch. Beach St Extension (between Water St and Beach Rd), Vineyard Haven. 693.9223. Bakery: Water St, Vineyard Haven. 693.4786

2 **The Shenandoah** With 7,000 square feet of sails, *The Shenandoah* (a 1964 reproduction of an 1849 vessel) achieves speeds in excess of 12 knots. Ten cabins on the 108-foot schooner house up to 26 passengers, who tend to bond quickly over hearty meals cooked up on the coal stove. The roomy main saloon, decorated with Civil War cutlasses and marine oil paintings, is lit by kerosene lamps, while a chanteyman and pump organ provide entertainment. The six-day cruises have no set route; depending on winds, ports of call might encircle the islands or extend to New London, Connecticut. ♦ M-Sa mid-June to mid-Sept. Beach St Extension, Vineyard Haven. Reservations required. 693.1699

3 **Wintertide Coffeehouse** The decor is meager, but the musical acts are excellent at this nonprofit cafe, run by volunteers since its founding in 1978. Folding chairs are brought out when bohemian improv gives way to folk, jazz, and blues headliners such as **Tom Paxton, Dave Van Ronk, Patty Larkin, Robin Batteau, Flor de Cana,** and islander **Kate**

Taylor (James' sister). Acts are scheduled throughout the year, but in September, when the tourist influx abates, the Wintertide mounts its **Singer/Songwriter's Retreat and Concert Series.** The players stay at Oak Bluffs' **Sea Spray Inn** and participate in workshops; the audiences enjoy a parade of top musicians playing for the fun of it. (The first such get-together, in 1992, resulted in *Big Times in a Small Town* for Rounder Records.) Though smoke- and alcohol-free, the cafe serves various coffees, dinner soups, salads, burritos, and desserts. ♦ Cover. Performances Tu-Su. At Five Corners, Oak Bluffs. 693.8830

4 Luce House Gallery & Vineyard Museum Artmakers One of the few buildings to survive the 1833 fire that leveled the town, this 1804 Federal house, owned by the **Dukes County Historical Society,** is enjoying a new life as a community arts center and exhibition space. The doorway, with its graceful fanlight and pediment, promises interesting sights within, and the shows, organized by sculptor and gallery manager **Mary Etherington,** fulfill that pledge. Keep an eye out for the work of local artist **Lucy Mitchell,** whose watercolor-bordered collages of mysterious stamps and envelopes suggest delightful imaginary journeys. ♦ Tu-Sa 10:30AM-5PM; Su 2-5PM. Beach Rd (between Water and Main Sts), Vineyard Haven. 693.5353

5 Bramhall & Dunn Dedicated to decorating people as well as homes, this stylish store features not only English country pine furniture, hooked and woven rugs, and all sorts of handsome accessories, but handknit sweaters, fabulous hats, delicate cotton lingerie, and smocked clothing for children. The stock, handpicked by owners **Emily Bramhall** and **Tharon Dunn,** will remind you of everybody you've been meaning to buy presents for, including yourself. ♦ Daily 9:30AM-10PM July-Aug; M-Sa 9:30AM-6PM, Su 11AM-6PM Sept-Dec; M-Sa 9:30AM-6PM Jan-June. 61 Main St (between Beach Rd and Union St), Vineyard Haven. 693.6437. Also at: The Red Barn, Old County Rd, W. Tisbury. 693.5221; 16 Federal St, Nantucket. 228.4688

6 Le Roux This shop fills a niche by providing everyday clothes for both sexes, with labels ranging from **Betsey Johnson** (at her least outrageous) to **Patagonia.** The look is neither staid nor trendy. ♦ M-Sa 9:30AM-9:30PM, Su 10AM-5PM June to early Sept; M-Sa 10AM-6PM, Su 11AM-5PM early Sept to June. 89 Main St (between Union St and Owen Park), Vineyard Haven. 693.6463. Also at: Winter St (Nevin Sq), Edgartown. 627.7766

6 Travis Tuck Sculptor **Travis Tuck**—typically wearing a leather apron and wielding an acetylene torch—employs the pre-Industrial Revolution repoussé method, whereby copper is warmed and then hammered from the reverse side. All work is by commission, and his copper weather vanes start at $3,000—or a good deal more for 23-karat gold leaf. His first project, in 1973, was a great white shark for *Jaws;* a more recent work, for a Menemsha summer home, was a seven-foot Mercury gliding through the air and holding up a cellular phone (representing the client's business). Tuck has also made a copper mask for **James Taylor** and a copper clock for **Beverly Sills.** ♦ M-Sa 10AM-5PM. 89 Main St (between Union St and Owen Park), Vineyard Haven. 693.3914

6 Martha's Vineyard National Bank Step inside this 1905 fieldstone building, designed by Boston architect **J. William Beals** in the shape of a Greek cross; friendly tellers will explain how to use the lobby's acoustic "sweet spot" to effect an eerie echo. The magnificent interior is adorned with milky stained glass, decorative plaster in fleur-de-lis, and acanthus side supports.

The bank was set in motion by gramophone magnate **William Barry Owen,** whose business interests took off when he paid a French artist $250 for an image of a dog, head cocked, listening to a record player (the famous logo for RCA and now EMI). Retiring to his native island, Owen became a director of the bank founded in Edgartown in 1855 by prominent whaling merchant **Dr. Daniel Fisher** and decided to move the operation closer to his home in Lambert's Cove.

Following the stock market crash of 1929, Owen's successor, **Stephen Carey Luce,** obeyed President Roosevelt's order to close the vault to stem withdrawals but called a meeting at Edgartown's **Whaling Church** to announce that he would offer a personal checking account with his own backing to anybody who desired one, so that the island's economy would not suffer. Despite federal disapproval, the strategy was legal, and "Lucebucks" saw the islanders through the crisis. ♦ M-F 8:30AM-3PM. 91 Main St (between Union St and Owen Park), Vineyard Haven. 693.9400

"The seashore is a sort of neutral ground, a most advantageous point from which to contemplate this world. Creeping along the endless beach amid the sun-squall [jellyfish] and foam, it occurs to us that we, too, are the product of sea-slime."

Henry David Thoreau, *Cape Cod*

7 The Lothrop Merry House $$ The ambience of this rambling 1790 B&B (shown above), with a broad lawn sloping down to a sliver of placid beach, will loosen memories of summers past for many guests. The seven bedrooms, some with fireplaces, are on the plain side, though far from austere. The implicit message is that sleeping is but a prelude to the pleasures at hand—knocking about in a loaner canoe, perhaps, or just lounging in an Adirondack chair and observing the harbor. Innkeepers **John** and **Merry Clarke** actually live out on the water in summer, aboard their 54-foot Alden Ketch; they offer half-day and daylong cruises, as well as overnight charters to Nantucket or Cuttyhunk. ♦ Owen Park (off Main St), Vineyard Haven. 693.1646

8 Deux Noisettes $$ No froufrou clutters the lines of this starkly beautiful 1840 Greek Revival house, which now functions as a bed-and-breakfast inn. The pale yellow parlor is a vision, with its floor-to-ceiling windows and pair of wingback chairs. French doors lead from the dining room to a rose-covered porch. The four bedrooms, each with a fireplace and some with harbor views, are equally spare and dramatic. Innkeeper **Barbara Grant,** a Cordon Bleu-trained pastry chef, concocts exquisite breakfasts, from fresh brioches and croissants to *chaussons* (apple turnovers) and fruit-filled crepes. ♦ 114 Main St (at Colonial Ln), Vineyard Haven. 693.0253

Colonial cookery was certainly a challenge, but accomplished cooks knew how to use the various areas of a brick fireplace to achieve any number of culinary effects, from frying and roasting to boiling and baking. The "beehive" oven found at the rear of most colonial fireplaces could, when filled with burning coals and blocked with a plug of charred wood, achieve temperatures of more than 400 degrees. Lacking a thermostat, cooks used their bare hands or perhaps a bit of flour or damp straw to test the degree of heat.

Restaurants/Clubs: Red **Hotels:** Blue
Shops/ Outdoors: Green **Sights/Culture:** Black

9 Old Schoolhouse Museum and Liberty Pole The town's first school building, raise in 1829, now contains the **Martha's Vineyar Preservation Trust's** collection of artifacts relating to the island's glory days as a whaling port. The pole is a replacement, erected in 1898 by the **Daughters of the American Revolution** to honor the three young girls who blew up the original during the **War of 1812** rather than let a British warship appropriate it for use as a mast. ♦ Donation. M-F 10AM-2PM mid-June to early Sept. 110 Main St (at Colonial Ln), Vineyard Haven. 627.8017

10 Le Grenier ★★$$$$ With the rise of the nouvelle school of cooking, it has become increasingly difficult to track down traditiona French cuisine. Chef-owner **Jean Dupon** hai from Lyon, France's gastronomic capital, an handles both modes well. Choose between modern dishes—monkfish in a tomato basil vinaigrette, for instance—and high-cholesterol classics: calf's brains Grenobloise with beurre noir and capers or lobster Normande flambéed with Calvados, apples, and cream. Though the restaurant's name means "The Attic," it's a romantic place, especially when aglow with hurricane lamps. ♦ French ♦ Dinner; call for schedule Oct-Mar. 96 Main St (between Church St an Colonial Ln), Vineyard Haven. Reservations recommended. 693.4906

Beneath Le Grenier:

la patisserie française ★$ At street level, the prices descend, but the quality doe not. The fare's a bit more casual (pasta, grilled fish, etc.), but the homemade croissants and pastries are at their freshest. ♦ French/Takeout ♦ Breakfast and lunch; Sunday brunch. 693.8087

10 Betsey, Bunky & Nini This branch of the Madison Avenue boutique founded by designer **Betsey Johnson** and friends in the late '60s purveys slinky European styles in conservative colors. Women who wouldn't dream of shopping outside Manhattan will feel right at home here. ♦ M-Th 10AM-6PM; F-Sa 10AM-7PM; Su 11AM-5PM. 90 Main S (at Church St), Vineyard Haven. 693.7003

11 Lorraine Parish If this gifted designer of women's clothing has yet to become a household name, that's by design, too. After seceding from Manhattan's Garment District Parish marketed her line for a long time by means of subscription-only catalogs and invitation-only trunk shows. Her local coterie includes **Carly Simon,** who commissioned a wedding dress. For outfits with that Vineyard look of free-flowing, effortless chic, this is the first place to look. ♦ By appointment Apr-Dec. 18 S. Main St (between Camp and Look Sts), Vineyard Haven. 693.9044. Also at: The Summer House, Siasconset, Nantucket. 257.9699

12 C.W. Morgan Marine Antiques **Frank Rapoza,** a nautical woodworker, has amassed an extraordinary collection of models, paintings, instruments, chests, and whatnots. A visit is rewarding for anyone interested in sailing relics and also for the merely curious. ♦ M, W-Su 10AM-noon, 1-5PM. Tisbury Wharf (at Beach Rd), Vineyard Haven. 693.3622

13 Wind's Up! Set on protected **Lagoon Pond,** this windsurfing/sailing school and rental shop is ideally situated for beginners. Lessons and boards are available for those as young as four as well as for wary adults. Those with experience can gear up and head out, using the establishment's handy map. An eight-hour certification course starts with a simulated lesson on land, moves onto the water (wet suits and booties are included), and concludes with three hours of supervised practice. ♦ Daily 9AM-6PM late June to early Sept; daily 10AM-5PM late May to late June, rest of Sept. 95 Beach Rd (between Beach St Extension and the Drawbridge), Vineyard Haven. 693.4252. Store annex at: Tisbury Market Place (Beach Rd), Vineyard Haven. 693.4340

13 Portside ★$ When you're tuckered out from the water sports, come here for a great burger, phyllo lamb pie with feta and pine nuts, or the vegetarian "Maui Special" (avocado, sprouts, cheese, tomato, and onion on whole wheat). Some weekend evenings you'll luck into a barbecue of chicken, ribs, and seafood kebabs. ♦ International/Takeout ♦ Lunch and dinner. Closed mid-Sept to mid-June. 95 Beach Rd (between Beach St Extension and the Drawbridge), Vineyard Haven. 693.5580

14 Admiral Benbow Inn $$ Built for a minister at the turn of the century, this seven-bedroom house, topped by a cupola and encircled by a shady porch, has the dark, ornate woodwork typical of that time. Yet the B&B has a young, energetic feel to it, and it's owned by the **Black Dog Tavern Co.,** which means for breakfast you can polish off a few of those pastries you may have eyeballed in the restaurant's display cases. There's no ocean view, and it's on a busy road somewhat removed from Oak Bluffs; by bike, however, it's a quick glide into town or to the Sound beaches. ♦ 520 New York Ave (at Oak Ave), Oak Bluffs. 693.6825

15 Wesley Hotel $$ Though not as grand as it started out in 1879, this 82-room behemoth has been thoroughly spruced up. Fortunately, the current owners don't subscribe to founder **A.G. Wesley's** notion of a make-over: to fund his expansionist plans in 1894, he committed arson; he then confessed, spent three years in prison, and returned to his creation as a chef. Actually, this establishment could use a good cook, not to mention a full-scale dining room. Still, the lobby and guest rooms are spacious and nicely furnished with Victorian reproductions. The first-come, first-served policy on rooms with harbor views (they're priced the same as those without) means reservations should be made early. If you end up at the back of the building, or in the Wesley Arms annex (where the rates, with shared bath, are half the norm), you can find comfort in a rocking chair on the vast front porch. ♦ Closed mid-Oct to May. 1 Lake Ave (at Dukes County Ave), Oak Bluffs. 693.6611

16 Cottage Museum The minute you pull into town you'll see the raison d'être for this museum: winding rows of colorful cottages ornamented with intricate Carpenter's Gothic woodwork. (The first such house was erected in 1859 to replace one of the Methodist revivalists' 500-odd canvas tents, and within the next two decades more than 300 cottages sprouted in **Wesleyan Grove,** each vying with its neighbors for most elaborate trim and garish color combinations.) The museum, a cream-and-orange 1867 cottage, is fairly typical in design, its tiny veranda topped by a small balcony with French doors shaped like church windows. Perusing its contents, from a portable organ to an ancient bathing suit, will give you a feel for those evangelistic campers' early days; recreational activities had to be squeezed into a schedule packed with prayer, with preachers holding forth at 10AM, 2PM, and 7PM daily. Following a tradition that began in 1869, one evening every August is designated "Illumination Night" (the date is kept secret to discourage crowds): the entire campground is lit with Japanese lanterns. ♦ Nominal admission. M-Sa 10:30AM-4PM mid-June to mid-Sept. 1 Trinity Park (within the Camp Meeting Grounds), Oak Bluffs. 693.0525

> "A wind's in the heart of me, a fire's in my heels,
> I am tired of brick and stone, and rumbling wagonwheels;
> I hunger for the sea's edge, the limits of the land,
> Where the wild old Atlantic is surging on the sand."
>
> **John Masefield**

17 **Trinity Park Tabernacle** When crowds for the Methodist revivals surpassed 16,000 in the late 1860s, it was clear that something more solid—and permanent—than a circus-size tent was required to shelter worshipers from the elements. Designed by architect **J.W. Hoyt** of Springfield, Massachusetts, and built in 1879 for just over $7,000, this open-air church, now on the **National Register of Historic Places,** is the largest wrought-iron and wood structure in America. Its conical crown (shown above) is ringed with a geometric pattern of amber, carmine, and midnight blue stained glass. Old-fashioned community sings take place Wednesdays at 8PM, and concerts are scheduled irregularly on weekends. **James Taylor** and **Bonnie Raitt** have regaled the faithful here, though the musicians are usually less-renowned acts. The **Martha's Vineyard Camp Meeting Association** publishes a schedule of events open to the public, including interdenominational services and flea markets. ♦ Service Su 9:30AM July-Aug. Trinity Park (within the Camp Meeting Grounds), Oak Bluffs. 693.0525

18 **Butterflies in Flight** In 1993, **Joe** and **Karen Kornacker** established a butterfly "aviary" on Martha's Vineyard. That first summer, having been warned about the bay's sometimes chilling wind, they skimped on ventilation, so that the temperature in the cheerful yellow tent often approached sauna levels. But the thousand winged denizens, representing 25 species, didn't seem to mind. These days visitors walk through a profusion of tropical plants, reading up on butterfly lo as the delicate creatures flutter about. Though the aviary stays open into the evening, daylight hours offer optimal viewin because butterflies, as Joe Kornacker points out, are "solar-powered." ♦ Admission. Dail 9AM-9PM mid-May to mid-Sept. At the Oak Bluffs Harbor Marina (off Circuit Ave Extension), Oak Bluffs. 693.4006

19 **Flying Horses Carousel** These horses have quite a pedigree. Declared a **National Historic Landmark** and operated by the **Martha's Vineyard Preservation Trust,** the 1876 carousel on which they ride hails from **Coney Island** and is purportedly the oldest one in the country still in operation. The 22 hand-carved steeds only go round and roun not up and down, but they have genuine horsehair manes and soulful glass eyes. M riders attend less to the horses than to grabbing rings; snagging the brass one means a free spin. ♦ Nominal fee. Daily 10AM-10PM late May to early Sept; M-Th 11AM-4PM, F 11AM-9PM, Sa-Su 11AM-5P mid-Apr to late May, early Sept to mid-Oct. 33 Circuit Ave (at Lake Ave), Oak Bluffs. 693.9481

20 **Zapotec Restaurant** ★★$$$ Anyone whose tastebuds thrive on spicy food shoul head for this cafe, decked in Christmas colo and festooned with chile-pepper lights. Everything's fresh in these gourmet Mexica dishes, and the chiles are seemingly calibrated to offset a dozen Mexican beers, including several rarely spotted north of the border. ♦ Mexican ♦ Dinner. Closed Monda and Tuesday mid-Apr to late May, early Sept to Oct; closed late Nov to mid-Apr. 10 Kennebec Ave (between Lake and Park Aves Oak Bluffs. 693.6800

21 **Ray's Barbecue** ★★$$ Introduced in 199 by **Raymond Schilcher,** chef-owner of the spiffy **Oyster Bar,** this down-home hickory p is just what the island was lacking. The men will make your mouth water and your lips whistle "Dixie." St. Louis ribs, Texas beef brisket, North Carolina pulled pork. . . . The indecisive, or gluttonous, can opt for the "Real Deal," a little of everything. Sides include corn bread, biscuits, sweet potato fries, collard greens, and mashed yams with brown sugar-bourbon butter. Should you survive this far, there's watermelon or strawberry shortcake to look forward to, perhaps washed down with homemade pink lemonade. At street level you can watch the meats slow-cooking as you wait to place an order; if you would rather eat here, have a seat upstairs in the small dining room. ♦ American/Takeout ♦ Lunch and dinner. Closed Sept-Apr. 113 Circuit Ave (between Lake and Park Aves), Oak Bluffs. 693.7444

21 Mad Martha's The homemade ice cream here comes in exotic flavors. (**President Clinton** chose mango sorbet.) Oldies on the jukebox encourage lingering over a cone rather than strolling away with it. ♦ Daily 11AM-midnight early July to early Sept; daily noon-9PM May to early July, early Sept to mid-Oct. 117 Circuit Ave (between Lake and Park Aves), Oak Bluffs. 693.9151. Also at: 8 Union St, Vineyard Haven. 863.9674; 4 Main St, Edgartown. 627.9768

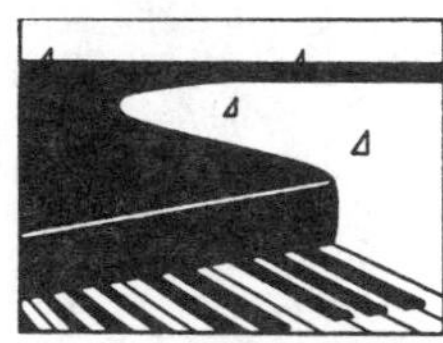

22 David's Island House $ The hotel's 18 rooms are eminently affordable but rather dreary. If all you require is a place to lay your head after exhausting Oak Bluffs' nightlife, they'll do just fine. ♦ Closed early Sept to late May. 120 Circuit Ave (between Lake and Park Aves), Oak Bluffs. 693.4516

Within David's Island House:

David's Island House Restaurant ★★$$$$ The vaguely Victorian dining room with bentwood chairs isn't especially appealing. The mostly Italian cuisine is a touch overpriced, if good (try the *arancini* of risotto and cheese). What draws people here is proprietor/pianist **David Crohan** with his vast repertoire and infectious enthusiasm. ♦ Italian ♦ Lunch and dinner. Closed Oct-Apr. 693.4516

22 The Atlantic Connection The island's own rock-and-roll icons (**Carly Simon, James Taylor,** and recent inductee **Billy Joel**) come to this dance club to hear their peers and to check out the up-and-comers. DJs alternate with live performers, from **Peter Wolf** (former lead singer of the **J. Geils Band**) to **Taj Mahal** and **Queen Ida.** ♦ Cover. Call for schedule. 124 Circuit Ave (between Lake and Park Aves), Oak Bluffs. 693.7129

23 Papa's Pizza ★★$ Along with a slice of good pizza, have a slice of the past. Long wooden tables line this old-fashioned storefront, which has a marble counter, brass lamps, a tin ceiling, and tin walls. Take a look at the vintage photographs of "campers" past. ♦ Italian/Takeout ♦ Lunch and dinner. 158 Circuit Ave (between Park and Narragansett Aves), Vineyard Haven. 693.1400

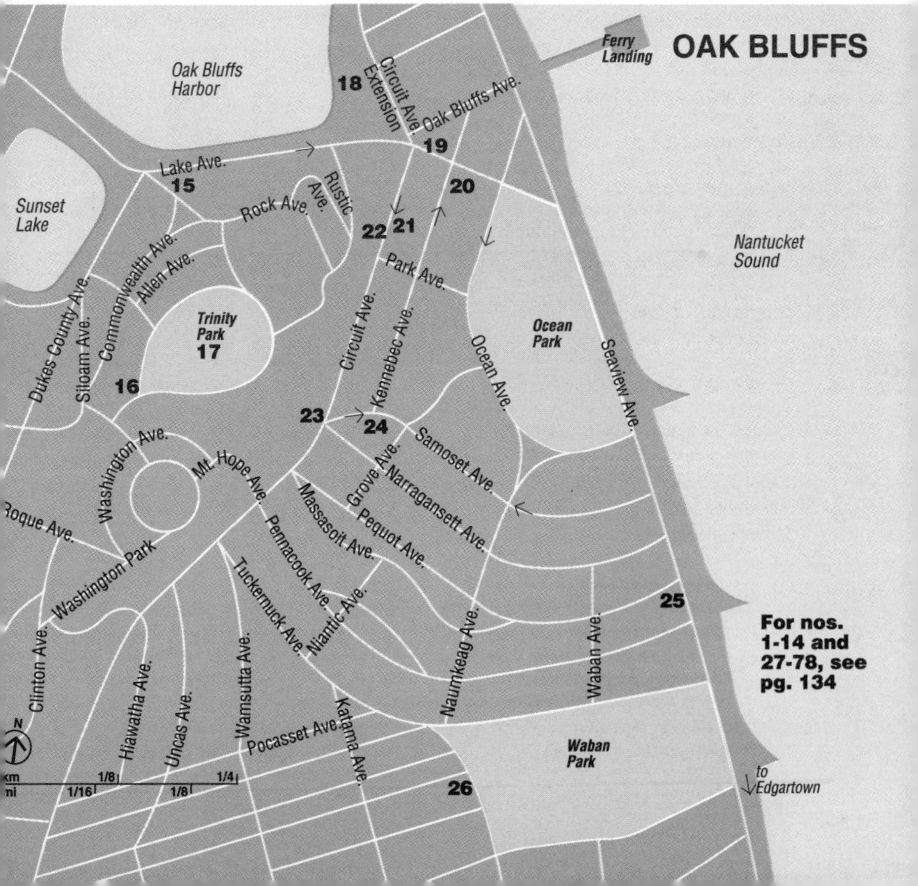

OAK BLUFFS

Ferry Landing
Oak Bluffs Harbor
Sunset Lake
Nantucket Sound
Trinity Park
Ocean Park
Waban Park
to Edgartown

For nos. 1-14 and 27-78, see pg. 134

23 **The Oyster Bar** ★★★$$$$ This 1930s-style bistro is one of the Vineyard's most glamorous restaurants. French doors in the cream-and-forest-green facade open onto a lofty space with 14-foot-high tin ceilings. A 40-foot mahogany-and-brass wine and raw bar takes up one side, an open kitchen the other. In between is a sea of white tablecloths interspersed with towering tropical plants and the faux-marble columns. The food is a fantasy, too: white truffle polenta and porcini soufflé, Tuscan grilled quail, veal tournedos with grilled red endive, a bouillabaisse perked up with cassis. Chef/owner **Raymond Schilcher's** creativity never lets up, but if you like to call the shots yourself, and prefer things relatively simple, you can order a half-dozen types of seafood grilled, blackened, sautéed, or steamed, as well as steak, veal, or lamb. ♦ International ♦ Dinner. Closed Tuesday mid-May to June, Sept to mid-Nov; closed mid-Nov to mid-May. 162 Circuit Ave (between Samoset and Narragansett Aves), Oak Bluffs. 693.3300

23 **Hilliard's Kitch-in-vue** This cottage/candy store is so cute—painted pink, blue, and white, and trimmed with heart cutouts—you half expect to find a witch inside, whipping up sweets for unsuspecting children. Instead it's **David Hilliard,** scion of a line of confectioners going back to the early 1900s; he's carrying on a tradition of handmade chocolates in this 50-year-old shop. ♦ Daily 9AM-10PM late May to early Sept; M-Sa 10AM-6PM, Su noon-3PM early Sept to late May. 164 Circuit Ave (at Narragansett Ave), Oak Bluffs. 693.2191

24 **Union Chapel** Built in 1870 as a monument to the grievous war won five years earlier, **Samuel Freeman Pratt's** octagonal wooden building (now on the **National Register of Historic Places**) is a beauty inside and out. Triangular windows high in the three-tiered roof cast a summery glow on the woodwork, painted robin's egg blue and dark green. Superb acoustics intensify the organ's warm, rumbling tones and the eloquent voices of ministers of various denominations convened from around the country. ♦ Service Su 10AM July to early Sept. Kennebec and Samoset Aves, Oak Bluffs. No phone

---

The commercialism that grips Cape Cod is nothing new, judging from Henry Thoreau's discovery, in mid-19th century Provincetown, of a sign advertising "Fine sand for sale." Thoreau chalked up the gambit as "a good instance of the fact that a man confers a value on the most worthless thing by mixing himself with it."

25 **The Oak House** $$$ When Massachusetts **Governor William Claflin** bought this Queen Anne house overlooking Nantucket Sound, h jacked up the roof to add another floor of bedrooms, all paneled in the manner of ship cabins. The rooms toward the back are quieter; then again, the front ones have views all the way to Cape Cod. Opulent Victorian furnishings create a mood of pampered leisu that's complemented by the aroma of fresh pastry wafting from the kitchen. A professionally trained chef, owner **Betsi Convery-Luce** enjoys baking peach cake for breakfast and caramel cookie tarts to go with tea or lemonade served on the glass-enclose porch. ♦ Closed mid-Oct to mid-May. Seaviev and Pequot Aves, Oak Bluffs. 693.4187

26 **Sea Spray Inn** $$ Separated from the wate by a grassy field, this comfortable seven-bedroom B&B reflects the personality of its owner, artist **Rayeanne King.** Her pastel drawings of flowers grace the walls of the dining room/parlor. She knows the island we and is happy to steer guests to its many pleasures. ♦ 2 Nashawena Park (off Waban Park), Oak Bluffs. 693.9388

27 **Felix Neck Wildlife Sanctuary** Nearly wiped out by DDT in the 1960s, the osprey, a hawk with a five-and-a-half-foot wingspan, is making a promising comeback at this 350-acre **Audubon Society** preserve. With nesting platforms provided by the sanctuary, these fish-eating birds have now graduated from th endangered list. Six miles of trails transecting woods, fields, marshes, and beaches should afford glimpses of many other species; be sure to inspect the aquariums and turtle tank at the visitors' center, as well as the **Raptor Barn.** Various interpretive exhibits are on view and nature programs are scheduled throughout the year. ♦ Admission. Trails: dai dawn-7PM. Visitor center: daily 8AM-4PM June-Oct; Tu-Su 8AM-4PM Nov-May. Off Edgartown-Vineyard Haven Rd (between County and Beach Rds), Vineyard Haven. 627.4850

28 **The Arbor** $$ It looks modest from the outside, but innkeeper **Peggy Hall** treated her 1880 farmhouse to a dramatic addition: a house-size sitting room with a cathedral ceiling. Crocheted bedspreads and eclectic antiques adorn the pretty rooms, but come ou and spend some social time on the chintz sofas in the living room, where you can solicit the advice of your charming and knowledgeable hostess. An elegant Continental breakfast is served. The inn is about a five-minute walk from the center of

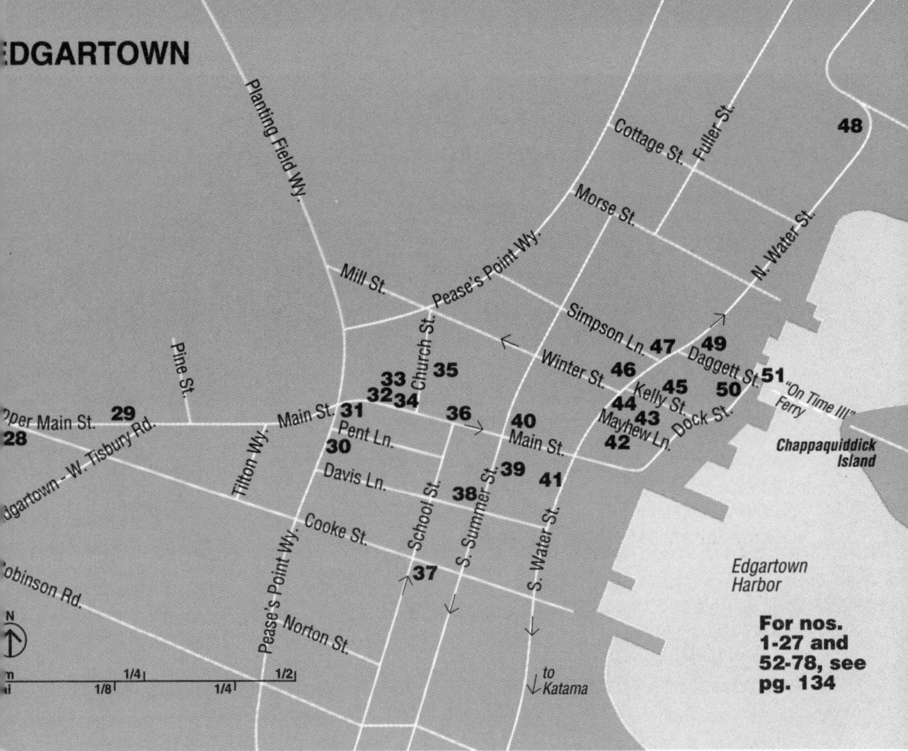

For nos. 1-27 and 52-78, see pg. 134

town or a minute of pedaling via the bike path. ♦ Closed Nov-Apr. 222 Upper Main St (between Chase and Edgartown-W. Tisbury Rds), Edgartown. 627.8137

29 Andrea's ★★$$$$ The rose garden, set with Roman parasols, is a lovely spot for partaking of classic Italian fare, from carpaccio garnished with curls of Reggiano to crab and lobster "scampi" on squid-ink fettuccine. The indoor dining room, in a house that dates from the 1890s, is appealing, too, with salmon sponge-painted walls and trompe l'oeil ivy trailing along the cross beams. Downstairs, the dimly lit, brick-walled bistro offers live jazz. ♦ Italian ♦ Dinner. Closed Tuesday May-June, Sept-Oct, late Nov to Dec; closed early Nov, Jan-Apr. 137 Upper Main St (at Edgartown-W. Tisbury Rd), Edgartown. 627.5850

30 Shiverick Inn $$$$ One of the more imposing mansions in town, this mansard-roofed Victorian was built for the town physician in 1840. Today, everything about the B&B is still formal: mahogany front doors, a black walnut staircase, crystal chandeliers, and a square cupola. The 10 high-ceilinged bedrooms (six with fireplaces) are distinctively decorated with antiques, Oriental rugs, patterned wallpapers, and, typically, a four-poster or canopy bed. Some will appreciate owner **Mary Turmelle's** efforts to protect the inn's romantic mood; others will find this place too fussy and stiff. Children under 12 aren't welcome. ♦ Pent Ln (at Pease's Point Wy), Edgartown. 627.3797, 800/825.3997

31 Point Way Inn $$$$ More than a decade ago, **Linda** and **Ben Smith** concluded an 18-month, 4,000-mile cruise on their ketch by settling into this 1840 sea captain's house and turning it into a 15-room B&B. It's clear that a real family lives here—not just because mementos of happy times crop up everywhere, but because visitors are made to feel as though they're house guests. Indications of the Smiths' hospitality are the honor bar (with chip-in kitty), a loaner car, and invitations to go clamming or play croquet with Ben. (He's among the top-ranked croquet players in the country; the inn's arborvitae-bordered lawn is the official headquarters of the **Edgartown Mallet Club**, where every July such celebrities as **Art Buchwald** participate in the charity Croquet Classic.) For breakfast, Linda prepares fresh juice in the '30s-style farmhouse kitchen, along with homemade granola, breads, and popovers. ♦ 104 Main St (at Pease's Point Wy), Edgartown. 627.8633, 800/942.9569

A tip for samurai grave-seekers: the easy-to-find John Belushi headstone in Chilmark Cemetery (just look for the votive beer cans placed there by devotees) is a decoy; the real one is unmarked.

Dr. Daniel Fisher House

32 Dr. Daniel Fisher House **Fisher,** an eminent physician in the mid-1800s, was also a whaling magnate, owner of what was said to be the largest spermaceti candle factory in the world, and founder of the **Martha's Vineyard National Bank.** Naturally, his house, built in 1840, was the grandest in town. Now headquarters for the **Martha's Vineyard Preservation Trust,** it's open only for private functions, but the exterior view of the front portico with its fluted columns crowned by acanthus capitals is worth a lingering walk-by. The decorative roof walk displays a complementary motif, and more columns appear in the graceful semicircular side porch.

During his lifetime, Fisher was more admired than envied. His obituary in the *Vineyard Gazette* read: "His continuous efforts for the good of his fellow-men will ever be remembered by his townsmen, who have saved thousands upon thousands of dollars by purchasing flour, corn, meal, coal, wood, etc., from him at a very small advance from first cost." This was a man, the paper concluded, "who adorned all the relations of life with manifold virtues. . . . He leaves behind him a respectable fortune, not one mill of which was dishonestly obtained." ♦ 99 Main St (between Planting Field Wy and Church St), Edgartown. 627.8017

33 Vincent House One of the oldest houses on the island, this 1672 shingled full Cape was moved here from Mashacket Cove in 1977 and restored by the **Martha's Vineyard Preservation Trust** to demonstrate 17th-century building techniques. Though the house contains a few archaeological finds from the move, it is unfurnished so as to offer a unique opportunity to observe architectural details, from the wide white-pine floorboards to a central chimney made of island-fired brick. Plexiglas panels permit visitors to view layers of wattle-and-daub insulation. ♦ Admission. Tours by reservation June-Sept. Off Main St (between Planting Field Wy and Church St), Edgartown. 627.8017

34 Old Whaling Church The magnum opus of local architect **Frederick Baylies, Jr.,** this 1843 Greek Revival church (at right) was built by the same construction methods used for whaling ships; the infrastructure consists of 50-foot hand-hewn red pine beams barged down from Maine and assembled with wooden pegs. Everything is on a grand scale. The portico has six massive columns, the 92-foot spiked square tower is visible far out to sea, and the 27-foot windows, arranged four to a side, bathe the interior in sunlight. Elegant whale-oil lamps (since electrified) were used to illuminate the short, gloomy days of winter. Originally, the churchgoers owned their pews and furnished them with carpets, footstools, and foot warmers; now the cushions are a uniform burgundy. In 1980, the Methodist congregation asked the **Martha's Vineyard Preservation Trust** to take charge of the building. Services are still held, but the church functions primarily as a 500-seat performing arts center offering lectures, films, plays, concerts, and so on. Such island luminaries as actress **Patricia Neal** and photographer **Alfred Eisenstaedt** have edified the populace from the pulpit. ♦ Service Su 9AM. Call for events schedule. 89 Main St (between Planting Field Wy and Church St), Edgartown. 627.8017

35 Savoir Faire ★★★$$$$ Edgartown embodies the resort-town dictum of "Don't eat on the water," where restaurants are frequently overpriced and mediocre. Hence one of the town's best restaurants can be found inland, beside a small parking lot. Ensconced beneath Savoir Faire's dainty white pergola, the immediate environment doesn't matter; one can dine by candlelight off the raw bar. Sit indoors if you prefer to watch the floor show provided by the open kitchen.

Owner **Scott Caskey** opened this place in 1985 as a gourmet shop; threatened with competition from the mainland (which never materialized), he turned it into an intimate restaurant. He attends to the *garde-manger* (salads, desserts, and other cold preparations), chef **James Bradley** to the stove, and their collaboration yields beautifully balanced meals: exquisite bitter greens with pear, Gorgonzola, and toasted walnuts, for instance, followed by duck with braised endive and a white bean ragout. The menu is constantly evolving, but you can count on thoughtful presentations in the New American mode, with a sunny Mediterranean influence. Desserts are Italianate and sophisticated; try the tart, cakey lemon soufflé. ♦ New American ♦ Lunch and dinner; dinner only on Sunday; call for schedule early Sept to Oct. Closed Nov to late Apr. 14 Church St (between Main St and Pease's Point Wy), Edgartown. 627.3389

35 Warriner's ★★$$$$ To your right is **Sam's,** the bistro wing of this popular restaurant; to your left is the pale-lemon **Library Room,** Warriner's formal dining area, with Queen Anne chairs, dark paneling, and rows of leatherbound volumes. The menu crosses over, and also covers many styles; hamburgers are available, as are entrées such as veal loin chop with shiitakes, leeks, and cognac-grape sauce. If you really want to live dangerously, thumb through the 300-odd wine listings. Read carefully: transpose a few digits, and the sommelier could be uncorking a $650 bottle of Chateau Lafite Rothschild. ♦ New American ♦ Dinner; call for schedule Apr-May, early Sept to Oct. Closed Nov-Mar. Old Post Office Sq (off Main St), Edgartown. 627.4488

36 Sandcastles Restaurant ★★$$$$ Owned in part by restaurateur **Sam Warriner,** Sandcastles sets its sights on a younger set than the clientele that frequents his more established operations. Evidence of this is found in the upstairs bar, where autographed lipstick smooches cover the ceiling. The relatively restrained dining rooms have chunky wooden chairs and peach walls and banquettes. The preparations are fairly straightforward, the flavors assertive. Roast asparagus wrapped in red pepper chevre and prosciutto is a great idea, and anyone weary of overwhelming sauces will appreciate the simplicity of grilled chicken breast that's been marinated in orange juice and tamari. ♦ New American ♦ Lunch and dinner; Sunday brunch. Closed Nov-Apr. 71 Main St (at School St), Edgartown. 627.8316

37 The Vineyard Museum Covering a square block, this complex houses the intriguing collections of the **Dukes County Historical Society.** Changing displays in the 1765 **Thomas Cooke House**—a full Cape constructed by shipbuilders for the customs collector—concern island history; keep an eye out for the mammy bench in the pantry, the inlaid boxes made on whaling ships, the homely portrait of early resident **Ephraim Pease** (oil paint on mattress ticking, and remarkably well preserved).

Within the larger institution, the **Francis Foster Museum** is devoted to the maritime trade and exhibits some exceptional scrimshaw, an 1840 ship's log with primitive watercolors by **Richard Norton,** and a portrait by **Thomas Hart Benton.** The **Captain Francis Pease House,** an 1845 Greek Revival structure, contains prehistoric, pre-Columbian, and Native American artifacts, including Wampanoag pottery made of multicolored Gay Head clay. Also on the grounds are a carriage shed housing an 1830 hearse, a fire engine from 1855, a 19th-century peddler's cart and whaleboat, and tombstones for **Nancy Luce's** pet chickens (a West Tisbury eccentric of the late 19th century, Miss Luce supported herself by selling postcards and poems about her beloved bantams). Outside, the transplanted **Gay Head Light Tower** shines for a few hours every summer evening. ♦ Admission. Daily 10AM-4:30AM early July-early Sept; W-F 1-4PM, Sa 10AM-4PM early Sept-early July. Thomas Cooke House closed mid-Oct to June. 8 Cooke St (at School St). 627.4441

A must-have item among cognoscenti, the Black Dog's trademark T-shirt has been successful enough (100,000 sold a year) to attract imitators, or rather parodists. In 1993, when Black Dog restaurateur Robert Douglas sought an injunction against an islander cranking out "black hog" T-shirts in his basement, U.S. District Court Judge Joseph L. Tauro opined that no copyright infringement had occurred, since there was no mistaking the two: "Unlike plaintiff's somewhat noble depiction of man's best friend," he wrote, "defendant's swine strikes a less inspiring pose."

Happy Trails: Scenic Cycling Routes

If theme-park developers ever wanted to come up with "Bikeworld," they'd do well to look to the Cape and the nearby islands. After all, the terrain is predominantly flat—with a few mild hills for kicks—and unrelentingly scenic. For these very reasons, bike trails have branched out through the area in recent years. You can bring your own bike, borrow a B&B loaner, or rent one from the many shops situated along the trails.

Among the longer paths is a 14-mile loop, spanning both banks of the **Cape Cod Canal,** maintained by the U.S. Army Corps of Engineers (759.5991). The **Shining Sea Bikeway** (548.8500) runs 3½ miles from Woods Hole to Falmouth, connecting with 24 miles of marked blacktop routes. A former Penn-Central right-of-way, the **Cape Cod Rail Trail** (896.3491) cuts a 19-mile swath that's eight feet wide, originating in South Dennis at Route 134 and running parallel to Route 6A up to Eastham. Within the **Cape Cod National Seashore** (487.1256) are Eastham's **Nauset Trail,** which covers the 1.6 miles between the Salt Pond Visitor Center and Coast Guard Beach; Truro's **Head of the Meadow Trail,** which leads from the beach along the old 1850 overland route to Provincetown, ending at High Head Road, two miles from start to finish; and Provincetown's **Province Lands Trail,** a seven-mile rollercoaster of loops and spurs that gyrates through forests and swooping dunes.

Both islands are also ideal for biking, either on or off a path. On **Martha's Vineyard,** a six-mile bike path links Vineyard Haven and Edgartown, and proceeds from there to South Beach. On **Nantucket,** bike paths radiate from Nantucket town to the beaches at Madaket (about six miles), Surfside (three miles), and Sconset (eight miles).

The more professional stores will ask about your biking proficiency before suggesting a route and sending you off with a map; it's better to be honest than to end up gasping for breath in some remote cul-de-sac. Many also offer parking and easy access to trails, and stock such essentials as helmets, car racks, and child seats. Among the top bike shops are:

Brewster: **Rail Trail Bike Shop,** 302 Underpass Road; 896.8200

Eastham: **The Little Capistrano Bike Shop,** Salt Pond Road; 255.6515

Falmouth Heights: **Holiday Cycles,** 465 Grand Avenue; 540.3459

Martha's Vineyard: **Anderson's Bike Rentals,** 14 Saco Avenue, Oak Bluffs; 693.9346

Nantucket: **Young's Bicycle Shop,** Steamboat Wharf; 228.1151

Provincetown: **Arnold's,** 329 Commercial Street; 487.0844

For those who'd prefer a guided tour, **Cape Cod Cycle Tours** (255.8281) offers day-long excursions—including lunch and a glimpse of local attractions—covering the areas of Sandwich, Brewster, Eastham, Wellfleet, and Provincetown. They can also arrange longer itineraries with van support and stopovers at deluxe inns.

---

38 Vineyard Gazette The circulation may be a modest 14,000, but this influential little paper—now edited by **Richard Reston**—goes out to all 50 states and a dozen or so foreign countries; no matter where they spend most of the year, its readers don't want to miss any news of "their" island. All are welcome to wander in and look around. For a full tour of the presses, it's best to make arrangements in advance. The operation is housed in the shingled **Benjamin Smith House,** built by a Revolutionary War captain around 1760.

The very first issue of the *Gazette,* dated 14 May 1846, is preserved under glass. The paper's mission can be read above its name: "A family newspaper—neutral in politics, devoted to general news, literature, morality, agriculture and amusement." Subscriptions cost $2 a year, and front-page news consisted of poetry and columns on such burning issues as "Covetousness" and "Married Life." ♦ M-F 9AM-5PM. 34 S. Summer St (at Davis Ln), Edgartown. 627.4311

Bayberry candles, made of fragrant wax culled from the green-gray berries, were said to bring "health to the home and wealth to the pocket" if burned to the socket.

39 Charlotte Inn $$$$ "Can an inn qualify as a national treasure?" *New York* magazine asked. Definitely, in the case of one so exquisite. Since 1971, **Gery** and **Paula Conover** have been assembling and polishing a charming compound connected by English gardens and brick walkways. They're now up to five houses comprising 24 lavish rooms and two dazzling suites. Each is distinctively decorated, and four-posters and fireplaces abound. The history of the formal white-clapboard main house goes back to 1860, when it belonged to merchant **Samuel Osborne,** whose daughter **Charlotte** turned it into an inn in the 1920s. Today, the downstairs sitting rooms double as the **Edgartown Art Gallery,** showcasing English and American antiques, as well as 19th- and 20th-century paintings and prints. The 1705 Garden House across the street is done up in French country furnishings, while the Coach House Suite, perched above the inn's collection of antique cars, combines English antiques, a walk-in dressing room ornamented with hats and fans, and a Palladian window that allows a sliver of harbor view. In the Summer House, one room has a fireplace and a baby grand. Tucked away amid wisteria vines, the Carriage House (which Gery built without blueprints in 1980) encloses a suite whose English hunting theme is enhanced by a huge brass bed, bold striped wallpaper, and vintage equestrian paraphernalia. ♦ 27 S. Summer St (off Main St), Edgartown. 627.4751

Within Charlotte Inn:

l'étoile

l'étoile ★★★★$$$$ A healthy collection of ferns and potted palms share the dining room with patrons, as brass hurricane lamps cast their flickering light across the glass canopy and the splendorous gold-edged china. The setting is ideal for dishes concocted by chef **Michael Brisson,** formerly of Boston's famed **L'Espalier,** who has a deft, light touch and a gift for pairing complementary ingredients. He uses warm Mission figs, for instance, to offset roasted pheasant breast with wild rice and roasted corn in a sauce of cognac, honey, and thyme. Every flavor is played to its full effect, whether it's in the torte of mascarpone and spring onions enhanced with Ossetra caviar or ice cream topped with Bailey's crème anglaise and caramelized macadamia nuts. When dinner runs to $100 or so a head, you expect perfection, and you are very likely to find it at l'étoile. ♦ Contemporary French ♦ Dinner; Sunday brunch; call for schedule late Sept to May. Reservations recommended. 627.5187

40 Edgartown Woodshop Toward the front of this warehouse-size store are little wooden gewgaws meant to tempt tourists. Press on and things get more interesting (as well as bigger and pricier): handsome Oriental rugs; antique sandalwood chests, cupboards, and ceremonial doorways from Pakistan; a sleek white spruce canoe with sail (for $4,200). ♦ Daily 9AM-10PM late June to mid-Oct; call for off-season hours. 55 Main St (at N. Summer St), Edgartown. 627.9853

41 Summer Solstice **Jennifer Gardner** collects colorful textiles from all over the world and turns them into comfortable clothing for women and children. The same stars and moons in indigo and aqua that make a great summer shift, for instance, might also turn up as a toddler's romper suit. Heavily beaded batiks become vests, jackets, and elegant evening slippers. The shop is located in a greenhouse tucked away in a bamboo grove, and across the street is Edgartown's famous **Pagoda Tree,** a voluminous Chinese Huai tree brought by ship as a seedling in the early 19th century. ♦ Daily 10AM-9PM late May to early Sept; daily 10AM-5PM early Sept to mid-Oct. 6 S. Water St (between Main St and Davis Ln), Edgartown. 645.3499

42 The Great Put On The name sounds like it belongs to the mod era only because this clothing shop dates back to 1969; but the stock is absolutely up to the minute, if not ahead of its time. Owner **Ken Bilzerian** is the brother of **Alan Bilzerian,** Boston's cutting-edge couturier, and their tastes are similar. Women will find designs by **BCBG, Norma Kamali,** and **Sue Wong,** plus an impressive array of outrageously fashionable footwear. There's also a fine selection of men's fashions in casual Italian tweeds and silks. ♦ Daily 10AM-11PM May to early Sept; daily 10AM-7PM early Sept to Dec. Mayhew Ln (between N. Water and Dock Sts), Edgartown. 627.5495

The mooncussers of Cape Cod legend were nefarious scavengers who would sometimes "prearrange" a wreck by tying a lantern to a donkey's tail to imitate a listing ship at anchor. Once their prey drifted to shore, they'd pick it clean by morning.

Restaurants/Clubs: Red **Hotels:** Blue
Shops/ Outdoors: Green **Sights/Culture:** Black

43 **Among the Flowers Cafe** ★$ This is one of the few spots in town where you can grab a pleasant meal without taking out a second mortgage, though getting a table can be tough in the summertime. The omelets, crepes, waffles, and quiches, all prettily garnished with fresh fruit, are available at lunch as well as breakfast. For dinner try lemon chicken, fettuccine Alfredo, or a lobster Newburg crepe—all painlessly priced. Most of the seating is outdoors, under an awning where you can glimpse the harbor. ♦ American/ Continental ♦ Breakfast, lunch, and dinner; breakfast and lunch only May-June, Sept to mid-Nov. Closed mid-Nov to May. Mayhew Ln (between N. Water and Dock Sts), Edgartown. 627.3233

44 **The Fligors of Edgartown** An all-purpose department store for year-round residents, this emporium is a handy source of preppie essentials for vacationers. The selection of gifts is extensive; for children there are **Steiff** stuffed animals, **Madame Alexander** dolls, and terrific outfits. Don't overlook the bargain basement, full of stuff that never goes out of style. ♦ Daily 9AM-11PM late May to early Sept; daily 9AM-5PM early Sept to late May. 27 N. Water St (at Kelly St), Edgartown. 627.4722

45 **Kelley House** $$$$ Renovated in 1991, the inn's 59 rooms are thoroughly modern with a country veneer. There's a heated outdoor pool, and those who place a premium on such amenities might prefer Kelley House to a more intimate B&B. In any case, milk and cookies at bedtime add a personal touch. ♦ Closed Nov-Apr. 23 Kelly St. 627.4394, 800/225.6005

Within Kelley House:

The Newes from America ★$ When the renovators started clearing out this basement space they found the original walls and hand-hewn timbers of the tavern that operated here in the mid-1700s. Etched-glass partitions and captain's chairs padded with green leather are modern additions to this resurrected pub, but the incongruous decor doesn't matter by candlelight, especially after you've imbibed a "Rack of Beers"—any five samples from a menu of 10 outstanding international brews. The food is an afterthought; however, the wood smoker does yield a tasty smoked oyster poorboy. ♦ American ♦ Lunch and dinner. 627.7900

46 **Colonial Inn** $$$ Since 1911, this hotel ha served as the unofficial center of town—a status reinforced, in the summer of 1993, by the opening of **Isola,** instantly the island's hottest restaurant. Because the lobby is also conduit to the **Nevins Square** shops beyond, it's a somewhat impersonal space, while breakfast is a casual, self-service affair in the atrium. The inn's attraction is the soothing comfort of its 42 rooms, prettily appointed with pine furniture, pastel fabrics, and brass beds. Some have views of the water, and all guests have access to the roof veranda, wher the waterfront view is unsurpassed. ♦ 38 N. Water St (between Winter St and Simpson Ln), Edgartown. 627.4711, 800/627.4701

Within Colonial Inn:

Isola ★★★$$$$ Despite a sprinkling of fin restaurants, Martha's Vineyard didn't really rate on the gourmet map until **Todd** and **Oliv English** of Boston's celebrated bistro **Olives** decided to branch out to the island. The plac has been packed since day one, luring patror not just with the off-chance of spotting such celebrity backers as **Michael J. Fox, Glenn Close,** and hockey star **Cam Neeley,** but wit the certainty of experiencing exciting meals. Todd English (who alternates kitchen duty with head chef **Paul Borras**) has a reputatio as an inspired innovator, and fans couldn't wait to see what he'd make of the fruits of their fair isle. A few intriguing dishes on the first season's menu were house-cured tuna tartare and oyster mignonette on toasted barley salad with cilantro, red onion, and lim oil; whole grilled striped bass over fennel branches with creamy Parmesan semolina; and New England blueberry buckle with ging ice cream, drizzled with caramel. The capacit crowds create a festive atmosphere, while th decor mellows the mood, with the colors of moss, white wine, and rust predominating. ♦ Northern Italian ♦ Lunch and dinner. Close mid-Oct to May. Reservations recommende 627.7899

47 **The Edgartown Inn** $$ **Nathaniel Hawthorne** spent the better part of a year at this 1798 Federal way station, writing *Twice Told Tales.* Other notable guests have included **Daniel Webster** and **John F. Kennedy,** while still a senator. The quarters in the main building are pleasant, though a bit stodgy; the stunners are the Garden House's two airy, modern rooms, suffused with the light of a Monet painting and bestowing utter privacy. For an additional charge, a full breakfast is served in the country-style kitchen wing, whose extreme quaintness will charm some and irritate others. ♦ Closed Nov-Mar. 56 N. Water St (at Simpson Ln), Edgartown. 627.4794

48 **Harbor View Hotel** $$$$ In 1891, this grand, sprawling establishment was actually two hotels, which were later linked by a 300-foot veranda. Since its $2 million centennial renovation, the amalgam has reclaimed the showplace status it enjoyed long ago. A palette of off-whites and neutral tones has been used to restful effect everywhere from the lobby, with its massive stone fireplace, to the 124 spacious rooms. Behind the hotel (away from the waterfront), a heated pool is flanked by eight cottages and the Mayhew building, a more motel-like arrangement with porches. The best rooms overlook **Lighthouse Beach,** accessible down a grass-lined path. ♦ 131 N. Water St (at Starbuck's Neck Rd), Edgartown. 627.4333, 800/225.6005

Within the Harbor View Hotel:

Starbuck's ★★★$$$$ Making no concessions to the barefoot style of beachside living, this restaurant is unabashedly formal. But for those willing to lace up their good shoes and keep their elbows off the table, the rewards are ample. An elaborate breakfast menu features Yankee red flannel hash and choose-your-own-combo griddle cakes (how about raspberries, Brazil nuts, and chocolate chips?). At lunchtime, a panfried crab-cake sandwich with tomato herb aioli is among the intriguing options, while for dinner you could select the preparation and sauce for one of six types of fish and in eight months never repeat the same meal. To simplify matters, opt for the traditional shore dinner, which begins with chowder and culminates in a classic strawberry shortcake. ♦ American ♦ Breakfast, lunch, and dinner; Sunday brunch. Reservations recommended. 627.7000

If you think modern bureaucracy is bad, consider the official name of Dukes County (which covers Martha's Vineyard and the Elizabeth Islands). The correct nomenclature, if you please, is the County of Dukes County.

49 **The Daggett House** $$$$ This inn was built in 1750 around the core of a 1660 tavern, where, in his first year in business, owner **John Daggett** was fined five shillings for "selling strong liquor," in addition to the sanctioned ale and beer. The tavern's old beehive fireplace has been incorporated into the dining room; beside it, a revolving bookcase hides a secret stairway leading to a bedroom with a harbor view. For all its colorful history (the tavern later became a boardinghouse for sailors, then a private school), the interior feels slightly bland. Paper place mats and piped-in music are careless touches that detract from the atmosphere. Still, some rooms are impressive; for instance, the Widow's Walk Suite, in the **Warren House** across the street, has a skylight that opens onto a rooftop deck with a hot tub. The central location is a plus, as is the secluded lawn that stretches down to a private swimming dock. ♦ 59 N. Water St (at Daggett St), Edgartown. 627.4600

Within The Daggett House:

The Daggett House Restaurant ★$$$ Dinner choices in this intimate, sconce-lit room are limited (four appetizers and entrées) but—for Edgartown—reasonably priced, especially the three-course prix fixe, which may start with a salad of island greens and radicchio and finish with a chocolate truffle tart. In between, try the grilled veal chop with caramelized onions or the salmon baked in parchment with orange-thyme butter. Breakfasts are hearty; a specialty is French toast made with the inn's signature Grapenut bread. ♦ American ♦ Breakfast and dinner; breakfast only on Monday and Tuesday mid-June to mid-Oct; breakfast only on Monday through Wednesday and Sunday mid-Oct to mid-June. 627.4600

50 **Old Sculpin Gallery** Would that this beautiful old building sheltered more consistently worthy work. It was originally a grain storage house belonging to **Dr. Daniel Fisher,** and in the first half of the century noted boatbuilder **Manuel Swartz Roberts** used it as his workshop. Now the nonprofit **Martha's Vineyard Art Association** mounts exhibitions and holds classes here, but the output shows more enthusiasm than skill. Of course, some pieces may take you by surprise and the wood-beamed structure itself merits a look. ♦ M-Sa 10AM-5PM, 8-10PM; Su 2-5PM, 7-10PM June to early Sept. 58 Dock St (at Daggett St), Edgartown. 627.4881

51 **On Time III** The original ferry to Chappaquiddick (Wampanoag for "the separated island") got its name because the builder promised to have it ready on time for the 1920 summer season. Most users figure it's a meaningless honorific because, with no schedule, how could the flatboat be late? It takes about five minutes to cross the 200-yard divide, carrying three cars and however many passengers want to crowd on. The ride is fun, but, other than taking a hike, there's not much to do on "Chappy" if you don't belong to the beach club. ♦ Fee. Daily 7:30AM-midnight June-Oct; call for hours Nov-May. Dock and Daggett Sts, Edgartown. 627.9794

52 **Mytoi** Less than three miles from the ferry landing is a 14-acre Japanese garden, created in 1958 by **Hugh Jones.** Badly damaged by Hurricane Bob, it's on the mend. The azaleas still bloom in spring, the Japanese iris in summer, and the goldfish glide in their picturesque pool beneath an ornamental bridge. ♦ Free. Daily sunrise-sunset. Off Dyke Rd, Chappaquiddick. 693.7662

53 **Wasque Reservation and Cape Poge Wildlife Refuge** These unspoiled tracts, 200 and 509 acres respectively, cover most of the island's eastern beaches. A great variety of shorebirds live here—kestrels, ospreys, oystercatchers, snowy egrets, great blue herons, and such rare and endangered species as least terns and piping plovers. Humans and their off-road vehicles are admitted for a fee and under strict regulations. One way to see the wildlife is to go on a "Saturday safari."

At the land's northernmost tip sits the **Cape Poge Lighthouse,** built in 1893 after the first two lighthouses here succumbed to the sea. Automated in 1964, this 40-foot tower originally stood 500 feet farther out, 150 feet from what was then the coast; in 1987, when its foundation had been undercut to a 25-foot margin, the Coast Guard moved it inland by crane and helicopter. During the fall, look for small boats scalloping offshore. Well-protected Cape Poge produces half of the state's scallop harvest. ♦ Admission. Closed mid-Sept to mid-June. Wasque Rd (off School Rd), Chappaquiddick. 693.7662

54 **Katama Shores Inn** $$ It may lack charm, but it's come a long way. This 67-room motel started out as an army barracks. Enticing **South Beach** is a mere two-minute walk away, and as most beaches on Martha's Vineyard are privately owned, this three-mile public expanse gets crowded. It's accessible by car, bike, and shuttle bus from Edgartown, so only serious beach bums need to stay this close. ♦ Closed mid-Oct to mid-May. Katama Rd (at South Beach), Edgartown. 627.4747

55 **Hot Tin Roof** Years ago **Carly Simon** was a co-owner of this hangar-turned-nightclub. These days the idiosyncratic schedule assigns some nights to DJs and others to live country music and comedy. Otherwise, live blues, R&B, and funk bands prevail. ♦ Cover. M-Sa 7PM-closing, Su 4PM-closing May to mid-Sept. Airport Rd (off Edgartown-W. Tisbury Rd), W. Tisbury. 693.1137

56 **Martha's Vineyard Riding Center** In all kinds of weather, beginning and accomplished horseback riders can take lessons in an indoor ring at this large, well-tended center. Horses can also be ridden on forested trails from dawn to sunset—and even by moonlight. ♦ By appointment. Scrubby Neck Rd (off Edgartown-W. Tisbury Rd), W. Tisbury. 693.3770

57 **Long Point Wildlife Refuge** Nature lovers must brave some bumpy roads to reach this 586-acre preserve, where a mile-long loop trail passes through a forest of pines and oaks, then sandy grassland and heath, to reach **Long Cove Pond,** home to songbirds, blue-claw crabs, and river otters. Another mile-long path leads to a secluded stretch of **South Beach;** it's a popular spot in summer, so get to the parking area very early in the day. ♦ Parking fee. Daily 10AM-6PM mid-June to mid-Sept. Off Waldron's Bottom Rd (off Edgartown-W. Tisbury Rd), W. Tisbury. 693.7662

"The Vineyard is not a way station, it is a destination," wrote Henry Beetle Hough, revered editor of the *Vineyard Gazette* for 65 years. "It is not a place of rush and hurry, it is in a state of rest."

"It is a mistake to talk of the monotone of ocean," naturalist Henry Beston observed. "The sea has many voices. Listen to the surf, really lend it your ears, and you will hear in it a world of sounds: hollow boomings and heavy roarings, great watery tumblings and tramplings, long hissing seethes, sharp, rifle-shot reports, splashes, whispers, the grinding undertone of stone, and sometimes vocal sounds that might be the half-heard talk of people in the sea."

Restaurants/Clubs: Red **Hotels:** Blue
Shops/ Outdoors: Green **Sights/Culture:** Black

58 **Manter Memorial AYH-Hostel** $ A homey cedar shake saltbox (see above) at the edge of a vast state forest, this excellent youth hostel hums with wholesome energy, from the huge group kitchen with recycling bins and two communal refrigerators to the five dorms accommodating some 80 beds. Notices of local attractions plaster the hallways, and the check-in desk also serves as info central. (Note that some stores offer discounts to hostelers.) Outside, there's a volleyball court, a chicken coop, and a sheltered bicycle rack. By the bike path, the hostel is a little more than seven miles from the Vineyard Haven ferry; shuttle buses are another option in summer. There's a lock-out period from 9:30AM to 5:30PM. ♦ Closed mid-Nov to Apr. Edgartown-W. Tisbury Rd (between Airport and Old County Rds), W. Tisbury. 693.2665

59 **The Granary Gallery at the Red Barn Emporium** At the core of this gallery's collection are the photographs by **Alfred Eisenstaedt,** who first came to Martha's Vineyard in 1937 on assignment for *Life.* Portraits run the gamut from scoundrels to stars (such as a radiant young **Katharine Hepburn**); one of the best-known among the many images is *Children at Puppet Theatre, Paris, 1963: The Moment the Evil Dragon Was Slain* (with a purchase price of almost $5,000). Other rooms showcase talents such as *Vineyard Gazette* photographer **Alison Shaw,** whose vivid color still lifes are studies in pure pattern, and **David Potts Wallis,** who approaches ships at odd angles to create his watercolors. Assorted antiques are scattered among the artworks, and an entire room is devoted to the **McAdoo** family's hooked wool rugs, an island enterprise for five generations. ♦ M-Sa 10AM-5PM, Su noon-4PM late May to Aug; M-Sa 11AM-4PM, Su noon-4PM Sept to mid-Oct. Old County Rd (off Edgartown-W. Tisbury Rd), W. Tisbury. 693.0455, 800/472.6279

60 **The Field Gallery** **Tom Maley's** frolicking white statues have been island emblems since the early 1960s when he built a larger-than-life dancing lady in an open field. Many more have followed, and visitors are welcome to wander among them any time of year. Set on this field is the gallery itself, designed by **Robert Schwartz** in 1971. It exhibits the work of local and regional artists in summer, from collagist **Lucy Mitchell** to cartoonist **Jules Feiffer,** who resides here during that season. The Sunday evening openings (held from 5 to 7PM) are a lively "insider's" tradition open to all. ♦ M-Sa 10AM-5PM; Su 2-7PM. State Rd (between Edgartown-W. Tisbury and South Rds), W. Tisbury. 693.5595

61 **Alley's General Store** "Dealers in almost everything" since 1858, this country store/post office/social nexus was struggling to stay afloat in 1993, beset by competition from the supermarkets. Fortunately, the **Martha's Vineyard Preservation Trust** came up with a plan to buy it, fix it up (the architectural firm of **Moore II** in West Tisbury is in charge of the restoration) and lease it to someone who appreciates its crucial role in the community and can make a go of it year-round. Regular customers such as Pulitzer Prize-winning historian **David McCullough,** who lives on nearby Music Street, contributed to the fund-raising efforts, and the store is slated to be reborn in summer 1994. ♦ Call for hours. State Rd (between Edgartown-W. Tisbury Rd and Music St), W. Tisbury. 693.0088

62 **Breakfast at Tiasquam** $$$ This modern Cape, with its pastoral grounds, is unusual among B&Bs in that it was designed to be one, rather than adapted from a private home. **Ron Crowe,** formerly in charge of **Bowdoin College's** food services, fell in love with the island while on a cycling vacation and decided to relocate in style. The eight-bedroom house, designed by **Doug Richmond** of Brunswick, Maine, incorporates a two-story greenhouse atrium, no fewer than 20 skylights, and a generous allotment of decks to make the most of the setting. The interior is a veritable catalog of fine crafts, with ceramic sinks created by local potter **Robert Parrot,** burnished cherry woodwork, and minimalist, Shaker-inspired furniture, some by **Thomas Moser.** For the morning meal, Crowe happily strives to satisfy virtually any craving; his specialties include corn-blueberry pancakes and freshly caught fish. He also provides passes to pretty, private **Lucy Vincent Beach,** and after a visit, the inn's heated outdoor showers are a treat. ♦ Off Middle Rd (between Music St and Meetinghouse Rd), Chilmark. 645.3685, 800/696.3685

63 **Allen Farm** As you round this hilly corner, with the ocean on one side and ancient stone fences lining the other, you might think you were in Hebrides—or perhaps New Zealand, the homeland of the 70 sheep in residence. They are shorn yearly to allow skilled hands to knit the sweaters, scarves, hats, and shawls stowed in the tiny shop here. ♦ Odd hours (call ahead). South Rd (between Meetinghouse and Middle Rds), Chilmark. 645.9064

Building Character: The Architecture of Cape Cod and The Islands

When imagining the Pilgrims landing in the New World, you might picture the settlers diligently constructing simple plank houses. Truth be told, upon arriving in the bitter cold of winter, they were desperate to cobble whatever shelter they could fashion. Their first efforts copied Native American wigwams made of arched saplings covered with bark, hides, cornstalks, grass—anything that was handy. As soon as they were able, however, the settlers replicated familiar English styles, adapting them to the harsh seaside environment. The simple yet effective post and beam method of construction, initially filled in with wattle and daub, later with interior walls of vertical board, more than sufficed for most people's needs well into the early 1800s.

The archetypal Cape Cod cottage (circa 1630-1720)—many of which still exist—was a one-and-a-half-story building with a steep side-gable roof, designed to deflect wind and precipitation. (The settlers replaced thatch, which blew away with the first gust of a northeastern, with native slate; the pitched roofs also helped distribute this added weight.) The first Cape Cod cottages were one-room structures built by the settlers—usually about 16 feet square, in accordance with the English measurement known as a rod—that were put up around massive fieldstone fireplaces cemented with clay. Perpendicular to the fireplace, transecting the ceiling, was a "summer beam," a massive wood support of the upper floor, which was usually low-ceilinged and served as a child's bedroom or storage area.

Such an arrangement, with two windows and the door set to one side, is today classified as a "half-Cape." The design proved adaptable as families grew. A "three-quarter cottage" extended far enough to permit an additional window on the other side of the door. A "full Cape" was about 30 feet deep by 34 feet wide, with a center door, a hearth, and two front rooms—the "hall," or master bedroom, and the parlor—each with two front windows. The back of the house became a combination cooking and all-purpose living room known as a keeping room. Its sun-warmed southwest corner was typically walled off as a small "borning room," which could also serve the sick or the elderly, and the cold northeast corner partitioned into a pantry and buttery.

As the settlers prospered and multiplied, many a half-Cape grew to a full Cape and then some, with connected outbuildings referred to as "warts." Some houses extended up as well as out—into the "saltbox" style, imported from Kent, which resembles the slope-lidded boxes in which colonists stored that precious commodity. The result was greater height but limited living space. By the mid-17th century, however, builders realized the walls could support roofs at a 45-degree angle. Extending the roof over rear lean-tos, they achieved the "colonial mansion" style, spacious enough for two large front-corner rooms and a kitchen extension in back. Usually the second floor boasted two corner bedrooms, but to create even more space, carpenters introduced the gambrel roof, which flares out before dropping downward, much like a barn's roof.

Eager to optimize the sun's warmth, the colonists quickly abandoned casement windows made of parchment, opting instead for six-by-eight-inch panes of glass shipped from England. Depending on their net worth—glass was extremely expensive—homeowners arranged these double-hung windows in multiples of four across, as in "8 over 12" or even "12 over 16."

By the close of the 17th century, all of these hastily improvised styles were beginning to merge. Around the same time, English architects traveling abroad

A Typical Modern Cape

were amassing bold new ideas about classical proportions, inspired by the work of 16th-century Italian architect **Andrea Palladio.** Gradually, asceticism gave way to a new trend toward self-expression and a deliberate aesthetic—which was eagerly embraced by the affluent, cosmopolitan seafarers along the colonies' coast. Whereas Georgian England (circa 1714-1830) constructed its grand symmetrical mansions in brick and stone, its New England counterpart favored wood as a building material, sometimes carved or painted to resemble brick. Stylistic variations abounded and were often superimposed right over the plainer colonial boxes. Doorways became especially ornate, flanked by fluted pilasters (pretend columns), topped with rectangular, triangular, and even elliptical pediments; when the elliptical pediments began to frame glass, the fanlight was born.

American designers developed and refined their own architectural vocabulary in the Federal period (1775-1820), so named for its association with the fledgling government, and returned to classicism during the Greek Revival of 1820 to 1860. Beginning in 1860, religious camp meetings spawned cottages of a modest Greek Revival mien, which soon blossomed into the no-holds-barred ornamentation of the Carpenter Gothic style; marvelous examples survive in **Oak Bluffs** on **Martha's Vineyard.** Victorian influences continued late into the 19th century, as the moneyed classes embraced the Second Empire (1865-80) and Queen Anne (1885-1920) modes. By the late-19th century, New England architects had matured sufficiently to create their own vernacular, the Shingle style, which peaked from 1880 to 1920. Many a grand summer house was fashioned in this style; these mammoth wooden buildings, while made of humble materials, may have seemed a sort of back-to-basics "reverse snobbery," but with their flowing open spaces and airy verandas, they were actually easier to maintain than their more formal predecessors.

Low-slung veranda-fronted bungalows—modeled on the heat-deflecting Indian *bangla* and suited to the modest means of the middle class—popped up on the Cape from 1890 to 1930. With the Depression came a revival of the plain Cape Cod cottage design, which began carpeting new suburban developments from coast to coast, as well as on Cape Cod itself. Then came building booms from the '60s to the '80s that introduced characterless structures that have never fit in well with the landscape, much less the older dwellings surrounding them. However, in recent years, responding to zoning and design restrictions, as well as the potential for profitability, developers have shown an interest in reviving and respecting the aesthetics that inform the traditional Cape house.

---

64 Chilmark Store Dating from 1941, Chilmark's general store lacks the bounteous old-time charm of **Alley's** in West Tisbury, but its porch is equally crowded thanks to **Primo Lombardi's** excellent, puffy-crusted pizza, generously topped with spicy linguica or homemade pesto. To complete your repast, try another kind of pie stocked by the store: fresh apple, blueberry, raspberry, or strawberry-rhubarb from the **Menemsha Bakeshop.** ♦ M-Tu, Th-Su 7AM-6PM May to mid-Oct. State Rd (at Beetlebung Corner), Chilmark. 645.3739

64 The Feast of Chilmark ★★★$$$$ The hidden treasure in this plain clapboard house is a two-level restaurant and cafe that ascends to surprising heights, in both interior space and culinary sophistication. The smart black-and-white cafe/bar serves as a permanent gallery for local-color photos by **Peter Simon** (Carly's brother). The main dining room extends into a mezzanine with vaulted ceilings and plenty of room for revolving art shows (lucky diners will catch the bold still-life pastels of **Thaw Malin,** also featured at **Savoir Faire**). Artistry on the dinner plates includes lobster turnovers with shrimp and lemon cream and roasted rack of domestic lamb with a spinach and cognac glaze. ♦ New American ♦ Dinner. Closed Monday May-June, Sept-Oct; closed Nov-Apr. State Rd (at Beetlebung Corner), Chilmark. 645.3553

65 Chilmark Chocolates The chocolate lollipops are luscious, the truffles transcendent. You can watch them being made at the risk of sharpening your sugar craving. ♦ W-Su 11:30AM-5:30PM July-Aug, Nov-Dec; call for off-season hours. State Rd (near Beetlebung Corner), Chilmark. 645.3013

66 Duck Inn $$ **Elise LeBovitt** realizes that some people consider her bed-and-breakfast farmhouse "too much," and that's fine with her. Set on a meadow above the Gay Head cliffs, it's like a post-hippie pensione with a hot tub. Duck Inn is perfect for visitors who want a place with a strong personality and glorious ocean views at every turn. The rooms, including one tucked into the 200-year-old stone foundation, are romantic and fancifully decorated, though not fancy. The pink stucco living room is agreeably cluttered and comfy, while the gourmet organic breakfast might involve pear couscous muffins. ♦ Off State Rd (near Moshup Trail), Gay Head. 645.9018

For a cheap, reliable, and easily accessible, if dim, source of light, the early settlers used a "rush lamp," consisting of a rush soaked in tallow and suspended above a wooden base with a metal clamp. Each rush burned for less than half an hour.

67 Gay Head Cliffs In midsummer, you will have to make your way past belching tour buses and tacky snack-and-souvenir stands to see these 150-foot-tall clay cliffs formed by glaciers some 100 million years ago. It's worth it, though, not just for the colorful striated layers but for the dramatic views of **Noman's Land Island** and the **Elizabeth Islands.** These cliffs started out as a section of coastal hills on the mainland. The exposed strata represent various geological epochs and contain related fossils; the gravel at the top has yielded the remains of whales and sharks along with the partial skeleton of a camel (extinct in North America for about 12,000 years).

Most of this area is now owned by the **Wampanoag Indians,** who have occupied Gay Head for at least 5,000 years. The natives' rights to Aquinnah (the "high land") were established definitively in a 1987 government settlement granting the tribe $4.5 million with which to buy back approximately 475 acres. Wampanoag legend holds that the gargantuan deity **Moshup** once lived at Gay Head in "Devil's Den" and used to roast whole whales in fires made with trees he ripped from the ground; the cliffs were said to be his garbage heaps, their gray layers ashes from his fire. When the American colonists arrived, they used the chromatic clay to paint houses, make bricks, and even build roads. Fossil hunters of the past two centuries tore up huge chunks of the cliffs, and in the 1970s, hippies used to soak in mud baths at their base. These actions are unthinkable now, when every effort is being made to stem the erosion that could ultimately destroy this great natural wonder. ♦ State Rd (at Moshup Trail), Gay Head

68 The Outermost Inn $$$ Built in 1971 by **Jean** and **Hugh Taylor** (of the musically gifted clan), this gray-shingled house (see above), with wraparound water views, was converted into a seven-room inn several years ago. The living room is full of instruments ("We encourage guests to play if they know how—and not to, if they don't," Jean says with a laugh). The guest rooms are sparsely furnished to show off the rich woodwork in beech, ash, cherry, and hickory. Outside, 35 acres of grassy dunes ramble toward the sea. The porch is a splendid place to sip a drink and enjoy the scene; a hammock in a tree beyond reminds guests that any time can be nap time. ♦ Closed Nov-Mar. Lighthouse Rd (between State and Lobsterville Rds), Gay Head. 645.3511

Within The Outermost Inn:

Outermost House Restaurant ★★★$$$ The simplicity of the inn's accommodations carries over to its kitchen. Chef **Barbara Fenner,** who trained at the **Culinary Institute of America,** prepares a straightforward prix fixe menu for two seatings in the dining room with its sea view. The main course might be a slab of grilled Menemsha swordfish or charbroiled sirloin, accompanied by homemade oatmeal rolls, a fresh garden salad, and steamed vegetables. "Brownies ecstasy" (with hazelnut ice cream), fruit shortcake, or white chocolate mousse may follow. ♦ New American ♦ Dinner. Closed Tuesday and Wednesday May to early Sept; closed Monday through Wednesday early Sept to mid-Oct; closed mid-Oct to late May. Reservations required. 645.3511

69 Arabella **Hugh Taylor** and two other captains sail his 50-foot catamaran on day trips to Cuttyhunk and sunset cruises of the harbor and Nantucket Sound. (Also located at this slip is a bike ferry that, for a small fee, wi save cyclists about 10 miles of backtracking to circumvent Menemsha Pond.) ♦ Daily 11AM-5PM, 6PM-sunset mid-June to mid-Sept. Menemsha Harbor (at North Rd), Menemsha. 645.3511

69 Home Port ★★$$$$ Fresh-off-the-boat fis has been this restaurant's selling point since 1931. Many of the more impressive specimens have ended up on the walls, and if trophy fish, paper place mats, and clamorous crowds aren't your idea of the ideal shore dinner, do as the locals do and call in a take-out order. Pick your meal up at the kitchen door and bring it to the scenic waterside locale of your choice for a sunset feast. ♦ New England/Takeout ♦ Dinner. Closed mid-Oct to May. North Rd (at Menemsha Harbor), Menemsha. Reservations recommended. 645.2679

70 Pandora's Box This tiny store is packed with ready-to-wear women's clothes perfectly suited to the island's laid-back lifestyle. Some make a statement, some are just loaf-around comfortable; all have a certain flair and are affordably priced, especially at the phenomenal sale held at the close of summer ♦ Daily 10AM-6PM mid-June to mid-Sept. Basin Rd (off North Rd), Menemsha. 645.9696

70 The Menemsha Bite ★$$ "The Bite" is a quintessential seafood snack shack, flanked by picnic tables. Staples like chowder and fried fish come in graduated containers, with jumbo portion of shrimp topping out at around $25. ♦ American ♦ Lunch and dinner Closed mid-Sept to June. Basin Rd (off North Rd), Menemsha. 645.9239

70 Poole's Fish Owned by **Everett H. Poole** since 1946, this is *the* source for fresh seafood. The store does its own smoking, and one refrigerated case serves as a makeshift raw bar where staffers shuck the crustaceans while you wait and even provide cocktail sauce. ♦ Daily 8AM-6PM July-Aug; M-Sa 8AM-5PM, Su noon-5PM May-June, Sept-Dec. Dutcher's Dock (off Basin Rd), Menemsha. 645.2282

71 Beach Plum Inn $$$$ Vibrant perennials surround the rambling white farmhouse (pictured below) with a broad lawn overlooking the harbor. Its comfortable living room/library, lovely grounds, and 11 airy rooms (some in surrounding cottages) make this a wonderful place to stay put and unwind. Your company will be high-placed and well-heeled. ♦ Closed mid-Oct to May. Off North Rd (between Menemsha Harbor and Menemsha Cross Rd), Menemsha. 645.9454

Within Beach Plum Inn:

Beach Plum Inn Restaurant ★★★$$$$ With windows on three sides, this simple white room captures the full glory of Menemsha's supreme sunsets. The prix fixe menu changes nightly, but among the stellar standards are *Brie en croûte,* beef Wellington, and a classic crème brûlée. ♦ Continental ♦ Breakfast and dinner. Closed mid-Oct to May. Reservations required. 645.9454

71 Menemsha Inn and Cottages $$ A dozen cottages (rented by the week), nine rooms, and six suites share a secluded setting on 10½ verdant acres with westerly views of the water. **Alfred Eisenstaedt** has been a regular guest since the 1950s, and the interior aesthetics would please any artist; as important as what you see is what you don't see: needless frills and pretense. There's a tranquil breakfast room with a piano, but no restaurant to create bustle. The most luxurious suites are in the Carriage House, which has a spacious common room with a fieldstone fireplace and inviting rattan and chintz couches. These rooms have private decks, perfect for restorative hours of sitting and gazing out to sea. ♦ Closed Dec-Apr. Off North Rd (between Menemsha Harbor and Menemsha Cross Rd), Menemsha. 645.2521

72 The Captain R. Flanders House $$ A whaling captain built this farmhouse in the late 18th century. Although it's now a bed-and-breakfast inn, little about it has changed over 200 years. The broad plank floors of the living room are the appropriate setting for some exceptional antiques; the furnishings have none of that "don't touch" feel common in more ostentatious B&Bs. This is a genuine working farm, positioned on 60 acres of rolling meadows crisscrossed by stone walls. After fortifying themselves with homemade muffins, honey, and jam at breakfast, guests can fritter the day away however they like. Passes are provided to nearby **Lucy Vincent Beach,** though the environs may inspire a long country walk. At some point, most guests find themselves echoing the sentiments of one regular visitor: "I hope this place never changes." ♦ Closed mid-Nov to Apr. North Rd (between Menemsha Cross and Tabor House Rds), Chilmark. 645.3123

73 Takemmy Farm Llama breeders **Frank** and **Mary Bailey** open their farm twice a week to visitors in the interest of introducing these intelligent, low-maintenance pack animals to the public. Shaded by willows and elms, it's an impressive spread. Hand-knit llama-wool sweaters are available for purchase, and those who want to become better acquainted with these extraordinary beasts can take the Baileys up on their "Bed and Make Your Own Breakfast" offer; guests stay in an antique-appointed one-bedroom apartment within the 300-year-old farmhouse. ♦ Free. W, Sa 1-5PM. State Rd (between Indian Hill and North Rds), W. Tisbury. 693.2486

74 Lambert's Cove Country Inn $$ A lengthy drive through pine forests on a meandering dirt road will bring you to a 1790s farmhouse, expanded by an author and amateur horticulturist into a seven-acre estate in the 1920s. This man's most endearing legacy at the inn today is the library, with shelves on all four walls promising innumerable opportunities for intellectual escape. Meanwhile, a set of French doors beckon flower lovers into the English garden. Everything about the house invites relaxation. The decor isn't a calculated design scheme; it's more the comfortable aftereffects of affluence. Many of the 15 rooms have decks overlooking the gardens, and, in spring, lilac and wisteria perfume the air. ♦ Lambert's Cove Rd (off State Rd), W. Tisbury. 693.2298

Within Lambert's Cove Country Inn:

Lambert's Cove Country Inn Restaurant ★★★$$$$ In fine weather dinner is served on an outdoor deck with a view of the apple orchards; if it gets chilly, the indoor dining room is pretty, too, with peach tablecloths covered with lace and glass. The constantly changing menu may venture into the likes of scallop and oyster pan stew with chives and crostini; cheese and walnut ravioli with asparagus, roasted red pepper, and fresh basil in a Gorgonzola cream sauce; veal saltimbocca; or barbecued Muscovy duck. Sunday brunch here is a beloved tradition, where indulgence is incited not only by the usual savory dishes but by such rich sweets as strawberry-mascarpone crepes with chocolate sauce. ♦ New American ♦ Dinner; Sunday brunch. Call for schedule mid-Sept to May. Reservations recommended. 693.2298

75 The Chilmark Pottery **Geoffrey Borr** has been hard at work in this rural studio since 1982, producing sturdy, useful ceramics in a range of rich, multihued glazes. Pick up an oversize coffee cup to take home. ♦ M-Sa 9:30AM-5:30PM; Su 11AM-5PM. Off State Rd (between Lambert's Cove and Old County Rds), W. Tisbury. 693.6476. Also at: 170 Circuit Ave, Oak Bluffs. 693.5910

76 Chicama Vineyards On a hunch that the soil here might prove hospitable to cultivated grapes, former San Franciscans **George** and **Catherine Matheisen** planted 75 vinifera vines in 1971. They now produce more than 8,000 cases a year. There are more than a dozen Chicama varieties, including Chardonnay, Cabernet, Riesling, Pinot Noir, and the island's first appellation Merlot. A tasty offshoot of the viticulture is a superb line of herb vinegars (almost 20 kinds), plus salad dressings, mustards, jams, jellies, chutneys, and ice cream toppings. Several handsome gift packs can be purchased in the shop or by mail order. Anytime of year, visitors are treated to a tasting (given a choice, opt for the creditable Chenin Blanc). In high season, a lively 20-minute tour is offered. ♦ Tours and tastings: M-Sa 11AM-5PM, Su 1-5PM late May to mid-Oct. Tastings: daily 1-4PM mid-Oct to mid-Nov; M-Sa 11AM-4PM, Su 1-4PM mid-Nov to Dec; Sa 1-4PM Jan-Apr; Sa 1-5PM early May. Stoney Hill Rd (off State Rd), W. Tisbury. 693.0309

76 Thimble Farm Those not daunted by the rutted dirt road leading to the farm can pick their own strawberries and raspberries here. (Children must be at least 12 years old). Also for sale are vegetables, flowers, melons, and pumpkins, according to the season. Much of this prime produce is grown in vast greenhouses that look like a science-fiction film set. ♦ Tu-Su 10AM-5PM mid-June to early Oct. Stoney Hill Rd (off State Rd), W. Tisbury. 693.6396

77 Scottish Bakehouse **Isabelle White** of Peebles, Scotland, opened this homey bakeshop in the early '60s, and islanders hav come to depend on her high-calorie handiwork. In addition to about 10 signature breads (one is called "Scotch Crusty"), the bakery produces sausage rolls, Cornish pasties, "Forfer Bridies" (pork and onion turnovers), and shortbread—plain as well as irresistible versions like chocolate hazelnut. ♦ Bakery ♦ Daily 8AM-7PM July to mid-Sept daily 8AM-5PM mid-Sept to June. State Rd (between Old County and Lambert's Cove Rds), Vineyard Haven. 693.1873. Also at: 3 Union St Mall, Vineyard Haven. 693.5582

78 On the Vineyard Gallery In 1978, **Doug Parker,** art director of Boston University's *Bostonia* magazine, turned the barn of his summertime home into an artists' co-op. It was more or less a philanthropic gesture. An artist himself, he considers the typical gallery sales commission of 60 percent to be an injustice, so he charges none; artists pay only a nominal fee to cover overhead. The shows here are ambitious, sophisticated, and worth a deliberate detour. ♦ Daily 2-6PM May-Oct. State Rd (at Lambert's Cove Rd), Vineyard Haven. 693.1338

Bests

Toby Wilson

Actor, The Vineyard Playhouse; Manager, Adam Cab

On Martha's Vineyard:

Sunset at **Gay Head** on Friday and Saturday. For a small donation, you can watch the sun set from the tower of the 19th-century brick lighthouse at Gay Head. On the clearest days, you get a sweeping view of the Clay Cliffs, the Elizabeth Islands, and even the Newport Bridge 40 miles in the distance.

Oak Bluffs is a town made up entirely of Victorian gingerbread cottages painted in bright pastel colors. In early August, the residents decorate their porches with antique Japanese lanterns. The following evening (Illumination Night), there's a fireworks display in Ocean Park overlooking Nantucket Sound A great family activity.

The **West Tisbury Agricultural Fair** in late August. A real old-fashioned country fair featuring rickety rides cheesy games, and great food ranging from cotton candy to tempura. **Bonnie Raitt** based a song called "Stayed Too Long at the Fair" on it.

The **Possible Dreams Auction** in early August at the Harborside Inn. Lunch with **Christopher Reeves,** a day's sailing with **Walter Cronkite,** a tour of the Brooklyn Bridge with **David McCullough**—all these prizes are auctioned off by gavel master **Art** uchwald to benefit Martha's Vineyard Community ervices.

unset concerts by **Der Künster Drum.** Every onday evening a sunset concert is held at various eaches around the island by a nine-piece drum band laying Afro-Caribbean rhythms. Dance, swim, roove, hang. Look for weekly locations on posters round the island.

ggs Galveston at the **Black Dog Tavern.** Pesto and mato wheat bread pizza at **Papa's Pizza.** Breakfasts the **Lost Pelican.** Banana Boats and cappuccino at **Taste of Italy.** Lemon poppy seed muffins and hocolate streusel coffee at **Mrs. Miller's.**

he **Newes from America,** an 18th-century pub eaturing a huge variety of beers and ales. With each rder you get a wooden nickel. Turn in 500 nickels nd you get a glass mug with your name carved in it. urn in a thousand and you get a stool with your ame carved in it. Turn in 5,000 and you get a liver ansplant with your name carved in it.

he **Home Port** in Menemsha (the fishing village here **Robert Shaw** kept his shack in the movie *aws*). The Home Port isn't a fancy place, just basic urf 'n' turf, but the food is great, the atmosphere errific, and the backdrop as serene and tranquil as nywhere on the east coast. BYOB; reservations must.

he **Atlantic Connection,** a dance club on Circuit venue in Oak Bluffs. "Circus Avenue" is where most f the nightlife is.

leidi Vanderbilt

Vriter

n Martha's Vineyard:

unrise over the **Vineyard Haven Harbor.**

reakfast at the **Black Dog Tavern.** Go early, when it rst opens, around 7AM, and sit on the porch. The est breakfasts on earth, and a perfect view.

sunny morning, a rainy afternoon, a late evening at he **Bunch of Grapes Bookstore.** In winter, the BOG is anity itself to those of us who live on the island. Pull ut a book and roll yourself into a ball on the floor. est-sellers, budget buys, how to build a house, nake a quilt, lose weight, knit, navigate, repair your ar. In summer, you might see **William Styron** help ut behind the counter—yes, he really did once. Or **acqueline Onassis, Michael J. Fox,** or **Spike Lee.** Vith or without summer celebs, this is a lavishly tocked dream of a small-town bookstore. Browse as ong as you like, even all day, but I defy you not to uy a book.

or tapes and CDs, stop by **Hear Say** in the little mall n Beach Road across from where the New Bedford erry *Schamonchi* docks. Also, for devotees of fabric rts, **The Heath Hen Quilt Shop** is just a few loors down.

unch at **The Patisserie** on Main Street. Sit on the orch. Watch people go by and the seasons change. at French bread with extra butter and extra jam.

ainy Day for your house, your bath, your child.

Afternoons, go to the **Wooden Tent Gallery** on State Road just outside Vineyard Haven. Top island artists (like my husband) sit their own shows. Great prices (almost no gallery mark-up). If you're just not buying art these days—shame on you—you can get wonderful note cards of the artists' work for a few dollars. Go for the openings and enjoy free food and wine and lots of friendly chatter. Linger over the work and talk to the artists (who are frantic with boredom during beach hours and will treat you like their very best friend ever) on less crowded days. Then go down the road a few hundred years to **On the Vineyard Gallery.**

Open studios: **Michele Ratte's** incredible silks and velvets; **Barney Zeitz'** unique stained glass and wrought-iron furniture.

Pick any holiday weekend—Memorial Day and July Fourth are the absolute best—and hang out by the standby line at the **Steamship Authority.** Count the cars trying to get on to the ferry. More than 300? Go buy a ginger cookie and some coffee at the **Black Dog Bakery** and settle in to watch and listen. Sometimes fights break out. You can feel superior because *you* are not in the standby line. (My personal record for being on standby was 16 hours.)

Go to the **Mary Wakeman Center** off Lambert's Cove Road and pick up a map of trails and ancient ways. Most Vineyard beaches are private or town-owned. But these trails are for everyone, and you and your dog can amble past farms, through woods, over meadows, and around ponds.

A massage at **Body and Soul.** You deserve it.

Sunset by the drawbridge between **Vineyard Haven** and **Oak Bluffs.**

Nights at **Wintertide Coffee House.** Everything from open mikes to national folk stars to the Japanese folk-rock group **Tsubasa.** For the spoken word, catch a reading there—or anywhere else—by the rapturous and entrancing award-winning poet **George Mills.**

A careful moonlit stroll along the great jetty that protects the harbor. Bring a flashlight.

Shooting stars. Lie on your back in August and look up. Be patient.

Ann Nelson

Owner, Bunch of Grapes Bookstore, Inc.

Bunch of Grapes Bookstore in Vineyard Haven—5,000 square feet, more than 30,000 titles. Island books are just one of the specialties.

Before the l870s, shipwreck victims had virtually no chance of survival unless they happened upon a "charity house" (a crude shed with fireplace) erected along the shore by the Massachusetts Humane Society. In 1872, Congress approved the building of nine life-saving stations on Cape Cod; four more were added in 1902 (one survives as a Life-Saving Museum at Race Point in Provincetown).

Nantucket

The Wampanoag natives—7,000 strong befor the advent of colonists—called the island of Nantucket **Nanaticut**, "the faraway land," and whaling captains nicknamed it "the Gray Lady," because of its frequent shroud of fog. The shape of this 14 by-3½-mile landmass has been variously described as a pork chop, a whale flipping its tail, and a strutting swan; in fact, it resembles nothing so much a a jellyfish billowing as fast as it can to get away from the mainland.

A good 30 miles out to sea, Nantucket is a truly retrograde destination, preserved—originally by a postwhaling depression, then by concerted community effort—from the incursions of modernity. Tourists undaunted b the two-hour ferry ride are greeted by weather-silvered wharves linked by cobblestoned streets to a town that is quintessentially quaint. The square-mile **National Landmark Historic District** encompasses no fewer than 800 structures predating 1850, the largest such concentration in the United States.

Compared to Cape Cod and the Vineyard, Nantucket was settled late. Early explorer **Bartholomew Gosnold** didn't even bother to debark, and **Thomas Mayhew**, having bought the whole chain of islands for £40 in 1642, sold Nantucket, sight unseen, in 1659 to a group of would-be settlers for £30 and "two Beaver Hatts, one for myself and one for my wife." One of the nine "original purchasers," and the first to settle in, was sheep farmer **Thomas**

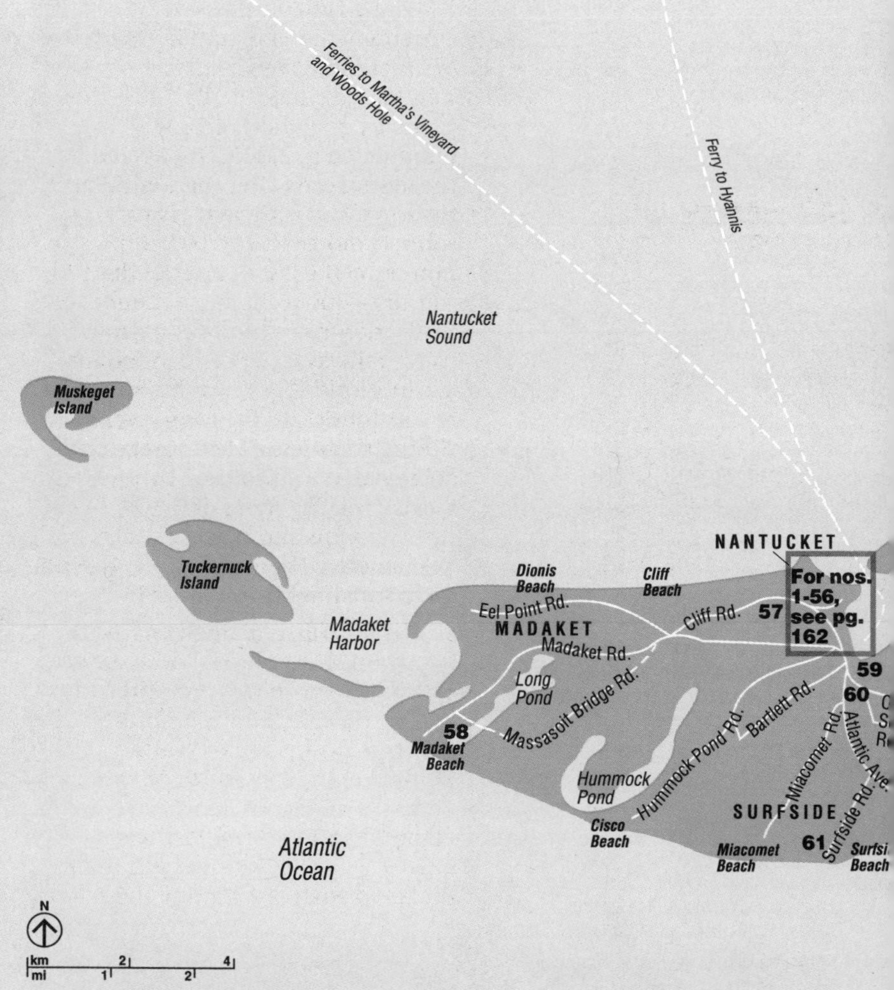

Macy of Salisbury, Massachusetts, who had been threatened on the mainland with hanging for sheltering Quakers during a thunderstorm. Over the next few years, the nine original purchasers sold "half-shares," thereby enlarging the number of shareholders to 27. The bitter dissension that soon grew up between the two "classes" was assuaged when proprietor **Tristram Coffin's** grandson **Jethro** married newcomer **John Gardner's** daughter **Mary** in 1686—à la Romeo and Juliet, only with a happy ending. The couple moved into a house built on Gardner land of lumber from the Coffin sawmill; their saltbox abode survives as Nantucket's oldest house.

At the start of the 18th century, some 300 settlers and 800 natives (their numbers already decimated by disease) were peacefully coexisting, cultivating maize, beans, squash, and tobacco, raising sheep, and catching cod off **Siasconset** at the island's eastern end. The Native Americans also thoughtfully taught their new neighbors how to spear the slow-moving sperm whales that passed within striking distance of shore—a pastime that in the coming centuries would turn the tiny island into a whaling center. Nantucketers built **Straight Wharf** in 1723; within 50 years the island became the biggest whaling seaport in the world.

The boom years went bust, however, with a series of blows. First, the **Great Fire of 1846** (which started in a milliner's shop) swept through the town's wooden buildings and oil- and tar-soaked docks, razing the port and destroying a third of the town. In 1849, the Gold Rush lured entrepreneurs west, and in the 1850s, petroleum-derived kerosene supplanted whale oil. By 1861, the island's population of 10,000 had plummeted to 2,000. Discovered by the leisure class after the Civil War, the town had sufficient visitors to support more than 50 boarding-houses by the last quarter of the 19th century—about the same number of B&Bs that thrive today. A narrow-gauge railway (later dismantled for use in World War I) was built in 1884 to cart tourists to the rose-covered fishing shanties of Siasconset (fondly abbreviated to "Sconset" by the locals). Among those drawn to the rustic charms and bracing waters of the remote village were actors **Joseph Jefferson** and **Lillian Russell.**

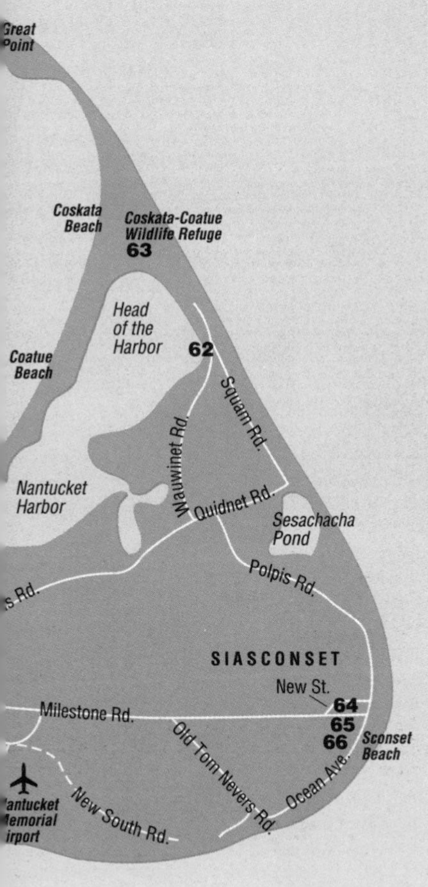

Still, island life remained relatively sleepy until the tourist boom of the early '70s, which was prompted in part by the late-'50s restoration efforts of businessman **Walter Beinecke, Jr.** (benefactor of Yale's Beinecke Library of Rare Books). Beinecke ruffled a few feathers by gussying up the fishing shacks along the town wharves, turning them into boutiques and restaurants attractive to tourists. Fortunately, he also helped initiate extremely strict zoning and building codes that protected the community from the ensuing onslaught.

As a result, there's not so much as a traffic light to jar you from the contemplation of a centuries-old aggregate of glorious architecture, much of which you can shop in, eat in, and even sleep in. Where other towns might boast a handful of historic B&Bs, Nantucket has literally dozens; you can pick one at random, or with the guidance of the **Nantucket Information Bureau** (228.0925) or the **Chamber of Commerce** (228.3643), and be assured of getting a beauty. Similarly, intriguing shops—many specializing in rarefied home decor and women's clothing—are packed along Main Street and Centre Street (once known as "Petticoat Row" for all the whalers' wives who maintained dry goods businesses there). The rare rainy day is a good excuse to plunder and pillage here, with rest stops at the many winning restaurants in the area.

Perhaps the most remarkable aspect of Nantucket is its miles upon miles of beach open to all comers, unlike the mostly private shores of Martha's Vineyard. Although it's sometimes a strain on property owners, the great majority are committed to maintaining public access. And thanks in large part to the early efforts of the **Nantucket Conservation Foundation**, about a third of the island's 30,000 acres is already under some kind of protective stewardship. A network of beautiful bike paths stems out from the tightly clustered houses in town, past rolling meadows carpeted with scrub oak, blueberry bushes, and heather to broad beaches where the capricious surf can be challenging one day and calm the next. Though peaceful and protected, Nantucket is never dull—the ocean sees to that. There's a popular superstition that if, when departing, you throw a penny off the ferry as you pass **Brant Point**, you're sure to return. And almost everyone does both.

---

1 Rope Walk ★★$$$$ Open to the bay breezes and with a front-row seat on the yachtly doings of the waterfront, this is a wonderful place to eat intelligently treated seafood while getting acclimated to island time. Stop for a briny nibble at the raw bar (in the evenings, you might find some sushi), or go all out and feast on grilled swordfish with sun-dried tomato *tapenade* and grilled onion and Gorgonzola polenta. The cuisine is more ambitious than the casual setting and service would suggest. ♦ American ♦ Lunch and dinner. Closed mid-Oct to mid-May. Straight Wharf (off Main St). 228.8886

1 The Sparrow Naval architect **Rand Watkins** modeled his 40-foot sailboat on a Norwegian North Sea pilot boat but gave it some nonworking-class finishing touches: the varnished teak interior is warmed by stained glass and brass accents. Rates for group sails are well within reach, but for a real treat spring for a private charter and escape to a secluded beach on **Coatue,** sipping champagne en route. ♦ By appointment early June to mid-Sept. Slip 18, Straight Wharf (off Main St). 228.6029

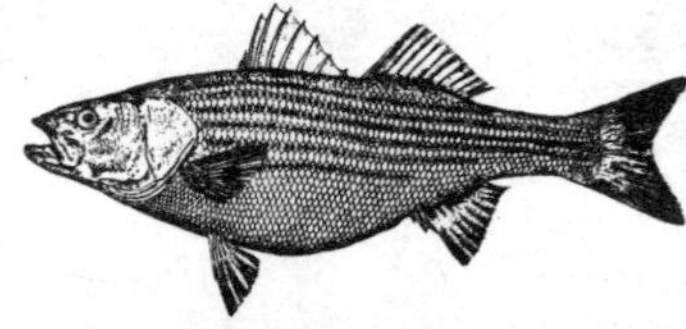

2 Straight Wharf Restaurant ★★★$$$$ In 1982, **Marion Morash** of PBS' "*Victory Garden*" founded this handsome restaurant, a sail-loft- type space with canvas panels ribboned through the rafters. She also served as chef until 1989, when **Sarah O'Neill** took over. The menu changes weekly, but the fare, served at two or three seatings, is fairly straightforward in concept and superb in its simplicity (e.g., sautéed soft-shell crabs with lemon caper meunière, or a dessert of melon, kiwi, and berries with lemon crème fraîche and biscotti). The adjoining bar-cum-patio serves a lower-priced, smaller-portion grill menu and stays open to mid-October. ♦ New American ♦ Dinner. Closed Monday; closed mid-Sept to mid-June. Straight Wharf (off Main St). 228.4499

3 The Morning Glory Cafe ★$$ It's worth venturing down this gauntlet of tourist-oriented "art" studios to splurge on breakfast (eggs in various exotic guises, such as *à la Genovese,* or an "ecstasy sandwich" of French toast made of Portuguese bread with sweetened cream cheese). Lunch features somewhat pricey but scrumptious sandwiches, such as the muffaletta (focaccia with caponata, mozzarella, prosciutto, and roasted red peppers) or a veggie pita stuffed with "broccamole" (*hummus*-like broccoli spread). For dinner, there are designer pizzas (e.g., "potato pepperoni" dressed up with pesto and fresh rosemary) and entrées as elaborate as Cajun honey-roasted duckling breast served over arugula with a rhubarb confit. Whatever the hour or hankering, you should be able to come up with a match. The dining room proper features blond-wood booths and a farm-motif mural, but most people favor the outdoor deck, set amid a crushed-shell walkway. ♦ International ♦ Breakfast, lunch, and dinner; breakfast and lunch only early Sept to mid-Oct. Closed mid-Oct to late May. 15 Old South Wharf. 228.2212

3 Wharf Cottages $$$$ These 25 properties, sprinkled through **Old South** and **Swain's** wharves, are nautically compact but charm incarnate, with crisp navy-and-white decor and a sitting area and garden, however tiny. Each sleeps two to eight and you can bring your own boat; docking facilities are offered. ♦ Closed mid-Oct to late May. New Whale St (between Main and Commercial Sts). 228.4620

4 Museum of Nantucket History The sturdy brick **Thomas Macy Warehouse,** which was used to outfit ships, was one of the first buildings erected after the Great Fire of 1846. A 13-foot diorama re-creates the pre-conflagration waterfront and recounts the disaster. Other displays chart the island's history from its geologic origins to its present state (there's even a cautionary exhibit of beach trash). Although not of paramount interest in and of itself, the museum offers a good overview of other points of historic interest, a dozen of which are also owned and run by the **Nantucket Historical Association.** If you plan to check out more than two or three sites, it makes sense to purchase a reasonably priced, all-inclusive pass, good for the season, right here at the outset. ♦ Admission. Daily 10AM-5PM, 7-10PM mid-June to early Sept; daily 11AM-3PM late May to mid-June, early Sept to mid-Oct; call for hours mid-Oct to mid-Dec. Straight Wharf. 228.3889

5 The Club Car ★★★$$$$ The bar part is a real train car (from the narrow-gauge that used to run to Sconset), and here pianist **Scott Olsen** holds forth nightly. The adjoining dining room is much more haute: Ossetra caviar figures among the appetizers, as do—less pricily—cold, grilled marinated scallops with lobster vinaigrette. Chef **Michael Shannon** keeps in mind that, even on Nantucket, fine diners appreciate an occasional break from seafood, so the menu also features premium veal, sweetbreads, sirloin, lamb, and squab, all inventively accoutered, in addition to salmon, soft-shells, and swordfish. The "curry Bombay" makes for an unusual surf-and-turf combo: chicken, shrimp, and lobster, with traditional accompaniments of basmati rice, *masoor dal,* and *papadums.* ♦ International ♦ Dinner. Closed Tuesday and Wednesday mid-May to July, mid-Sept to early Dec; closed early Dec to mid-May. 1 Main St (at Easy St). 228.1101

6 Pacific Club This three-story brick building was built as a counting house and warehouse in 1772 by shipowner **William Rotch,** whose *Beaver* and *Dartmouth* carried the English tea that was dumped during the **Boston Tea Party.** The *Beaver* later became the first whaler to round Cape Horn. Rotch himself achieved some notoriety in defending the case of a slave whose name survives simply as **"Boston."** Boston's master, **William Swain,** attached his earnings at the end of a successful whaling voyage; Boston sued to reclaim the money and, with Rotch seeing to his defense, was granted his freedom as well. (Although a few slaves numbered among the early settlers, Quaker disapproval had all but eradicated the practice by the 1770s.) In 1789, the building became one of the first **U.S. Customs Service's** houses, and in the mid-1800s it was turned into a club exclusively for captains of the Pacific whaling fleet. The club survives, as a social rather than a professional entity, and the building also houses the **Nantucket Chamber of Commerce,** which—among other activities—fields lodging requests. ♦ Chamber of Commerce: M-F 8AM-6PM, Sa 11AM-4PM late May to early Sept; M-F 9AM-5PM early Sept to late Apr; M-F 8AM-6PM late Apr to late May. Main and S. Water Sts. 228.3643

Among the animals you *won't* find on Nantucket are squirrels, chipmunks, raccoons, foxes, weasels, skunks, muskrats, and porcupines; deer and rabbits are plentiful, though, as are colorful pheasants.

Restaurants/Clubs: Red **Hotels:** Blue
Shops/ Outdoors: Green **Sights/Culture:** Black

For nos. 57-66, see pg. 158
Indian Ave.
Jefferson Ave.
Bathing Beach Rd.
Lincoln Ave.
Hulbert Ave.
Charles St.
Walsh St.
Dix St.
Johnson St.
James St.
Henry St.
N. Beach St.
Highland St.
Grant St.
Nantucket Ave.
Cabot Ln.
Walsh St.
Willard St.
Delaney St.
Cliff Rd.
E. Lincoln Ave.
Derrymore Rd.
N. Liberty St.
Swain St.
Folgers Ln.
North Ave.
Hite Hill Ln.
Easton St.
Wyar's Ln.
Mackay Wy.
Harbor View Wy.
Sunset Hill Rd.
Chester St.
N. Water St.
S. Beach St.
West Chester Rd.
Gull Island St.
Wesco Pl.
Centre St.
Sea St.
Lily St.
Step Ln.
Whalers Ln.
Franklin St.
Church Ct.
Ash St.
Ash Ln.
Academy Ave.
Easy St.
S. Water St.
Westminster St.
Gay St.
Broad St.
Grove Ln.
Oak St.
Chestnut St.
Quince St.
Liberty St.
Hussey St.
Federal St.
New Ln.
Brocks Ct.
India St.
Rose Ln.
Union St.
Liberty Ln.
Woodbury Ln.
Liberty St.
Winter St.
Walnut Ln.
Main St.
Stone Alley
Barnabas Ln.
Lowell Pl.
Howard Ct.
Quarter Mill Hill St.
Gardner St.
Rays Ct.
Fair St.
Orange St.
Main St.
Howard St.
Traders Ln.
Moores Ct.
Lucretia Mott Ln.
Madaket Rd.
Quaker Rd.
Summer St.
School St.
Martins Ln.
Pleasant Ave.
Charter St.
Bloom St.
Plumb Ln.
Hiller St.
High St.
Vestal St.
Darling St.
Tattle Ct.
Vestal St.
Cooper Ln.
Saratoga Ln.
Farmer St.
Pine St.
Twin St.
Lyon St.
Winn St.
Mt. Vernon St.
Candle House Ln.
Jefferson Ln.
Mill St.
New Mill St.
Angola St.
Eagle Ln.
Prospect St.
Silver St.
Joy St.
Milk St.
Chicken Hill St.
S. Mill St.
W. Dover St.
N. Mill St.
Mill Hill Park
W. York St.
1 2 3 4 5 6 7 8 9 10 11 12 13 14 15 16 17 18 19 20 21 22 23 24 25 26 27 28 29 30 31 32 33 34 35 36 37 38 39 40 41 42 43 44 45 46 47 48 49 50 51 52 54 55 56

NANTUCKET

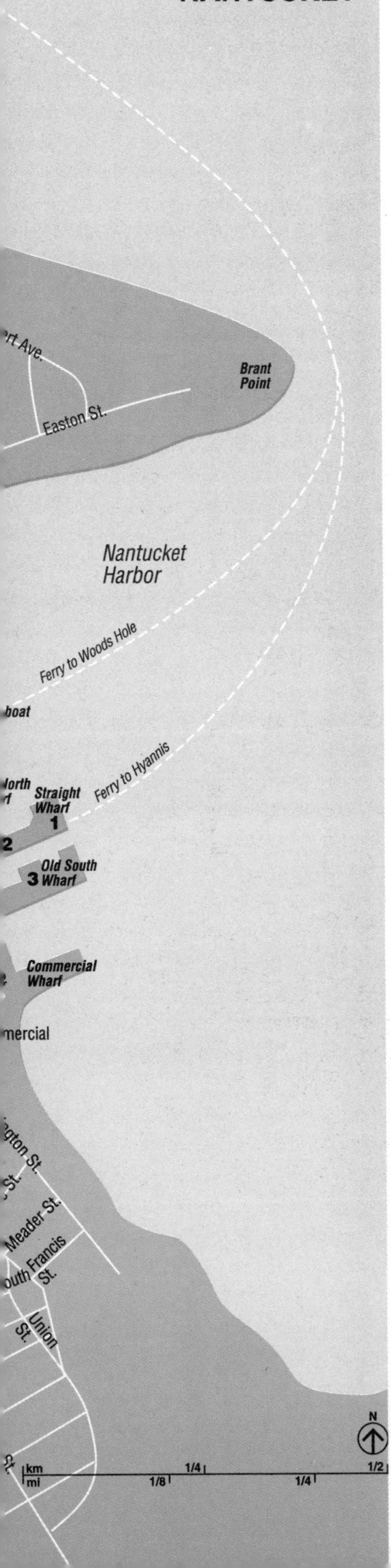

Brant Point
Easton St.
Nantucket Harbor
Ferry to Woods Hole
Ferry to Hyannis
Straight Wharf
1
2
Old South Wharf
3
Commercial Wharf
Meader St.
Francis St.
Union St.
N
km 1/4 1/2
mi 1/8 1/4

7 Main Street Gallery Like many a seaside resort community, Nantucket tends to foster pretty imagery more than serious art. **Reggie Levine** has an eye for the exceptional, and exhibits works that strike out in new directions, from **Will Berry's** inchoate colorist landscapes and figures (which invite the viewer to fill in from memory or desire) to **John Devaney's** often surreal subaqueous portraiture, where the subject may turn out to be an unexpected species. Of the 20 or so artists Levine represents, each receives a week-long show, and all generally have several pieces on view throughout the summer. As president of the **Nantucket Arts Alliance,** Levine works year-round to maximize the impact of the arts on the island, and vice versa. ♦ Daily 9AM-6PM June-Sept; call for hours Oct-May. 2 S. Water St (at Main St). 228.2252

8 Erica Wilson Needle Works When designer **Erica Wilson,** author of more than a dozen books and star of both a PBS and a BBC series, came to Nantucket in 1958, within a few years of graduating from London's **Royal School of Needlework,** the Historical Association commissioned her to provide period textiles for the newly restored **Jared Coffin House.** She stayed on, opening this casual counterpart to her Madison Avenue boutique and offering hands-on guidance for hundreds of grateful adepts. The shop spills over with her latest enthusiasms: not just the needlepoint kits one would expect (although these are abundant, and feature designers she admires as well as her own handiwork), but richly textured sweaters, sweet smocked baby clothes, home accessories both silly and recherché (check out the **Gianni Versace** china), and her latest discovery, from **Kitsch 'n Couture:** colorful shifts, shorts, and shirts fashioned from '40s-era tablecloths. Nantucket has many other, more high-concept shops focusing on home design, but this one is especially warm and welcoming, and an impulse purchase could just become a fulfilling project. ♦ Daily 9AM-10PM mid-June to mid-Sept; daily 9:30AM-5:30PM Apr to mid-June and mid-Sept to Jan. 25 Main St (between Union and Federal Sts). 228.9881

The fishing trawlers' most prolific, and least popular, catch is dogfish, a small and aggressive shark with skin like sandpaper. They wreak havoc on nets and have no domestic market.

9 Stephen Swift Although certain influences are evident (from Queen Anne to Shaker), **Stephen Swift's** fine hand-fashioned furniture (like the chair pictured here) is far too individualized to pass as reproduction—not that he'd want it to. Such is its classicism, though, that his work would blend in at the most traditional of homes, or just as easily adapt to a modern setting. Among his signature pieces are wavy-backed Windsor chairs and benches (as sturdy as the original but more comfortable) and delicate, pared-down four-posters that would dress up any bedroom. At the top of the line ($4,200) is a "scallop" bed with hand-carved headboard. Also appealing are his dressers with graduated drawers, and "huntboards" that conjure visions of lavish breakfast buffets. You can wander about this spare and roomy second-floor space, mentally furnishing your dreamhouse. ♦ M-Sa 9AM-5PM. 34 Main St (at Federal St). 228.0255

9 Espresso Cafe ★★$ But for the relentless eddy of ravenous devotees, this self-service restaurant resembles an old-fashioned ice cream parlor, with tin ceilings, black-and-white tile floor, and little marble tables. You can get ice cream all right (trendy **Ben & Jerry's**), but the main reason to stop in is to partake of the tastiest and most affordably priced grazing food on the island, from impromptu frittatas, quiches, and pizzas to an ever-changing array of hearty international dishes scrawled on the blackboard. The pastries, starting with morning croissants and culminating in a ne plus ultra lemon almond pound cake, are superb; regulars scoop up the "day olds," charitably reduced to half-price and just as delicious. They also know that hidden behind the restaurant is a secluded patio where you can linger as long as you like, shielded from the upscale hurly-burly of Main Street. ♦ International/Takeout ♦ Breakfast, lunch, and dinner. 40 Main St (at Federal St). 228.6930. Take-out store at: Fast Forward, 117 Orange St. 228.5807

9 Mayo & McClure Nantucket abounds in clothing stores for women, ranging from Victorian froufrou to country-wholesome to tasteful taupes. Each school has its own appeal; however, regardless of bent, a certain similarity invariably creeps in. Here, the selections veer wildly from subdued and sensuous (drapey cottons, linens, rayons, and velvets) to the intentionally outrageous (e.g., tapestry *Cat in the Hat* concoctions). The partners also dabble in Art Deco/moderne home accessories, especially barware, and th retro jazz and blues they favor could well inspire you to take up gimlet making. ♦ Daily 10AM-10PM late May to early Sept; Tu-Sa 10AM-5PM early Sept to Jan; call for hours Jan to mid-Apr; Sa-Su 10AM-5PM mid-Apr t late May. 44 Main St (between Federal and Orange Sts). 228.1258

9 Golden Basket Glenaan Elliott originated the miniature golden lightship basket in 1977, and although the concept has since been copied, her designs are still the most delicately proportioned and exquisitely made; each has working handles and hinges, and comes with a tiny gold penny tucked inside. Basic baskets in gold run roughly $200 to $1,600; they're also available in all sorts of variations, including pavé diamond (about $10,000). Be sure to check out the other local charms, such as a golden whelk shell lined in delicate pink porcelain. ♦ Daily 9AM-10PM July to early Sept; daily 9AM-5PM early Sept to July. 44 Main St (between Federal and Orange St). 228.4344, 800/582.8205. Also at: Straight Wharf, Nantucket. 228.1019; Kelly and Dock Sts, Edgartown. 627.4459; 827 Main St, Osterville 428.1016

10 Tonkin of Nantucket Brass and silver knickknacks are a forte of this perennially well-stocked antiques store, an island fixture since 1971. Many of the rarefied trappings seem to derive from English manor houses, but there are a few native artifacts on hand, such as a marvelous sculpted fairgrounds pig ($3,350) and a select assortment of antique lightship baskets. ♦ M-Sa 9AM-5PM. 33 Main St (between Federal and Centre Sts). 228.9697

10 Force 5 Water Sports Christopher and **Francie Bovers'** shop rides the surfer mystique, with up-to-the-minute music to browse by and a full line of wetsuits, windsurfers, boogieboards, and surfboards for sale or rent; kayaks, Sunfish, and Daysailers are also available, as are lessons in the various pursuits. The bathing suit selection is the best in town, and for off-water wintertime wandering there are plenty of Patagonia cover-ups. Kids are catered to, with minuscule Aqua Socks starting at size 3 and plenty of polar-fleece bunting for brisk days at the beach. ♦ Daily 9AM-10PM mid-June to Aug; call for hours Oct to mid-June. 37 Main St (between Federal and Centre Sts). 228.0700. Also at: Jetties Beach. 228.5358

10 Arno's ★★$$$ Arno's has long been a reliable if uninspired choice for an in-town meal. New owners **Jeanne** and **Richard Diamond** and **Jeff Evans** have spiffed it up quite a bit. Overscale paintings of bathers and tennis buffs by **Molly Dee,** like sepia-toned blowups of vintage photos, enliven the brick walls, and a tall, spiky flower adds style to each glass-topped table. The menu is looking livelier, too, starting with lobster-Boursin omelets for breakfast and culminating in a "Nantucket Mixed Grill"—grilled swordfish, scallops, shrimp, and linguica—with a cranberry barbecue sauce. The windowed storefront right on Main Street still creates a slight fishbowl effect; the difference is, now onlookers are peering in enviously. ♦ American/Takeout ♦ Breakfast, lunch, and dinner. 41 Main St (between Federal and Centre Sts). 228.7001

11 Mitchell's Book Corner The "hand selling" of books is an endangered art, but **Mimi Beman** (who took over this bookstore from her parents in 1978) is an avid practitioner, matchmaking for regular customers and steering drop-ins straight to the appropriate shelf: "I don't have to look on a computer," she says, "to know what we have in the store." If you're hoping to get to know the island in depth, head back to the **Nantucket Room,** where you'll find every conceivable title on island lore (including some out-of-print gems), plus tomes on whaling, yachting, and the sea in general. ♦ Daily 9AM-10PM mid-June to mid-Sept; M-Sa 9:30AM-6PM, Su 10AM-4PM mid-Sept to Jan, Apr to mid-June; M-Sa 9:30AM-5PM Jan-Mar. 54 Main St (at Orange St). 228.1080

12 Essense A colorful fellow by the solo moniker of **Harpo** (there's a definite resemblance) is behind this unusual store. A self-professed "nose," he has assembled 180 essential oils with which he can duplicate designer scents or customize blends; uncut by alcohol (unlike their commercial counterparts, which typically consist of 94 percent alcohol), these perfumes purportedly do not cause associated problems such as allergies and headaches—and instead of rapidly vaporizing, they linger on the skin. You'll get the full rap while being treated to a free dab on the wrist. Says Harpo: "We do people, and then kick them out so they'll come back—amazed at how long the scent lasted." These "elixirs" can also be mixed with various bases to create moisturizers, soaps, shampoos, conditioners, and massage oils; there's even a **Kama Sutra** line, which you can sample in the Weekender package. The shop, which looks like an ancient pharmacy, is actually a neologism fashioned from recycled mantelpieces and doors. Harpo, who started out in St. John and Martha's Vineyard (that branch is now a franchise), is loath to discuss his clientele but admits to creating a custom scent for a certain megastar who also goes by one name, this one starting with an M. ♦ Daily 10AM-10PM mid-Apr to Oct; M-Th, Su 10AM-6PM, F-Sa 10AM-10PM Nov-Dec; Sa-Su 10AM-5PM Jan to mid-Apr. 5 Centre St (at Rose Ln). 325.4740, 800/223.8660. Also at: 38 N. Water St, Edgartown, Martha's Vineyard. 627.3840

13 The Boarding House ★★★$$$$ This is one terrific restaurant, topped only by its own bar and sidewalk cafe, a magnet for low-key socializing late into summer evenings. The restaurant is set slightly below ground and, with its arched walls, feels like a sanctum. That sense is reinforced by the creations of chef **Seth Raynor** (a graduate of the **New England Culinary Institute**), who straddles the fine line between stark, bold flavors and "comfort" foods: e.g., grilled quail with crisp-fried onion rings, or lobster tail with mashed new potatoes and beurre blanc. Several of the restaurant's greatest hits, including a sublime lobster bisque, reappear on the bistro menu for stylish off-hours snacking. ♦ New American ♦ Dinner. Closed Tuesday; closed Jan-Feb. Call for schedule Mar-May, mid-Oct to Jan. 12 Federal St (at India St). 228.9622

13 Company of the Cauldron ★★★$$$$ If atmosphere is what you seek, look for this vest-pocket restaurant lit by sconces and tin lanterns. Lavish flowers and a few apt antique decorative elements impart an elegant mood. The prix fixe menu—there's only one—changes daily, and is set a week ahead, so you can call to pick the optimal night (perhaps one when the harpist is playing). The well-considered cuisine, issuing from a home-size kitchen, is such that every night's a good night, as the full house of convivial diners—there are two seatings nightly—will attest. ♦ New American ♦ Dinner. Closed Monday; closed mid-Oct to late May. 7 India St (between Federal and Centre Sts). Reservations requested. 228.4016

"The humpback," Melville wrote in *Moby-Dick,* "is the most gamesome and lighthearted of all the whales, making more gay foam and white water generally than any other of them."

Restaurants/Clubs: Red **Hotels:** Blue
Shops/ Outdoors: Green **Sights/Culture:** Black

13 DeMarco ★★★$$$$ Downstairs, with its dark wood paneling, is too taverny a space to do justice to *haute* Italian; see if you can secure a table on the lofty second floor. Once ensconced, you can enjoy exquisite antipasti and pasta (e.g., lemon fettuccine with poached lobster, chanterelle mushrooms, cognac, and asparagus) and bracing *secondi,* such as roast rack of lamb drizzled with basil-infused olive oil and accompanied by an eggplant Napoleon. The entrées are among the priciest around, but the clientele is not exactly pinching pennies. ♦ Northern Italian ♦ Dinner. Closed Oct-Apr. 9 India St (between Federal and Centre Sts). Reservations required. 228.1836

14 Obadiah's ★★$$$ **Andrew** and **Lynda Willauer,** who turned this 1840s captain's house into a restaurant in 1978, started out with modest but admirable ambitions: to serve good seafood at good prices. They've succeeded all these years. Eat outdoors, on an awning-covered brick patio with punched-tin lanterns and hanging baskets, or indoors, in an atmospheric brick-walled cellar. "No pretense" is the unspoken code: the servers are friendly and responsive, and you can choose from about 20 traditionally derived entrées, such as pan-cooked, cornmeal-coated yellowtail sole. Dinners come with native-grown accompaniments (perhaps homey mashed red potatoes) and a regularly replenished bread basket featuring addictive cranberry bread. That same concoction turns up in a delectable bread pudding, and other sweet endings include strawberry shortcake and "Obadiah's Bad Bad Dessert," a dark chocolate cake with mocha frosting, topped with walnuts, coconut, and whipped cream. Whether you partake or not, you'll feel very good by meal's end, and even after the check arrives. ♦ New England/Takeout ♦ Lunch and dinner. Closed late Sept to mid-June. 2 India St (between Federal and Centre Sts). 228.4430

14 Lynda Willauer Antiques You'd have to look far and wide for a better selection of American and English furniture, all painstakingly tagged as to provenance and state of repair. Slant-front desks are a particular interest: these might range from a mahogany Chippendale ($4,800) to an 18th-century North Shore example ($15,000). Other specialties include Chinese export porcelain, majolica, paintings, samplers, quilts, and brass and tortoiseshell accessories. Take your time and browse at length; it will be worthwhile, if only in terms of aesthetic pleasure. ♦ M-Sa 10AM-6PM July-Aug; daily 10AM-6PM late May to July, early to late Sept. 2 India St (between Federal and Centre Sts). 228.3631

The Gallery

14 The Gallery at Four India Street The work displayed in this bright second-story space is quite traditional: even the 15 contemporary artists shown (such as landscape painter **John Osborne**) visibly demonstrate their allegiance to 19th-century schools of painting. Most of the pieces are n[o] homages, but the real thing (for example, a **Rembrandt Peale** portrait priced at $37,000). There's also a smattering of antiques: a few decoys, silver cigarette cases, Bakelite bracelets—whatever happens to catch galler[y] director **Kathleen Knight's** eye. ♦ M-Sa 10AM-5PM Feb-Dec. 4 India St (between Federal and Centre Sts). 228.8509

15 Nantucket Atheneum In 1836, two small library associations, motivated by "the desire we have to promote the Cultivation of Literature, the Sciences and Arts and thereby advance the best interests of our Native town," formed a "proprietorship" to create a temple of learning. Local savant **Maria Mitchell,** then only 18, was appointed the firs[t] librarian. When the first building and all its contents were lost to the Great Fire, the proprietors rebuilt within six months, funded by donations that poured in from across the country. Local architect **Frederick Brown Coleman** (whose previous credits included the "Two Greeks," a pair of showplace house[s] on upper Main Street), designed this exemplary 1847 Greek Revival building, fronted by fluted Ionic columns. **Ralph Waldo Emerson** gave the inaugural address, to be followed by visits—at Mitchell's instigation—by such luminaries as **Henry David Thoreau, Horace Greeley, Louis Agassiz, John James Audubon, Herman Melville,** and **Frederick Douglass.** All the vital topics of the day, from abolition to suffrage, were heatedly discussed upstairs in the Great Hall, which also hosted concerts and "theatricals."

The tradition of lectures and readings continues to this day, not only in the multihued hall (painted mustard yellow with mauve, violet, green, and gold trim) but, in summer, in the adjoining garden. The library itself (which, although privately funded in part, doubles as the town's public library) contains some 40,000 volumes, including many rare 19th-century books and manuscripts; venerable portraits and display cases full of whaling and shipping artifacts ar[e] on hand to remind visitors of the community's illustrious history. ♦ Great Hall: Tu, Sa 9:30AM-noon, Th 2-5PM; call for schedule of public events. Library: M, W-F 9:30AM-4:30PM, Tu 9:30AM-8PM, Sa 9:30AM-1PM. Lower India St (between Federal and S. Water Sts). 228.1110

16 21 Federal ★★★$$$$ A sensation ever since it opened in 1985, this austere yet handsome restaurant is still going strong after several changes of chefs. Paneled dining rooms, illumined by pewter sconces, fill the 1847 Greek Revival house, and in summer the feasting overflows onto a flowery courtyard. The menu changes weekly, but you might encounter the likes of salmon tartare with buckwheat blinis and caviar, or potato-crusted salmon; the flavors are robust and uncomplicated, and all the more memorable. Desserts are also inspired; consider a simple yet artful gingerbread with apples, caramel, and cider sabayon. ♦ New American ♦ Lunch and dinner. Closed Jan-Mar. 21 Federal St (at Oak St). Reservations recommended. 228.2121

17 Dreamland Theatre This much-moved building started out at 76 Main Street as the **Atlantic Hall,** a Quaker meetinghouse that was the largest building in the rebuilt town; it then became the **Atlantic Straw Company** (a hat factory), was transported to Brant Point to serve as the central building of the **Nantucket Hotel,** and, after being floated across the harbor by barge, ended up here in 1905. The drab interior gives no hint of the structure's colorful former lives, but the steady stream of first-run movies, changing every other day or so, are a summertime staple. ♦ Daily 7PM, 9PM (generally) June-Sept. 19 S. Water St (at Oak St). 228.5356

17 Claire Murray As a New York transplant running a Nantucket B&B in the late 1970s, **Claire Murray** took up the traditional art of hooking rugs to see her through the slow season. She proved so well suited to the task, especially the design element, that she now runs a retail company grossing $3 million a year. Too busy creating new collections (**Winterthur, Colonial Williamsburg,** and the **Museum Folk Art Collection** have all inspired special lines), she has 300 "hookers" working for her around the world. Of course, customers can also hook their own: kits costing about two-thirds the price of finished rugs (a few hundred dollars to over $1,000) come with complimentary lessons in case you get hopelessly entangled. In addition to needle arts supplies, this pretty store (the first of five so far, coast to coast) stocks ready-made quilts and sweaters, hand-painted furniture, flowery tableware, and Nantucket Wildflowers toiletries and scented stationery. One gets the sense that Murray is just warming up, with a world of island-inspired home accents still to come. ♦ M-Sa 10AM-6PM, Su 10AM-4PM June-Sept; call for hours Oct-May. 11 S. Water St (at India St). 228.1913. Also at: 867 Main St, Osterville. 420.3562

18 Vincent's Italian Restaurant ★★$$$ It would be a shame to overlook this 1954 establishment (pictured here) just because it looks run-of-the-mill, with its red-and-white-checked tablecloths and the obligatory Chianti bottles strung from the rafters. Plenty of restaurants offer more polished Italian food, but you'd be hard-pressed to come up with stuff this all-out good. Vincent's has kept up with the times, offering, for example, a killer white pizza loaded with ricotta and roast garlic, and some very tasty neo-pastas, such as scallops pesto *primavera* and grilled swordfish *puttanesca.* Then again, the traditional dishes (seafood canelloni, risotto *pescatore,* and many more) are just as mouth-watering. There's a good reason why you'll see so many young couples and families packed in here: it's one of the few places in town where you can eat your fill for under $20. ♦ Italian/Takeout ♦ Breakfast, lunch, and dinner; call for schedule mid-Jan to early Apr, Nov to mid-Dec. Closed mid-Dec to mid-Jan. 21 S. Water St (between Oak and Broad Sts). 228.0189

19 The Juice Bar You can indeed get juice here, from lemonade to fresh carrot—and pastries, too. But most people come for the homemade ice cream, in such tantalizing flavors as mocha macadamia nut brittle, preferably in the form of a "minisundae" (quite substantial) cloaked in homemade hot fudge. A word of warning: Once you've tasted one, you'll be gravitating back every night till the ferry carries you off. ♦ Daily 8AM-11PM Apr to early Dec. 12 Broad St (at S. Water St). 228.5799

Architectural historian Clair Baisley approaches the challenge of dating Cape houses with a grain of salt. "Except for Ranch houses, Garrison houses and other obvious productions of the 1900s," she writes in *Cape Cod Architecture* (Parnassus Imprints, 1986), "all houses on Cape Cod are at least two hundred and fifty years old, and about one third of them are the oldest house in town."

20 **Young's Bicycle Shop** Since 1931, transients right off the boat have been coming here to outfit themselves with the quintessential Nantucket accessory: a bike. Three-speed clunkers with "baskets 'n bells" should suit the merely curious; serious sportifs might spring for purple Cannondale mountain bikes (the rates are quite reasonable). Young's also rents scooters, cars, and Jeeps, but keep in mind that Nantucket is a small island, best seen up close and quietly. Even if you're not planning to pedal, stop in to see their collection of antique two-wheelers. ♦ Daily 8AM-8PM early July to early Sept; daily 8AM-6PM early Sept to early July. Steamboat Wharf (between S. Beach and Easy Sts). 228.1151

21 **Nantucket House Antiques** When many of the *antiquaires* along the main drag have added mass-produced "country" accessories to cater to the tourists, it's nice to find this shop still full of genuine treasures—including, for instance, a 1720 oak chest on stand (asking price: $65,000). Most of the stock is a lot more affordable: a 1740 burled mulberry chest or 1780 fruitwood slant-front desk, for example, each under $10,000. From the ivy-patterned majolica to the rugged trestle tables, everything's so well chosen, you can't help picturing the rooms these items were meant to grace. To help with the visualization, owners **Sandy** and **Hudson Holland, Jr.**, also offer an interior design service. ♦ Daily 9:30AM-12:30PM, 2:30-5:30PM June to early Sept; daily 10AM-12:30PM, 2:30-5PM late Apr to June, early Sept to early Dec; call for hours early Dec to late Apr. 1 S. Beach St (between Broad St and Whalers Ln). 228.4604

21 **The Second Story** ★★★$$$$ Virtually unknown to off-islanders, this intimate second-floor restaurant overlooks a cluster of tennis courts and the Sound beyond. Painted a moody marbleized teal, it's a refreshing spot for Sunday brunch and a romantic hideaway at dinner. Chef-owner **David B. Toole** scans the globe in search of exciting ideas to spark his menu, which changes almost daily. Predominant influences are Asian, Southwestern, and European; you might start, for instance, with Vietnamese scallop and red pepper wontons and move on to grilled pork tenderloin with roasted corn and black bean salsa, or perhaps Ligurian-style braised salmon with white beans and saffron. Even the desserts are multicultural: to wit, an "Asian Napoleon" fashioned from fried wontons and citrus pastry cream. For armchair adventurers, it's a heady whirlwind tour. ♦ International ♦ Dinner; brunch also o[n] weekends. Call for schedule mid-Sept to Jun[e]. 1 S. Beach St (between Broad St and Whaler[s] Ln). Reservations recommended. 228.3471

22 **Peter Foulger Museum** While researchers toil in the archives upstairs, the **Nantucket Historical Association (NHA)** mounts temporary exhibits on the ground floor of this 1971 brick building (cleverly camouflaged to resemble the older buildings that surround it) recently, for instance, the NHA solicited islanders' attic caches of China Trade artifacts. **Peter Foulger** was an early settler who served as an interpreter when settlers were negotiating to purchase land from the natives in 1659; his daughter **Abiah** gave birth to **Benjamin Franklin.** Other members of his distinguished line include astronomer **Maria Mitchell,** abolitionist **Lucretia Mott,** and coffee mogul **James Folger,** all born on Nantucket. ♦ Admission. Daily 10AM-5PM mid-June to early Sept; daily 11AM-3PM late May to mid-June, early Sept to mid-Oct. 15 Broad St (at N. Water St). 228.1894

"Nantucket! Take out your map and look at it," Melville enjoined in *Moby-Dick*. "See what a real corner of the world it occupies; how it stands there, away off shore . . . a mere hillock, an elbow of sand, all beach without a background." Melville himself had done little more than pull out a map and listen to some wild whaling tales before penning his epic novel. He had never visited Nantucket when he wrote about it, instead drawing on characters from his own voyage aboard the *Acushnet* out of New Bedford, and adapting the story line from the tragic tale of Captain George Pollard, Jr., whose whaleship, the *Essex,* sank in the Pacific in 1819 after twice being front-ended by an 85-foot sperm whale. Pollard and a handful of his 19-man crew survived three months at sea, eventually resorting to cannibalism; the cabinboy, his nephew, was the first to be consumed. (First-mate Owen Chase recorded their ordeal.) Pollard went to sea once more, was again shipwrecked, and retired to Nantucket to work as a night watchman. On first visiting the island in 1855, the year after his novel was published, Melville caught a glimpse of the elderly Pollard looming through the fog, and on inquiring as to his identity, was shaken by the sight of this "most impressive man," whom by now islanders regarded as "a nobody."

22 Whaling Museum Housed in a former spermaceti-candle factory, this museum is a must-visit; if not for the awe-inspiring skeleton of a 43-foot finback whale (stranded in the '60s), then for the exceptional collections of scrimshaw and nautical art (check out the action painting *Ship Spermo of Nantucket in a Heavy Thunder-Squall on the Coast of California 1876,* executed by a captain who survived). A map occupying one entire wall depicts the round-the-world meanderings of the *Alpha,* accompanied by related log entries. The price of admission includes several lectures, scheduled throughout the day, that give a brief and colorful history of the industry, starting with the beachside "whalebecue" feasts natives and settlers enjoyed when a cetacean happened to ground. Pursued to its logical conclusion, this booming business ultimately led to the tragic near-extirpation of some extraordinary species, but that story must await another museum; this one is full of the glories of the hunt. There's quite a nice gift shop, too. ♦ Admission. Daily 10AM-5PM late May to mid-Oct; call for hours mid-Oct to Jan; Sa-Su 11AM-3PM Jan-Mar. 13 Broad St (at N. Water St). 228.1736

23 Le Languedoc Restaurant ★★★$$$$ At street level there's a pleasant patio; upstairs, a cluster of small formal dining rooms (some painted a deep tomato red); and downstairs a casual bistro with Breuer chairs and blue-and-white-checked tablecloths. Don't expect Provençale homilies: this is highly competitive contemporary cuisine (e.g., porcini-dusted rack of lamb *persillade* with quinoa pudding), accordingly priced. The cafe menu, on the other hand, lends itself to low-capital ventures—for instance, the lobster scallion hash with saffron aioli—and some very impressive wines are available by the glass. ♦ New American ♦ Lunch May to late June; dinner July-Oct. Closed Monday May to late June, mid-Sept to mid-Dec; closed Sunday mid-Apr to July, Nov to mid-Dec; closed mid-Dec to mid-Apr. 24 Broad St (between Centre and Federal Sts). Jacket advised and reservations recommended for dining room. 228.2552

23 Cioppino's ★★$$$$ This newer restaurant (opened in '92) also has a pretty side patio, and a houseful of handsome dining rooms painted the faintest of mauves; the upstairs is especially nice, illumined by a skylight and enhanced by a large garden diptych by local painter **William Welch.** Aside from the namesake dish (a spicy San Franciscan shellfish stew), the approach is mostly evolved Continental: Nantucket bay scallops *niçoise,* wild mushroom vol-au-vent, tournedos Roselli (with lobster and lemon hollandaise). The garden's great for late-night drinks and desserts, whether sensible mango sorbet or go-for-broke warm pecan pie with bourbon ice cream. ♦ New American ♦ Lunch and dinner; Sunday brunch. Closed mid-Oct to mid-May. 20 Broad St (between Centre and Federal Sts). 228.4622

24 Jared Coffin House $$ If there were posthumous awards for trying to please one's spouse, **Jared Coffin** would surely qualify. A wealthy shipowner, he built this grand three-story brick house, the largest in town, in 1845 because his wife decided that their original home, **Moor's End** (built in 1834 at Mill and Pleasant streets, now privately owned), was too remote to suit her social aspirations. After living in their new mansion only two years, the Coffins decamped for the more civilized pleasures of Boston, leaving their showplace —with its impressive Ionic portico (illustrated above) and lofty cupola—to become an inn. Had Mrs. Coffin only stuck around another century-plus, she would have seen her dream realized, for the Jared Coffin House has indeed become the social center of town—not just because it's such a popular place to go, but because innkeeper **Phil Read,** who leased the inn from the **Nantucket Historical Trust** in 1963 and bought it in 1976, has been such an active force in promoting tourism and ensuring that visitors get the warmest possible welcome. In fact, as soon as you've checked into the antique-filled lobby, you'll probably be steered to the full-time concierge, who can tell you what's going on and what has been going on for the past three centuries.

The house itself has 11 gracious rooms; 45 more are distributed among five surrounding houses, the most elegant of which is the 1841 Greek Revival **Harrison Gray House,** named for the owner of the whaleship *Nantucket.* Queen-size canopy beds are the norm, but some very reasonably priced singles are scattered about, a boon for solo explorers. ♦ 29 Broad St (at Centre St). 228.2405, 800/248.2405

Within the Jared Coffin House:

Jared's ★★$$$$ Decorated with nautical paintings and a 19th-century portrait of the Coffin grandchildren, its salmon walls aglow with candlelight, this formal dining room is ideal for a dressy night out—even if the culinary output can be uneven. You might encounter, for instance, a celestial lobster bisque, followed by an undressed salad garnish or lamb that's more charred than grilled. The hits outnumber the misses, though, and you've got to grant points for originality: consider the Nantucket blue salad, with spinach and bleu cheese in a blueberry vinaigrette. It was not so long ago that this dining room was as stuffy as it looks (side dishes included an "appropriate starch"); customers willing to ride out the growing pains will be rewarded in the long run. Meanwhile, the breakfasts manage to maintain the beloved traditions (eggs Benedict, prime rib hash) while introducing such yummy innovations as lemon blueberry bread French toast with pecan honey butter. ♦ New American ♦ Breakfast and dinner; Sunday brunch; breakfast only Monday through Thursday and Sunday Oct-Dec, May. Closed Monday. Reservations and jacket recommended. 228.2400

The Tap Room ★$$ If you miss the old standards, you have only to head downstairs to this dark-paneled pub for chowder, steaks, burgers, fried fish, Welsh rarebit, and the "Pride of New England" combo: fishcakes, baked beans, brown bread, and coleslaw. In summer the same menu is served outdoors on a patio overflowing with flowers. ♦ American ♦ Lunch and dinner. 228.2400

24 Brotherhood of Thieves ★★$$ Look for the lines invariably loitering outside. This low-beamed, semisubterranean 1840 whaling bar (its name derives from an 1844 antislavery pamphlet) is so popular that patrons willingly wait an hour or more to work their way inside, where it's so dark that candles are required in full daylight. What you'll be eating (in case you can't see it) are great burgers, sandwiches, and blackboard specials served with curly fries on pewter plates at plank tables. Folk singers hold forth every weekend (plus a few weekdays in summer), but not so stridently that you can't talk over them. Some tourists penetrate here, but mostly it's a fraternity of long-term Nantucketers. ♦ American ♦ Lunch and dinner. Closed Feb to mid-Mar. 23 Broad St (between Centre and Federal Sts). No phone

25 The Quaker House $$ Congenial owners **Carolyn** and **Bob Taylor** run this pretty seven room B&B right in the center of town—a plus for those who like to be centrally located, maybe a minus for those who prefer to retire early. It's not that the street life is rowdy, but people do tend to stroll and socialize till all hours, and the houses are closely packed. ♦ 5 Chestnut St (at Centre St). 228.0400

Within The Quaker House:

The Quaker House Restaurant ★★$$ Breakfast may strike you as expensive, if elaborate (e.g., baked apple pancakes); however, the four-course prix fixe dinners, from lasagna to tournedos au poivre, are a real bargain for this high-roller town. Two small rooms, with lace curtains and raspberry-pink trim, accommodate 12 tables. ♦ Regional American ♦ Breakfast and dinner. Closed mid-Oct to late May. 228.9156

26 Paul LaPaglia Antique Prints The prints—mostly maritime, botanical, and regional—are companionable, the framing beautifully selected and executed in burled woods and simple gilt. There's also an occasional oil: for instance, a magnificent 1905 portrait of a striped bass by **Charles Storer.** This is an excellent place to pick up a memento of lasting value. ♦ M-Sa 9AM-5PM late May to mid-Oct; call for winter hours. 38 Centre St (at Chestnut St). 228.8760

27 The Off Centre Cafe ★★$$ This tiny restaurant, tucked away in a former meetinghouse turned minimall, is loved for its ornate breakfasts and its skillful Mexican dinners, ranging from burritos and enchiladas to vegetable corn pudding and chicken mole. Chef/owner **Liz Holland** started out at Boston's chic **29 Newbury Street,** and what her eatery lacks in space it makes up for in panache. The breakfasts—featuring such blackboard specials as "strawberry-peach popover with caramel goo"—are enough to revive your will to live. ♦ International/Takeout ♦ Breakfast and dinner; Sunday brunch; breakfast only on Saturday and Sunday mid-Sept to Jan, Apr-May. Closed Jan-Apr. 29 Centre St (at Hussey St). 228.8470

Those peculiar woven purses you see dangling from tanned, moneyed arms are Nantucket lightship baskets, a.k.a.—somewhat disrespectfully—"Nantucket minks." With prices ascending into the thousands and future collectibility virtually assured, these handbags date back to crude baskets fashioned by sailors on lonely "lightship" duty, warning boats off the shoals to the south and east end of the island in the mid-18th century. Back on shore, they refined their craft, and a cottage industry catering to tourists was soon spawned.

28 **United Methodist Church** This slightly derelict but still magnificent 1823 building, with its imposing Doric-columned 1840 facade, is not only an active church but a haven for the performing arts. The basement houses the professional-caliber **Actor's Theatre of Nantucket** (223.6325) founded by islander **Richard Cary** in 1985; upstairs, in a space carved out of the church's back balcony, a tiny proscenium showcases various enterprises, including the **Island Stage** (228.6620) and photographer **Cary Hazlegrove's** long-playing slide presentation "On Island" (228.3783). ♦ Service Su 10AM. 2 Centre St (between Liberty St and Rose Ln). 228.0810

29 **Pacific National Bank** It's business as usual at this elegant 1818 brick bank, spared by the Great Fire. Above the original teller cages are rather vapid murals of the whaling days executed by **Robert Charles Haun** in 1954. Perhaps the most exciting thing ever to have happened here was **Maria Mitchell's** rooftop discovery of a comet in October 1847 (further information on her extraordinary career can be found at the **Maria Mitchell Science Center**). So gently illuminated are the streets, you can still see stars from "downtown"; farther out, the nightly light show is dazzling. ♦ M-F 8:30AM-3PM, Sa 8:30AM-noon June-Oct; M-F 8:30AM-3PM Nov-May. 61 Main St (at Fair St). 228.1917

30 **Murray's Toggery Shop** A town landmark since the early 1900s, this minidepartment store (featured in *The Preppy Handbook*) specializes in **"Nantucket Reds,"** cotton pants, shorts, and skirts guaranteed to fade to a ruddy pink recognized in certain circles as a badge of belonging. Of course, anyone can wander in and buy some; the stuff even comes in baseball caps now, as well as toddlers' overalls. For the most part, the rest of the stock is pretty conservative, with a few nods to junior preps in the form of **Birkenstocks** and **Doc Martens.** Part of this building was the early 1800s shop of **John Macy,** whose son **Roland** worked here before leaving in 1837 to try whaling and gold prospecting; failing in both, he fell back on his sales skills and, in 1858, opened a New York shop that would soon balloon into a retail giant. ♦ M-Sa 9AM-6PM, Su 10AM-6PM mid-Apr to mid-Oct; M-Sa 9AM-5PM, Su 10AM-2PM mid-Oct to Dec; M-Sa 9AM-5PM Jan to mid-Apr. 62 Main St (between Orange and Fair Sts). 228.0437, 800/368.2134. Bargain outlet: New St. 228.3584. Also at: 75 Main St, Vineyard Haven, Martha's Vineyard. 693.2640; 150 Circuit Ave, Oak Bluffs, Martha's Vineyard. 693.2640

31 **Unitarian Universalist Church** A familiar part of the Nantucket "skyline," this 1809 church (in the **National Register of Historic Places**) didn't get its clock until 1823 and its bell (smuggled from Portugal during the War of 1812) until 1830; the 109-foot wooden tower had to be rebuilt to support its ton-plus weight. In 1844, the congregation commissioned Swiss artist **Carl Wendte,** who had recently decorated the original Treasury Building in Washington, DC, to create a trompe l'oeil false dome; newly rich from the whaling trade, they wanted their place of worship to sport a more continental look. The skylight that casts a heavenly glow about the altar was discovered intact during a recent renovation. ♦ Interior: M-Sa 10AM-4PM July to mid-Sept. Service Su 10:45AM. 11 Orange St (at Stone Alley). 228.5466

32 **Four Chimneys** $$$$ The plain facade of this 1835 B&B gives no hint of the lovely proportions inside, much less the Japanese garden hidden in the back. Ten large and beautifully appointed rooms boast canopy beds with down comforters; half have fireplaces as well. The elegant yellow parlor, with crystal chandelier, is flanked by twin fireplaces that add a warming glow to the evening. It's here that you'll be treated to hors d'oeuvres, accompanied by innkeeper **Bernadette Mannix's** recommendations for yet another well-spent day. ♦ Closed Jan-Apr. 38 Orange St (between Plumb Ln and Flora St). 228.1912

33 **The Woodbox Inn** $$ Built in 1709, this shingled house (pictured above) is the oldest inn on the island, and easily the most evocative. The sleeping quarters include seven queen-bedded rooms and two suites with fireplaces. Breakfasts in the keeping room feature delicious egg dishes and popovers. ♦ Closed mid-Oct to June. 29 Fair St (between Hiller and Darling Sts). 228.0587

Within The Woodbox Inn:

The Woodbox Restaurant ★★★$$$$ The three small dining rooms, including a colonial kitchen, are so low-beamed that even small adults have to duck to get through the doorways. It's hard to imagine anything further from dinner theater, yet more dramatic: the two seatings are staged as carefully as a show. Host **Dexter Tutein** ushers guests into dark-paneled rooms set with pewter and flickering by candlelight. Dinner unfolds as a ceremony of classics, from chowder or perhaps home-smoked salmon or goat cheese tart, on to beef Wellington (the Woodbox's signature dish), filet mignon with a cognac, shallot, and black cherry reduction, or grilled quail with a honey and star anise glaze. These are just a few of the mouth-watering choices, and if none of these dishes is cooked over a open hearth, as would have been the custom, they're all the more succulent done the modern way. ♦ Yankee/Continental ♦ Breakfast and dinner; dinner only Monday through Wednesday mid-Oct to Jan. Closed Monday June to mid-Oct; closed Jan-June. Dinner reservations required. 228.0587

34 Ships Inn $$ Whaling captain **Obed Starbuck** built this handsome three-story home in 1831; it would become the birthplace of abolitionist and women's rights activist **Lucretia Coffin Mott.** The exterior is Quaker-plain, the only decoration being the square-paned sidelights surrounding the door. The 12 rooms, all named for Starbuck's ships, are decorated like summerhouse guest rooms—they're not especially fancy but quite comfortable. ♦ Closed mid-Oct to mid-May. 13 Fair St (between Lucretia Mott Ln and School St). 228.0040

Within Ships Inn:

Ships Inn Restaurant ★★★$$$$ This peach-hued restaurant is halfway below street level, but so opened up, with small-paned windows lining two sides, that it feels roomy; the gentle lighting enhances the convivial mood. Chef/owner **Mark Gottwald** has come up with many appealing and healthy dishes, such as a creamless chilled carrot soup with cumin and fresh basil, and grilled tuna with plum sauce and sweet rice. You can abandon your good intentions for dessert: the chocolate soufflé cake and lemon curd tart make a worthwhile downfall. ♦ New American ♦ Dinner. Closed Tuesday; closed early Oct to June. Reservations recommended. 228.0040

35 Quaker Meetinghouse Built as a Friends' school in 1838, this building is simplicity itself, the only decorative element to speak of being the 12-over-12 antique glass windows. Visitors are always welcome at Friends' meetings; sitting in may give you a feel for the high-minded forces that shaped this island during its two most formative centuries. ♦ Service Su 10AM mid-June to mid-Sept. 1 Fair St (between Rays and Moores Cts). 228.0136

35 Fair Street Museum This concrete 1904 annex to the Meetinghouse, owned by the **Nantucket Historical Association** and used to house the collection of the **Nantucket Artists Association**, is an egregious eyesore, all the more shocking for its rarity. Still, no one's likely to complain as long as it provides a safe haven for works by **John Singleton Copley, Gilbert Stuart, Childe Hassam,** and children's illustrator **Tony Sarg.** ♦ F-Sa 11AM-3PM July-Aug. 1 Fair St (between Rays and Moores Cts). 228.0722

36 Macy-Christian House Dry-goods merchant **Thomas Macy** built this lean-to saltbox in 1740 and it stayed in the family until 1827; the **Reverend George P. Christian** and his wife bought it in 1934 and spent years renovating it in the Colonial Revival style. Thus, all is not strictly authentic, but the Christians' collections exert an interest all their own, especially as explicated by knowledgeable guides. They'll point out the lustreware (which in the dim light of an old keeping room really could pass for silver), the Nantucket-made Windsor chairs, and the curious lighting devices, including a cylindrical skater's lantern with mica windows. The upstairs bedrooms are a bit more pure in appearance, but even the overdone kitchen renovation is worth seeing for all the fascinating gadgets it contains—including a "beebox," a trap that helped plunderers track wild bees to their hives. ♦ Admission. Daily 10AM-5PM mid-June to early Sept; daily 11AM-3PM late May to mid-June, early Sept to mid-Oct. 12 Liberty St (at Walnut Ln). 228.1894

Substitute "Jeep" for "calash" and Mary Cushing Edes' 1835 letter home to her sister Charlotte Cushing still rings true: "The streets [of Nantucket] are sandy and they run in every direction. When you go out walking you return with shoes full of dirt, although some of the streets have sidewalks. The houses set any way. Travel over rutted roads is mostly in a calash, a two wheel open box wagon and standing mostly to soften the jolting. It is good fun once in a while but such exercise is not desireable often. You never saw anything like the place."

37 **The Coffin School** Among the original purchasers, **Tristram Coffin** and his wife, **Dionis,** were unusually prolific, producing nine children and 74 grandchildren. When Boston-raised **Sir Isaac Coffin,** a British loyalist, decided to resettle in Nantucket in the early 19th century, he established a school for Coffin descendants, who were estimated at that time to comprise half the island population. (There was no public education offered then, only "cent schools," an arrangement whereby parents paid a penny a day per child to have them taught reading and writing in various homes.) This 1852 brick temple, which replaced the original Fair Street building, is worth visiting not only for its grand Greek Revival architecture, complete with marble columns and steps, but for its collection of paintings by **Elizabeth Rebecca Coffin,** who studied with **Thomas Eakins** (notable among her works is a remarkably retiring self-portrait, in a three-quarters pose, as seen from the back). The basement houses a permanent collection of rather contrived paintings by British marine artist **Rodney Charman** depicting the history of Nantucket. The juxtaposition is an object lesson in the difference between artworks with soul and those without. ♦ Free. Daily 10AM-5PM late May to mid-Oct; Sa-Su mid-Oct to late Nov. Winter St (between Liberty and Main Sts). 228.2505

38 **Hadwen House** The three **Starbuck** sisters ended up living across the street from their brothers. One married Newport candle merchant **William Hadwen** (whose former factory is now the **Whaling Museum**), and their house, built in 1845, was one of two soon nicknamed the "Two Greeks"—neighboring Greek Revival houses designed by local architect **Frederick Brown Coleman.** The mansion, with its imposing Ionic portico and rooftop cupola, is now the property of the **Nantucket Historical Association** and open for guided tours. The interior decoration has been restored to the appropriate period, 1840-60, with the last owners' more recent belongings sequestered in a back room. Docents will point out such features as the sterling doorknobs, the Italian marble mantels, and the whalebone "mortgage button" installed in the newel post, a traditional way of celebrating a paid-off mortgage (the document itself, or its ashes, would be stored within). To the rear of the house is a period garden.

Next door, under private ownership and not open to the public, is the other "Greek," this one with Corinthian capitals purportedly modeled after Athen's Temple of the Winds; built for Hadwen's adopted daughter, **Mary Swain Wright,** it features a second-story domed ballroom with a sprung dance floor and an oculus opening to the sky. ♦ Admission. Daily 10AM-5PM mid-June to early Sept; daily 11AM-3PM late May to mid-June, early Sept to mid-Oct. 96 Main St (between Pleasant Ave and Traders Ln). 228.1894

39 **The Three Bricks** Whaling mogul **Joseph Starbuck,** who owned 23 ships, commissioned these three identical (but for their iron fences) Georgian mansions for his sons **George, Matthew,** and **William.** Built by Cape Cod house carpenter **James Child** and mason **Christopher Capen** in 1840, they cost a grand total of $40,124 and set a new standard for in-town elegance (certain details are echoed in the **Jared Coffin House,** built five years later). Starbuck handed over the keys to his sons but prudently held title for another decade, until they were full partners in the business. The family ties have held to this day: one house is still owned by a descendant. ♦ Not open to the public. 93-97 Main St (at Pleasant Ave)

40 **Old Mill** Adapting his design from mills he'd seen in Holland, sailor **Nathan Wilbur** built this windmill out of shipwreck wood in 1746. Originally one of four that stood on the hills west of town, it's the only one remaining, and the only mill on the Cape and islands still in its original location. A 50-foot Douglas fir pole (the original was a mast) turns the 30-by-6-foot arms, covered with sailcloth, into the wind, setting in motion a wooden gear train that grinds corn between millstones weighing more than a ton apiece. You can buy some fresh meal after watching it (wind permitting) being made. ♦ Admission. Daily 10AM-5PM mid-June to early Sept; daily 11AM-3PM late May to mid-June, early Sept to mid-Oct. S. Mill and Prospect Sts. 228.1894

41 **The Maria Mitchell Science Center** Born on the island on 1 July 1818, the third of 10 children, **Maria** (pronounced "mar-EYE-a") **Mitchell** was lucky enough to have, in Pacific National Bank president and amateur astronomer **William Mitchell,** a father who believed in equal educational opportunities for girls. By the time she was 12, she was helping him chart the solar eclipse; within the next year, whaling captains were bringing her their navigational devices to be set according to astronomical calculations. At 18, she was appointed the librarian of the **Nantucket Atheneum;** in her 20-year tenure, she would attract a phenomenal roster of speakers, including **Emerson, Thoreau,** and **Melville.** At age 29 she discovered a comet while skygazing from the roof of her family's quarters in the bank. The feat brought her international fame; she was feted throughout the U.S. and in Europe, and was the first woman to be admitted to the **American Academy of Arts and Sciences** (the second would not succeed her for more than a century). Setting another precedent, she became the first female college professor in the U.S., teaching astronomy at Vassar from 1865 until her death in 1889.

In 1902, three of her cousins founded the **Maria Mitchell Association** to commemorate her remarkable life and continue her work. The nonprofit foundation is dedicated primarily to the study of the island's environment, with a special focus on passing along Mitchell's love of science to local children: "We especially need imagination in science," she once wrote. "It is not all mathematics, not all logic, but it is somewhat beauty and poetry." Five of the association's six facilities are open to the public (the exception is the **Maria Mitchell Observatory,** used for undergraduate research). The **Science Library** (2 Vestal Street, 228.9219) is located in a former schoolhouse where William Mitchell taught celestial navigation; nearby is the **Hinchman House** (7 Milk Street, 228.0898), a natural history museum that houses specimens and hosts lectures and walks. Across the street is the **Mitchell House** (1 Vestal Street, 228.2896), Mitchell's birthplace, built in 1790, which contains extensive memorabilia, including the telescope she used to spot the comet. Some distance away is the **Loines Observatory** (Milk Street Extension, 228.9273), which holds lectures on Monday nights and viewings on Wednesday nights (weather permitting) in summer. And in town, on the water, is a tiny shack housing the association's **Aquarium** (28 Washington Street, 228.5387), which holds a few fresh- and saltwater tanks, and where science interns field curious children's questions. ♦ Library: Tu-Sa 10AM-4PM mid-June to mid-Sept; M-Th 2-5PM mid-Sept to mid-June. Other facilities: Tu-Sa 10AM-4PM early June to late Aug. 2 Vestal St (at Milk St). 228.9198

42 **Old Gaol** Sturdier than it looks, the shingled facade, which seems right at home in this residential area, conceals a frame built of massive timbers bolted with iron; the petty thieves, embezzlers, and murderers who did time here, from 1805 right up until 1933, had little hope of escaping this crude facility, with its plank bunks, open privies, and iron grates for windows. Lest you suspect the islanders of cruel and unusual punishment, however, keep in mind that most prisoners were allowed to go home at night, the risk of flight being slim. The **Nantucket Historical Association** keeps the building open, but there's rarely anyone on hand; you can poke about at will, imagining whether **Mike Milken,** say, would have benefited from such a school-of-hard-knocks setting. ♦ Free. Daily 10AM-5PM mid-June to early Sept; daily 11AM-3PM late May to mid-June, early Sept to mid-Oct. 15R Vestal St (between Bloom St and Quaker Rd). 228.1894

43 **Fire Hose Cart House** Little neighborhood fire stations sprung up all over town after the devastating conflagration of 1846. This one, built in 1886, is the only one remaining; it houses the strictly decorative late 19th-century fire pumper *Siasconset,* an elaborate beauty. ♦ Free. Daily 10AM-5PM mid-June to early Sept; daily 11AM-3PM late May to mid-June, early Sept to mid-Oct. 8 Gardner St (at Howard St). 228.1893

44 **India House** $$ The circa 1803 home of ropemaker **Charles Hussey** makes a splendidly spare seven-room B&B, with wide plank floors and plenty of canopied four-posters. Guests have first crack at one of the best breakfasts around, featuring such treats as blueberry-stuffed French toast and soft-shell crabs filled with scallop mousse, in addition to fresh juice and homemade breads and muffins. The private garden out back is a lovely spot to sip a cocktail while recapping the pleasures of the day. ♦ 37 India St (between Centre and Gardner Sts). 228.9043

Within India House:

India House Restaurant ★★★$$$$ Three small dining rooms, with listing floors and low-slung ceilings, make a lovely, intimate setting for superb candlelit dinners. A favorite of many years' standing is Lamb India House enrobed in rosemary-studded breading and cloaked in béarnaise, but new influences have surfaced of late: e.g., Asian (pepper-encrusted tuna on gingered wild rice) and Southwestern (Texas wild boar ribs with peach barbecue sauce). The menu changes weekly, so you can be sure that this wonderful restaurant won't be resting on its well-deserved laurels. ♦ New American ♦ Breakfast and dinner; Sunday brunch. Closed Dec-Apr. Reservations recommended for dinner. 228.9043

45 **Jethro Coffin House** This circa 1686 saltbox, the oldest surviving structure on the island and a **National Historical Landmark,** is also known as the **Horseshoe House** for the brick design on its central chimney. Whatever the intended symbolism (it may have been just a Jacobean decoration), this has indeed been a lucky dwelling. It was built for **Jethro** and **Mary Gardner Coffin,** offspring of two of the island's earliest settlers; their marriage helped to quell a simmering feud between the "original purchasers" (the Gardner side) and mere shareholders (Coffin's status). Lightning struck and severely damaged the house in 1987 (in fact, nearly cut it in two), prompting a long-overdue restoration. Dimly illumined by leaded glass diamond-pane windows, it's filled with period furniture such as lathed ladderback chairs and a clever trundle bed on wooden wheels. **Nantucket Historical Association** docents will fill you in on all the related lore. ♦ Admission. Daily 10AM-5PM mid-June to mid-Oct; Sa-Su 11AM-3PM late May to mid-June. Sunset Hill Rd (off West Chester Rd). 228.1894

46 American Seasons ★★★$$$$ Dinner here is fancy but fun, thanks to a playful yet sophisticated folk-arts decor featuring high-backed wooden benches, tables with painted-on game boards, and an exuberant harvest mural by **Kevin Paulsen.** Chef-owner **Everett G. Reid III** makes the most of domestic multiculturalism with a menu divided into four quarters: New England, Down South, Wild West, and Pacific Coast. You get a continent's worth of options: grilled Maine salmon with fennel sauce and black olive risotto, for instance, or New Orleans oyster loaf with fried collard greens, marinated kid with cinnamon Navaho fry bread, confit of duckling with a sauce of black huckleberries. Novelty-seekers will be in multiple-choice heaven. All dishes, including the elaborate desserts, are delivered on plates as large as platters, beautifully arrayed. ♦ New American ♦ Dinner. Closed late Dec to Apr. 80 Centre St (at Chester St). Reservations recommended. 228.7111

47 Centerboard $$$ There are not that many Victorian houses in town, and none as luxuriously updated as this 1890s example, replete with parquet floors, Oriental rugs, lavish fabrics, and lace-trimmed linens. The overall look is lighter and less cluttered than the original mode, and thus more in line with modern tastes. Of the six bedrooms, the first-floor suite is perhaps the most romantic, with a green-marble Jacuzzi and a private living room with fireplace. ♦ 8 Chester St (between Centre and Easton Sts). 228.9696

48 Martin House Inn $$ Of the many historic B&Bs in town, **Ceci** and **Channing Moore's** place—an 1803 mariner's home—has the most congenial atmosphere, combined with the most reasonable prices; in fact, the tiny single rooms tucked at odd angles under the eaves are among the cheapest available on the island, yet utterly charming. Like the occupants of the more opulent rooms boasting four-posters and fireplaces, attic dwellers have access to the large, impeccably decorated living room with its own roaring fire (in season); beyond the window seats is a porch with conversational groupings of wicker settees, plus an inviting hammock. Breakfast—a buffet affair featuring tasty homemade breads and coffee cakes—is served at a long gleaming table where strangers fast become fond acquaintances as they trade tips for pleasurable explorations. ♦ 61 Centre St (between Step Ln and Lily St). 228.0678

49 Anchor Inn $$ This comfy 11-room B&B (pictured above), with period furnishings, was built in 1806 by **Archaelus Hammond,** the first captain to harpoon a whale in the Pacific. Visitors are likely to have lesser pursuits in mind, such as heading off to the beach after a breakfast of homemade bran-and-fruit muffins and classical music on the enclosed sunporch; innkeepers **Ann** and **Charles Balas** are happy to provide beach towels as well as directions. The brick patio out back offers an inspiring view of the **First Congregational Church.** ♦ Closed Jan-Mar. 66 Centre St (at Step Ln). 228.0072

49 First Congregational Church Built in 1834 by Boston housewright **Samuel Waldon,** this spiky Gothic Revival church lost its steeple in 1849 (it was judged too precarious to withstand the island's high winds, and removed). A better-engineered replacement was installed via helicopter in 1968; photos documenting the miraculous restoration are on display en route to the viewing platform 120 feet up. This aerie allows a staggering 360-degree perspective of the island. On the way out, have a look at the neoclassical trompe l'oeil painting behind the altar, executed by **E.H. Whitaker** of Boston in 1852. The circa 1730 vestry behind the church has been moved from its original site but remains Nantucket's oldest house of worship. ♦ Service Su 10AM. Tower: Nominal fee. M-Sa 10AM-4PM mid-June to mid-Oct. 62 Centre St (at Step Ln). 228.0950

Nantucket nearly squeaked into the automobile age as a carless sanctuary. Such vehicles were banned there until 1918, when a vote admitted them by a narrow margin.

Restaurants/Clubs: Red **Hotels:** Blue
Shops/ Outdoors: Green **Sights/Culture:** Black

50 The Folger Hotel $$ This somewhat faded 60-room behemoth may have seen better days over the past century-plus (it was built in 1891), but it still enjoys a comfy charm and is fun for families who aren't too fussy as to decor. (The bedrooms, though clean and airy, are rather drab.) The lobby, painted a deep blue and white, is full of life; often there's an auction brewing that you can preview, and the front desk sells sodas and candy bars, a tradition that kids find endearing. The best feature of all is the lengthy wraparound porch, complete with relaxing swings, leading to a secluded garden with lily pond. ♦ Closed mid-Oct to mid-May. 89 Easton St (at North Ave). 228.0313, 800/365.4371

Within The Folger Hotel:

The Whale Restaurant ★$$$ If you've had your fill of jicama and porcini it's nice to know you can find a good square meal in this big, boxy dining room: there's prime rib, if that's your pleasure, or plain baked Boston scrod with lemon butter, even corny surf 'n turf, and every entrée comes with an all-you-can-eat salad bar. Some effort has been made to dress up this space with hanging plants and Victorian touches such as kerosene lamps. ♦ American ♦ Breakfast and dinner. Closed Nov-May. 228.0313

51 Harbor House $$$ A virtual village has grown up around this 1886 summer hotel: 112 rooms in all, the larger, more luxurious (with country-pine furniture and private patios and decks) located in six town houses linked to one another and to an outdoor heated pool by nicely landscaped brick walkways. Just as some find the entire complex overbuilt, others consider it just the right mix of privacy and communality. Either way, the service and amenities—including priority time on nine clay tennis courts—are all one could wish for. ♦ 7 S. Beach St (at Harbor View Wy). 228.1500, 800/475.2637

Within the Harbor House:

The Hearth at the Harbor House ★★$$$$ With cinnabar red paneling dramatically offsetting a snowy field of white tablecloths, this is one of the larger, more formal dining rooms in town, and a traditional spot for lavish Sunday brunches. The restaurant tries to keep pace with the ultratrendy competition (offering such entrées as pan-seared smoked pork roast with chipotle fruit barbecue sauce), but you might do better here to stick to such classics as filet mignon with wild mushrooms or swordfish steak with chive beurre blanc. The Hearth is the only island restaurant so far to offer an early-bird discount (labeled more tastefully a[s] "sunset dinner specials"), and it's a very goo[d] deal, especially given that two under-12 children are fed free for each adult. A singing duo holds forth evenings in the adjoining **Hearth Lounge,** a barnlike space with a carve[d] whale hanging over the fireplace and a huge chandelier sporting brass weathervanes hun[g] amid the massive beams. ♦ New England ♦ Breakfast, lunch, and dinner; Sunday brunch. Closed for lunch Monday through Thursday mid-Sept to May. Reservations recommended. 228.1500

52 Downy Flake ★$ This beloved institution o[f] several decades' standing is just a modest cottage fronting the **Children's Beach** playground. Let the kids run wild while you breakfast on blueberry pancakes or the renowned homemade doughnuts. ♦ America[n] ♦ Breakfast and lunch. Closed mid-Sept to May. 6 Harbor View Wy (between S. Beach and Walsh Sts). 228.4533

53 White Elephant Hotel $$$$ There's not a trace of downward mobility about this ultraluxurious resort, so the name is either an outdated relic or someone's idea of a little joke. A mere lawn's width from the picturesque harbor, the complex comprises a shingled L-shaped building with 22 large rooms with decks, scattered cottages containing 34 more rooms, and the Breakers addition, containing 26 concierge-attended rooms even more opulently appointed than the English country norm (floral fabrics, stenciled pine armoires, sponge-painted walls). Every space is fresh and breezy, and none more so than the outdoor heated pool and hot tub surrounded by tasteful gray arbors. The hotel's location allows it to welcome "sail-in" guests. ♦ Closed mid-Oct to late May. Easton and Willard Sts. 228.5500, 800/475.2637

Within the White Elephant Hotel:

The Regatta ★★★$$$$ If the weather's fine, you'll surely want to sit out on the terrace, under a crisp white Roman parasol, to watch the boats come and go. The indoor dining room has its own allure, with celery-and-white-striped walls topped by pink latticework. Lunches feature such clever innovations as a "lobster Reuben," and dinners take a more elegant tack—for instance, lobster and asparagus *feuilleté*. The only distraction will be the glimmering view. ♦ New England ♦ Breakfast, lunch, and dinner; Sunday brunch. Closed mid-Oct to May. Reservations recommended. 228.2500

54 **Beachside Resort** $$$ Once you poke your head in, you'll realize that this is no ordinary motel. The lobby and bedrooms have been lavished with Provençal prints and handsome rattan and wicker furniture; the patios and decks overlooking the central courtyard with its heated pool have been prettified with French doors and latticework. If you prefer the laissez faire lifestyle of a motel to the sometimes constricting rituals of a B&B, you might find this the ideal base. ♦ Closed mid-Oct to mid-Apr. 31 N. Beach St (at E. Lincoln Ave). 228.2241, 800/322.4433

55 **Cliffside Beach Club** $$$$ The nucleus of this luxury hotel, the only one on the island located right on the dunes, was a 1920s bathing club that went private in 1949, thus setting a troublesome precedent for ownership of this four-acre chunk of **Jetties Beach:** Here, as the club's brochure brags, "the beach was divided into sections and . . . members waited years to secure one of the more prestigious spots." This scrambling for position seems downright comical—and more than a little pernicious—in light of the fact that the rest of Nantucket's shoreline has been kept open to the public all these years. If you don't mind partaking of a questionable heritage, it *is* a lovely stretch of gentle bay beach, and it's certainly pleasant to walk right out of your contemporary room (decorated with diagonal wooden wainscoting and island-made modern furniture) and down the wooden deck to your own colorful beach umbrella. And at least the traditional, low-profile, shingled exterior gives no hint of the modern amenities concealed within the 17 rooms, four studios, two suites, apartment, and cottage. The cathedral-ceilinged lobby is especially striking, its rafters hung with boldly patterned quilts to set off the white wicker furniture. ♦ Closed late Sept to late May. Jefferson Ave (off Spring St). 228.0618

Within the Cliffside Beach Club:

The Galley Restaurant on Cliffside Beach ★★★$$$$ You couldn't pick a prettier spot right beside the beach to plunk yourself down at, surrounded by flower boxes and the gentle thrum of the surf. Waiterly attitude may be a problem (lest anyone mistake this shingled shack for a *snack bar,* heaven forfend, they tend to treat unannounced visitors as probable rubes), but once you've established your honorable intentions you can dine like a king—Neptune, perhaps—on **Daniel Fourquot's** masterful bistro fare. Lunch might feature cold poached salmon with a lemon basil coulis; dinner, grilled lobster with coral beurre blanc. For dessert, don't miss the classic *tarte Tatin.* ♦ French ♦ Breakfast, lunch, and dinner. Closed mid-Sept to mid-June. Reservations recommended for dinner. 228.9641

56 **Fair Winds** $$ Just far enough from town that you feel you've found the "real" Nantucket, yet close enough that you can stroll in for dinner, this seven-bedroom B&B offers the peace many visitors are seeking: in fact, says innkeeper **Kathy Hughes,** a lot of first-time guests spot the house while out cycling and, after coming in for a look, make it their "second visit" destination. The light-drenched common rooms lead to a 50-foot deck with a panoramic view of the Sound; it's here that guests tend to bring their breakfast of fresh-baked breads and muffins. Four of the prettily decorated bedrooms enjoy that same priceless view. ♦ Closed mid-Oct to mid-May (except certain weekends); call for off-season schedule. 29 Cliff Rd (between Folgers and Cabot Lns). 228.1988

57 **Westmoor Inn** $$$ Longtime summerer **W.H.N. Voss** had this yellow Federal-style mansion, designed by New York architect **Frederick P. Hill,** built in 1917 for his new bride, *née* **Alice Vanderbilt.** During the transformation from summer home to luxury country inn, all the delightful detailing—from the grand portico to the widow's walk—was retained, but the interior design maximizes the effect of the mansion's light-suffused hilltop setting. The spacious living room is full of thoughtful touches, such as the vase of magnificent gladiola on the baby grand, and a 1,000-piece puzzle of Nantucket arrayed as a work in progress. There's even a cozy little TV room (anathema at most B&Bs) sporting cheerful blue-and-white splatter paint and framed architectural blueprints. The 14 bedrooms, including a ground-floor suite with a full-size Jacuzzi and French doors leading to the lawn, are as fully romantic as one would expect. After breakfasting to classical music in the conservatory, one can head off down a sandy lane to a quiet stretch of bay beach or hop on one of the mountain bikes provided and explore the island. ♦ Closed early Dec to May (except certain weekends); call for off-season schedule. Westmoor Ln (at Cliff Rd). 228.0877

Traditional fishers may have some peculiar superstitions (e.g., that whistling summons the wind), but their meteorological tricks are surprisingly reliable. For instance, birds wheeling in small circles generally augur a storm. "Sundogs," small rainbows spotted at dawn, may suggest where the wind will come from next.

Thar' She Blows: Whale Tales

Before the colonists came along, Native Americans had always killed whales while canoeing close to shore. Harpoons attached with vines to "drogues" (large chunks of wood) impeded the whales' progress until the hunters could catch up and lance their lungs. The settlers of Southampton, New York, in the mid-17th century were the first colonists to try sailing in search of whales; they would stay out for up to three weeks, camping along the shore and cutting the blubber first into "horse pieces" (large strips), then mincing it into "books" and rendering the books into oil in large iron "try-pots." The practice spread up the coast, and in 1690, Nantucket islanders hired **Ichabod Paddock** of Truro to instruct them in how to hunt whales.

Noting the profits to be gleaned from the "Royal Fish," the English crown established regulations whereby the government received a portion of the spoils from any beached whales. Another elaborate set of rules was developed to divvy up whale meat and return harpoons to their rightful owners. As incentive, whaling vessels were exempted from paying taxes for their first seven years at sea, and whalers were released from military service during the whaling season.

By the turn of the century, coastal whaling was so prevalent that the south side of Nantucket was divided into four half-mile stretches, each with its own lookout mast, a hut to house five or six men, and a "try works" to render the blubber on the spot. The preferred prey was the 50-foot, 50-ton right whale, so-called because it swam close to shore and remained afloat after it was killed. The "baleen"—bony upper jaw slats—was fashioned into fishing rods, corset stays, umbrellas, and the like. By the early 18th century, however, not only had the right whales become wise to whalers' tactics and moved offshore, they'd all but disappeared (some 300 are thought to survive today). By happenstance, in 1712, **Captain Christopher Hussey** was blown off-course into deep water, where he speared the first sperm whale, a feisty mammal with teeth in lieu of baleen; in its head cavity, whalers found spermaceti, an oil far superior to that rendered from blubber and which, when exposed to air, hardened into a waxy substance ideal for candlemaking. The pursuit of sperm whales was perilous, often involving a death-defying "Nantucket sleigh ride" through rough seas; nevertheless, tiny Nantucket rapidly outflanked England's own whaling fleet, maintaining its ascendancy for more than a century.

With the need for bigger boats came backers willing to invest on a share basis for a shot at "greasy luck"—whaling profits. Soon, the economy blossomed all along the coast: shipwrights, coopers, and chandlers alike had their hands full. Gradually, **New Bedford,** a Massachusetts fishing town west of Cape Cod with an exceptionally deep harbor, nudged its way to the forefront of the whaling industry; between 1825 and 1860, its fleet ballooned to 735 ships. Whaling captains in search of marketable spermaceti braved the South Atlantic and ultimately ventured into the uncharted waters of the Pacific and Indian oceans, where their voyages often lasted as long as seven years. As **Herman Melville** wrote in *Moby-Dick:* "These Sea Hermits conquered the watery world like so many Alexanders." The challenges were daunting, indeed; not only did whalers brave the whims of the ocean, but they were up against Spanish privateers, militant French (at war with the Crown and the colonies until 1763), the British themselves (who made a practice of conscripting any crews they came across during the Revolution and the War of 1812), and run-of-the-mill island cannibals. Add the daily reality of on-board rats,

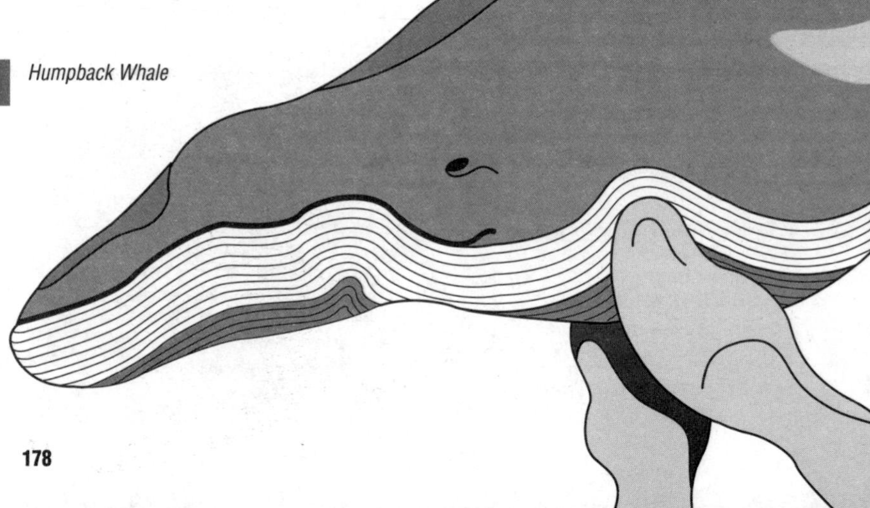

Humpback Whale

paches, moldy stores, and a high incidence of scurvy to an intrinsically dangerous and lonely profession, and it's no wonder crews became increasingly hard to round up. The discovery of petroleum-derived kerosene in Pennsylvania in 1836 and its introduction on the market in 1859 sounded a death knell for the industry.

Still, a few whaling fleets persisted, employing Norwegian whaler **Sven Foyn's** late-1860s invention: a harpoon cannon capable of spearing the elusive blue whale (the world's largest mammal) and the finback. Within 20 years, big blues and finbacks nearly disappeared from the Northern Hemisphere. In 1923, Norwegian **Carl Larsen** brought in factory ships capable of processing an entire whale within an hour—that is, as many as 39,000 animals a year. In 1946, 17 nations formed the **International Whaling Commission (IWC)** to regulate (and thereby preserve) the industry. Alarmed by the prospect of the species' extinction, the United States ceased all its whaling efforts in 1971. The IWC called for a worldwide ban in 1986—a call that Japan (which uses whale meat for food and animal feed), and Iceland, Norway, and the Soviet Union (which use whale oil for such products as soap, cosmetics, paint, and machinery lubricant) have yet to heed.

It was not long after America's whaling activity stopped that **Captain Al Avellar** of Provincetown's Dolphin Fleet hit upon the idea of enabling ordinary landlubbers to go "whaling" armed with cameras instead of harpoons. In 1975, with marine biologist **Charles Mayo** as a guide, Avellar offered whale-watching cruises to the Stellwagen Bank, a major marine feeding ground seven miles off Provincetown. Stellwagen Bank is an 840-square-mile, crescent-shaped undersea cliff some 80 to 100 feet high; here, ocean currents force cool, nutrient-rich water to the surface, attracting small fish and, in turn, whales. Avellar's innovation soon spawned imitators, whose numbers have increased so rapidly that on any given day you're apt to spot more boats than behemoths. Still, there's nothing quite like the thrill of coming upon a 50-ton mammal playfully breaching on the surface of the water, or gliding by, huge and mysterious. Although no charter company can absolutely guarantee sightings (at best they will let you go again for free), you can improve your odds by venturing out in spring or fall, when many whales make the 4,000-mile journey between their seasonal feeding grounds. The three species you're most likely to see are finbacks (typically 50 to 70 feet long), humpbacks (at 40 to 50 feet, they're the type known for their lovely, eerie "singing"), and pilots (averaging 13 feet). The tourist fleets all have on-board naturalists; some are expert researchers who can recognize distinctive patterns on the flukes and bodies and offer a life history of individual whales.

Whale-watching cruises generally cost under $20 per person, and last about three or four hours, depending on the distance covered. It makes more sense to depart from Provincetown, which is closest to the Bank, but if you don't mind whiling away a bit of extra time on the water, the particular port-of-call doesn't much matter. The following companies are all well regarded:

From Plymouth: **Capt. John Boats.** 746.2643, 800/242.2469.

From Barnstable Harbor: **Hyannis Whale Watcher Cruises.** 362.6088, 800/287.0374.

From Provincetown: **Dolphin Fleet.** 255.3857, 800/826.9300; **Portuguese Princess.** 487.2641, 800/442.3188; **Ranger V.** 487.1582, 800/992.9333.

If you come home feeling a special fondness for the whales you've met, you might consider contributing to the **Whale Adoption Project** (563.2843), a Falmouth-based fund-raising effort dedicated to whale research, rescue, and education, sponsored by the International Wildlife Coalition.

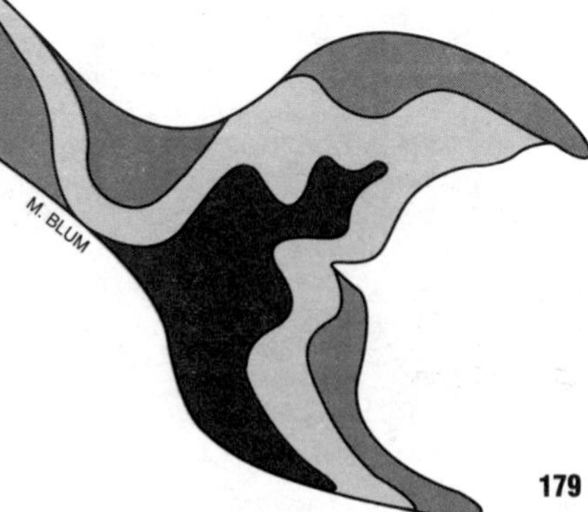

58 The Westender ★$$$$ Stop in for the bathrooms (**Madaket Beach** has none) and stay for a reviving drink—perhaps a four-rum "Magnet Mystery"—at the small but voluble downstairs bar, presided over by the head of a wild boar. The loftlike restaurant upstairs is handsome, with windows all around to catch the ocean view, but the menu overreaches and is overpriced—true, too, of the lunch stand the restaurant operates. The management seems to count on the fact that, having come this far (especially by bike) and lacking other options, visitors will be grateful for what they can get; on the contrary, it's that very situation that makes for a sense of exploitation. ♦ American ♦ Lunch and dinner. Closed mid-Oct to late May. 326 Madaket Rd (at Madaket Beach), Madaket. 228.5197

59 Beach Plum Cafe ★★★$$$ A bit of a jog from town, but not far from the Sconset bike trail, this charming little restaurant is definitely off the beaten path but well worth seeking out; don't be surprised if scores of savvy residents have already beaten you to it. It's a tiny place, with about a dozen tables and accompanying mule-ear chairs squeezed into two rooms. Local artwork (look for **Dee Macy's** still lifes) enlivens the white walls. Chef **Jean ("Buddy") Dion** trained at the **Culinary Institute of America** and has cooked in such illustrious Cape Cod kitchens as **Chillingsworth** and the **Captain Linnell House;** the fact that he's here out of love for the island is evidenced in the lack of lunch in summer—he'd rather get in a few hours of beach time. As an example of his capabilities once he's back at the range, consider spicy shredded duck wrapped in phyllo with a honeyed ancho chili sauce, or grilled loin of lamb in a Cabernet Sauvignon reduction sprinkled with rosemary.

The beach-bound can stop in for a bracing breakfast: perhaps a sun-dried tomato, mushroom, pesto, and Brie omelet, or French toast (made from fresh-baked baguettes) slathered in cranberry-orange butter. The brunch offers many of the same sensational dishes; if you get a late enough start (after noon, when the "blue laws" let up), you can compensate yourself with a mimosa or a "Nantucket Red"—cranberry juice and champagne. ♦ New American ♦ Breakfast and dinner; Sunday brunch; lunch also from mid-Oct to mid-May. 11 W. Creek Rd (between Pleasant and Orange Sts). 228.8893

59 Chin's Restaurant ★★$$$ Chef **Chin Manasmontri,** a Chinese native of Thailand who once cooked in some of the finest restaurants in Bangkok, has been working his magic here since the late '70s, long before Thai became trendy. Lucky Nantucketers have been feasting all the while on such delicacies as *tom kha gai* soup (chicken chunks in coconut milk with lemongrass, lime juice, and chile), skewered chicken satay with spicy peanut dipping sauce, and *ton mun,* curried fried fishcakes made of fresh local bluefish—and those are just the appetizers. Several entries among the dozen Thai entrées, such as spicy cold grilled beef, will severely test even those who claim asbestos mouths, and leave them weeping with pleasure.

As for the Chinese side of the menu (all MSG-free, naturally), you'll find all your old favorites, from *moo goo gai pan* to *kung pao* beef, with a few interesting oddities such as clay-baked chicken with honey and soy sauce. You can eat in, in a crisp little dining room decorated in black and white, with Indonesian carvings, or carry your cartons home or off to the beach. ♦ Classical Chinese/Thai/Takeout ♦ Lunch and dinner; dinner only from Sept to mid-Dec, Feb-May. Closed Tuesday Sept to mid-Dec, Feb-May; closed mid-Dec to Feb. 126 Chin's Wy (off Pleasant St). 228.0200

60 The Muse If you're young and have the urge to dance, it's easy enough to find this roadhouse/rock club on the way to **Surfside Beach.** Decor is your usual campy detritus (e.g., an airplane's tail end, with a mannequin pilot suspended over the dance floor) and decent pizza is produced on the premises. ♦ Cover. Daily 9PM-1AM June-Aug; F-Sa 9PM-1AM Sept-May. 44 Atlantic Ave (between Bartlett and Miacomet Rds). 228.6873

61 Robert B. Johnson AYH-Hostel $ Of all five hostels on the Cape and islands, this one takes the cake for location—as well as local color. Set right beside **Surfside Beach,** the former "Star of the Sea" is an authentic 1874 lifesaving station, Nantucket's first. Where seven Surfmen once stood ready to fish out shipwreck victims (preferably still alive), some 50 backpackers now enjoy sex-segregated bunk rooms; the women's quarters, upstairs, still contain a climb-up lookout post. The usual lockout (9:30AM-5PM) and curfew (10:30PM) rules prevail. ♦ Closed Nov-May. Surfside. 228.0433

The name for johnnycakes, a kind of dry cornmeal pancake the settlers adopted from the natives, evolved from the expression "bread for the journey."

Restaurants/Clubs: Red **Hotels:** Blue
Shops/ Outdoors: Green **Sights/Culture:** Black

62 **The Wauwinet** $$$$ This ultradeluxe retreat, renovated by summerers **Stephen** and **Jill Karp** in 1988 for roughly $3 million, has earned several nicknames, including "The Ultimate," or, as the staff has been known to joke, the "We Want It." With 25 rooms in the main building (which started out as a restaurant in 1850) and 10 more in five modest-looking shingled cottages, the capacity is only about 80 spoiled guests, tended to by 100 staffers. Whatever your pleasure is, they'll try to see to it, jitneying you into town, for instance, in a 1936 "Woody," or dispatching you on a 21-foot launch across the bay to your own private strip of beach.

But why leave the grounds—ever? (Unless you go broke: the cottage suites run up to $1,200 a night.) Everything is thoroughly delightful right here. The inn is optimally located between the ocean and the vast harbor; the distance between these two bodies of water is so slight this spot used to be called the "haulover," because fishers would drag their boats across it to avoid circumnavigating **Great Point.** This pristine little complex, the last stop on an eight-mile road to nowhere (actually, a wildlife sanctuary), contains several clay tennis courts with a pro shop and pro, a croquet lawn, a platform for nearly life-size "beach chess," and plenty of boats and bikes to borrow.

Then again, the rooms—all provided with a cozy nook from which to gaze out across the water—are so lovely, you may just want to stay indoors. New York interior designer **Martin Kuckley** created individualized decors featuring pine armoires, plenty of wicker, exquisite Audubon prints, handsome fabrics, and a lovely array of antique accessories. The respectful yet playful style is demonstrated in a lobby where bleached pine floors have been painted with trompe l'oeil throw rugs and marble trim, and in a warm and colorful library where everyone convenes for sherry and port at day's end. ♦ Closed Nov to mid-Apr. 120 Wauwinet Rd (off Squam Rd), Wauwinet. 228.0145, 800/426.8718

Within The Wauwinet:

Toppers ★★★★$$$$ Named not for the dapper ghost but the family terrier (whose portrait enjoys a place of honor), this accomplished restaurant offers deluxe "shore dinners": You can debark from **Straight Wharf** on the *Wauwinet Lady* for a round-trip luncheon or dinner cruise. The tariff ($29 or $48 prix fixe) usually suffices to discourage the tackier tourists, and in any case, there's a dress code. Those who come for dinner in the restaurant proper (which, for an additional fee, can culminate in an optional "sunset dessert" cruise) are in for a ritual of surpassing peacefulness. The seating consists of wicker armchairs pillowed in pale-blue plaid, or comfy chintz-covered banquettes with fringed linen antimacassars. A double-tailed gilt mermaid gazes down on a flickering fire, and brass-shaded candles warmly light each luxuriously set table.

Chef **Peter Wallace's** menu is a carefully considered study of seasonal peaks; in September, for instance (an especially lovely time to go), you might encounter champagne risotto with golden chanterelle mushrooms and pancetta cracklings, and pan-seared tenderloin of beef with potato-leek rösti and Moroccan cherry tomato jam. Desserts are generous and fanciful, and the homemade ice creams and sorbets (imagine: prickly pear!) will be unlike any you've ever encountered. ♦ New American ♦ Breakfast, lunch, and dinner. Closed Nov to mid-May. Reservations recommended. 228.8768

63 **Coskata-Coatue Wildlife Refuge** Shaped like a fishhook, **Great Point** reaches toward the Cape as if hoping to snag it. The entire point is an 1,100-acre preserve maintained by the **Trustees of the Reservations,** who offer three-hour tours guided by a naturalist. Rumbling along in a pickup truck, you can expect to see all sorts of shorebirds, including, possibly, piping plovers, egrets, and blue herons. You'll also get an up-close look at the **Great Point Lighthouse**—not the 1818 original, demolished by a storm in 1984, but a rubblestone replica erected in 1986, which relies partly on solar energy. ♦ Fee. W-Su 8:30AM, 3:30PM. Leaves from Wauwinet Inn parking lot. Wauwinet. 228.6799

64 **The Chanticleer Inn** ★★★★$$$$ Chef **Jean-Charles Berruet's** glorious country *auberge* has enjoyed a long reign as Nantucket's premier restaurant. One enters through a bower, past a courtyard full of white flowers. There the choices get more complex: to the right is a clubby dining room with dark wood-paneled walls and fireplace; upstairs is a peach-hued, arched hall with private alcoves overlooking the garden. Either of these settings would suit a particular mood (chummy or romantic), but there's no mistaking the power room: the formal ell straight ahead, with decorative paneling in muted tones setting off massive sprays of cut flowers.

The unifying theme is very serious cuisine, of the sort you'd ordinarily have to hop a Concorde for. To highlight just a few options on the $60 prix fixe menu (the dishes sound all the more glamorous in French): *gateau de grenouilles aux pommes de terre* (yes, a frogs' legs "cake" in a potato crust), *tournedos de lotte marinee au gingembre, sauce au rhum, croquettes d'ail* (a gingered monkfish scallopini with a lemon-rum sauce and sweet garlic fritters), and *pain perdu, glace au chocolat blanc, coulis d'abricots secs* (a very classy bread pudding with white chocolate ice cream and apricot sauce). Don't even look at the à la carte listings unless you're prepared for extreme sticker shock: appetizers run to $25, desserts $15 to $20. And yet you'll rarely hear of anyone who comes away complaining. ♦ Classical French ♦ Lunch and dinner. Closed Wednesday; closed mid-Oct to mid-May. 9 New St (between W. Chapel St and Park Ln), Siasconset. Reservations recommended; jacket required. 257.6231. Take-out outlet at: 15 S. Beach St, Nantucket. 325.5625

64 Siasconset Casino **This magnificent Shingle-style private tennis club, built in 1899, might on rare occasion have a court available for rent by nonmembers at 1 or 2PM; give a call. Evenings in summer, the delightful lattice-raftered theater—once used for productions in the community's heyday as an actors' colony—shows first-run movies; viewers are advised to bring cushions to mitigate the metal folding chairs. ♦ New St (between W. Chapel St and Park Ln), Siasconset. 257.6661**

65 Sconset Café ★★★$$$$ This plain and tiny restaurant looks like somebody's oversize kitchen. Actually, it's the working lab of chef/owner/cookbook author **Pam McKinstry**, who succeeds in conjuring a sophisticated international menu for a steady clientele of admirers. A midsummer's night feast here might meander through crab cakes remoulade or carpaccio drizzled with truffle-and-olive oil; "veal Portofino" grilled with a Parmesan-basil crust, or confit of duck with lemon caramel sauce and nectarine chutney. Breakfasts are just as enticing, with such specialties as waffles made with oatmeal and oranges. At lunch, try the succulent *melanzane* sandwich: grilled eggplant with pesto and fresh mozzarella, on a baguette. ♦ New American ♦ Breakfast, lunch, and dinner. Closed mid-Sept to mid-May. Post Office Sq (at Main St), Siasconset. 257.4008

65 Claudette's You can eat on the little wooden deck, but if you're beach-bound, just pick up a reasonably priced box lunch: a meat loaf or seafood salad sandwich, for instance, with a brownie or lemon cake for dessert. ♦ Daily 9AM-4PM mid-May to mid-Oct. Post Office Sq (at Main St), Siasconset. 257.6622

66 The Summer House $$$$ It seems straight out of a dream, this cluster of eight rose-covered cottages, built of salvaged wood in the 1840s on a bluff overlooking the sea. Tiny to begin with, they're all but dwarfed by the enveloping greenery: Fragrant honeysuckle aswarm with greedy bees tumbles over the low, shingled roofs, and the ivy is so avid, it climbs right into the rooms, probing the skylights and window frames. Furnished with English country antiques, the bedrooms are not overdecorated, thankfully, although the bathrooms are certainly fancy enough, with marble Jacuzzis in all but one, and the beds are draped in fine linens and lace. Basically, owners **Peter Karlson** and **Danielle deBenedictus** have tried to keep this a very special place where time stands still, the kind of place you could find only in Siasconset. Adirondack chairs are scattered casually across the lush, shady lawn encircled by the cottages. The view is due east, where you can watch the sun rise—and sometimes the moon. Wooden steps lead down to a jewellike pool set in the dunes and surrounded by the inn's kitchen gardens; you can order a splendid poolside lunch on the bluestone patio, or take a refreshing dip. From here, a short walk through the compass grass brings you to an endless, untouched beach. ♦ Closed Nov to mid-May. Ocean Ave (at Magnolia Ave), Siasconset. 257.4577

Within The Summer House:

The Summer House Restaurant ★★★$$$$ A blissful summery mood descends as **Sal Gioe,** a seasoned pianist, riffs his way gently through Gershwin and Porter. The rambling dining room, a comforting jumble of white wicker, pastel linens, and abundant informal flowers, displays none of the pomp and pretense it could get away with, for this is quite distinguished cuisine, presented by a knowledgeable and personable staff. One course after another delights, from a seductive lemon-buttermilk pancake with lobster medaillons in a cognac-vanilla syrup (it's as sweet as a sundae, and superb), to a salad of warm smoked duck on wild greens with a sweet-tart dressing of ginger and brandied cherries, and on to pistachio-crusted rack of domestic lamb roasted on a bed of fresh rosemary with black currant mint sauce. The desserts (key lime pie, "chocolate sin cake," etc.) are also hard to choose among, assuming you make it that far. Abundance—of pleasures, and the time that makes them possible—is the impression you'll come away with. You won't want to stay away long. ♦ New American ♦ Lunch (at the pool) and dinner. Closed mid-Oct to late May. 257.9976

Bests

rank Conroy
riter

antucket:

ichael Shannon's truly perfect food at **The Club ar,** at the foot of Main Street.

morning walk through the old streets behind the **acific National Bank**—an architectural time-trip.

conset, with its small, rose-covered cottages and ny town square out of the 18th century.

alking the moors in September.

ary Keller's harp at **Company of the Cauldron.**

ocktails at the **Rope Walk** while watching the boat ction on the harbor.

aking the ferry instead of the plane.

enny Theroux Garneau
eneral Manager, *Nantucket Beacon*

n Nantucket, I love:

he smell of flowers everywhere. You are totally onsumed by every sense.

he beautiful wide-open beaches.

unset champagne at **The Wauwinet** and then dinner t **21 Federal.** Watch out for **Michael**—he doesn't now how to pour a half glass of wine.

he magic of **Christmas Stroll.**

he yellow of **Daffodil Weekend.**

he fact that you really have to want to be here to get o this beautiful faraway island.

eslie Linsley
uthor/Photographer of *Nantucket Style*

on Aron
hotographer/Graphic Designer

Nantucket, a romantic island that cannot be reached y car (only ferry or plane), is protected under a National Trust and all its beaches and moors are pen to the public. It's a wonderful place for oneymooners, families, and people who love nature. Although it's mostly known as a summer resort, the est-kept secret is the fall season. September and October provide the best weather, the water is warm nough for swimming, and it's less crowded. Year-ound residents look forward to this time of year when the population goes back from 35,000 to 7,500.

On Nantucket:

Sunday brunch at the **Beach Plum Cafe.** Great home-baked breads and muffins.

Picnic on **Tuckernuck** after a long sail; pick up picnic sandwiches of chicken salad from **5 Corners.**

Walking the full length of **Jetties Beach** at the end of the day after most of the crowds have left and the sun is starting its descent.

Watching the sunset from **Madaket Harbor.**

A late-day stroll along the **Marina** to see the variety of ships docked there.

Scalloping in October at **Hither Creek.**

Supper at the **Straight Wharf Restaurant** in August.

On a cool or rainy evening, supper at the **Brotherhood of Thieves,** an old-fashioned whaling bar with communal tables.

A long bird-watching walk in **Sanford Farm** (off Madaket Road).

Biking or roller skating on the **Sconset Bike Path** and having lunch on the porch at **Claudette's** in Sconset.

Stan Grossfeld
Associate Editor, *The Boston Globe*

Listening to WCBS Radio describe the rush-hour bottleneck on the FDR Drive while opening a long-necked beer and watching the Canada geese cruise during sunset at **Madaket.**

At **Shucker's Restaurant** in Woods Hole, try Murph's Nobska Light Beer, homebrewed by **Murph.**

Watching the 7AM ferry round Brandt Point Light from the flower-covered balcony at **The Overlook Hotel.**

Try a "Dark and Stormy"—ginger beer and rum—as concocted by **Michael Sturgis** at **21 Federal.**

Go to the backdoor of the **Homeport** in Menemsha; order the broiled swordfish to go and eat it while sitting on the pier watching all of the fishing boats come home.

David Sarnoff, founder of the RCA network, got his start as a wireless operator at a Marconi station in Siasconset.

Henry David Thoreau visited the Cape four times between 1849 and 1857, "wishing to get a better view than I had yet had of the ocean," and was duly blown away: "There I had got the Cape under me, as much as if I were riding it barebacked," he enthused upon reaching the beaches of the Outer Cape. "It was not as on the map, or seen from the stagecoach, but there I found it all out of doors, huge and real, Cape Cod!" He was less than prescient about its potential appeal for the masses: "At present [this coast] is wholly unknown to the unfashionable world, and probably it will never be agreeable to them," he wrote in *Cape Cod* (1865). "It is a wild rank place," he concluded, where "a sort of chaos reigns still."

Detours

If approaching the Cape from the north or west, you'll pass within minutes of **Plymouth** and **New Bedford**, two towns intimately linked with its history, and deserving of a stopover. Plymouth is the tourist mecca of Cape Cod Bay—the launching pad of U.S. history. Aside from the rather nondescript **Plymouth Rock**, the other main attraction is **Plimoth Plantation**, a "living history" museum that convincingly re-creates the early days of colonization. Fans of the Cape's maritime history will be well-rewarded by a stopover in New Bedford, on Buzzards Bay. During the early 19th century, New Bedford vied with the Islands for preeminence in the whaling trade, and vestiges from its glory days are plentiful. New Bedford is also the ferry terminus for **Cuttyhunk**, the outermost of the Elizabeth Islands, which trail off the Cape's southwestern corner. Fourteen miles out to sea, the island is primarily a nature preserve where deer actually roam the streets. To read up on the sights before heading off to these towns, ask the **Massachusetts Office of Travel and Tourism** (100 Cambridge Street, 13th floor, Boston, Massachusetts 02202, 617/727.3201 or 800/447.6277) and the regional tourism offices listed below for brochures.

Plymouth

Calling itself "America's Hometown since 1620," Plymouth has not exactly been shy about courting tourists. The harborside community is a curious amalgam of breathtaking historic homes that open their doors to visitors and garish commercial properties. If you can tolerate the architectural mishmash, there are several sites worth seeking out. Note that virtually all the attractions close from Thanksgiving to late May (and most of the historic houses shutter their doors even earlier, around Labor Day or Columbus Day). Call ahead to **Destination Plymouth** (747.4161) if you plan to visit off-season.

As many as one million visitors a year make a beeline for **Plymouth Rock** (Water Street, 866.2580), a chunk of Dedham granodiorite that may or may not mark the spot where the *Mayflower* passengers first alighted on 20 December 1620. No one is certain, but in 1741, a 95-year-old man claimed that one of the original passengers told him *this* was the location, and the rock has been in history books ever since. If Plymouth Rock looks slightly puny, that's because hordes of souvenir-seekers reportedly chipped away some 3,000 pounds, or three quarters of its bulk, before it was placed under protective custody (**Pilgrim Hall Museum** has a good-size sample). The rock also changed locales quite a bit from 1870 until the tricentennial year of 1921, when—with the help of the **National Society of the Colonial Dames of America**—it finally found a home under an elaborate neo-Grecian portico designed by **McKim, Meade & White.** The monument today is the centerpiece of Massachusetts' smallest state park.

That large, gaudily painted vessel at the end of State Pier is the ***Mayflower II*** (admission; 746.1622), a full-scale replica (106.5 feet long) made in England. When it sailed over in 1957, the passage took two months, as long as the original *Mayflower* voyage. The reproduction rigging matches the original down to the last detail, and so convincing are the actors playing passengers and crew, you'd swear they were the real thing too. On board, time is frozen in February 1621, two months after the Pilgrims arrived in Plymouth; most still live on the ship, as they work to build their colony. The pseudo Pilgrims will answer questions, such as why they made the journey and what they hope to gain, with thoughtful and often humorous responses. (The boat is a harborside extension of **Plimoth Plantation,** 2.5 miles down the coast; combination tickets are available.)

The Mayflower

M. BLUM

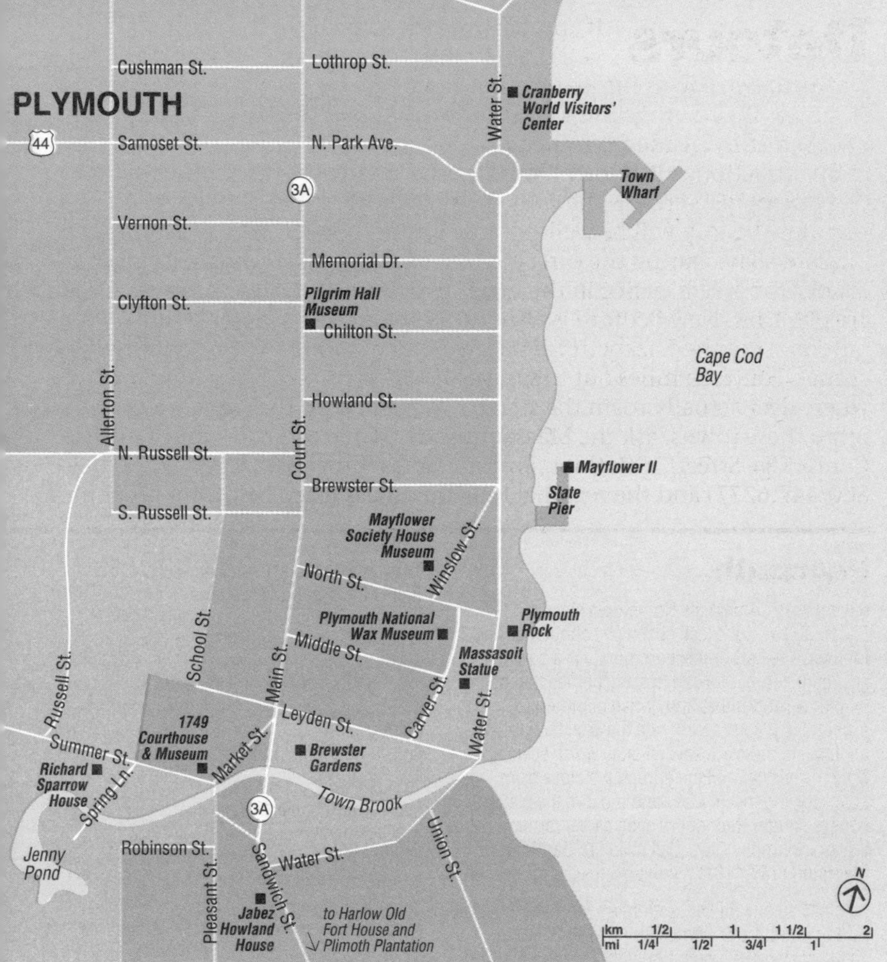

From the pier, it's only a mile or two to tour the town on foot, but if you prefer, hop aboard the **Plymouth Rock Trolley** (734.3419), which makes a circuit of all the usual stops. You can get off to look around, or scale **Coles Hill,** where half the Pilgrim community was buried that first bleak winter—secretly, at night, so the natives wouldn't learn how severely their numbers were depleted. The hill is now topped by a statue of the great sachem **Massasoit** (erected by the Improved Order of Red Men in 1921), who agreed to treaties in the spring of 1621 that gave the Pilgrims the stability they needed to prosper. Trollies run every 20 minutes.

More Pilgrim adventures are depicted nearby at the corny but colorful **Plymouth National Wax Museum** (admission; 16 Carver Street, 746.6468). In the spookily lit tableaux, the Pilgrims' linens may look too starched, but for a young audience, this is a fun way to absorb history. Also on this bluff are two historic houses to tour: the humble 1749 **Spooner House** (admission; 27 North Street, 746.0012), packed with the belongings and tales of five generations of the family who built it, and the **Mayflower Society House Museum** (admission; 4 Winslow Street, 746.2590), headquartered in the 1754 home of **Edward Winslow,** the great-grandson of **Governor Edward Winslow.** This magnificent white colonial house contains a gravity-defying double "flying staircase," and nine rooms of 17th- and 18th-century furnishings, including original Pilgrim items. Next door is a delightful bed-and-breakfast, the **1782 Jackson-Russell-Whitfield House** ($; 26 North Street, 746.5289). The three bedrooms behind the pretty brick Federal facade boast antique bedsteads and hand-painted, stenciled walls.

In *Cape Cod Pilot* (1937), WPA writer Josef Berger provided this assessment of putative *Mayflower* relics: "The only thing to bear in mind is that Lloyds of London has the measurements of the *Mayflower* on record as 90 feet from stem to stern and 20 feet in the beam, with a depth of hold of 11 to 14 feet, and that enough objects have already been established in this country as genuine *Mayflower* cargo to fill a warehouse of a hundred times this cubic area."

One block west is **Station One + 1** (★$$$; 51 Main Street, 746.1200), a turn-of-the-century firehouse converted into a Continental restaurant. A block south on Main Street is the **1749 Courthouse & Museum** (free; Town Square, 830.4075). Before becoming President, **John Adams** argued a few cases here, in the oldest wooden courthouse in America. Today, the building houses various artifacts, including an elaborate 1740 hand-carved oak bench and an 1828 fire pump. On **Burial Hill** behind the courthouse, you can wander among centuries-old graves and gaze down on the harbor, where the mast of the *Mayflower II* sports a British flag.

On the southern slope of the hill is the modern **John Carver Inn** ($; 25 Summer Street, 746.7100, 800/274.1620), complete with outdoor pool and the **Hearth 'N Kettle Restaurant** (★$$). At the inn, value-conscious visitors can purchase a "Plymouth Passport" good for discounts at most local attractions. Across the street is the 1640 **Richard Sparrow House** (donation requested; 42 Summer Street, 747.1240), Plymouth's oldest surviving home (and one of the oldest in the country). Inside this plain frame house with diamond-pane windows is a pottery shop where resident artisan/caretaker **Lois Atherton** creates richly glazed stoneware for Plimoth Plantation and others. Watch her work, and then visit the keeping room and upstairs bedrooms, where a remarkable 1649 wooden wingback "master chair" (the wings were intended to block drafts) is on display. Around the corner, stop off at the country-style **Run of the Mill Tavern** (★★$$; 6 Spring Lane, 830.1262), offering reasonably priced sandwiches, burgers, and fish entrées. Or follow Town Brook (the source of the Pilgrims' drinking water) through Brewster Gardens down to the harbor to **Cafe Nanina** (★★$$$; 14 Union Street, 747.4503), where the close-up view of the harbor is complemented by hearty Italian country cuisine served in a sophisticated setting.

Heading north along the harbor, past the pier, you'll see **Hedge House** (admission; 126 Water Street, 746.9697), an 1809 Federal home refurbished with period antiques, including Chinese porcelains and local textiles, as well as exotica ranging from wallpaper bandboxes to a "magic lantern." Beyond, in a former clam factory on the harbor, the **Cranberry World Visitors Center** (free; 225 Water Street, 747.2350) exhibits attractions such as a scaled-down demonstration bog, displays on the history of cranberry cultivation, and free samples from **Ocean Spray,** the Center's sponsor.

On Court Street (Route 3A), parallel to Water Street, one block west, is the **Pilgrim Hall Museum** (admission; 75 Court Street, 746.1620). Operated by the **Pilgrim Society,** the oldest public museum in the nation is housed in an 1824 Greek Revival building designed by **Alexander Parris** (the Bulfinch protégé who, two years later, completed Boston's Quincy Market). No high-tech interactive exhibits here, just an astounding haul of Pilgrim artifacts—including **John Alden's** halberd and Bible, **William Brewster's** wooden chair, and the hooded wicker cradle of **Peregrine White,** who was born aboard the *Mayflower* when it was anchored in Provincetown. Among the other fascinating objects displayed are the remains of the *Sparrow-Hawk,* the first recorded shipwreck off Cape Cod. This 40-foot bark, its hull constructed from naturally curved tree trunks and branches, struck Chatham Bar around 1626 en route to Virginia and lay on the ocean floor until 1863, when it surfaced after a storm. It was displayed on Boston Common and went on tour before coming to rest here in 1889.

South on Route 3A toward Plimoth Plantation, two more houses welcome history buffs. Just past Town Brook, the **Jabez Howland House** (admission; 33 Sandwich Street, 746.9590) is the only surviving house (pictured above) to have been inhabited by *Mayflower* Pilgrims (Howland's parents, **John** and **Elizabeth**). Built around 1667, it more than doubled in size over the next 80 years. Today, it's maintained by the **Pilgrim John Howland Society,** a group of descendants, and contains period furnishings. The 1677 **Harlow Old Fort House** (admission; 119 Sandwich Street, 746.3017) was built with timbers from the original 1622 fort that stood atop Burial Hill. Here, you can observe and even participate in 17th-century homemaking crafts, such as spinning and candle-making.

Any visit to Plymouth must include a stop at **Plimoth Plantation** (admission; Route 3A, 746.1622), a few miles south of the center of town. Start at the quadrangular **Visitors Center** designed in 1986 by **Graham Gund,** an architect from Cambridge, Massachusetts. Exhibits include a choice selection of 17th-century furniture and an auditory comparison of Jacobean dialects. Then it's off to the reproduction **1627 Pilgrim Village,** where, according to the museum's roadside signage, "history repeats itself." (On the way, you can watch artisans demonstrate pottery, weaving, joinery, and basketry at the **Crafts Center.**) Once inside the village's wooden barricades, you're introduced to a full sensory understanding of another age. Here, in a compound of thatched, wattle-and-daub houses set on a slanting hillside, skilled actors portray colonists going about the business of daily life: tending the livestock and herb gardens, performing military drills, cooking and eating (while swatting the ubiquitous flies), and gossiping in the dialects prevalent at the time. They'll engage your participation whenever possible and entertain endless questions—as long as they're chronologically correct. Any discussion of post-1627 events will only elicit bewilderment. So

comprehensive is Plimoth Plantation's portrayal of the past that even the farm animals have been back-bred to 17th-century standards.

On the way back to the Visitor Center, visit a re-created Wampanoag camp, **Hobbamock's Homesite.** Hobbamock, a Wampanoag, lived alongside the colonists in the 1620s and helped them to adapt. While here, you can learn about the bark-covered huts called *wetus* and watch dugout canoes being made.

Open from April through November, Plimoth Plantation mounts a full schedule of special reenactments, such as trials and weddings, as well as concerts, workshops, and authentic colonial dinners. Try to call ahead to learn what's planned, though even an impromptu visit is sure to be rewarding. And allow yourself a few hours to get into the 17th-century spirit.

New Bedford

Settled in 1652, New Bedford, located at the mouth of the **Acushnet River,** got a slow start as a boomtown. By 1752, it was still a sleepy hamlet, an outpost of Dartmouth, harboring a dozen or so farming families, mostly Quaker. Its deep waters, however, had caught the attention of early whaler **Joseph Russell,** who in the 1740s renamed the port for the **Duke of Bedford.** The first ship launched was the *Dartmouth,* in 1767; six years later, this same vessel dumped cargo during the Boston Tea Party. The British pretty much demolished New Bedford in 1778, but 10 years later it was rebuilt on the western side of the river. (The original site, now the town of **Fairhaven,** still boasts a residential area, **Poverty Point,** dating from the 18th century.) In the heyday of whaling, New Bedford competed with Nantucket for the title of whaling capital, finally taking the lead in 1857, just as the industry was about to go bust.

The town lost much of its affluence with the decline of whaling, but not its will to survive. Today, it's an active fishing port (with the largest commercial fleet on the East Coast) and an industrial center with a great deal of civic pride. Townspeople have worked for more than a decade to restore more than a hundred buildings of historic significance, partly in hopes of appealing to a tourist market. The odds they face are considerable. The integrity of the downtown and harbor area has been compromised by some rather hideous 20th-century additions, including intrusive roadways seemingly designed to discourage pedestrians. Nor has the recession been kind: the town has a downtrodden, dispirited air. Yet admirers of old architecture will find much to savor, and the city offers perhaps a more realistic glimpse of seafaring life today than do the carefully preserved fantasy-fulfilling towns along the Cape. At the very least, you'll want to stop at the **New Bedford Museum of Whaling** to enjoy the collections, and visit the nearby **Seamen's Bethel,** immortalized in *Moby-Dick.*

A good place to get your bearings is the **New Bedford Visitors Center** (47 North Second Street, 991.6200 or 800/288.6263), maintained by the **Bristol County Convention & Visitors Bureau;** they'll provide suggestions and brochures, including a series of walking itineraries prepared by the **New Bedford Preservation Society.** Guided one-hour tours of the **Waterfront Historic District** are offered in summer, or you can wing it anytime; in summer, a 25-cent trolley makes the circuit of popular spots. You might start by repairing to the restaurant on the corner, **Freestone's** (★★$$; 41 William Street, 993.7477), an 1833 Richardsonian Romanesque brownstone that once housed a bank. Plot your course while enjoying affordable ethnic entrées, or refreshing smoothies, "mocktails," or full-octane blender drinks. A few blocks toward the water is **Candleworks** (★★$$; 72 North Water Street, 997.1294), an elegant Italian trattoria that extends, conservatory-style, from the granite cellar of an 1810 factory decorated with graceful Federal ornamentation; the patio is a summer oasis.

One block south is the **New Bedford Whaling Museum** (admission; 8 Johnny Cake Hill, 997.0046), which houses a fully rigged half-scale model (89 feet long) of the 1826 whaling bark *Lagoda;* you can climb right on board, or get a good view from the balcony. Other nautical treasures range from figureheads, models, and trade signs to sea chests, nautical paintings (including an extraordinary naif triptych by whaler-turned-painter **C.S. Raleigh**), and outstanding scrimshaw. The museum also boasts a collection of dolls and toys, and glass pieces, including the holdings of the now defunct **New Bedford Glass Museum.** When you've exhausted the possibilities, head across the street to the refreshingly spare **Seamen's Bethel** (donation requested; 15 Johnny Cake Hill, 992.3295). **Herman Melville** visited this 1832 Greek Revival chapel when it was still relatively new, and noted: "Few are the moody fishermen shortly bound for the Indian or Pacific oceans who failed to make a Sunday visit to the spot." Although it has been architecturally amended over the past century and a half—the bow-shaped pulpit didn't exist in Melville's day—it remains a poignant monument to those lost at sea, as well as a comfort to those still plying it.

One of New Bedford's architectural treasures began as an instant failure. The **Zeiterion Theatre** (684 Purchase Street, 994.2900) was built in 1923 to host vaudeville shows; **George Jessel** was the opening act. Within months, the stage was dark, a victim of bad timing. That fall, the tapestry brick building with its opulent ivory-and-rose interior and gilded Grecian frieze reopened as a moviehouse and over the next six decades hosted five world premieres—including *Moby-Dick.* A 1971 renovation, however, completely obscured the theater's original charm. With the help of local benefactors, it was restored in 1982 and donated to the town as a not-for-profit performing arts center, which hosts concerts, plays, dance, and film screenings throughout the year.

The 19th-century nabobs of New Bedford built their mansions away from the wharf, along the ridge of County Street, originally a native trail. Some of the residences, like the **William Rotch Rodman Mansion** (388 County Street), resemble institutions more than private homes. Now an office building, this granite Greek Revival structure, designed by Providence architect **Russell Warren** in 1833-36, was rumored to be the most expensive house of its time. It's still an

imposing sight. On the next block, the **Rotch-Jones-Duff House and Garden Museum** (admission; 396 County Street, 997.1401) is open for tours year-round. Built by English carpenter/architect **Richard Upjohn** in 1833 of clapboard-covered brick, the 22-room Classical Revival mansion (illustrated above) was commissioned by whaling merchant **William Rotch, Jr.,** and changed hands only twice over the next 150 years. In 1981, it was bought by the **Waterfront Historic Area League (WHALE)** and preserved as an architectural sampler of the many periods it survived: there's a Greek Revival sitting room, a Victorian parlor, and upstairs, the 1940s bedroom of the last owners, appended by a full-size dressing room with two centuries' worth of hatboxes. The grounds are particularly appealing, and encompass a wildflower walk, a dogwood allée, and a boxwood parterre.

Families with restless young children in tow might enjoy the **New Bedford Fire Museum** (admission; Bedford and South Six Streets, 992.2162). Open weekdays in summer, the museum—next door to the oldest active station in Massachusetts—features restored fire trucks, including an 1840 hand-pump engine. Visitors can slide down a brass pole, try on uniforms, ring bells, and play firefighter. If you've time to spare, the **Buttonwood Park Zoo** (admission; Hawthorne Street, 991.6178) is a fun place to stretch your legs while marveling at the mountain lions, black bears, harbor seals, and assorted other wildlife. Set within a 970-acre park designed by noted landscape architect **Frederick Law Olmsted,** the 1894 zoo does not quite measure up to the grandeur of his original design, and features none of the "habitat" settings of more contemporary zoos, but little kids probably won't notice.

No visit to New Bedford would be complete without a glimpse of the active waterfront, and at **Lisboa Antiga** (★$$), a Portuguese cafe housed in the **Durant Sail Loft Inn** ($; 1 Merrills Wharf, 999.2700), you can get a sense of the waterfront's past as well as its current configuration. The building itself, now

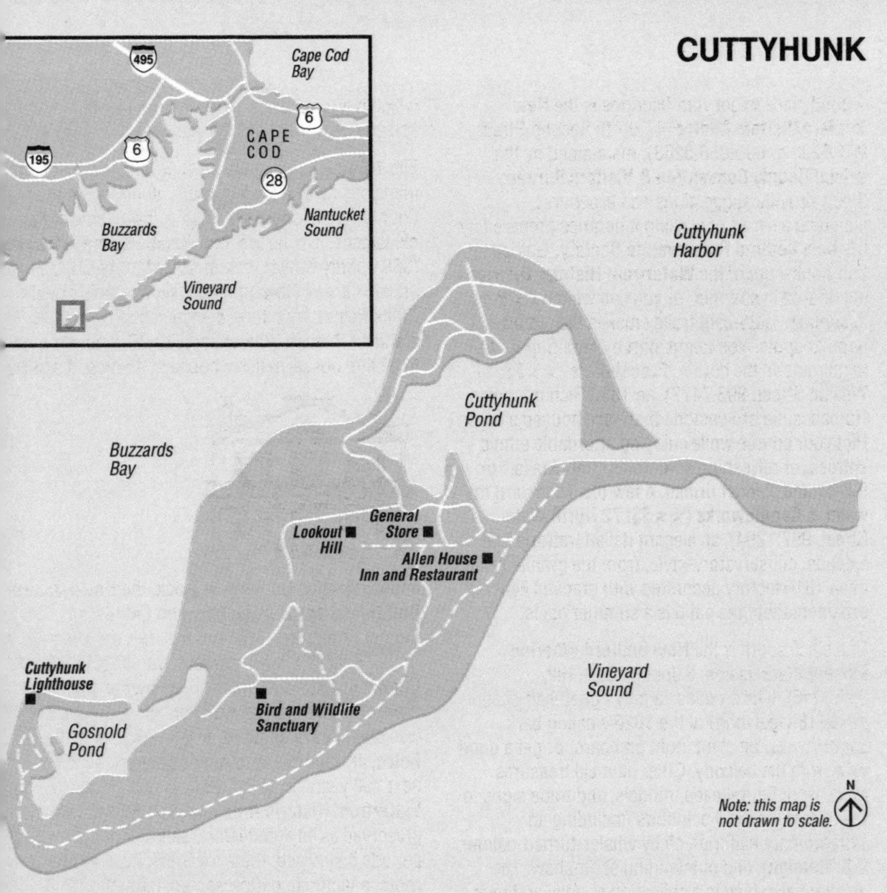

an architectural shell containing a modern 17-room hotel, is the former **Bourne Counting House,** an 1847-48 granite warehouse used by Cape Cod grocery-clerk-turned-whaling-magnate **Jonathan Bourne.** In 1925, it became a sailmaking factory, but the interior was twice destroyed by fire. Although the late 1970s renovation was perhaps overzealous, the ground-level cafe, with its sidewalk patio, provides a lively meeting ground for tourists and local workers, who come to enjoy such classic Portuguese specialties as *mariscada* (seafood stew), *bacalhau assado* (baked cod), and *carne de porco a Alentejana* (marinated pork with littleneck clams). The prices, happily, are geared to workers, not tourists.

The West Coast doesn't have a lock on earthquakes. Governor William Bradford documented a 1638 temblor in Plymouth: "It was very terrible for the time, and the earth shooke with that violence, as they could not stand without catching hould of ye posts."

Herman Melville set off on a whaler from Fairhaven (across the river from New Bedford) on 3 January 1841; his ship, the *Acushnet,* would become, as he later wrote, "my Harvard and my Yale."

Cuttyhunk

If you're longing to "get away from it all," there is no better place than this final link in the Elizabeth Islands chain. In summer, at least one ferry a day makes a round-trip, a little over an hour each way, to the tiny—2½-by-¾-mile—island 14 miles out to sea (its native name meant "a thing that lies out of the water"). Off-season, from Columbus Day to Memorial Day, there are only two ferries a week, to accommodate the 30 or so year-round residents. In July and August, the population expands to all of 300, mostly descendants of the early settlers of 1688. It's *quiet.* More than half the island is a nature preserve, and, not surprisingly, deer roam the streets—all 1.3 miles of them. The principal entertainment, naturally, is long, bracing walks. For so much as a nightcap, you'll have to bring your own—the island is "dry." There's one general store, and there's one 12-room inn ($) that serves three meals: open only in season, the **Allen House Inn and Restaurant** (★★$$; 996.9292) is, ipso facto, the best in town. It is in fact good, with cheerful though not fancy rooms, and a menu that reflects the sea's proximity. Leave behind your briefcase, beeper, and woes, and just bring a good book and sturdy walking shoes to enjoy an elemental encounter with an island scarcely touched by the 20th century.

Index

D

E

F

G

H

L

M

T

U

V

W

Y

Z

Restaurants

Only restaurants with star ratings are listed below and at right. All restaurants are listed alphabetically in the main (preceding) index. Always call in advance to ensure a restaurant has not closed, changed its hours, or booked its tables for a private party. The restaurant price ratings are based on the average cost of an entrée for one person, excluding tax and tip.

★★★★ An Extraordinary Experience
★★★ Excellent
★★ Very Good
★ Good

$$$$ Big Bucks ($20 and up)
$$$ Expensive ($15-$20)
$$ Reasonable ($10-$15)
$ The Price Is Right (less than $10)

★★★★

★★★

Hotels

The hotels listed below and at right are grouped according to their price ratings; they are also listed in the main index. The hotel price ratings reflect the base price of a standard room for two people for one night during the peak season.

$$$$ Big Bucks ($250 and up)
$$$ Expensive ($175-$250)
$$ Reasonable ($100-$175)
$ The Price Is Right (less than $100)

$$$$

$$$

$$

$

Features

Bests

Maps